This is a translated collection of essays by a leading German economic historian on nineteenth- and twentieth-century Germany up to recent times. Though the articles were published originally in a variety of places, the issues dealt with are connected: economic growth, fluctuations, structural change, changes in socio-economic institutions and in the economic system as a whole, all in interaction with other historical phenomena.

Among the essays is a study of whether Germany's comparatively late start as an industrial nation was the result of a specific lack of capital. Borchardt also shows in which particular ways the value of human capital was already being calculated by the mid-nineteenth century. The west–east developmental gradient, which became of increasing importance for the wealth of the nation, is also analysed. Other articles deal with key patterns of long-term economic development, and unusual changes in the phenomena of business cycles and their characteristics are described and analysed. The collection also contains several essays which have become the subject of so-called 'Borchardt controversies', in which hypotheses are presented on the economic causes of the collapse of the parliamentary regime by 1929–30, at the very end of the 'crisis before the crisis'. He also explains why there were no alternatives to the economic policies of the slump, and in particular why there was no 'miracle weapon' against Hitler's seizure of power.

These are among the most original and stimulating contributions of recent years to the economic history of modern Germany. Together they will provoke discussion and controversy among English-language readers, while illustrating the power of economic history and its usefulness for political historians and anyone who ponders deeply the meaning of history.

Perspectives on modern German economic history and policy

Perspectives on modern German economic history and policy

KNUT BORCHARDT

TRANSLATED BY PETER LAMBERT

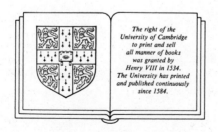

The right of the
University of Cambridge
to print and sell
all manner of books
was granted by
Henry VIII in 1534.
The University has printed
and published continuously
since 1584.

CAMBRIDGE UNIVERSITY PRESS

Cambridge

New York   Port Chester   Melbourne   Sydney

Published by the Press Syndicate of the University of Cambridge
The Pitt Building, Trumpington Street, Cambridge CB2 1RP
40 West 20th Street, New York, NY 100114211, USA
10 Stamford Road, Oakleigh, Melbourne 3166, Australia

Originally published in German as *Wachstum, Krisen, Handlungsspielräume
der Wirtschaftspolitik: Studien zur Wirtschaftgeschichte des 19. und 20. Jahrhunderts*
by Vandenhoeck & Ruprecht, Göttingen, 1982
and © Vandenhoeck & Ruprecht 1982
First published in English by Cambridge University Press 1991 as *Perspectives on modern
German economic history and policy*
English translation © Cambridge Universty Press 1991

Printed in Great Britain at the University Press, Cambridge

British Library cataloguing in publication data

Borchardt, Knut
  Perspectives on modern German economic history and policy.
  1. West Germany. Economic policies
  I. Title   II. Wachstum, Krisen, Handlungsspielräume der
  Wirtschaftspolitik. *English*
  330.943087

Library of Congress cataloguing in publication data

Borchardt, Knut
  [Wachstum, Krisen, Handlungsspielräume der Wirtschaftspolitik.
  English]
  Perspectives on modern German economic history and policy/ Knut
  Borchardt: translated by Peter Lambert.
      p.   cm.
  Translation of: Wachstum, Krisen, Handlungsspielräume der
  Wirtschaftspolitik.
  Includes bibliographical references and index.
  ISBN 0 521 36310 1 – ISBN 0 521 36858 8 (pbk)
    1. Germany – Economic conditions.   2. Germany – Economic policy.
  3. Economic development.   I. Title.
  HC286.B6613   1991
  338.943 – dc20   90–1854   CIP

ISBN 0 521 36310 1 hardback
ISBN 0 521 36858 8 paperback

CONTENTS

FIGURES

TABLES

PREFACE TO THE ENGLISH EDITION

This volume is basically the translated edition of a collection of essays on German economic history of the nineteenth and twentieth centuries which was published with Vandenhoeck & Ruprecht, Göttingen, in 1982. Only the first contribution to that volume ('Europe's economic history: a model for developing countries?') was replaced by the later essay on 'Protectionism in historical perspective'.

As in the German edition, the original articles were included with only minor corrections (and no revision). Thanks go to Peter Lambert for the difficult work of translating the German text, to Anne Rix from Cambridge University Press for her admirable work of editing and to my staff in Munich for their assistance. Above all, I wish to thank Harold James, formerly of Cambridge University, now at Princeton, for everything he did for this book.

December 1989   Knut Borchardt

PREFACE TO THE GERMAN EDITION

The present collection unites essays and lectures on the history of economic development – mostly of nineteenth- and twentieth-century Germany. They came into being over the course of twenty years, as contributions to the important but at the same time difficult task of bringing the disciplines of economics and history closer together. However, the reader will notice in the selection of themes and in the manner of the treatment, that it is a matter here of historical studies produced by an economist.

In fact it was stimuli from current problems in economics which repeatedly led me to see the subject 'in historical perspective' and to ask whether, and what, might be learnt from history (especially in contributions 1, 5 and 11). But one does not only learn from history for the benefit of the present. One also learns from the present for the purpose of viewing history. Even at the risk of being accused of an unhistorical prejudice, I would like to acknowledge that this assumption underpins the majority of the essays in this collection. This is especially true of those essays which are concerned with conditions of growth in the nineteenth century, and of those devoted to the economic history of the Weimar Republic. Changed experiences in the present, and new economic insights, seemed to suggest a new look at the history of the nineteenth century and at that of Weimar.

Though the origins of these essays differed, and the author's special interests and working methods changed over the course of time, nevertheless the inquiries presented here are connected. They all have as their subject economic development: that is growth, fluctuations, structural change, changes in socio-economic institutions, as well as in the economic order as a whole – all in interaction with other historical phenomena. Economic development is a complicated story of collective phenomena and individual activity. This subject permits and even demands quite different approaches and presents individual researchers with the possibility of contributing to the division of labour in accordance with their comparative advantages.

Economic development can and even must often be observed and analysed on the high level of economic aggregates. I hope that the contributions show how interesting such questions and the answers which emerge can be for a non-specialist as well. However, an analysis of economic development which grasps the motive forces concretely also requires a breakdown of the large macro-economic pattern, and an investigation of the details of sectors, branches, regions and groups of actors. The macro-economic figures are in any case always suspect: it could be a case of 'spurious sums and averages' or of unhistorical or artificial constructs. The collection also contains studies which develop in this direction, even if the task of disaggregation is generally not taken very far here. Finally, although economic development is indubitably concerned to a great extent with large anonymous forces, the question of achievement, failure and blame can and must also be posed here, because there is always room – which must of course first be explored in each case – for historically effective decisons. It is a fascinating task for the economic historian (as it is for the economic policy-maker) to find out how possibilities of individual action and supra-individual determination relate to one another in a concrete situation. How 'makable' is history? The collection contains a number of contributions to this theme (above all in 7, 8, 9, 10 and 11).

The essays reprinted here are up to twenty years old. The conclusions appear to me still to be defensible today, but the arguments and evidence do not necessarily correspond with the latest state of research. The publishers and I planned a collection of already available studies, and not a collection of new contributions with old titles. It was precisely several of the older essays which sparked lively discussions. Re-working or even re-writing these essays would reduce their value as a reference source for these discussions. The result is that the essays remain substantially intact, with some contemporary formulations removed and occasional stylistic improvements and clarifications. Postscripts were added to the oldest essays (2, 3 and 4), which refer to the development of research since the publication of the original essays. On occasion footnotes were supplemented and new ones inserted where this appeared particularly useful. New footnotes are distinguished from the numerical sequence by a figure followed by the letter a or b, so that they may be rapidly identified as new.

Rules of etiquette demand that an author who presents a collection of his essays and lectures declares that he has by no means done this of his own accord, but has rather yielded to the pressure of esteemed colleagues, who had long regretted the absence of such a volume. Such rules not only give the author the chance to show himself to be modest, but also allow the responsibility for the project in part to be shifted on to the shoulders of others. I gladly avail myself of this opportunity. In fact, the editors of the *Kritische Studien zur Geschichtswissenschaft* repeatedly enquired whether I too would not like to entrust my altogether too scattered contributions to economic history to their care. And after all, most of these essays really were scattered, as the index of the places of first publication testifies. They were scarcely accessible to the direct field of vision of historians. I am sincerely grateful to Helmut Berding, Jürgen Kocka and Hans-Ulrich Wehler for opening up this opportunity, as well as for their encouragement.

Munich, August 1981   Knut Borchardt

ORIGINAL CHAPTER TITLES AND FIRST PLACES OF PUBLICATION

1 Protektionismus im historischen Rückblick, in A. Gutowski (ed.), *Der neue Protektionismus* (Hamburg 1984), pp. 17–48.

2 Zur Frage des Kapitalmangels in der ersten Hälfte des 19. Jahrhunderts in Deutschland, in *JNST*, 173 (1961), pp. 401–21.

3 Regionale Wachstumsdifferenzierung in Deutschland im 19. Jahrhundert unter besonderer Berücksichtigung des West–Ost–Gefälles, in W. Abel, *et al.* (eds.), *Wirtschaft, Geschichte und Wirtschaftsgeschichte, Festschrift für F. Lütge* (Stuttgart 1966), pp. 325–39.

4 Zum Problem der Erziehungs- und Ausbildungsinvestitionen im 19. Jahrhundert, in H. Aubin, *et al.* (eds.), *Beiträge zur Wirtschafts- und Stadtgeschichte, Festschrift für H. Ammann* (Wiesbaden 1965), pp. 380–92.

5 Wandlungen des Konjunkturphänomens in den letzten hundert Jahren. Bayerische Akademie der Wissenschaften, Sitzungsberichte der Philosophisch-historischen Klasse, 1976, 1 (Munich 1976).

6 Trend, Zyklus, Strukturbrüche, Zufälle: Was bestimmt die deutsche Wirtschaftsgeschichte des 20. Jahrhunderts?, in *VSWG*, 64 (1977), pp. 145–78.

7 Die Bundesrepublik Deutschland in den säkularen Trends der wirtschaftlichen Entwicklung, in W. Conze and M. R. Lepsius (eds.), *Sozialgeschichte der Bundesrepublik Deutschland* (Stuttgart 1983), pp. 20–45.

8 Die Erfahrung mit Inflationen in Deutschland, in J. Schlemmer (ed.), *Enteignung durch Inflation?* (Munich 1972), pp. 9–22.

9 Zwangslagen und Handlungsspielräume in der großen Weltwirtschaftskrise der frühen dreißiger Jahre: Zur Revision der überlieferten Geschichtsbildes, in: Bayerische Akademie der Wissenschaften, Jahrbuch 1979 (Munich 1979), pp. 87–132.

10 Wirtschaftliche Ursachen des Scheiterns der Weimarer Republik, in K. D. Erdmann and H. Schulze (eds.), *Weimar, Selbstpreisgabe einer Demokratie. Eine Bilanz heute* (Düsseldorf 1980), pp. 211–49.

11 Zur Frage der währungspolitischen Optionen Deutschlands in der Weltwirtschaftskrise, in K. Borchardt and F. Holzheu (eds.), *Theorie und Politik der
internationalen Wirtschaftsbeziehungen. H. Möller zum 65. Geburtstag* (Stuttgart 1980), pp. 165–82.

ABBREVIATIONS

AER	*American Economic Review*
ASG	*Archiv für Sozialgeschichte*
BA	Bundesarchiv Koblenz
BkAr	Bank-Archiv
CEHE	*Cambridge Economic History of Europe*
CJEPS	*Canadian Journal of Economic and Political Science*
DBBk	Deutsche Bundesbank
EDCC	*Economic Development and Cultural Change*
EEH	*Explorations in Entrepreneurial History*
EHR	*Economic History Review*
EJ	*Economic Journal*
ESS	*Encyclopaedia of the Social Sciences*
EurEH	*European Economic History*
FA	*Finanzarchiv*
GdS	*Grundriß der Sozialökonomik*
GuG	*Geschichte und Gesellschaft*
GWU	*Geschichte in Wissenschaft und Unterricht*
HdFW	*Handbuch der Finanzwissenschaft*
HdSt	*Handwörterbuch der Staatswissenschaften*
HdSW	*Handwörterbuch der Sozialwissenschaften*
HdWSG	*Handbuch der deutschen Wirtschafts- und Sozialgeschichte*
HdWW	*Handwörterbuch der Wirtschaftswissenschaft*
HJ	*Historical Journal*
HPE	*History of Political Economy*
HZ	*Historische Zeitschrift*
IfK	Institut für Konjunkturforschung Berlin
IfZG	Institut für Zeitgeschichte München
IWK	*Internationale Wissenschaftliche Korrespondenz zur Geschichte der Arbeiterbewegung*
JEH	*Journal of Economic History*

JEL	*Journal of Economic Literature*
JMCB	*Journal of Money, Credit and Banking*
JNSt	*Jahrbücher für Nationalökonomie und Statistik*
JPE	*Journal of Political Economy*
JSW	*Jahrbuch für Sozialwissenschaft*
JWG	*Jahrbuch für Wirtschaftsgeschichte*
KuK	*Kredit und Kapital*
NA	National Archives Washington
N.F.	*Neue Folge*
NWB	Neue Wissenschaftliche Bibliothek
OEP	*Oxford Economic Papers*
ORDO	Ordo. Jahrbuch für die Ordnung von Wirtschaft und Gesellschaft
PA	Politisches Archiv des Auswärtigen Amtes Bonn
Pap. a. Proc.	Papers and Proceedings
PRO	Public Record Office London
QJE	*Quarterly Journal of Economics*
RES	*Review of Economics and Statistics*
RGBl	*Reichsgesetzblatt*
SchJb	*Schmollers Jahrbuch für Wirtschafts- und Sozialwissenschaften*
SchVfSp	*Schriften des Vereins für Socialpolitik*
SEJ	*Southern Economic Journal*
SP	*Soziale Praxis*
SR	*Social Research*
StatBA	Statistisches Bundesamt
StatRA	Statistisches Reichsamt
StJbb	Statistisches Jahrbuch (für die Bundesrepublik bzw. für das Deutsche Reich)
SVR	Sachverständigenrat zur Begutachtung der Gesamtwirtschaftlichen Entwicklung
TG	*Technikgeschichte*
VfKf	*Vierteljahrshefte zur Konjunkturforschung*
VfZ	*Vierteljahrshefte für Zeitgeschichte*
VjhStDR	*Vierteljahrshefte zur Statistik des Deutschen Reiches*
VSWG	*Vierteljahrschrift für Sozial- und Wirtschaftsgeschichte*
WA	*Weltwirtschaftliches Archiv*
WD	*Wirtschaftsdienst*
WiSta	*Wirtschaft und Statistik*
ZAA	*Zeitschrift für Agrargeschichte und Agrarsoziologie*
ZfGS	*Zeitschrift für die Gesamte Staatswissenschaft*
ZfN	*Zeitschrift für Nationalökonomie*
ZPStB	*Zeitschrift des Königlichen Preußischen Statistischen Bureaus*
ZStA	Zentrales Staatsarchiv der DDR Potsdam
ZUG	*Zeitschrift für Unternehmensgeschichte*

1 PROTECTIONISM IN HISTORICAL PERSPECTIVE

1 When in Britain in the 1900s a debate broke out about Joseph Chamberlain's proposals for protective tariffs, one consequence – among other perhaps more important repercussions – was to split an academic economic community which until then had been held together with some difficulty by Alfred Marshall. Now it was possible to discern alongside theoretical economists a group of economic historians. The historians welcomed Chamberlain's view, while the theoreticians who were still deeply committed to classical traditions opposed it.[1]

How should I see my present role in the light of this historical background? There are certainly economic historians who today take the same side as their early predecessors. Among them are not just old-fashioned enemies of theory, but also historical econometricians – so-called cliometricians, who do not simply pronounce value judgements but attempt to test hypotheses with the help of carefully constructed mathematical models.

Despite this I should perhaps join the impressive majority of theorists who since the end of the eighteenth century have again and again opposed the growth of protectionism. In 1930, over a thousand university teachers signed an appeal to the US President not to sign the now infamous Hawley-Smoot tariff law if it were to receive the support of Congress (as seemed likely). An interesting sample survey recently cast light on the opinion of economists in the Federal Republic. Of the academic economists asked, about 70 per cent agreed in general to the proposition that 'Tariffs and import quotas reduced society's economic prosperity'. A further 24 per cent agreed with some reservations, and only 6 per cent rejected the proposition altogether.[2] The majority view is clear – but is its influence on events as obvious?

2   If anything should give occasion not to overestimate the significance of the majority view of economists, it is the history of protectionism.[3] Despite all the emphasis by economists on the adverse effects, such as welfare losses, there has always – with the exception of brief time periods – been protectionism. For understandable reasons, politicians today are certainly not as candid as Bismarck was when he said in the Reichstag debate on tariffs on 2 May 1879: 'In all these questions I hold as little of science as in all other issues concerning organic forms . . . The abstract theories of science leave me quite cold in this respect, and I judge on the basis of experience. I see that countries that protect prosper, and that countries which are open fall back in the race.'[4]

Today it would not be possible to argue quite like this; but the facts still seem to indicate that commercial policy is not made on the basis of the normative theories of free trade and protection expressed in our textbooks.

How then is policy made? This is a question which has occupied the attention of historians, and thus there is a substantial quantity of historical investigation available. Over the past thirty years this material has increasingly been used by economists in developing what is now known as the 'positive theory of protectionism' (in distinction to a 'normative theory').[5] Currently we are reflecting on how the increase in protection is to be explained, and how protectionism could be limited. Perhaps we can learn from history?

In the nineteenth and twentieth centuries there were several waves of protectionism. In the following, I will concern myself with the turning points in the swings towards and away from protectionism, and will ask what constellations led to demands for protection and also to its dismantling.

3   The framework for my story is the supposition that there is a market for protection, a political market.[6] Here supply and demand meet, and attempt to derive benefits from an exchange of services. The demand for protection is usually provided by economic interests threatened by foreign competition. The suppliers of protection are state – or in the case of customs unions supra-state – institutions. Their services are clearly protectionist measures, which protect the buyers of protection from competition and thus secure their incomes from economic rent. What do the buyers in this market offer to the suppliers in exchange? Here there are different options to be investigated: the possibility of reelection for politicians, the securing of parliamentary majorities, or the solving of budget problems. As economic interests in the nineteenth century clamoured for protection, they made it easier for the state to increase its revenue.[7]

The experts among you know that this market model is very rough and ready, and that we need further to explain:

(1) how economic conditions influence the utility of protection for economic interests, and thus affect the demand for protection;
(2) how the economic interests are organised;
(3) how the state institutions which meet the demand are organised.

The role of economics and economists should also be included in this model. They presumably influence market sentiment, and the prices prevailing on the market for protection.

At present I can only offer hints, since my task is not to make theoretical constructions but to present historical material.

4 When Adam Smith was writing, Europe was a long way away from free trade, but was moving in that direction. Frequently trade barriers were dismantled as a result of the influence of enlightened men. It is not surprising that this process was interrupted by the wars at the turn of the eighteenth and nineteenth centuries. Wars were then in part economic wars, and the continental blockade was only a particularly large-scale effort to defeat the opponent by economic means. However, why did the movement towards free trade not resume after the Napoleonic wars? Why was there first in most countries a phase of vigorous protectionism? The major cause was the severe and long-lasting economic crisis. Almost all countries attempted to protect their producers from foreign competition by means of high tariffs. Even Britain surrounded her farms with sliding duties designed to secure a high price level.

5 The development in Prussia was rather surprising. In France, the weak restoration government yielded to the concentrated pressure of economic interests and imposed a radical solidarity protectionism with import prohibitions and high tariffs for manufactures and agriculture. In Prussia, however, a similarly restorationist political system in 1818 introduced a tariff system which even at the time was reckoned to be liberal. Import and transit duties were set at an extremely low level.[8]

These were certainly not popular – but Prussia was not a constitutional monarchy. She was dominated by a bureaucracy educated by free trading professors. Political conservatism and economic liberalism did not exclude each other. What was even more important, the free trade ideology of the bureaucracy corresponded exactly with the interests of the politically crucial land-owning aristocracy in the Prussian east. The agrarian producers wished to sell their surplus production through the Baltic ports to western Europe. This was however only possible, as they rightly recognised, if the Prussian market were left open for the export products of the grain buying countries.

I have already stated that this policy was not popular. But the opposition to protection from manufacturers had no opportunity either to organise or to assert influence because of Prussian censorship and the limitations on the freedom of assembly. This changed with the foundation of the customs union (Zollverein) of 1834.[9] In particular south German manufacturers living in constitutional monarchies gained influence in their parliaments. These states then transmitted their interests to the Zollverein.[10] Now Prussia had to calculate new costs and benefits, since the existence of the Zollverein might be challenged by the southern states. But the Zollverein constituted an important instrument for the central European power politics of Prussia, which hoped to use it to exclude Austrian influence. The political market for protection thus underwent a structural change.

On the other hand the clash of interests between the manufacturers who either suffered or thought they suffered from British competition and the export-oriented agrarians remained until the 1870s in Prussia. It was a nobleman from the Mark Brandenburg named Otto von Bismarck who, probably in 1847, described the clash in this way for a local newspaper: 'In the same way we hear with reference to indirect taxation more said about a protective system for the benefit of domestic manufacture and commerce than about the free trade needed by the cereal farming population.'[11] How remote now seems the idea that German farmers might be free traders!

6   The English landlords of the early nineteenth century were not free traders. After 1815 they felt threatened by the continental grain surpluses, with the result that England introduced the well-known corn laws. From the 1820s there was increasing bitter conflict over them, until they were repealed between 1842 and 1846.

We economists derive considerable satisfaction from the traditional version of history in which economists played a leading role in supporting the right cause in the clash between the urban middle classes and the workers on the one hand and the landed aristocracy on the other – and in helping free trade to triumph. Unfortunately, this version of history is not quite correct.

We should not accept the rhetoric of the 'victors', the Manchesterites. The fact that the repeal of the corn laws was the work of the Tories and was supported by the agrarian aristocracy in parliament should suggest another interpretation. Of course, it could be cited as an example of how great was the economists' power to convince. But the economists' agitation only contributed to making the tariff reform *necessary* for the maintenance of domestic peace. Repeal only became *possible* because of the changed conditions of demand and supply in the market for protection.[12]

After the end of the 1830s the demand for protection was reduced because of significant changes in the competitive position of agriculture. Continental grain exporters now found adequate opportunities in their rapidly growing domestic markets, while the new technology of 'high farming' reduced production costs for British agriculture. From the late 1830s, most landlords did not need to fear undercutting by foreigners any longer. They were proved right after the repeal of the corn laws: these were the golden years of British farming. There was no distribution of income in favour of the urban producers and away from landowners as had been suggested in the Ricardian model. The contraction of British agriculture began only thirty years later, when large quantities of American and Russian grain came onto the European market.[13]

In the 1840s it was not just the buyers of protection, but also the supplier, the state, which became less interested in import duties. The state could finance itself in other ways. In any case, revenue from grain tariffs played only a marginal role in the budget at this point.

The structural changes in the demand and supply of protection would probably not have made the reduction of corn tariffs politically possible. A skilful strategy on the part of Peel was needed to obtain the necessary majorities in parliament. He linked repeal with a 'Grand Design' which gave compensating advantages to those who believed that they would lose. Taxes on agriculture were reduced before the repeal of the corn laws, and credit for productive purposes such as drainage offered on very generous terms by the state. In short, part of the presumed damage was compensated for, both materially and symbolically.

If we examine all these circumstances, the contribution of economists in the triumph of repeal was relatively slight. Of course no one can calculate precisely what changes in sentiment the economists had managed to produce over the course of decades.[14]

7 The unilateral repeal of the corn laws inaugurated the era of free trade. In 1860 the previously most protectionist country (with the possible exception of Russia), France, concluded a treaty with the country that had advanced most towards free trade, Britain. The still existing trade barriers between the two countries were dramatically reduced. The Most Favoured Nation clause made the Cobden-Chevalier Treaty a model for a series of treaties between many European states. Thanks to these treaties Europe

became within a few years a free trade zone – though this only lasted two decades. What made the Anglo-French treaty necessary and possible?

It was not the outcome of organised producer interests in either France or Britain. If anything at all was heard from French producers, it was protests – expressed even in the Chamber of Deputies. The majority of deputies strictly opposed opening France to the products of her arch-rival. But, because Cobden-Chevalier was an international treaty, it did not need the consent of the Chamber; this was an important element in making the treaty possible. Foreign policy was the domain of the Emperor and his government; and this was largely a question of foreign policy.

France had just embarked on the war with Austria, and wished to annex Nice and Savoy. This led to substantial criticism in Britain, where people said that Napoleon III was beginning to take 'revenge for Waterloo'. A vigorous campaign for rearmament began in Britain. This disconcerted not only Napoleon, but also the British government, which would have preferred to reduce taxes in order to aid an economy still suffering from the after effects of the 1857 crisis. The government did not want a war with France.

Berndt Wendt has described the Cobden-Chevalier Treaty as an early example of British appeasement policy; it was indeed a treaty of neutrality.[15]

France bought peace with trade political concessions. In order to appease the domestic interests outraged by the Treaty, Napoleon needed to pay a domestic price. In the same way that Peel had offered concessions to British farmers, Napoleon now gave loans on favourable conditions to French producers.

It was not just the Cobden-Chevalier Treaty that was motivated by foreign policy interests. The series of successor treaties also stood in most countries for the securing of European hegemony or peace. They were not supported by a broad consensus of domestic interests. K. Graf rightly believed that 'in view of the state of interests the reforms in the respective areas probably could not have been carried out on a democratic path'.[16] With a few exceptions, the liberalisation of European commerce was carried out by authoritarian states.

Ninety years ago Walter Lotz wrote that 'the political conjuncture required free trade, the economic conjuncture permitted it'.[17] In fact the favourable economic circumstances of the 1860s until 1873 meant that agrarian and manufacturing producers in most countries encountered no increased and certainly no ruinous competition despite the vigorous growth of international trade.[18] There was a sustained upswing. Free trade sentiment now gripped wide circles.[19] But it is more likely that the free trade atmosphere was a consequence rather than a cause of the favourable economic climate.

8   The rapid change in the climate of commercial policy, which occurred in almost all European states a few years later, cannot be otherwise understood. During the 'Gründerkrise' ('Foundation Crisis') beginning in 1873, which was soon followed by a structural and secular agrarian crisis, the weakness of the liberal position soon became evident. With the exception of Britain and the Netherlands at the end of the 1870s the European states turned once more to protectionism. A few states, for instance Denmark, protected manufactures but left agriculture unprotected. Other states, such as Switzerland, left manufactures open but aided agriculture. In France however the idea of solidarity protectionism revived, and this after 1879 became Bismarck's maxim for the German Empire.

We cannot depict this rather complex development in detail and show for instance how in the various states between 1875 and 1895 average duties on manufactures doubled and how particularly those highly concentrated industries which already employed large numbers of workers benefited.[20]

The general transition of central and southern European agriculture to protectionism was of particular importance. In Germany there was a break with previous history; farmers under the leadership of the exporting east German Junkers had been the chief proponents of free trade ideas. Strictly speaking even at the end of the 1870s the Junkers still did not stand in the forefront of the protectionist movement, because the structural agrarian crisis was only in its initial phases and the devastating consequences had not yet become clear.[21] This was to change quickly after 1880.

What was the origin of the agrarian malaise? Initially there was a debt crisis as a consequence of the deflation after 1873. Then came the flooding of European markets with Russian and American grain. This was possible after the end of the Crimean War for Russia and the Civil War for the USA, and when the revolution in sea and land transport reduced freight rates to a fraction of their former level.[22] Overseas grain did not always conquer the market as quickly as in Barcelona, where the share of domestically produced grain fell from 57 per cent to 11 per cent between 1884 and 1886; but grain prices sank everywhere.[23]

If we wish to examine why Germany altered course in tariff policy, then grain prices played a role, but not a dominant one: otherwise the result would not have been merely an *ad valorem* rate of 5 to 7 per cent. Probably even the changes in the interests of manufacturing and agriculture wrought by the foundation crisis and the agitation of industrialists, workers and farmers did not produce this change of tack. There certainly was agitation, and there were demands for protective tariffs, but there is much to be said for the view that at least in Germany the crucial change was in the supply of protection.[24]

The architect of the Empire, Bismarck, recognised that his creation was constitutionally weak as long as the Empire depended on financial contributions from the federal states. He dreamt of making the Empire more independent through an income of its own; and even of turning the table round and making the states financially dependent on the Empire. A financial constitution is a constitution of political power. Because the Empire only received indirect taxes and customs duties, Bismarck turned his attention to these.

The crux of the matter was a constitutional alteration for the federal state, the supplier of protection.[25] Protection was possible, because at the time there were interests which demanded it. The protectionist movement corresponded with Bismarck's intentions perfectly, and secured an otherwise impossible majority in the Reichstag in support of his ideas.

Both buyers and sellers of protection were already then motivated by a slogan which we often assume only became a political objective during the inter-war world economic crisis: employment. It was a general belief that 'national labour' should and must be protected by tariffs.[26] The Reich Chancellery received large quantities of petitions from workers who feared for their jobs, or who feared pressure on wages. Even the social democratic party was unsure whether it should represent producers' or consumers' interests. At the 1876 Congress the party avoided the issue, and resolved 'that the question of whether there should be a protective tariff or not is a practical matter which should be decided in each case individually'.[27] Only at the end of the nineteenth century, when it was above all a matter of agrarian tariffs, did the SPD clearly take the point of view of consumers.

9   Bismarck's policy had wide-ranging consequences that went beyond the specific circumstances that had occasioned the policy. It led to a general wave of protectionism throughout Europe. Now the departure from free trade became legitimate. With this the economic interests had easier access to state authority. In Germany it was above all farmers who made use of this as grain prices continued to decline. In 1882, 1885 and 1887 the specific duty rates were increased in rapid succession, so that in view of falling world market prices *ad valorem* protection for rye was around 46 per cent in 1889/90, and for wheat 33 per cent.[28]

Now however two painful consequences made themselves felt:[29] on the one hand the increased burden on consumers in comparison with a situation without tariffs became an urgent issue. The workers protested against the tariff and voted for the left. On the other hand, it became clear that the protectionist spiral in Europe damaged the sale of Germany's industrial exports. Industry needed to export, however. A different economic and social climate existed from that of the foundation crisis. It demanded a revision of tariff policy.

It is difficult to be sure whether this change in climate was sufficient to risk a correction of the protectionist trend of the type attempted by Reich Chancellor von Caprivi between 1891 and 1894. There were other foreign political influences at work, as at the time of the Cobden-Chevalier Treaty.[30] The political alliances in Europe were reshaped in the years after 1890. The Dual Alliance with Austria became the axis of German security policy and required trade political support. At the same time, there was a threat of military conflict with Russia after the German-Russian Reinsurance Treaty was not renewed and after Russia sought a rapprochement with France. Within a short space of time, a trade war broke out in the East, in the course of which the powers blocked off their markets against each other's exports. It was high time to secure peace. That was the purpose of the Caprivi trade treaties, and especially of that concluded with Russia in 1894. Both sides reduced protection: on the German side it was above all agrarian tariffs that were reduced and made general through the still prevailing Most-Favoured Nation system.

There may have been much to be said for Caprivi's logic, and his tariff policy might even have been domestically and internationally necessary – but it was only possible for a brief space of time. It excited the passionate protest of the agrarians. They would not let themselves be bought off by a series of measures designed to be favourable to their interests.[31] In light of the preponderance of other allegedly damaged interests, Caprivi's policy of compensation could not be successful. In 1893 the Agrarian League (Bund der Landwirte) was formed as a powerful interest organisation. The first point at issue it raised was: 'Adequate tariff protection for the products of agriculture and associated trades'. The second point stated: 'For that reason there can be no reduction of existing duty rates, no commercial treaties with Russia or other countries which may lead to the reduction of tariffs; there should be a corresponding regulation of our relationship with America.'[32] Already in 1894 the position of the Chancellor became hopeless because of the new constellation of power in the Reichstag and because of his political isolation. He resigned. But the treaties concluded remained in force until 1906, and probably contributed to the further industrial development of Germany.[33]

It is often alleged that agrarian protection operated solely in the interest of the large east German cereal farmers, while the small peasant farmers who grew no grain but bought feedstuffs for their animals were victimised. If this were true, it would be difficult to understand why peasant farmers initiated the demand for protection before the Junkers and remained powerfully protectionist. Were they as Kindleberger supposes dominated by the Junkers or too stupid or insufficiently organised politically?[34] None of these was the case. The answer is that they too derived a benefit from tariffs since they applied also to animal products. They gave a high degree of effective protection – if we use the method of calculation supplied by Max Corden.[35] It is true that the relative rates of protection were greater for the large cereal farmers than for small livestock rearers. But in the case of livestock there were non-tariff barriers, in particular highly restrictive veterinary regulations, which explain more of the difference between domestic and foreign prices than does the duty. This is thus not a case of Junker minorities who pushed through their interests in some mysterious way.

If Bismarck's policy had avoided stirring up the old conflict between manufacturing and agrarian interests, Caprivi could hardly avoid this issue. Germany had become an exporting country. Her future economic fate depended on the development of exports.[36] But was this really *necessary*? Many, and not just agrarians, thought otherwise, with the result that there was an extraordinarily massive conflict over principle, which also stirred economists. Should the Empire in future be an 'Agrarian State' or an 'Industrial State'? Military, strategic, social hygienic, cultural philosophical and social political aspects were raised.[37] It was less a question of theories than of preferences and even of issues of conscience. People denounced each other as 'Growth Fanatics' who could not see any distributive case, or as 'Agrarian Romantics' who could not understand that the good old days were over, to use the modern term.[38] Every interest stance could be interpreted by its adherents, citing major authors, as the generally most socially responsible position.

The contradiction between growth and distribution policies could not be solved in the way familiar to modern economists who suggest that a larger cake might bring something even for those disadvantaged by change. The disadvantaged were concerned with so-called 'positional goods', with distribution and with the quality of the cake. These really were interests which could not be reconciled by means of the prospect of a 'general compensation' from an increased national income: even if in retrospect we think little of the arguments advanced by the interests at the time.[39]

I will avoid here the issue of how in 1902 the tariff levels were again raised to around the level of 1885. The political weight of the united agrarian front together with heavy industrial interests played a significant role because of the majorities held in the Reichstag and in the Bundesrat (Federal Chamber). The agrarians had reached a veto-position concerning all sorts of political schemes – including for instance the naval expansion desired by industry. The government was forced to obtain majorities – in this case for 'Weltpolitik' – by making a deal in which tariffs were offered in response to demand. As this development became apparent, those interests in Germany which represented a counter-position began to organise. In 1895 a free trade 'Bund der Industriellen' (Industrialists' League) was formed in opposition to the protectionist 'Centralverband Deutscher Industrieller' (Central Association of German Industrialists), and in 1909 several free trade organisations, including the banks, merged to form the 'Hansabund'.[40] The political market for protection became more and more organised.

10   In retrospect we may see some things in a gentler light than did the disputing parties. Despite agricultural tariffs, the Empire did not remain an agrarian state, and indeed imported one quarter of the world's grain exports before the First World War.[41] Whether and to what extent European and American tariffs at the end of the nineteenth and at the beginning of the twentieth centuries represented a brake on general economic development in the industrial countries is still a matter for dispute.[42] Some even argue that they favoured growth. Paul Bairoch attempts to prove this from the fact that average growth in GNP in most countries was higher in the phase of high protectionism than earlier.[43] But this is a rather naive way of arguing. After all there are a multitude of rival theories to explain faster growth. Because we cannot isolate the effect of tariff measures from other influences, we unfortunately have no method of resolving the dispute about the effect of tariffs. But this is also not our theme: we are concerned with the turning points in waves of protectionism.

11   Let us attempt to draw a preliminary conclusion for the nineteenth-century experience.

We have examined two beginnings of general European waves of protectionism. Both were in times of deep depression, and this meant at the time also of deflation. Then we investigated four episodes in which protectionist barriers were dismantled. The first case, that of Prussia, was rather exceptional, since here a country went over to low rates although it was in a deep economic crisis. Here we emphasised the particular political circumstances. The next two cases, in which there was a breakthrough to free trade, were at a time of prosperity – which tends to lessen distributional conflicts. The fourth instance, Caprivi's attempt to reduce barriers, again occurred at a relatively unfavourable point in time, at the end of the years 1873–96 which Spiethoff characterised as a phase of stagnation in which the price trend was downwards. And this attempt failed, at least in the longer term. The recovery phase after 1896 should have offered favourable conditions for softening the anger of the tariff political revisionists, but we must remember that contemporaries obviously could not know that this accelerated growth would last until the outbreak of the First World War. Just at the moment, when the debates about the new Bülow tariff reached their peak, Germany was in the depth of one of the most severe business cycle depressions in her history. This was not an opportune moment for generosity in distributional issues.

If we are to draw a lesson from these experiences, it might be that we should expect trends in economic growth and trends in the growth of protectionism to run in opposite directions. This conclusion would not be contradicted by the experiences of the twentieth century. Keynes in 1933 drew the consequence: 'It is not within practical politics to make serious progress [in reducing tariffs] so long as prices are falling and exchange strained. Tariffism, *as history shows*, is an inevitable . . . concomitant of falling prices.' (emphasis K.B.)[44] Like Keynes, Robert Baldwin in 1979 described it as being 'the first and most necessary step' in reducing barriers to trade 'to restore world economic prosperity'.[45] If this is true, then the chances of stimulating growth by reducing protection in conditions such as those of today are relatively small.

With this the capacity of history to provide comforting lessons is, however, not exhausted. As I attempted to demonstrate, it is not just those interests articulating protectionist *demands* that played a role in the story. At the turning points of protectionist waves the *suppliers* of protection had powerful motives either to increase or decrease the *supply* of protection. It is not easy to derive economic policy recommendations from a 'supply side theory of protection', since the constitutional and foreign policy motives of the suppliers are not easily alterable variables. But we can always observe situations in which for instance the foreign policy interests become predominant: when the suppliers of protection in order to preserve peace or maintain alliances are obliged to exchange tariff reductions and stimulate neutrality or friendship by economic means – that is by allowing a freer access of foreign goods to the domestic market.

The decisive question would be whether in these situations policies that are necessary from a foreign policy viewpoint are also equitable in domestic politics. Can they be pushed through against powerful social forces? In some circumstances this is particularly difficult in democracies –

as can be seen from the history of the nineteenth century. Democracies are in essence the form of state which heeds the interests of the majority or of the holders of veto-positions.

However protectionist interests need not be those of the majority. This identity of the majority with protectionism is not an inevitable political fact. One of the most interesting experiences in the history of protectionism has been that 'economic and social packets of interests' have again and again been able to overcome opposing interests. I have examined the 'packet' assembled by Peel when he repealed the corn laws; but Napoleon's plan to give credit to the outraged producers after the conclusion of the Cobden-Chevalier Treaty belongs also in the same category. Caprivi on the other hand did not, and probably could not, offer sufficient symbolic or material compensation to the landowners. Perhaps this contributed to his failure.

Such compensation naturally should not just constitute an exchange of protective techniques (such as replacing open tariff protection by hidden subsidies) if the goal of dismantling protection is to be achieved. It would be best for free trade politicians if the accepted symbolic value of the compensation far exceeded the material value, and there are historical examples of this.

The cases of Peel and Napoleon show yet another possibility. I set out how the disadvantaged received cheap state credits. These were aids to structural adjustment.[46] They represented compensations that not only reduced opposition but also had a positive impact on growth and contributed to eliminating the protectionist interest altogether: the result was that there was no new request for protection or compensation.

12   I do not know if these 'lessons from history' are helpful in respect to the present task of stopping the protectionist wave or reducing levels of protection. There is at least one case in the twentieth century which can give us a certain measure of hope. Here, in a desperate situation, there was a successful transition from radical protectionism to a liberation from protectionist bonds. Later, when this policy was continued, it helped the whole world. I am referring to the change in American commercial policy in 1934/5. Here lay the seeds of Bretton Woods and Havana. I will now examine this transition briefly as a conclusion.

The story of how a few men around the Secretary of State, Cordell Hull, succeeded in breaking down the isolation of the USA is exciting. Before this there had not only been a catastrophic tariff policy but President Roosevelt had also allowed the 1933 World Economic Conference in London to fail because he believed that the situation in his country would not permit the burdens that an international commitment would necessitate.[47] At the time Keynes called this policy 'magnificently right'.[48] It was also popular in the USA. Nevertheless a few months later an admittedly internally divided administration set the points differently, and the Secretary of State succeeded in steering the 1934 Reciprocal Trade Agreements Act through Congress, a measure which laid the foundation for subsequent US external economic policy. This was the result of a series of particular circumstances, which can be fitted into the picture I have already derived from history.[49]

Politically this new trade policy of reciprocally agreed tariff reductions and use of most-favoured nation clauses only became *possible* because in the Act Congress explicitly agreed to surrender its right to approve commercial treaties. The Act was an enabling law. With it trade policy passed from the legislature to the executive and was thus largely removed from the open political clash of interests.

This gave particular groups of experts, and above all interest groups which had not yet been able to find congressional majorities, an opportunity for increased influence in politics. The reprisals that the USA faced from her traditional trading partners imposed heavy losses on American suppliers, and the future looked terrifying. The cotton exporting south, the grain exporting mid-west and the high technology areas in the north were all in danger of social and economic devastation. There were a few people in the New Deal Administration who still dreamed of a planned restructuring of the American economy, but they were gently eased out of power.

That this transformation was successful was the result of two further circumstances with which we should already be familiar: first, the foreign political threat to American leadership, and secondly skilled compensation deals which made the President's policy more marketable and secured for him victory in the 1936 election.

It is obvious that a consequence of the world depression had been to make the world less secure and to threaten peace. Japan was already fighting in Manchuria, and the USA was attempting to strengthen Chinese resistance. In Europe after Hitler's seizure of power the atmosphere became more ominous. Italy in 1934 was already preparing for an invasion of Abyssinia, which took place in 1936. It was time for the western democracies and those states dependent on them to end the suicidal economic war and the beggar-thy-neighbour policies. The national interest of the USA coincided now with a theory of the universal benefits of a freeing of world trade.[50] But how in a deeply depressed USA could this turn towards greater international involvement be explained? Was this not a policy desired above all by banks and representatives of multinational corporations? How could a President who had ridden into office on a populist wave carry out such a volte-face and still hope for reelection in 1936?

Here is not the place to describe all the steps of this volte-face. Two were particularly significant and successful. They cut a sufficiently large – even a massive – bloc of voters off from the previously isolationist and protectionist camp. It was precisely the major industrialists in export industries and the heads of the new investment banks, which stood close to the Democratic President, who encouraged him to put the Wagner Act (regulating the labour market and accepting autonomous negotiating parties) and the Social Security Act through Congress.[51] For the protectionist industries this was a doubly terrifying packet; for modern industries it was less appalling than the prospect of being cut off for a long time from foreign markets. In this way the risk of free trade was also reduced for labour, which in general had sought protection previously. The Reciprocal Trade Agreements Act, the Labour Act and the Social Security Law formed the packet in which the transition in US trade policy was sold. Accepted by the voters in 1936, it had enormous long-term consequences.[52]

13   With that I have reached a conclusion. Perhaps doubt remains as to whether the hypotheses that I have derived from history possess a general explanatory value. In the course of a presentation such as this I could not satisfy all demands for convincing proofs and demonstrations. It would be an advance if we could as a result of these historical reflections consider protectionism in a broader framework than that usually adopted by economists. For this is the task of economic history: to deepen our understanding of problems and to stimulate ideas on how to solve them. History in any case never presents any solutions that are capable of being copied directly.

2 WAS THERE A CAPITAL SHORTAGE IN THE FIRST HALF OF THE NINETEENTH CENTURY IN GERMANY?

I

Among the answers to the question as to why Germany's[1] economic development until the middle of the nineteenth century[2] remained so strikingly behind that of England, the argument that capital for industrialisation was lacking has played a comparatively major role for a long time.[3] It has only occasionally been challenged, and then rather in passing.[4] Certainly the sources themselves, and above all the records of companies, suggest a certain bias in this direction. Naturally we hear more of complaints about the lack of capital than about the opposite. But it will be demonstrated below that this thesis is not self-evidently correct, and that there are good grounds for examining it rather more precisely, and on the whole for relativising it.

When one reads of a 'lack of capital' we must appreciate that many different things can be meant. Here lies a source of great misunderstanding, because many authors do not clearly explain what they mean. By a lack of capital (or of finance) we can understand either

    (a) an inadequate *flow* of purchasing power, or
    (b) an inadequate *stock* of capital.

Depending on which *flow* is observed, judgements can be made in respect of the size of

    (1) the collective savings of an economic system,
    (2) the collective supply of investible funds, or
    (3) the credit supply in a specified period.

If one speaks of a shortage of capital in the sense of inadequate *stocks*, then one means either

(1) inadequate material assets, above all in the means of production,[5]
(2) inadequate stocks of liquid assets, or finally
(3) inadequate stocks of means of payment.

Below we test in which respect one can speak of a shortage of capital in early nineteenth-century Germany, and whether indeed this concept should be abandoned altogether.

II

In the more recent literature devoted to the explanation of economic growth, in particular in developing countries, the role of total savings as a limiting factor is stressed relatively heavily.[6] But, with respect to Germany, the assumption needs to be rejected that in the first half of the nineteenth century the ability or the will to save decisively prevented a more extensive industrial development and thus a faster growth of the economy as a whole. In essence, there are four reasons on which this hypothesis should be rejected.

1 The extent of voluntary savings within an economic system does not determine investment even today, when there is a developed banking apparatus. Given the resources of liquid assets, of which a considerable portion must have been hoarded, resources which were certainly far in excess of the volume of annual savings, a temporary expansion in the financing of (industrial) investments without an equally large planned renunciation of consumption would have been possible even at that time, and investment *ex ante* would have exceeded savings *ex ante*.[7] The propensity to save should have limited investment just as little in the first decades of the nineteenth century as it did subsequently.[8]

2 But, even were the savings ratio crucial, the assumption that in the first half of the nineteenth century it really was maximally high still appears to be unjustified. It is true that we do not know its exact size, but there exist indicators that it could have been higher (and at the same time that the consumption ratio could have been lower). It would have been a matter of a relative reduction of consumption without, on average, endangering the health or productive performance of the population.[8a] That this was possible is indicated by the not insignificant expenditure on goods for which there was no urgent demand,[9] so too does the ability of German society to withstand numerous crises, involving a necessary lowering of consumption, and the raising of funds in times of war and also for other forms of state consumption. Even in poor societies there are still hypothetical potentials for more saving.[9a]

3   An increase in the accumulation of material assets (real capital formation) would not necessarily even have required a lowering of consumption.
In view of the fact that in Germany in the first half of the nineteenth
century there was certainly no full employment for those fit to work, an
increase in the production of (investment) goods without an increased
financial outlay could have taken place. Those in open or concealed unemployment did in any case participate in consumption; employing them in
the generation of investment goods in those agricultural or industrial
occupations to which they belonged socially could have been a question of
institutional-organisational adaptation rather than of the quantity of dispo-
sible means for subsistence available.[10]

4   But is the explanation for the relatively low investment in the industrial
sector after all dependent on something like the aggregate savings ratio of
an economy? Very considerable resources for capital formation were supplied for agriculture, for commerce, for building houses, and for transportation. Industrial investment can only have accounted for a very small
portion of all the investments.

For instance at the beginning of the fifties the entire textile industry,
which was by far the largest industry at this time, and embraced more than
half those in industrial employment,[11] possessed plant and circulating
assets worth approximately 190 million Talers.[12] Comparing this with the
estimates of national income by W. G. Hoffmann and H. Müller yields the
following result:[13] capital in the textile industry amounted to 7 per cent of
the average national income for the years 1851–5. Even if errors in calculation need to be taken into account here,[13a] the result reveals the dimensions
involved in the comparison of industrial investment with the total production and consumption potential of the economy.[13b] It appears that the
textile industry, and thus over 60 per cent of all industry (if we measure in
terms of employment) could have been financed or even doubled in size on
the basis of the normal savings ratios – even in the middle of the nineteenth
century. In fact, of course, the financing of this capacity took decades and
therefore required only a marginal part of total savings.

Agriculture represented a much greater share of the total volume of
investment, for the value of livestock alone was substantially greater than
that of all industrial assets.[14] To be sure, for our purpose it is pointless to
estimate the *total assets* of agriculture, since from this nothing can be
inferred regarding the quantity of investment. This is because land values
form a considerable part of the total assets of agriculture, and these depend
in turn on the fluctuating production prices.[15] A calculation of national
wealth is therefore only an intellectual game.[16]

But, on the basis of other figures for wealth, we can still gain an impression as to what quantitative significance even considerably higher industrial investment would have had in relation to total capital formation. Annual investments in house construction, for instance, must have been several times greater than the sums invested in industry. The fire insurance value of buildings in the Zollverein in the middle of the century stood at around 3.2 thousand million Talers[17] (the actual value of the buildings was assuredly higher, but we are deliberately taking the lowest possible estimate). This means that, with depreciation and repairs at an annual 1.5 per cent, at least 50 million Talers annually were needed for reinvestment, for the upkeep of the assets. We know relatively little about new net investment in housing. According to Engel, it amounted to circa 6 million Talers annually in Saxony around the middle of the century. If we extrapolate on the basis of the population of the member states of the Zollverein, we obtain an aggregate net investment in house construction in the territory of the Zollverein of around 90 million Talers (= 270 million Marks).[17a] That would be equivalent to more than half the total assets of the textile industry![17b]

Such figures indicate that even a very considerable increase in industrial investment would have been possible within the limits of a nearly constant savings ratio. From the perspective of the economy as a whole, it was a question of rather small sums. All in all, it seems to me that the thesis of a shortage of capital, which focuses on inadequate savings, is disproved and therefore the reasons for the retardation of industrial investments must be sought elsewhere.

III

With that we come to the fifth reason which speaks against the thesis of a capital shortage. Among economic historians it was too long assumed – on the basis of outdated economic theories – that industrialisation was chiefly a problem of expanding capacity and of producers' capabilities of supply.[18] It was assumed (for the most part unconsciously) that there had always been a great propensity to invest; and this is why historians in the tradition of economists such as Adam Smith only examined whether investors had sufficient means at their disposal.

Such an assumption, however, is substantiated neither by theory, nor by the facts known to us. It would certainly be an exaggeration if one were to claim the opposite: because savings were made and because people were not consuming more, investors lacked sufficient incentives for investment.[19] But there can be no doubt about the fact that in Germany in the early nineteenth century industrial development was not characterised by a steady and growing demand, with the result that investment activity formed *the* critical bottleneck. Again and again, there were great incentives for liquid saving, with a resultant diminution of the domestic market. Again and again, foreign demand proved to be unstable – stagnating or even shrinking.[20] There were also lengthy periods in which public sector demand left much to be desired. Prussia, for instance, repaid bond debts amounting to a total of approximately 80 million Talers between 1821 and 1825.[21] Grain exports to Britain from 1821 to 1825 were only 15 per cent of the volume over the period 1801 to 1805.[22] The fall in prices of agricultural products before the mid-twenties did not lower the industrial production costs in Germany and thus provide German industry with a competitive advantage; rather it diminished the capacity of the agricultural market to absorb industrial products. At a time in which Baumstark's statement: 'industries and trade owe their bloom to the wealth of agriculture'[23] was still in general true,[24] this occurrence had the greatest significance. When there was a poor rye harvest in 1827, and prices rose, and when France also needed imported grain, the Cologne Chamber of Commerce was jubilant: 'A good year! As a consequence, the almost extinguished courage of the countryman has been rejuvenated, and it is pleasing to see how the gradual return of the previous prosperity to the inhabitants of the countryside also has a beneficial effect on the townspeople.'[25]

Only at the moment at which foreign countries and the state again played a greater role in the market did increased growth set in. Interestingly, the necessary capital was then available, and the various complaints about a lack of capital disappeared from the references.[26] In the forties and above all in the fifties (at least until 1857) these circumstances also coincided with autonomous increases of supply in several branches of the economy – above all, of course, in the railways. Almost until the middle of the nineteenth century, however, the leading industries were still the industries of mass consumer durables, and they needed demand in order to make substantial investments – unless there was a chance to use high prices and reduce costs by investment in improvements. Such investment might either eliminate previous imports, or might anticipate a future increase in demand. Such an opportunity, however, no longer existed for the German textile industry. The technical improvements had been used above all by English industry. Since the highly developed pioneering industry of England had not only conquered foreign markets previously supplied by German producers, but also substantially influenced prices on the German market, the profit level presumably no longer offered German producers incentives high enough to justify the considerable risks involved in the industrial outlay of capital. There was thus no stimulation for similar massive investment.[27] If a lack of capital had constrained industrial investment on a large scale, then those with sufficient means at their disposal – and of course there were such – would have been able to make considerable profits since they would have stood in a quasi-monopolistic position. But as a rule this did not occur before the end of the period that we are examining.

Opportunities for profit, generally still moderate, were matched by rising risks which also limited the demand for outside financing, even at low rates of interest, as well as for self-financing.[28] The risks of capital outlay to industry mounted up, since industrial output (at least in the case of a part of the capital) united a long-term commitment, as in agriculture, with the specific market risks of trading and banking, and finally with the risk of applying technical apparatuses which might be rapidly outdated as a consequence of technical progress. When, at the Munich meeting of the Estates in 1819, the project of a Bavarian national bank was deliberated, the delegate Schäzler, in a judgement which has subsequently become famous, judged the creditworthiness of factories sceptically:

> Whether factories can or should also be supported by the bank with sizeable advances of money is a question which still demands a great deal of discussion. Factories are, more than any other business concern, even at the apparently most advantageous moment, subject to great possible dangers, and the material assets of a factory which has come to a standstill, whatever they had cost, are worth almost nothing at all any more.[29]

In view of the very considerable fluctuations in the volume of production, even into the fifties,[30] Schäzler's warning was surely not unjustified; it applied not only to the creditors but also to debtors. In as much as banks and other 'capitalists' participated in the financing of industry at all, they probably really lent for the current needs of the enterprises rather than for fixed investment – even if they gave credit on mortgage. In the textile industry, inventories still played a very considerable role.[31] There are many examples of the risks of new technology given in a large number of monographs on entrepreneurs.

To emphasise the point: risk did not just deter the lenders, that is it not only limited the *availability* of capital, but it also influenced the entrepreneurs, and the potential *demand* for capital. Even where credit really was available, frequently they did not succeed in transforming it into investment. Here an example is given by the experience of the Bayerische Hypotheken- und Wechselbank (Bavarian Mortgage and Exchange Bank) whose fiftieth anniversary volume in 1885 states: 'The first result thus proved those right who feared the Bank would lack business . . . Artisans who could not enlarge their business operations and did not want to enlarge them either, and therefore did not need capital . . .'.[32] It further stated: 'A bank cannot create business transactions, it can only advance them, if the necessary conditions are given . . .'.

The very attitude to the problem of indebtedness hindered the easy use of a larger supply of credit, for it was still held to be unusual and even almost immoral to become indebted.[33] At this time a debtor who could not pay was shut out of society, and also lost his political rights since he was judged incapable and immoral. But it would be wrong to conclude from this, as does a great deal of recent historical writing concerned with business history research, that an inhibited willingness to become indebted was primarily a problem of the absence of a 'capitalist attitude', of a lack of entrepreneurial spirit. This was certainly a contributory factor, but there were also enough objective constraints limiting the demand for investment. Besides those already listed, mention should be made of the fact that in a period in which there were such considerable variations in sales, entrepreneurs were not necessarily interested in more productive but capital-intensive methods, which would have robbed the enterprise of flexibility. In view of the need to rapidly adjust the number of workers to the economic conditions of the time, a possible reduction in production costs under favourable economic conditions assuredly did not play a major role. At any rate, we still observe in the middle of the century, an increase in the number of labour-intensive small and micro-businesses.[34]

IV

The upshot thus seems to be that the demand for external finance from potential investors, as well as for self-financing, were much more limited than is allowed by the thesis of a shortage of capital. Not infrequently we even observe industrial disinvestment, in which the sums withdrawn were kept liquid. Everyone who balked at investment in capital goods was actually rewarded by a real increase in the value of cash and of monetary claims during the deflationary process which lasted until the thirties; as well as by the returns from a multitude of domestic and foreign securities.[35] Thus the *Augsburger Allgemeine Zeitung* reported in 1826: 'The continual sinking of all products, the stagnation of our factories . . . had the natural consequence that everything went into trading in securities.'[36] The effective rate of interest was relatively very high, and the risk, since the regulation of state debt, small in comparison; capital gains over the course of ten years at times amounted to as much as 100 per cent! All in all, this was an extraordinarily high premium on liquidity, which makes understandable the increasing creditor positions of both business in general and industry until the fifth decade of the century: they were thus engaged, as a sector, in a 'net capital export'. They were not – as they became in the later phases of industrialisation – the main debtors. The main debtors were public authorities at home and abroad, agriculture[37] and transportation. Whether, in view of the balance of trade surpluses of the Zollverein until around 1840, one can speak as Brockhage[38] claims of a German net capital export does not seem to me to be certain. France indisputably exported capital. But it is indisputable that for Germany in the first half of the century[38a] capital import for industry still had a comparatively minor quantative significance, even if it must also be admitted that in individual cases capital import had the function of stimulating pioneering achievements. This also is true rather for the middle of the century than for the beginning, and mainly for the west of Germany.[39]

Because the literature on the subject overestimates the capital requirement of industry, investment in securities and particularly in state securities has been criticised and condemned as a sign of irrational economic behaviour on the part of the wealthy at that time,[40] who were thus responsible for the slow rise of industry. They were said to have limited the supply of capital, which in principle was available. Now we have already indicated that at that time industrial demand for capital cannot have been as great as is often suggested. It should not be overlooked that the acquisition of securities was often not the cause, but the consequence, of slow industrial development.[41] In any case, the high returns for investment in securities – even without a consideration of the great propensity for liquidity – is evidence of 'rational' behaviour. That is not to deny that there were also class-determined investment habits – such as the tradition of the aristocracy to favour landed property, breweries, distilleries, etc.[42] But even here a purely economic explanation would be more obvious. After all, the markets were not transparent, the knowledge of the capitalists was very limited, and the possibilities of control over distant investments were too small. (Thus only a small social and economic area remained open for investment. That is how the small isolated capital markets came into existence; only the market for state securities already formed a large market.[43]) A behavioural norm, whose historical roots were no longer understood, doubtless grew out of an originally correct principle.

Capital in the early stages of development is not (if it ever has been) mobile for all purposes and between all persons; and there is no general capital market with a lively inter-regional and inter-sectoral arbitrage. But the cause lies not alone in the behaviour of the suppliers of credit. In view of the economic situation and of the structural imperfections of the money and capital markets, neither creditors nor debtors (apart from a few exceptions) are prepared for extensive credit operations involving fixed investment; the rate of interest therefore has only a small influence on the volume of investment.[44] A national supply of credit only became relevant to the growth of industry once a corresponding demand had been developed. This depended on the emergence of the banking system itself,[45] and above all on the contact between banks and other banks, as well as on modern transport and communication systems which became only available from the fifties.[46] The credit market was not so decisive because banks were willing to give longer-term credit on a large scale. We now know that they did this much more rarely than is widely supposed – and for the time being they were less prepared to extend credit after 1848 than before.[47] Much more decisive was the development of a national stock of liquidity, which transformed the terms of credit. Now that the credit givers also could find possibilities of refinancing themselves, and were therefore not dependent on calling in credit in the case of individual difficulties, the debtors were also prepared to take the now diminished risk of indebtedness; although joint stock companies still worked mainly with their own capital. So the credit market does not only stimulate a supply of credit and mobilises it, but also stimulates a demand for credit, at precisely that moment in time at which the demand for goods increases substantially.

If the above argument is correct, it is false to speak of a general lack of credit availability in the first half of the century. It only makes sense to speak of an insufficient availability in terms of an effective demand.

It was not a German peculiarity that industrial credit was still underdeveloped in the first half of the century; this was true also of more highly developed countries. Evidently the development of credit is no *sine qua non* of economic progress. In all countries the limit on the possibility of investment was – if a sufficient proclivity to invest existed – the extent of all privately owned capital in various forms. The capitalist himself transformed his funds or profits into material assets, in some circumstances in partnership with others, and later in joint stock companies.[48]

In the first half of the century it was, therefore, not so much capital that travelled as the capitalist. Hence the real problem of the time was that of the mobility of the capitalists. Mobility was doubtless already greater than ever before in Germany, but still less than in England at the end of the eighteenth and in the nineteenth century. As the demand for investment grew in the middle of the nineteenth century, the credit system developed as an adequate substitute for personal mobility. The so-called 'German path' of industrialisation began.

V

Two questions remain, which require once more an examination of the thesis of the shortage of capital in terms of the stock concept. What resources did the mobile capitalist have at his disposal; and what occasioned his, perhaps only limited, mobility? To begin with the first question. The decisive sources of finance apart from the profits of entrepreneurs – about which we unfortunately still know next to nothing in this context – were those liquid assets of whose favoured position we have already spoken: currency, stocks of precious metals in a non-monetary form, debt claims, and those stocks of goods which were liquid. We are considerably better informed about their use than we are about the size and use of profits, because a person leaves behind traces in records: concessions, founding contracts, disputes, etc. The successful use of such resources for investment did, it is true, presuppose a demand corresponding to an elastic supply of the means of production. In general, there would have been no shortage of supply of producer goods, in view of the increasing numbers of workers and of the efficiency of foreign suppliers. The development of prices of capital goods in any event reveals no bottleneck before 1845.

Theoretically, then, resources were available in the form of liquid assets. The question arises whether these were sufficiently large after the Napoleonic Wars. It is beyond doubt that many individual assets were reduced, but also that there were many 'new rich', who were able to increase their capital.[49] Presumably for the entire population a net loss of capital occurred; but it would be more important to know how the wealth of those who might have invested in industry – that is of traders and some manufacturers – changed. Apart from individual examples, we know very little about this. But it has already been indicated that after the end of the war not even the liquid resources – which were evidently available – were directed towards investment: the preservation of liquidity took priority over investment in business. Thus, at least for the first fifteen years after the wars, and probably for longer, it is impossible to speak of an inadequate total of liquid resources.

In view of the low propensity to invest, of the unwillingness to go into debt, and of the high proclivity to liquidity, the question arises whether a slight inflationary trend might not have promoted German development. Through the generation of profits, it might have made investment resources directly available to those who could have used them – to the entrepreneurs – as Earl Hamilton sought to show in the case of sixteenth- and seventeenth-century England.[50] But in an agrarian society, with an elastic supply of goods from abroad, such an effect should not be over-emphasised.[50a] It was by no means certain that it would have been industry that might have profited from inflation. All the increases in price indices in the history of the eighteenth and nineteenth centuries show that agriculture benefited in the first instance. Demand for consumer goods is more price and income elastic than for agricultural goods. Industrial demand thus diminishes with declining real incomes. It is true that it would now have been theoretically possible for agriculture to transfer profits to industry. But this did not occur to any substantial extent, even in England.[51] Given rising prices, farmers are more likely to hoard, and may even reduce their supply of goods to the market. If there had, however, been an inflation, the basis of the later export successes of Germany would have been taken away, as one can see from a study of the immediate consequences of the Napoleonic Wars.

What was it that finally induced the owners of liquid assets to invest in industry? Alongside the demand which developed in the forties, capital was finally exposed to a pressure for utilisation:[52] because in the traditional areas in which assets had been used, increased investment would have meant falling rates of profit, and even a steady capital stock encountered reduced profit levels. There are several reasons for this, which probably all worked together cumulatively.

1 Some monopolistic firms required only a certain size and a certain capital. Further profits were not used in the same enterprise but were invested in other sectors, for instance, by heirs.

2 With the improvement in the transport system the opportunities for profit and simultaneously the capital requirements of commerce grew less. In Cologne the shrinking of the carrying trade, which was for the most part associated with credit, released capital; a similar process is to be observed in many places. Since mercantile capital was still relatively substantial in the early stages of industrialisation, substantial sums for investment in industry, which in each individual case still required *relatively* small sums, resulted from that process.[53]

3 This coincided with the fact that the development of industry in principle altered the significance of commerce. Merchants, who had previously been lords over the producers, were threatened by dependence on ever bigger units of production. We have very early examples of this in England.[54] Dependence of this sort was avoidable, if vertical integration with production was pursued from a base in commerce.

4 Finally the decline of the cyclical and structural premium on

liquidity, and the increase in the real value of liquid resources, is also of great importance. The constant increase in the price of securities, associated with a decline in the effective interest rate to around 3.5 per cent which occasioned loan conversions in many states,[55] removed the preference for this type of asset among those who could choose between alternative investments.[56] The decline in the importance of the exchange business for all bankers operated in the same direction. In a town such as Augsburg, the way in which a liquidity which had once been highly prized finally had to be diverted into industrial investment due to low returns is clearly discernible;[57] in addition it was certain that the city, incorporated into the newly expanded state of Bavaria, and faced with altered economic circumstances, could not remain a finance and commercial centre of the first order.[58]

VI

What then is the answer to the question posed?

With regard to total savings we cannot speak of a shortage of capital. Total savings had little effect on actual investments in industry in the early nineteenth century. Whether or not a sufficiently large aggregate supply of investible credit and private resources was available is on the whole not decisive either, since the market was imperfect and contact between suppliers and borrowers in general was scanty. Moreover, there are good reasons to think that the demand for investment as a whole may not have been all that great, and that it is quite possible to speak of a limited demand rather than of a limited supply. It is thus also questionable whether insufficient liquidity could have been the obstacle to investment, although in individual cases such a conclusion can be demonstrated. We know that certain enterprises lacked resources in certain situations. And we shall never know how many enterprises never saw the light of day due to a lack of resources. But on the other hand we also know that at the same time those with money not infrequently encountered difficulties in finding *secure* debtors willing to pay even low interest rates. Banks refused to accept deposits because they could find no use for these resources, and many enterprises which came into being with considerable resources failed because they could not achieve sustained profits – which they would surely have done had there really been a shortage of investment funds. For in that case already established enterprises would have had a quasi-monopolistic position on the market. This may perhaps be observed in some branches of industry towards the middle of the century; in others it is certainly not the case before 1850.

In formulating a conclusion we encounter the following problem: what criteria do we have for deciding the answer to our question in the light of the heterogeneous developments in different regions and sectors of business? Since the markets were unconnected and the mobility of the capitalists was limited, it seems only possible to judge with regard to particular circumstances. If a supply pressure existed in some markets, and an excess of demand in others, then the issue cannot be summed up with a single statement without weighing up the importance of individual markets.[59] For this, however, there are no undisputed quantitative indicators. The view presented here is that the importance of capital shortage has, in all aspects of the literature on the subject, been overestimated.

Postscript

Since the appearance of this essay in 1961, a large number of works have touched on or referred to the subject treated here. My main theses have not been criticised; they have rather – with a few variations of emphasis – been confirmed. (See *inter alia* H. Winkel, 'Kapitalquellen und Kapitalverwendung am Vorabend des industriellen Aufschwungs in Deutschland', *SchJb*, 90 (1970), pp. 275ff; P. Coym, 'Unternehmensfinanzierung im frühen 19 Jahrhundert – dargestellt am Beispiel der Rheinprovinz und Westfalens' (thesis, Hamburg 1970); R. Tilly, 'Zur Entwicklung des Kapitalmarktes und Industrialisierung im 19. Jahrhundert unter besonderer Berücksichtigung Deutschlands', *VSWG*, 60 (1973), pp. 146ff – reprinted in R. Tilly, *Kapital, Staat und sozialer Protest in der deutschen Industrialisierung* (Göttingen 1980), pp. 77ff; R. Tilly, 'Capital Formation in Germany in the Nineteenth Century', *CEHE*, VII/1 (1978), pp. 382ff.)

Of course, international research has since shown that important arguments, which were presented here for Germany in the early nineteenth century, appear to hold true of all western European industrial countries in the phase of early industrialisation. (On this, see F. Crouzet (ed.), *Capital Formation in the Industrial Revolution* (London 1972); J. P. P. Higgins and S. Pollard (eds.), *Aspects of Capital Investment in Great Britain, 1740–1850* (London 1971); P. Mathias, 'Capital, Credit and Enterprise in the Industrial Revolution' in P. Mathias, *The Transformation of England. Essays in the Economic and Social History of England in the Eighteenth Century* (London 1979), pp. 88ff. Simultaneously with my article there appeared: A. Brusatti, 'Unternehmensfinanzierung und Privatkredit im Österreichischen Vormärz' in *Mitteilungen des Österreichischen Staatsarchivs*, 13 (1960), pp. 331ff.)

The essay has been reprinted in materially unaltered form. But the opportunity for some stylistic corrections and clarifications was taken.

Relevant conclusions of detailed research were also worked into the footnotes. The reader will find such addenda above all in the footnotes marked by additional letters. Where criticism is known of, the relevant statements were not, as a rule, altered; but here too the footnotes provide the relevant explanation.

I wish to take the opportunity of explicitly correcting a misunderstanding found in the case of several authors. In the preceding essay it was *not* stated that industrial entrepreneurs did not face a shortage of capital – if one understands this as their desire to obtain (more) finance at low prices and against only negligible securities. Nobody can deny this kind of shortage of capital, because it appears massively documented in the sources. But there has never been a capital market in which everyone who wanted financial resources also obtained them on conditions agreeable to him. (A 'perfect' capital market in this sense is indeed even unthinkable.) The characteristic of capital, along with goods, services and other economic activities, is that it is scarce; so that there are always some who are excluded from its use. This is why the sources are full of representations of this kind. The question posed in the essay was primarily one concerning the whole economy: whether a shortage of capital (in the economy as a whole) was a barrier to growth and which had particular significance in explaining instances of developmental backwardness or hesitant industrialisation before the forties or fifties of the nineteenth century.

3 REGIONAL VARIATIONS IN GROWTH IN GERMANY IN THE NINETEENTH CENTURY WITH PARTICULAR REFERENCE TO THE WEST–EAST DEVELOPMENTAL GRADIENT

I

It is the general scholarly opinion that regional differences in levels of prosperity developed in the course of the nineteenth century, in the wake of industrialisation, in Germany; and that the previous differences in the level of economic activity in the Kingdom of Prussia were accentuated. As everyone knows, it is possible to speak of a west–east gradient in Prussia, of the decay of several formerly industrial areas (for instance in the Eifel), and of the relative decline of large parts of Franconia, etc. But a *quantification* as well as a systematic *explanation* for the whole phenomenon of the regional differentiation of the growth process in Germany is still lacking.

That is no accident. The present state of research reflects a certain level of academic interest and of the possibilities open to academic enquiry. There is a large number of important local, provincial, or sectoral investigations, but almost all of them deal with a particular aspect, and only in passing do they treat the issue of a general economic-geographic analysis.

Three external circumstances perhaps at present lead economic historians to pursue more closely the problem of geographic development within highly industrialised countries.

1 Current observations of international variations in development sharpen our interest in regional variations in development as well.
2 Political economy is concerned more and more with regional economic analysis, and provides a number of interesting analytical tools, tested on current material.
3 The existence of a large number of national programmes for the development of distressed areas directs attention towards the causes of such distress. Since these often lie far back in history,

the economic historian is called on to cooperate in providing an explanation. But a purely local historian cannot do much. The concept of a 'distressed area' itself has meaning only in the context of a supra-localised conception of a 'norm' for regional growth. Often enough in regional investigations, such a clear term of reference is lacking, with the result that they contain assertions incompatible with those made about other areas. Thus we have no 'test of coherence' for the many individual studies of regional economic development.

The following important questions await clarification:

1 At present, we discuss the international mechanisms for transmitting economic growth from countries with a high per capita income to countries with a low per capita income. How did this transmission function within Germany, since Germany was by no means drawn into the developmental process evenly or all at once?

2 There is a well-founded hypothesis that average per capita income was not, even around 1800, uniform throughout Germany. What variations were there and how did they develop in the wake of industrialisation?

3 It may be assumed that (at least initially) variations increased. But where and why?

4 Are there regions with a developmental lag (or a lag in income) which did not catch up, as well as regions which were able to catch up? How can such variable fortunes be explained?

5 It may be assumed that the phases of industrialisation affected the development of regional income levels and that individual regions of Germany each experienced their 'take-off' in particular economic sectors. Is this correct, and if so, why?

One could further extend the catalogue of questions; and one should also note that several of them overlap, or at least stand in a close connection with each other. No doubt a problem such as this is a long-term research program rather than the subject for a single contribution.

Here the immediate issue at stake is to ascertain indicators of regional variations in nineteenth-century development. I should also like to contribute some initial hypotheses explaining the regional differentiation of growth in Germany. By growth, we understand an increase in the real national product per capita. Therefore, if regional variations are discerned, differences in the level and development of national product per capita in various regions of Germany must be demonstrable. Sections II and III of this essay are devoted to a discussion of the sources; section IV contains some hypotheses explaining the phenomenon.

II

The obvious first step is to undertake a careful investigation of the product per head in the individual regions of Germany in the course of the nineteenth and twentieth centuries. Unfortunately, such material is available to us only to a very limited extent, since the income tax system in the individual states of Germany is relatively recent. Table 3.1 contains the results provided by Hoffmann-Müller.

Table 3.1. *National income per capita in Germany in several states for selected five and three year periods (Marks)*

	1871/5	1881/5	1891/5	1901/5	1911/13
German Empire	364	381	445	538	716
Prussia	352	369	428	516	698
Saxony		402	549	655	870
Hamburg/Bremen	812	790	877	1011	1261
Hesse	310[a]	343	407	515	634
Baden			474	561	708
Württemberg					688
Bavaria					635

Note: [a] 1872–5.
Source: W. G. Hoffmann and J. H. Müller, *Das deutsche Volkseinkommen 1851–1957*, Tübingen 1959, pp. 20f.

A considerable disadvantage of this material lies in the fact that the political boundaries encompass areas of quite different size; and Prussia, which accounted for around 60 per cent of the population of the German Empire in 1871, is only represented by an average figure. Thus, the west–east gradient between the Prussian provinces, which is of pre-eminent interest, cannot be detected. Only the relatively favourable position of the north German city states, the special position of the Kingdom of Saxony, the slight backwardness of Württemberg and the greater retardation of Bavaria are noticeable.

For the years 1900, 1907 and 1913, there are estimates of the 'uncorrected incomes' in the Prussian provinces and for several German federal states, which permit a rather more precise observation of regional variations.[1] They can be taken from table 3.2, in which column 4 contains the officially estimated national per capita income. Table 3.3, drawn from the same source, shows the increases in real per capita income, using a single price index of the Reich to deflate national income. We will return to this point later.

Unfortunately, similarly detailed information is not available to us for earlier years. The picture afforded by the figures at hand is substantially clear, notwithstanding reservations about their exactitude. The result of table 3.1 is (as far as possible) confirmed in tables 3.2 and 3.3. Within Prussia there are, however, as table 3.2 shows, very considerable variations in incomes. Berlin and Brandenburg tower above the rest. Brandenburg is exceptional, among other reasons, because the as yet unincorporated suburbs of Berlin were statistically included in this province. Disregarding this narrowly limited local centre of Berlin, the west–east gradient appears

Table 3.2. *Unadjusted per capita income and national income per capita in selected years*

	Unadjusted per capita income (Marks)			NI per capita (Marks)	Unadjusted income as per cent of Prussian average		
	1900 1	1907 2	1913 3	1913 4	1900 5	1907 6	1913 7
Prussia	447	516	599	747	100,0	100,0	100,0
East Prussia	321	342	399	486	71,8	66,3	66,6
West Prussia	302	327	390	480	67,6	63,4	65,1
Pomerania	347	380	469	576	77,6	73,6	78,3
Posen	302	319	375	465	67,6	61,8	62,8
Silesia	396	437	492	603	88,6	84,7	82,1
Berlin	834	945	957	1254	186,6	183,1	159,8
Brandenburg	479	637	793	962	107,2	123,4	132,4
Berlin/Brandenburg	613	747	847	1058	137,1	144,8	141,4
Province of Saxony	442	494	564	700	98,9	95,7	94,2
Schleswig-Holstein	447	524	626	763	100,0	101,6	104,5
Hanover	422	467	563	697	94,4	90,5	94,0
Westphalia	445	508	582	735	99,6	98,4	97,2
Hesse-Nassau	549	625	723	899	122,8	121,1	120,7
Rhine province/ Hohenzollern	488	570	657	832	109,2	110,5	109,7
Kingdom of Saxony	509[a]	587	719	897	113,9[a]	113,8	120,0
Württemberg	—	510	576	672	—	98,8	96,2
Baden	422	548	612	710	94,4	106,2	102,2
Bavaria	—	—	—	629	—	—	—
Hamburg	870	1010	1115	1313	194,6	195,7	186,1

Note: [a] 1899.
Source: *Das deutsche Volkseinkommen vor und nach dem Kriege, Einzelschriften zur Statistik des Deutschen Reiches* Nr. 24, Berlin 1932, p. 72 table 12, p. 73 table 13, p. 76 table 15.

Table 3.3. *Changes of unadjusted per
capita income in constant 1913 prices
from 1900 to 1913 (per cent)*

Prussia	+ 7
East Prussia	0
West Prussia	+ 3
Pomerania	+ 8
Posen	− 1
Silesia	− 1
Berlin/Brandenburg	+ 11
Province of Saxony	+ 2
Schleswig-Holstein	+ 12
Hanover	+ 7
Westphalia	+ 5
Hesse-Nassau	+ 5
Rhine province/Hohenzollern	+ 8
Kingdom of Saxony	+ 13
Baden	+ 16
Hamburg	+ 2

*Source: Das deutsche Volkseinkommen vor
und nach dem Kriege*, p. 74 table 14.

quite clearly. All the eastern provinces lie far below the Prussian average.
Indeed, the eastern provinces, with the exception of Pomerania, had fallen
back even further by comparison with the average immediately before the
First World War, as is shown in table 3.3. Of course, the figures used for
'nominal per capita income' and also for real income in table 3.3, deflated
with a unitary Reich price index, cannot reveal much about precise differences in prosperity. In the first place, nominal income appears to have
been systematically underestimated, especially in rural districts; secondly,
not a difference in nominal income, but a difference in real income would
be decisive for a variation in prosperity. However, deflating using a unified
price index is almost certainly incorrect. Prices were regionally different,
and developed in different ways over time. In fact, consumer prices in the
German Reich had a distinct regional profile with a considerable gradient,
especially between agrarian areas and centres of consumption. To be sure,
the Zollverein, railways and other factors led to a certain levelling, but the
process was by no means complete.[2] Unfortunately, we do not as yet have
any possibility of conducting inter-regional comparisons of price indices,
and of converting regional nominal incomes into comparable real incomes.
It seems to be the case, however, that, particularly in those districts in
which nominal incomes were especially low, the most important consumer
goods prices were also below the Reich average. Thus the gradient in real

income in general will have been smaller than the gradient in nominal incomes. To what extent this hypothesis may be confirmed remains to be seen.[3]

As has already been said, one of the biggest gaps in table 3.1 is that Prussia and other federal states appear as undifferentiated units. Although tables 3.2 and 3.3 overcome this defect to some extent, they do not extend back in time sufficiently far to permit a study of the actual process of industrialisation. For the particular kind of income represented by wages we have a multitude of scattered pieces of information from much earlier periods, and even several official and non-official systematic statistics of regional wage differentials.[4] With a corresponding ordering of the regions, the material of R. Kuczynski and G. Bry also yields a west–east gradient for skilled and unskilled workers, and in the west a weak gradient from north to south. But wage comparisons between those in different occupations remain dubious. Grumbach-König's more ambitious wage comparison comprehends average industrial wages in different regions by sector. Unfortunately, the administrative boundaries of the respective units were very variably defined in the original material, and occupational associations (Berufsgenossenschaften) for the most part encompassed regions too large to be really useful. Nevertheless, in the textile industry as in iron and steel, a very considerable retardation in wages in Silesia compared with Rhineland-Westphalia can be observed for the whole period between 1888 and 1913.

Wage statistics emanating from the implementation of Sections 6 and 8 of the sickness insurance law of 1883 are very much more differentiated with regard to regions. The law specified that the level of the sickness benefit should be determined according to locally customary daily wage rates for labourers; with the result that the higher administrative authorities prescribed these rates of pay after consulting local government.[5]

Figure 3.1 shows as an example the geographic distribution of the established pay rates in 1906. This material too shows a clear downward gradient to the east. For many reasons, which need not be discussed here, the value of these statistics should be assessed quite critically. In addition, wage statistics are never a substitute for income statistics, since the wage is only one kind of income among many. And, in addition, these wage statistics only take us back in time a short distance.

The very regionally specific evidence from the Prussian class tax, from the classified income tax and from income tax, especially from the enfranchising tax on property, in relation to total regional population, go back somewhat further. Since income tax was only paid by recipients of higher incomes, the proportion of the population paying income tax may be

Figure 3.1   Wages of day labourers (1 January 1906)

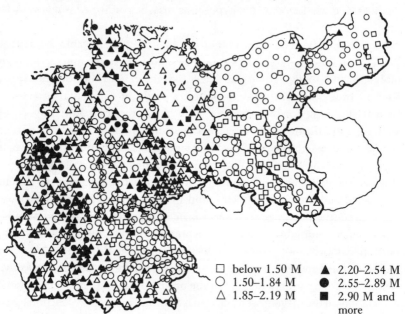

□ below 1.50 M	▲ 2.20–2.54 M
○ 1.50–1.84 M	● 2.55–2.89 M
△ 1.85–2.19 M	■ 2.90 M and more

understood as a wealth index for the region.[6] The results for the Kingdom of Prussia are presented in a simplified form as follows:

1 In general, over the entire period the proportion of those paying income tax was larger in the towns than in the country, and therefore urbanised regions in each case appear wealthier than rural ones.

2 Generally, the proportions in the central and western provinces through the whole of the surveyed period were higher than in the east: remarkably, this is true both of *Regierungsbezirke* (governmental districts) taken as a whole and for purely urban and purely country districts taken on their own. As early as 1875, among the ten most disadvantaged Prussian *Regierungsbezirke* there is only one which is not in the east; and among the top seven *Regierungsbezirke* there is none in the east. Of course, around this time, the measured variation did not extend across the entire state. It is true that the east was clearly disadvantaged, but the central *Regierungsbezirke* were not clearly differentiated from those in the west.

3 In general, the proportion of those paying income tax in Prussia

from the middle of the nineteenth century until the First World War grew faster in those *Regierungsbezirke* which already had a relatively privileged position than in the eastern provinces. That becomes especially clear if we examine specific periods of rapid growth. From 1896 to 1901, the nine *Regierungsbezirke* with the lowest increase of those paying income tax as a proportion of the whole population lay in the east.[6a]

The number and proportion of income tax payers does not yet tell us a great deal, if it is possible that in one region a few payers had much larger taxable incomes than did a great many payers in another. Such a possibility cannot be ruled out for Eastern Prussia in the middle of the century. In 1867, the actual income tax payers in East Prussia, for instance, paid more taxes on average than did their counterparts in the province of Saxony, but their share of the population was still substantially smaller, so that the average income of the population in the province of Saxony would have been higher than in East Prussia. Around 1822, the total class tax paid per payer was actually higher in East Prussia than in the province of the Rhine! However, since the class tax hardly reflected the real conditions of income, no importance need be attached to this observation. But it becomes apparent that the task of establishing precisely from *what date* the eastern provinces of Prussia can be characterised as relatively 'underdeveloped' becomes increasingly urgent.

Let us summarise the preceding argument: the regional distribution of income in the nineteenth century cannot, for many reasons, yet be studied with anything approximating to precision over a longer period. The material is largely absent. For the end of the nineteenth century a few general statements are possible. They are so interesting that an attempt should be made to advance further by means of a different route.

III

At this point it is clear that, since the direct path via tax statistics is not possible for periods lying further back, we must look for alternative ways. We cannot approach early regional incomes from the distribution side; neither, of course, is the value added available. But perhaps we could succeed in discovering differences in income by analysing personal expenditure. This becomes possible with the use of certain categories of expenditure which (1) clearly grow with per capita income and (2) are statistically available with a sufficient regional dispersion. Most kinds of expenditure do not, as far as I can see, fulfil these demands. In Germany there were considerable regional differences in habits of consumption. In most cases, where figures are available, a regional cross section cannot provide information about differences in average income.

Therefore we will attempt to arrive at such expenditure (and income) indirectly, with the help of two fairly unusual indicators: the density of doctors and the density of students in secondary schools. Although a whole number of reasons will immediately occur to the reader which make the exercise appear suspect, let us assume for the moment, until the opposite be proven, that the density of *doctors and school students* might be functions of the average income of a region. In fact, in the years 1908 to 1913, there was a surprisingly close correlation between the density of doctors and the per capita income in the Prussian provinces ($r = 0.8511$). It is even better if one correlates only the *rankings* of the provinces with regard to the density of doctors and the level of per capita income. (The rank correlation coefficient amounted to 0.9 on the Spearman-Pearson test.) Only the ranking in the density of doctors of Westphalia and Hanover deviate considerably from the rankings in the order of income: according to the density of doctors, Hanover appears in too positive and Westphalia in too severe a light. The Rhineland has a slightly worse rating in the density of doctors than in income, and Pomerania a somewhat better one (see figure 3.2). Unfortunately, in other parts of the Reich, the correspondence of this indicator was much poorer; and for this reason we have dispensed with a regionally extended application until such time as the causes of the variability may be clarified. That this close correlation between the density of doctors and per capita income in Prussia is not a chance outcome for the years 1908 to 1913 is shown by a very similar close correlation of the regional distribution of both quantities in the German Reich (both Länder and the Prussian provinces) in the years 1931/2 ($r = 0.96$) and 1936 ($r = 0.97$).

Table 3.4 presents the rankings of the Prussian provinces with regard to the number of inhabitants per doctor.[7] It contains several striking pieces of evidence. First, the long-standing retardation of three eastern provinces, East and West Prussia and Posen, is apparent. East Prussia does improve in the process and pushes Posen into first place (indicating the lowest density of doctors) but the principal gradient remains unchanged. The two other eastern provinces, Pomerania and Silesia, change their rankings in a very significant way. Silesia, which was still relatively highly developed in the early nineteenth century, deteriorated step by step until the census of 1867 and ended in a substantially worse position than at the beginning. Pomerania, by contrast, was able in the second half of the century to

Figure 3.2 Correlation of per capita income and number of physicians per 10,000 inhabitants

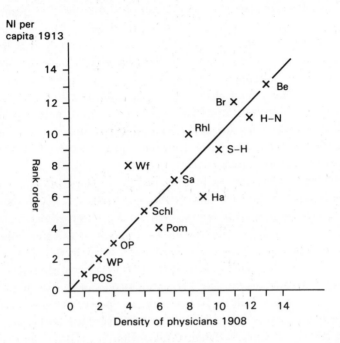

Table 3.4. *Ranking of Prussian provinces according to inhabitants per physician in selected years*

1825	1849	1861	1867	1882	1902–1908
1 East Prussia (EP)	EP	EP	PS	PS	PS
2 West Prussia (WP)	PS	PS	EP	EP	WP
3 Posen (PS)	WP	WP	WP	WP	EP
4 Pomerania (PO)	PO	PO	SI	BR	WE
5 Rhineland^a (RH)	SI	SI	PO	SI	SI
6 Brandenburg (BR)	BR	BR	BR	PO	POQ
7 Silesia (SI)	RH	WE	SA	SA	SA
8 Westphalia (WE)	WE	RH	WE	WE	RH
9 Saxony (SA)	SA	SA	RH	RH	HA
10 City of Berlin (BE)	BE	BE	Schleswig-H. (SH)	HA	SH
			Hanover (HA)	SH	BR
			Hesse-N (HN)	HN	HN
			BE	BE	BE

Note: ^a Including Hohenzollern.
Source: See footnote 7.

improve on its originally rather poor position. Movement of the Rhineland is very evident. It corresponds fairly precisely to the converse of the Silesian development. The dramatic changes in the positions of Brandenburg and Westphalia in the last period are perhaps to be explained by the fact that in those years the towns in Brandenburg near to Berlin became rich in doctors, whereas in Westphalia the large expansion of the working-class population in the Ruhr did not immediately attract new physicians. One should also note the high density of doctors in those areas annexed by Prussia in 1866, which thus considerably improved the Prussian average after that date.[7a] It seems to me that the facts just described are, on the whole, fairly plausible, and agree with what we know of regional economic development.

Similarly, an attempt was made to use the development of schooling as an indicator of regional wealth in Prussia. In various key years a fairly close correspondence between the order of the density of doctors and the order of the density of students in secondary schools actually resulted. Table 3.5 presents visually this correlation between the last respective surveys before the First World War.[8] The correlation of rankings between density of school students and per capita income (according to table 3.2, column 2) was also still fairly close, as the Spearman-Pearson rank correlation coefficient of 0.81 tells us. The indicator of the density of students in higher schools is less well suited for obvious reasons to comparisons of

Table 3.5. *Comparison of the rankings of Prussian provinces by inhabitants per physician and students of secondary schools*

Ranking by inhabitants per physician (1908)	Ranking by inhabitants per student (1910)
Posen	Posen
West Prussia	Silesia
East Prussia	Westphalia
Westphalia	East Prussia
Silesia	West Prussia
Pomerania	Saxony
Saxony	Pomerania
Rhineland and Hohenzollern	Rhineland and Hohenzollern
Hanover	Hanover
Schleswig-Holstein	Schleswig-Holstein
Brandenburg	Hesse-Nassau
Hesse-Nassau	Brandenburg
Berlin	Berlin

Source: For density of physicians table 3.4; for density of students: Stat. Jb. f.d. Preuss. Staat, Vol. 9, 1911, pp. 365 ff.

wealth, but it does not seem self-evidently an absurd supposition to assume a connection between regional income levels and density of school students.

The conclusions in short are as follows: in the first available overview of 1822 (according to Engel – see footnote 8), the eastern provinces of Posen, East and West Prussia and Pomerania, already lie at the top of the league showing the number of inhabitants per school student in a higher institution. Saxony, Berlin-Brandenburg and Silesia show a considerably higher density of pupils. The Rhineland still finds itself in the middle. Thus the surprisingly close agreement with the order of the density of physicians (table 3.4) is evident. But in the course of the nineteenth century, the picture then alters in favour of some of the eastern provinces. To what cause this may be attributed is hard to say without closer examination. Possibly the very much higher population growth in the east is responsible, since with a growing proportion of young people, the proportion of school students is also increased. But perhaps the prosperity of agriculture also made itself felt in the higher income brackets. In any case, the order is at this time quite different from that given by the statistics of physicians. Even the new territorial gains of 1866 do not fit in entirely seamlessly. Schleswig-Holstein – by contrast with the case of the physicians' statistics – still has a low ranking in the density of school students.[8a] After 1895, however, the improved position of some of the eastern states for the most part once more vanished. The order of density of school students in the year 1896 is, from the worst to the best provinces – Posen, East Prussia, Silesia, Westphalia, West Prussia, Pomerania, Brandenburg, Saxony, Schleswig-Holstein, Rhineland, Hanover, Hesse-Nassau, Berlin. The west–east gradient is, with the exception of Berlin, clearly recognisable.

If the assumption set out here, that the density of physicians and the density of school students are indicators of wealth, is really valid, then the facts supplied substantiate the supposition that in Prussia *the west–east gradient already existed before the Industrial Revolution*. Silesia, alone among the eastern provinces, was better off in terms of wealth; it had lost its position in the wake of the Industrial Revolution. For this, a whole series of reasons may be given. Presumably, in the course of industrialisation, the income of the traditional markets for Silesian craft producers grew more slowly, since the east of Europe remained visibly underdeveloped. Silesian goods had poor access to the western market, especially since the route to the west was blocked by the much more highly developed regions of central Germany. Furthermore, Silesia, as the traditional location of the linen industry, had as its crucial export that one trade which from the middle of the nineteenth century hardly showed any growth worth mentioning. So the traditional export industry was eliminated as a source of growth.[9]

IV

The hypothesis derived from the indicators, that an income gradient from west to east evidently already existed in the *pre-industrial* nineteenth century, now requires some tentative explanation.

Without a doubt there had already been a *price* gradient for agricultural products long before the nineteenth century. After all, we can already observe how in the fifteenth and sixteenth centuries the north-east German territories supplied grain to the developmental hub with the Low Countries as a centre. The system of von Thünen rings had come into being, with an increase of agricultural prices from the periphery to the centre.[10] But a price gradient is *not* identical with an income gradient. The reasons for the reported income gradient must be investigated more deeply.

It is tempting to seek the causes in the relatively poor development of manufacturers in the eastern area. In fact the east remained predominantly agrarian in the centuries in which pre-industrial crafts emerged; with the exception of Silesia, it scarcely developed an own export industry. In the eighteenth and early nineteenth centuries, the manufacturing zones lay elsewhere, in the central mountain regions and on their edges. There were two strips which ran across Germany forming manufacturing zones, one from Westphalia through Thuringia and Saxony to Silesia, and the other from Switzerland, on the left and right banks of the Rhine to the Netherlands Provinces.[11] In these zones, manufacturers were located which supplied a supra-regional market, and thus stood out above the norm of local crafts for basic needs.

Of course, one must not exaggerate the spread of manufacturing density around 1800. Even pronouncedly rural areas did after all have branches of secondary and tertiary employment in 'local manufactures'. Characteristically, in 1832, in several districts of the agrarian east the urban proportion of the population lay above the average for Prussia. Domestic provisions as well as agricultural exports required the town, and its supporting trades. Of course, the manufacturing population stayed within more modest limits in the east than it did elsewhere. In other parts of Germany, a manufacturing superstructure, whose location was determined either by raw material availability, or which for other reasons was able to attract distant demand, developed beyond the level of local crafts. As an example of the size of this superstructure, one could take two Württemberg *Kreise* (districts) of very different manufacturing structure. In 1861, the district which was by far the most developed in manufacturing, the Black Forest *Kreis*, still had

(only) 177 per thousand inhabitants employed in commerce and manufacture, as against 129 in the almost entirely agrarian Jagst *Kreis*. The
difference between these naturally very extensive areas, which are comparable with *Regierungsbezirke* in Prussia, thus amounted to only fifty
employees per thousand of the population. The difference is thus not yet
very great, yet it must already have been significant with regard to the
emergence of regional variations in income.

But does that really mean very much? We as the heirs of the 'Industrial
Revolution' too readily identify economic development with industrialisation, and rarely imagine that agricultural zones could have had a higher
average income than manufacturing zones. Conditions must, however, on
occasion, have once been like this. Schleswig-Holstein is a much later
proof of the prosperity of agricultural regions. Of course, this province lay
closer to the main markets and produced under what was surely on average
more advantageous conditions than the east. But the east also should not be
called backward just because it was agrarian. After all in the eighteenth and
early nineteenth centuries, the craft manufacturing zones were located in
the most distressed areas of Germany. The distress and poverty of the
population working at home and putting out production have often been
described. It was not a coincidence that pre-industrial crafts were concentrated in those areas where the free hereditary division of peasant property prevailed, and parcellised holdings could not fully feed a family. Yet
there are also concentrations of crafts in regions of single heir inheritance.
The impossibility of increasing the amount of land capable of cultivation
and/or the poor quality of the soil, which rendered economically unattrac-
tive an increased input of labour, often necessitated craft production as a
sideline. (We will not enter into the many social structural determinants
here.) Craft activity as a major occupation may later have developed on the
basis of this, perhaps also did prosperity. But that was not the rule.

Although negligible pre-industrial development of the east German
regions does not allow us to infer poverty, there is here a key to the
explanation of the separate development of the east. In the Prussian east,
the growth of population for a long time *did not* come up against barriers.
There were still vast reserves of land at the beginning of the nineteenth
century, so that from 1815 to 1864 acreage expanded two and a half times;
this was also a consequence of the disappearance of the fallow. As a result,
not only local requirements but also a growing demand from the Berlin
area and for exports could be met. The middle of the nineteenth century
became the golden age of the east German agrarian economy.

Rising agrarian demand was best satisfied to a large extent through an
increased application of the factors of production, land and labour, rather

than through technical progress and still less through an increased application of capital and credit. The great elasticity of factor supply was an obstacle to growth. In consequence, few linkage effects carried over from agriculture to the secondary sector. The condition of the agrarian economy did not affect the fundamental structure of the eastern economy. Furthermore, the profits from the favourable market situation in agriculture do not appear to have been equally distributed. The favourable position may have furnished a relatively small number of grain exporters with income, while the mass of estate labourers and peasant families had a lesser share, particularly since national minorities afforded a reservoir of cheap labour. The rent income of exporters, however, appears frequently to have found a direct route to the western parts of the country, either as expenditure in the capital or in other political centres, or for the direct purchase of western goods, or for capital transfer to the west. The east certainly could have pressed for tariff protection of infant industries against the western parts of Germany with much more justice than could the western industries of Germany demand protection against foreign markets. Of course, the specific social composition of the north-east of Germany stood in the way of such a demand, and also blocked more realistic state measures. The Junker owners of the great estates, as is richly documented, consciously and unconsciously conserved the basically growth-impeding economic conditions of their agrarian regions.[12] Thus the agrarian income of the east temporarily contributed to the development of the industrial west; the export multiplier operated in the Reich as a whole, but rather less in the eastern regions. In the east, the 'propagation effect' of the leading sector, agriculture, must have been relatively small. The consequence was that the area did not catch up with the development of the west after the first wave of industrialisation.

The attempt made here at explaining the observed, and probably undiminished, gradient of incomes is certainly all too simple, and the evidential base is not secure. But, for the moment, only the fundamentals need concern us. The conceptual basis of our explanation is a fusion of two growth models: the export hypothesis and the structural hypothesis. We follow D. C. North[13] in emphasising the strategic importance of regional export sectors for growth. As a rule, developmental effects are transferred intra-regionally from the export sector. The export sector of the east Prussian provinces, even in the prosperous phase, triggered relatively few internal secondary effects. Unfortunately it was that sector which was the real 'loser' in the process of industrialisation. The relatively small domestic income elasticity of demand for grain, combined with international competition on the world market after the seventies, prevented this export sector from growing even in proportion to national income in Germany, let alone faster than average. In the seventies and eighties, people left the eastern provinces in masses seeking a home abroad and in the central provinces. At this time, most German emigrants came from the east, shortly thereafter the Ruhr emerged as the destination of migration. This massive migration from the east did not have a parallel in central and western parts of Germany, where in general, if there was significant migration, it was short range. In the west and in the centre of Germany, industry (with the exception of raw material oriented industries) developed in those areas with an adequate supply of labour; industry in a way came to labour, but matters were different in the east. Labour moved to the industrial locations: to Berlin, to the Ruhr, and partly to Saxony.

In consequence, the east–west pattern of location of pre-industrial Germany remained in existence throughout the industrialisation process. With that, an income gradient was also maintained.

It is hard to imagine how the outcome could have been different. One can only dream of how German economic geography would have looked around 1900 if the Industrial Revolution had occurred for instance in Russia rather than in England, and incomes had risen faster there.

Postscript

As repeatedly happens in sciences, there was, in the second half of the sixties, a surprising coincidence of the efforts of various authors to solve a particular problem. When, at the 3rd International Congress for Economic History in Munich, 1965, I presented the paper reprinted here, I did not know that an extensive study by J. G. Williamson had just (in July 1965) appeared in *EDCC*, which had, in part, set itself a similar task.[14] Of course, Williamson limited himself to the period after 1900 with regard to the interpretation of German material and was interested in statements of general applicability to all countries. The 'Williamson Thesis' claims first an increasing regional disparity of incomes, which, in the developmental process, is followed (or still needs to be followed) by a period of convergence.

My study was published in two places, in 1966 in the Festschrift for Friedrich Lütge[15] and in 1968 in a collection published by the *Gesellschaft für Wirtschafts- und Sozialgeschichte*,[16] both of which were sources too obscure for foreign scholars to find. In any event, in 1966 there appeared an essay by T. J. Orsagh, who likewise enquired as to the probable geographical distribution of incomes in the course of German history before the First World War and knew nothing of my work.[17] Orsagh saw more clearly than Williamson, but similar to the way I did, the urgency (and possibility) of seeking other indicators beyond the official income data: 'Suppose one can discover a variable or set of variables which is functionally related to income and for which data are available in adequate geographic detail'.[18] With the help of the hypothesis that the sectoral employment structure could be a proxy for income variations, he goes back to 1882. His thesis is that there has since been a convergence of the disparity. It would certainly be timely to subject his method to a critical examination; but that cannot be achieved here. Because Orsagh believes that the differences in the sectoral employment structures between the regions simultaneously reflect the differences in income (through an equation of estimates), he is the most radical representative of the sector hypothesis. For him there need, at bottom, be no other explanation for regional disparities of income.

For the first time, H. Hesse in 1971 looked in a comparative way at the works already mentioned.[19] He described the differences in the statements of the authors respecting convergence/divergence of income variations and attempted, with the help of further indicators and also with coefficients of variation, to arrive at better results, above all for the early period beginning in 1820. In some series, one recognises in Hesse's work the picture of converging disparities, in others a certain confirmation of the (generalised) Williamson Thesis of the temporal sequence: divergence – convergence. Hesse does not go specifically into the west–east gradient, just as, in view of his academic interest, he does not devote attention to change in the positions of specific regions.

As against that, a book by J. P. Tipton, Jr, which appeared in 1976, explicitly set itself the task of analysing the concrete changes in the regional patterns of development in a broad framework of explanatory variables.[20] For this, he used a measure of regional specialisation as the variable to be explained, which bears a certain resemblance to the indicator used by Orsagh. But Tipton does not explicitly examine in detail any of the previously mentioned authors, and also leaves open how the 'growing specialisation' he diagnosed for the period after 1861 could affect income disparities.

The latest attempt to describe and also to explain regional development and income disparities, specifically of the west–east variation, in the nineteenth century, with the aid of new indicators is G. Hohorst's work published in 1977.[21] Here, there are also estimates of the regional per capita income in Prussian provinces from 1810 together with figures for sector shares. Hohorst's results agree surprisingly well with my expressed conjecture, and actually go beyond them inasmuch as he speaks with greater certainty of tendencies towards increasing disparity, that is, of divergence – especially with regard to the west–east gradient, which of course also already appears in his work in a pronounced form in 1816.

In the seventies, systematic research not only into the economic history of regions but also specifically into the structural differences within and between regions was enlivened in the Federal Republic, not least under the stimulation of S. Pollard.[22] It is precisely in this area that many questions have remained open, indeed that it is a matter of a 'standing task of research', as I have written above, is demonstrated by the overview, critically discussing previous studies and their problems, by R. Fremding, T. Pierenkemper and R. H. Tilly 'Regionale Differenzierung in Deutschland als Schwerpunkt wirtschaftshistorischer Forschung' which, at the same time, is an introduction to the essay collection edited by the authors.[23] The reader may now find an overview on the breadth of suggestions for the interpretation of regionally differing processes of industrialisation in H. Kiesewetter 'Erklärungshypothesen zur regionalen Industrialisierung in Deutschland im 19. Jahrhundert'.[24] The statement proposed by Myrdal, that growing divergence of incomes is irreversible in principle if the state does not intervene is finally pursued in a study of German development from 1870 (for which he assumes convergence of income) by W. Abelshaüer, in which he deals with the extent and significance of state infrastructural activity, to which he accords an equalising role in regional policy.[25]

It did not appear wise to work the wealth of the contributions just described into the old draft of the 1965 lecture, which was described by friendly critics as a 'pioneering work'.[26] But several footnotes indicate those points which would have to be rewritten on the basis of research today, while I see no occasion to alter the fundamental statements. With Hohorst, I am of the opinion that the thesis of sequence from divergence to convergence cannot be proven from the German material now available. Whether, on the other hand, the thesis of an enduringly growing divergence deserves preference, I do not yet dare decide. For this reason, I would like to hold on to my old formulation and to speak of an 'observed and undiminished(?) income gradient'. But, in the strict sense, no proof for this is produced in my work either, because the ranking figures (ordinal measurements) express nothing as to the respective intervals (cardinal measurement). The conclusion which, in the first place, seemed the most important to me, was that the west–east gradient already existed before the Industrial Revolution.

4 INVESTMENT IN EDUCATION AND INSTRUCTION IN THE NINETEENTH CENTURY

I

Since the 1950s, economic theorists have ceased to regard private and public expenditure on upbringing and instruction as consumption, as they had done previously, but at least in part as investment. They realised that labour was not an original factor of production, and that wages also include an element of interest or rent.[1] Individual ability, knowledge and capabilities were no longer held to be the result of birth, but required for their development the input of means of production. The accumulated 'investments' finally resulted in the resource 'human capital', whose productivity could now be evaluated. We now speak of education as being one among many other sectors of the economy, which may be analysed in economic terms.[2]

This trend in scholarship, which has become something of a fashion, produced considerable changes in economic theory and economic policy. Whereas originally in the theory of growth, the formation of real capital and a somewhat unspecified 'technical progress', stood at the centre of attention, authors like T. W. Schultz, E. F. Denison, F. Machlup and others[3] have succeeded in accommodating as an explicit variable in econometric research changes in the quality of labour, of its knowledge and ability. No wonder that the training and development of manpower in developing countries has now also become a focal point of aid provided by wealthy countries, and that the discussion of education in the Federal Republic has been enriched by terms derived from the discipline of economics. With all due respect to the fact that education is not predominantly, let alone exclusively, an economic problem, these beginnings at an economic comprehension of education should be welcomed.

As so often in intellectual history, however, this progress is really a step back to classical authors, who were quite familiar with the problem. Adam

Smith[4] already compared the educated individual with a machine and believed that the wage thus contains an element of profit. But Adam Smith was by no means the first to have interpreted education and training in the light of economics. Seventeenth- and eighteenth-century pedagogic practices showed the long tradition of this way of thinking, as also does the pre-classical economic literature. Petty, for instance, regarded 'art' alongside soil, labour and real capital as a fourth factor of production.[5] Among the classical authors, J. B. Say[6] was also of the opinion that it was necessary to pay interest on educational capital and that it earned a risk premium (because there was a possibility of premature death or of professional failure, or other catastrophes). J. H. von Thünen also emphasised the character of expenditure on education as investment, and consequently characterised emigration as a kind of capital export.[7]

This is not the place to go into the reasons why the interpretation advanced by these classical economists was later neglected in the text books and was finally forgotten except among some social politicians and in literature on insurance; with the result that it could be celebrated as a new intellectual development after the Second World War. It is at once necessary and useful to remind ourselves that in the nineteenth century there were authors in Germany who took the more theoretical indications of the classics seriously, and attempted to calculate the stock of educational capital.[8] The most frequent occasions for such considerations, and even for attempts at calculation, were efficiency problems of life and liability insurance, suggestions on hygiene and social policy and on a more just or more expedient system of taxation. Philanthropists sought to prove that a health service, slum clearance, the regulation of sewage, and medical research were not only charities, but formed one of the most economically productive tasks of society, since the death of an individual before the end of his normal working life would rob society of capital which had not yet been amortised, and because healthy individuals had a higher economic value.[9]

After 1856, the well-known statistician Ernst Engel (1821–1896) repeatedly investigated the specific form of capital formation in upbringing, training and education, and attempted to estimate the extent of these investments.[10] At the same time T. Wittstein[11] and R. Lüdtge[12] endeavoured to assess the value of the individual, whether in terms of costs or of expected income. The task of this contribution is to give an account of several of the most important sources, and to draw some conclusions.

II

Engel's work on the 'Price of Labour', in which he set out the main ideas which later he sought to verify, provides a starting point. In particular, Engel believed that the lifetime income of a working individual must contain to a very considerable degree an amortisation of expenditure on upbringing. In his study of the incomes of railway employees (1874), he thought that he had found a statistical confirmation of his views. For the incomes of railway employees in three different ranks, 25 per cent, 35 per cent, and 31 per cent respectively represented the amortisation quota of a specific educational 'cost value'.

The method of calculation was relatively simple, although the effort and the difficulty of obtaining material quite considerable. Engel extracted the income of employees from the extensive statistics of the Prussian railway system. He arranged them in three different categories: (1) employees with an elementary school education, (2) employees with secondary school education, though not necessarily with a certificate of completion (in grammar schools, non-classical secondary schools, commercial schools and higher schools for burghers), (3) employees with completed or interrupted academic education. Whether civil servants' incomes can be taken as representative of the absolute and relative level of incomes of all the earning population may be doubted for several reasons. In addition, Engel attributed groups of people to his qualification groups in a rather arbitrary way. But these sources of possible error are still relatively small compared with the rather weak foundations on which his estimates of 'cost value' rested.

Engel estimated the expenditure for support and education of children and young people in separate educational levels on the basis of criteria that are very crude, and cannot be substantiated or directly compared. He added these annual sums together to constitute the cost value. In 1874 he did not yet take into account the fact that interest had to be paid on investment over time in order to be able to calculate the full figure for capital value. Wittstein and Lüdtge recognised this weakness and they did calculate a cost value that included interest. Engel, however, rightly saw that a certain risk premium had to be included in the sum since quite a few children and young people failed to attain the educational target set. Their costs had to be included with the cost values of those who were successful, in order to avoid arriving at a false sum for total capital formation. To be sure, it may be doubted that it was really justified to include in the cost value a real capital risk – that is an allowance for the impossibility of being able completely to write off the capital value in the future.

Table 4.1 takes Engel's calculation of 1874, corrects the figures on cost value by allowing for a 5 per cent interest rate, and calculates the present value of the flow of income from the year of entry into a profession. The figures are average cost or discounted values of incomes at the beginning of professional life. The discounted 'net incomes' in line 3 equal the gross incomes minus an estimated annual minimum maintenance expenditure for an adult (150 Talers). A comparison of line 3 and line 1 shows that at educational level 1, the effective 'value of return' does not exceed the 'cost value' by a substantial amount. By contrast, the calculated 'rents' for the second and third educational grades are evidently considerable.

Table 4.1. *Cost value and discounted value by educational qualification, calculated on the basis of Ernst Engel's figures (1874)*

| Taler | Educational qualification and commencement of earning | | |
	I Age 15	II Age 20	III Age 25
Individual 'cost value', without risk premia, with interest	1645	5551	9336
Discounted value of expected gross income	4804	11072	19840
Discounted value of expected 'net income'	2155	8477	17335

Before one draws from this the conclusion that at this time investments in higher qualifications for labour forces must have yielded high returns, we should think about the dubious character of such 'rents'. As described above, the gainfully employed individuals in the various levels have been accorded the same maintenance costs during their working lives (by me). Engel did not do this. He rather proceeded from maintenance expenditures which varied according to status between the various grades. But his necessary annual maintenance costs corresponding to the professional status of the three categories of civil servants (which were, he held, the prerequisite for deriving a long-term income) appear to me heavily exaggerated with regard to categories 2 and 3. In the end, the expenditure of these groups was also a way of consuming the 'rents of education'. But because I do not know where the status lines should be drawn, I prefer the egalitarian solution in table 4.1; and in any event the value of these estimated figures should not be overrated. We are, after all, dealing with the incomes of railway civil servants (and in the study of 1876 with the salaries of civil servants). This was a very particular group of employees, whose employer had to guarantee an appropriate means of subsistence, and who were not vulnerable to the normal conditions of the labour market.

III

In his 1883 publication, Engel considerably corrected his earlier statements on the cost value of labour. He avoided all references to an income value. His promised second part on the value of the human being did not appear. But his corrections in his enquiry into cost value deserve our special interest.

Table 4.2 contains an overview of the various estimates of cost value by Wittstein, Lüdtge and Engel (in the case of Engel from the works of 1874 without interest paid as in the original, and with interest paid, and of 1883). We have avoided adding a separate column for the cost values of the 1876 study. They do not differ substantially from those given in column 5, except that Engel in 1876 assumed that civil servants of the third educational grade only commenced their full working life in their thirty-first year – and this of course raises the cost value.

Table 4.2. *Cost value of education and upbringing of males by educational qualification, on the basis of the figures of T. Wittstein, R. Lüdtge and E. Engel (Marks)*

1	2 Wittstein 4% Int.	3 Wittstein 5% Int.	4 Lüdtge 5% Int.	5 Engel 1874 no Int	6 Engel 1874 5% Int.	7 Engel 1883 4% Int.
I Elementary schooling, ending at 15	10341	11346	6357	3686	4935	3738
II Secondary schooling, ending at 20	–	–	19485	11484	16653	12138
III Tertiary education, ending at 25	45339	52605	31164	18630	28008	27547

The very considerable disparity in the estimates strengthens our scepticism concerning the data. Some deviations may be ascribed to the rate of interest, which matters a great deal especially in the case of lengthy periods of upbringing and instruction. But it is evident that the crucial differences are the result of varying assumptions regarding the necessary annual outlay on raising children. In 1867, Wittstein assumed an expenditure for the first year in the life of a child who would later attain an educational grade 1, a sum three times larger than that estimated by Engel in 1883.

Engel had originally conceived the figures in column 7 as multiples of an abstract base figure, but then came to the conclusion, after comparing the estimates with the household calculations of twenty families available to him, that at least for the first educational grade a constant cost sum might be applied. The values for the second and third grade he still estimated as multiples, and quite large multiples, of expenditures for the first grade.

We now provide a rough check of the reliability of the various estimates. Overall, Engel's data appear better, while Lüdtge and certainly Wittstein seem to give exaggerated figures. Possibly even the cost values given by Engel are too high. We can test his data by asking what annual 'investment sums' would have been necessary in order to realise the cost values for children at the appropriate ages. We use as a basis the 'annual contributions to the cost of males and females' given by Engel in 1883. The numbers of children and young people in the various age groups for 1880 come from the official Prussian statistics, as does the approximate distribution among the various types of school. Ninety-two per cent received elementary education at a Volksschule, 7.5 per cent had a secondary education (mostly at grammar schools) and around 0.5 per cent went on to universities and to higher and technical schools.[13]

The total annual investment sums up to 2,400 million Marks; on the basis of the Hoffmann-Müller figures for Prussian national income this would imply around 25 per cent of national income. Considering that at that time 35 per cent of the population was below sixteen, and that the greater part of the educational and training expenditures estimated by Engel and his colleagues lay in the maintenance costs of those growing up, the 'investment quota' for the formation of factors of production fit for employment must at any rate have had an upper limit in the proportion of the children in the whole population. In reality, the investment quota must have been lower because (i) only part of NNP was available for private and public consumption and (ii) the expenditure on those growing up must on average have been below that on the maintenance of adults. For this reason even Engel's estimate is still possibly too high; but it is certain that Wittstein exaggerated, for according to his calculation more than half of the national income would have been devoted to the raising, education and training of young people.

IV

What was the relation of private to public expenditure on these investments in upbringing and instruction in the years covered here? The average annual current expenditure per pupil in public elementary schools in Prussia amounted to 23.10 Marks in 1878 and 23.61 Marks in 1886 (in

1861 it amounted only to 10.37 Marks).[14] These sums are small compared with the total discounted value of those growing up as calculated by Engel. They amount to only 6.05 per cent of the total educational capital of a fifteen-year-old of the first educational grade. Naturally, the expenditure per pupil in secondary institutions, and even more so for higher education students, was greater. In 1882/3 these figures were respectively 170 Marks and 640 Marks per person per year.[15] But these categories represented a much smaller share of the total population. All in all, around 1880 state expenditure for the maintenance of public elementary schools, secondary schools and universities amounted to only 1.4 per cent of national income in Prussia, and this is clearly very far below the 25 per cent mentioned previously.[15a] Even if one includes expenditure on school buildings as well as the costs of non-public educational institutions (which are not contained in the above figures), it remains true that the major share of 'the total investment quota' for upbringing and education was taken up by the private expenditure of households for the maintenance of those in education.[15b]

Since, around 1880, 35 per cent of the population in Prussia was below the age of sixteen, and thus for the most part not yet capable of earning an income, a considerable part of GNP was spent on their maintenance. Perhaps in the nineteenth century relatively more was spent for the coming generation than is now. It is true that public expenditure on education as a share of national income now exceeds that of 1880, but the same age group as a proportion of the population today (1965) is only 22 per cent, as compared with 35 per cent then. The result is that the margin for expenditure on 'higher education' (or for real capital formation) is much greater than it was towards the end of the nineteenth century.

It is however certain that children were at that time not kept away from the work process as rigorously as they are in the twentieth century. The census of 1871, after all, still shows a fairly high proportion of illiteracy in Prussia.[16] But, in the towns, compulsory schooling decisively limited the possibilities of earning available to young people.

On the other hand, it should not be believed that the whole of the nineteenth century was a period of continuous educational progress. After 1825, the absolute and relative numbers of grammar school (*gymnasium*) pupils declined; so too from 1828 did the number of university students, which remained at a low level until the sixties.[17] It is not improbable that developments in personal incomes of heads of household exercised an influence on this contraction of education. This requires more detailed study, which should take into account the distribution of students among faculties. Evidently there were several waves. In the first, the number of students in philosophical-philological disciplines increased disproportionately; after 1870 the numbers in mathematical and natural science departments of the philosophical faculties increased, and reached their maximum in 1882. In the sharp decline in the numbers of all university students which followed, the philosophical faculties actually lost 44 per cent of their students, and only in 1896 were the student numbers of 1882 reached once more.[17a]

V

It is a fundamental problem of all investment in human capital in the modern age that those who invest generally no longer themselves directly enjoy the yield. In pre-industrial society this was in part still the case; and wherever those capable of earning a living directly supported their parents' generation, the children's occupational training could largely be regarded as private capital investment by parents. In general, however, it is other economic motivations which affect the choice of children's educational careers, indisputable though it remains that from a macro-economic viewpoint educational investments are a prerequisite for every generation's security in old age.

Educational investments are a showcase of external economies,[17b] and are thus correctly recognised from early on as an appropriate field for state activity. Yet, as has already been shown, the 'nationalisation of the education process' in the nineteenth century had not yet continued to the extent that the burdens were carried in large part by the state. The state had merely introduced general compulsory education, and agreed to contribute to the support of schools in association with communal authorities. In 1862 to 1864 parents still bore on average one quarter of the total expenditure of public elementary schools; in 1878 this figure was already as mentioned only 13 per cent. The portion of private fees in the financing of the current expenses of higher schools remained unaltered at its high level – it constituted almost one half of those expenses. However, the available figures permit the conclusion that even a complete absence of school fees would not have changed access to educational possibilities considerably, since school fees only represented a relatively small proportion of the total costs of the education process for a private household.[17c]

The nineteenth century was characterised by a vicious cycle of property and education, which was commented on by contemporaries. In 1856, Engel wrote: 'The entire system for fighting pauperism might be summed up with these words: provision for a constant rentability of the same and provision for its general amortisation'.[18] Thünen had already spoken of a 'monopoly' of manufacturing producers, which they secured through educational barriers. Workers' wages were, he said, so small that they could not let their children attain such occupational training that might have facilitated a rise into the class of industrial producers.[19] The truth of this sentence is demonstrated by Engel's figures.

For the masses, higher education was simply out of the question because of the high cost.[19a] When we consider that, in 1881, 93 per cent of all those who paid the classified income tax and the income tax (not to mention those beneath the tax threshold) had an annual income below 1500 Marks, and most even lay under 660 Marks, it becomes clear that parents could possibly afford the mounting costs per child for the first educational grade (estimated by Engel at between 100 Marks and 250 Marks). But they could not pay those of the second grade (from 200 Marks to 600 Marks) or of the third (from 300 Marks to 1,050 Marks). Even if Engel's cost estimates are somewhat too high (as we have tried to show above), his verdict on social and educational policy still seems apposite: 'Here it is again mainly property which stratifies people and divides them into classes. If one examines this manifestation more closely, one soon discovers that the property classes are perhaps not entirely, but nevertheless substantially, identical with the educated classes. Belonging to these educated classes practically determines the cost values of their members.'[20]

There was a singular redistributive characteristic of state education policy. The primary school system was already sufficiently 'nationalised' that the state carried the major burden of expenditure. For secondary schools, private fees still covered nearly half the costs; but at the level of the universities the relationship between private and public assumption of costs was quite decisively reversed. The share of fees paid by the institutions' users actually sank below that of those of primary school pupils; in 1882/3 students at Prussian universities paid an average of 60 Marks per annum or only 9.3 per cent of the total current expense (while the private share in costs in elementary schools was 13 per cent). If one wants to make the point dramatically, then the highest educational levels (which were necessarily subsidised) contained a strong measure of *subvention of the upper classes*. It was primarily members of the upper orders who were able to thrust their way forward right up to the gate of the university.

Postscript

In 1965 the original essay closed with a sixth section in which the suggestion was made that the questions treated here should be more closely pursued by social and economic historians. The question as to whether it would be possible quantitatively to formulate the contribution of the education system to Germany's economic growth in the nineteenth century, and not merely write the history of the institutions, was also put. In fact, within a fairly short space of time, the state of research has changed considerably. W. Krug in 1966, having already estimated the income lost through occupational training (the opportunity cost), published in 1970 his calculations on the development of 'non-material capital' after 1870.[21] By contrast with Engel, Wittstein and Lüdtge, and concurring with the educational economic school of the post-war period, Krug concentrated on more narrowly defined educational capital; consequently as a rule he excluded the maintenance expenditure and included the income lost by those educated beyond their period of compulsory schooling.[22] Direct comparisons with the calculations of the nineteenth-century authors are therefore impossible. H. von Laer's estimates of human capital[23] remain closer to the classical concept, that is to say, they include the costs of upbringing.

In the interim, the attempt quantitatively to determine the contribution of the education system to German economic growth in the nineteenth century has also been undertaken. For this, Thirlwall-Lundgreen[24] make use both of the methods suggested by Dennison (1962) and those of Schultz and Harberger (1960, 1965). In the first case, the additional school years are estimated as contributions towards input within the framework of a production function; in the second case, the contribution of the non-material capital stock to production is evaluated. In counterposition to what are after all at first sight very obvious assumptions, Thirlwall-Lundgreen calculate the part played by higher education in the increase of national product from 1870 to 1913 at only slightly over 2 per cent.

Lundgreen, agreeing with the modern tradition in educational economics, includes in investments only such expenditure as is devoted to more narrowly defined occupational training: private and public spending on primary school education, private and public spending on every kind of further school education, as well as the lost income from earnings for pupils and students above the age of compulsory schooling. He examines expenditure that was relevant to qualifications. Such limitations have much to recommend them, especially if one considers the factors in the individual decision, after the end of compulsory schooling, either to continue occupational training (to invest) or to start earning at once. Such a micro-economic point of departure for calculating motives at the end of compulsory schooling, however, misses several significant considerations, such as that of barriers in the educational system or the whole problematic of the reproduction of labour. Yet different questions will demand different concepts of non-material capital, with the result that Engel, Wittstein and Lüdtge can only conditionally be placed in the history of modern educational economics.

How rapidly historical research on education has developed since 1965 is shown by P. Lundgreen's overview:[25] in his bibliography, which includes 102 titles, there are only nineteen published before 1965. Yet contributions from economic history remain rare.

5 CHANGES IN THE PHENOMENON OF THE BUSINESS CYCLE OVER THE LAST HUNDRED YEARS

I

Striking shifts of focus are apparent in the development of economic thought in the twentieth century. From one decade to another, different themes stand at the centre of attention in economic conferences, and the subjects of contributions in economic journals change. One of the most striking examples is the change in interpretation of the phenomenon described by the concept of 'business cycle'.

In the period between the two world wars, both the theory and empirical research into business cycles were among the most interesting areas of economics, characterised by a lively scientific progress. After 1950, however, the business cycle was discussed less and less as a problem of theoretical analysis. It became a kind of appendix to the theories of growth, of income, or of money. The booms and slumps of the fifties and sixties, which were on the whole relatively mild by comparison with those of the twenties and thirties, certainly contributed to the optimistic notion that both the theories and the instruments necessary to make growth permanent were available. The opinion that the business cycle no longer even existed was much canvassed.[1] In several of the textbooks on macroeconomic theory in the sixties and early seventies, the term *Konjunktur* (business cycle) no longer appeared in the subject index.

In consequence hardly anyone connected with the discipline was surprised when in the years 1964/5 Lawrence Klein, in collaboration with other important American theorists and econometricians, began to plan a conference to be held on the theme 'Is the Business Cycle Obsolete?'. It is true that, when the planned conference eventually met in London in 1967, no one among the experts gathered there from all over the world wished to deny the cyclical deviations in the development of western post-war economies. It was also agreed that development after the Second World

War showed regular sequences of varying intensity of economic activity, although the pattern was considerably different from that in previous periods.[2] Although the term 'growth cycle' was not coined then, it has had since then a general academic validity.

By a growth cycle, we understand a movement in the economy of the type represented in the schematic diagram at top right in figure 5.1. Unlike the movement illustrated at top left in the same figure, which represents the schema often termed as the 'classical business cycle', in the case of a growth cycle growth and contraction in GNP (Y) do not follow each other in rhythmic succession. Production increases in every year, but the pace of movement alters in a rhythmic succession of slower and quicker growth. In figure 5.1, the growth rates belonging to the respective illustrations of the growth of GNP are entered in the lower charts.

The difference between the two kinds of cycle of economic development, shown in the lower graphs of figure 5.1, lies in the fact that, on the left-hand side, the growth rates regularly also reach negative values, whereas the respective minima on the right-hand side always show positive growth rates.

Until the beginning of the 1970s, the supposition that the growth cycle represented the new form of cyclical deviations in economic development was plainly the dominant view.[3] That is how matters were put in textbooks, in official publications and in numerous scientific contributions. As late as 1973 a collection of essays edited by Alfred E. Ott for the Theoretical Committee of the *Gesellschaft für Wirtschafts- und Sozialwissenschaften*, including contributions by German-speaking specialists on the theory of business cycles, appeared under a characteristic title, *Wachstumszyklen. Über die neue Form der Konjunkturschwankungen* ('Growth cycles: on the new form of business cycle fluctuations').[4]

Since then, experiences in the western world may have contributed to a repeated paradigmatic change. In the Federal Republic, NNP fell by 2.5 per cent in 1975, after it had already stagnated in 1974. In the summer of 1975, the unemployment rate reached 4.4 per cent – a level which, for twenty years, had been held to be unthinkable, or at least intolerable.[5] In the light of these occurrences, the theories of growth cycles rapidly lost their glamour: developed a few years previously, they had shown that only growth cycles were observable in the post-war period and why this could not have been otherwise. Several contributions had even explained why this process would necessarily continue in the future.[6]

Of course, it is still believed to be improbable that business cycles now will produce troughs comparable to those characteristic of the period between the two world wars. It is still generally believed that an appropri-

Figure 5.1 Classical business cycles and modern growth cycles

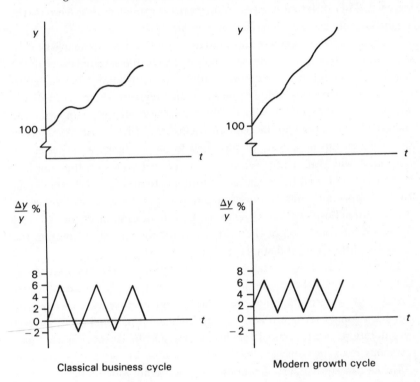

Classical business cycle   Modern growth cycle

ate economic theory, improved control instruments and an insightful economic policy on the part of governments will prevent worse things from
happening. These were the circumstances which, for more than twenty
years, were used to explain why in the post-war period there had only been
growth cycles rather than fluctuations of the old kind.[7] Economists, indeed,
took for themselves some of the credit for the fact that cyclical swings in
the post-war period were much milder than before, that unemployment
was far lower on average after 1945, and that, even in the years of cyclical
peaks of unemployment, rates in most countries remained well below the
rates attained in the inter-war period even in particularly good years.[8] Until
very recently it was believed that a difficult problem of capitalist development was now under control. That explains the economists' high spirits in
speaking of growth cycles rather than business cycles.

For the economic historian it is interesting to observe that the collective
experience of success described above has provided the basis for historical
generalisations in the academic literature, generalisations which are
presented in something like the following manner: *Now* the movement in

the business cycle is progressing in the manner described; *formerly* it had proceeded in a different manner. *Now* there are growth cycles; *formerly* the business cycle was characterised by regular downswings.[9]

Virtually all statements of this kind are based, not on an analysis of the historical evidence, but at the most on impermissible extrapolations of the experiences of the inter-war period into statements about the character-istics of a 'former' period. In the German literature there is, as of the present, no work which systematically concerns itself with comparing the picture of fluctuations in the economy before the First World War – when the 'classical business cycle' is supposed to have reigned – and after the Second World War. In foreign literature, contributions on this question are also rare.[10] I therefore began some time ago to make good the omission. In this connection, first the question as to whether the stated differences in the pattern of business cycles ever existed was to be examined; there should follow an interpretation of the evidence, with the aim of elaborating the causes of differences and similarities.

In the present study I would like to concentrate on the first part of the task, especially as the results for this are comparatively well established already. The interpretation of the evidence (and further work on sources) will be a longer-term project. Nevertheless, at the conclusion, several considerations are presented for discussion, which, however, raise more questions than they answer.[11]

In the descriptive part, I propose to corroborate four theses:

1 Growth cycles are not peculiar to the post-war period. Taking the same criteria and methods of measurement as are generally used today in business cycle analysis, the cycles in pre-1914 Germany appear also as growth cycles. The inter-war period, with its pro-found business cycle troughs, is not typical of the historical phenomena of business cycles.

2 Using not current criteria and methods of measurement, but rather those of researchers into business cycles of forty or fifty years ago (such as Spiethoff and Schumpeter), another conclusion emerges. For certain indicators, which were once thought of as more important than they are now, there are clear differences between the 'classical cycle' and post-war development. However, these indicators do not uniformly justify a contrast of the more recent development, described as a milder growth cycle, and the older business cycle.

3 Virtually all new and old indicators show that development in the post-war period proceeded on the whole more steadily than in the inter-war period. But that is not true for a general comparison

between development after the Second World War (henceforth called the post-war period) and development before the First World War (henceforth called the pre-war period). The dominant pre-conception, according to which post-war development was much steadier by comparison with the 'classical business cycle' of the pre-war period, requires extensive correction.

4 In contrast to received opinion, on the whole post-war development in the Federal Republic proceeded more along the lines of a classical cyclical pattern of regular deviation than did economic development before 1914. While cyclical movements can be discerned only with difficulty in numerous important series of indicators for the pre-war period, they may readily be recognised in virtually all important series after 1945.[12] It is true that the length of fluctuations in the post-war period, with a cyclical duration of four to five years, is considerably shorter than in the pre-war period, where the interval between one trough and the next or one peak and the next amounted to between seven and nine years.[13]

II

I now turn to the demonstrations. In what follows, I present and interpret several figures containing indicators of the course of the business cycle. Figure 5.2 shows the growth rates of NNP at constant prices.[14] The sequence of figures begins with this graph because today we usually describe cycles in terms of growth rates of GNP or industrial production. The current notion of business cycle fluctuations derives from an unsteady growth of GNP.[15] In our case we cannot use the more usual measurement of growth and of the business cycle in terms of rates of change in *gross* national product, because W. G. Hoffmann and his collaborators, who produced most of the pre-war series, estimated only *net* national product.[16]

In figure 5.2, as in most of the following figures, there are two large gaps. The first lasts from 1914 to 1924 and covers the First World War and the period of the post-war inflation including the year of the stabilisation crisis, 1924. The second gap covers 1939 to 1949 and includes the Second World War and the period before the foundation of the Federal Republic at the end of 1949. In both cases, because of the statistical sources it is not possible, and because of the exceptional circumstances it is not necessary to include them in a historical comparison of business cycles. For the inter-war period, the sources permit a comparison of the years 1925 to 1938 with other periods: but the present figure and several of the following graphs show that the inter-war period was clearly a quite exceptional case in terms of the pattern of the business cycle.[17]

Figure 5.2   Growth rates of NNP (constant market prices)

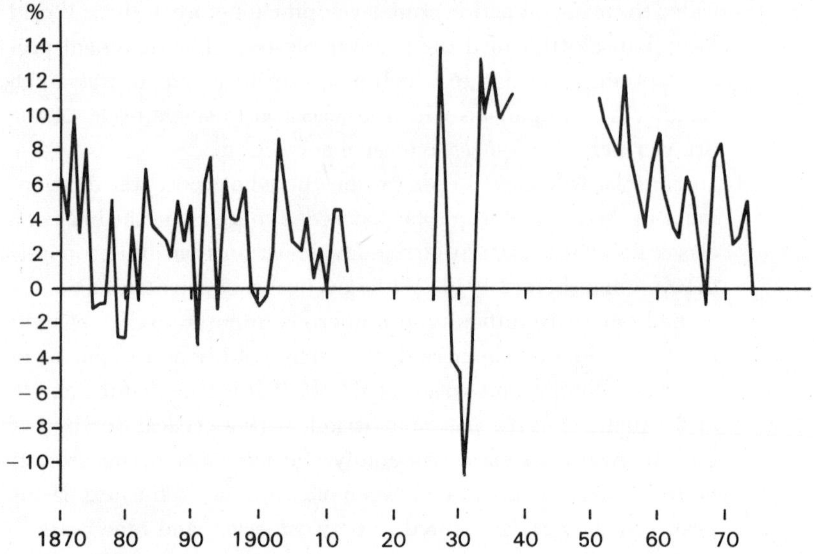

Sources:
1870–1938: W. G. Hoffmann, *et al.*, *Das Wachstum der deutschen Wirtschaft seit der Mitte des 19. Jahrhunderts*, Berlin–Heidelberg–New York 1965, pp. 827f.
1950–1974: StatBA, *Lange Reihen zur Wirtschaftsentwicklung 1974*, Stuttgart 1974, pp. 144f. No means or variances were calculated, as the growth rate series after 1951 shows a trend

I now turn to the pre-war period. The series from which figure 5.2 is derived shows eleven years between 1870 and 1913 in which the real national product shrank. Of these, five years were in the so-called 'promoters' crisis' (*Gründerkrise*) of 1873 to 1880, which was in many respects an exceptional occurrence in the economic history of the nineteenth century, just as the preceding boom from 1869 to 1873, whose very high growth rates are shown at the left side of the graph, was an unparalleled event. Leaving out this extraordinary fluctuation of the seventies, there are six years before the First World War in which real national product fell; and only one sequence of two consecutive years of fall, 1900 and 1901. The maximum fall from one year to the next (1891) was 3.4 per cent. This depression was caused above all by considerable harvest failures, whereas manufacturing output, according to Hoffmann, continued to grow.[18] Of the six falls between 1880 and 1913, three were under 1 per cent, and the overall average was a decline of 1.2 per cent. We may characterise these contractions as mild. As a comparison, recent calculations of growth rates of national product in Great Britain in the nineteenth and twentieth centuries by Feinstein also reveal contractions in the period between 1870 and 1913 with an average downward movement of only 1 per cent.[19] In the case of the German Empire, as well as in that of Great Britain, average growth rates in the pre-war period lay substantially below those of the post-war period. Figure 5.2 and the following figures show that the pre-war cycles did not have the same intensity of contraction as characterised those of the inter-war period.[20] It also emerges from figure 5.2 that, although the movement in growth rates before the First World War doubtless followed a cyclical course, the pattern was not anything like as clear as in the period after 1950, when there was a regular alternation of years of rapid and years of slower growth.[21]

Figure 5.3 also demonstrates that the fluctuations in economic activity in the post-war period were far more regular than in the pre-war period. It uses the same sources as figure 5.2 (net national product at constant prices according to W. G. Hoffmann), but depicts not growth rates, but movement around a calculated trend.[22] Whereas cyclicality is evidently greater in the post-war period than before the war, instability (above all due to the fluctuations of the 1870s and the boom and slump around 1900) is somewhat greater before the First World War than in the post-war period.

Figure 5.3   Deviations from trend of NNP (constant market prices)

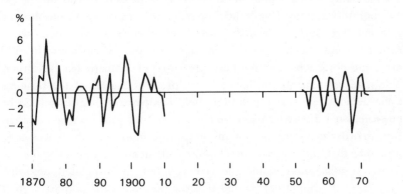

Sources:
1870–1910: W. G. Hoffmann, *et al.*, *Das Wachstum*, pp. 827f. For the period 1870–82 the NNP at market prices includes, contrary to normal usage, the external balance of capital movements and services.
1952–72: StatBA, *Lange Reihen 1974*, pp. 144f. and StJb 1975 für die Bundesrepublik Deutschland, p. 508. Trend: 5 year moving average.
1870–1910: variance = 6.2
1952–72:   variance = 3.3

At this point the description of the historical-statistical evidence has to be interrupted once more because a central methodological problem of comparative business cycle history was initially almost overlooked in both the figures presented – it should now be examined. Are the series of economic variables upon which the figures are based equally reliable over the entire time period? These figures, and most of the following figures, are derived from different sources (see the list in the appendix). For the post-war period, the sources are official statistics; but for the inter-war and above all for the pre-war periods there are often only historical reconstructions of time-series calculated by later researchers on the basis of all manner of records. As a rule these are not the same sources as those used by modern official statistics. Since the sources for the most recent past are so different from those of the more distant past, like is clearly not being compared with like. It is true, however, that many critical objections which may be raised against a long-term comparability of the absolute dimensions (e.g. of the real national product of 1870, 1900, 1930 and 1970) do not in our case matter, since we are concerned with the fluctuations of growth rates and deviations from a trend. The critical questions regarding comparabilities still remain. However, there are no answers to them. If we had such answers, we could assuredly provide 'better' historical series.

If we believe it is impossible to make statements on earlier economic movements just because the time-series of the national product before 1914 are only available to us in the form of estimates of Hoffmann and his collaborators and not from official sources, the entire line of questioning pursued here must be rejected. It would not then be susceptible to scientific treatment. Such a position has not been put in the literature until now, and objections have not been presented in comparable cases either. The many statements on 'former' and 'present' courses of the business cycle demonstrate that the authors hold comparisons in principle to be possible, even if they have not been supported yet with detailed research. But, in order to secure the conclusions of this study from the objection in principle that the material used is not sufficiently similar to make the desired comparisons possible, the results ought to be formulated somewhat differently. It should not be said that the post-war cycle *is* more regular than the pre-war cycle, or that deviations from the trend *were* not substantially greater after 1950 than before 1914. It is more correct to say: the *available material* does not contradict such a statement – and other material is not currently at hand. If, in the following, statements are formulated on the basis of historical facts, then henceforth they stand explicitly as abbreviations of the otherwise somewhat more cumbersome formulations about the material that we have.

After these methodological provisos, we can proceed with the examination of the material. Comparing growth rates of industrial production in the Federal Republic between 1950 and 1974 with those growth rates calculated from Rolf Wagenführ's estimates of industrial production in the nineteenth and twentieth centuries,[23] the greater regularity of the cyclical fluctuations in the post-war period (figure 5.4) is again apparent. It is true that, in fluctuations before 1914, periodic movements are evident, but they stand out less clearly. In the nineteenth century, there was a cumulation of declines of industrial production only in the *Gründerkrise*, but from then until the First World War only three years of falling industrial production were ascertainable, namely 1892, 1907 and 1908. Disregarding the *Gründerkrise*, the magnitude of fluctuation too seems to have been no more intense in the pre-war period than in the post-war period. The inter-war period again shows itself to be a completely unusual case.[24]

Fortunately we are in a position not only to make long-term comparisons of perhaps questionable growth rates of net national product and industrial production, but we are also able to examine the original

Figure 5.4   Growth rates of industrial production

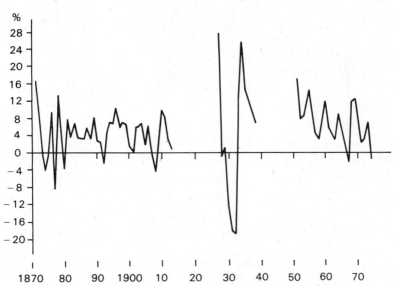

Sources:
StatBA, *Bevölkerung und Wirtschaft 1872–1972*, Stuttgart 1972, p. 176f.; *Bevölkerung und Wirtschaft. Langfristige Reihen 1871 bis 1957*, Stuttgart 1958, p. 46; WiSta 1975/9, p. 558
No means or variances were calculated, as the growth rate series after 1951 follows a trend

magnitudes of production recorded in several areas and branches of industry. From these figures it emerges that neither in the pre- nor in the post-war period did numerous branches of industry show a regular pattern of fluctuations in growth rates, corresponding with the general course of the business cycle. In both cases in which such a correlation came closest to being realised, in the production of pig-iron and steel, surprising results emerge from the comparison of the two periods.

Pig-iron production in the post-war period (figure 5.5) shows regular cycles, which conform fairly precisely to what was described in figure 5.1 as the 'classical business cycle'. By contrast, the pre-war period was characterised far less by regular cycles. Certainly the two crises of 1901 and 1908

Figure 5.5   Growth rates of pig-iron production

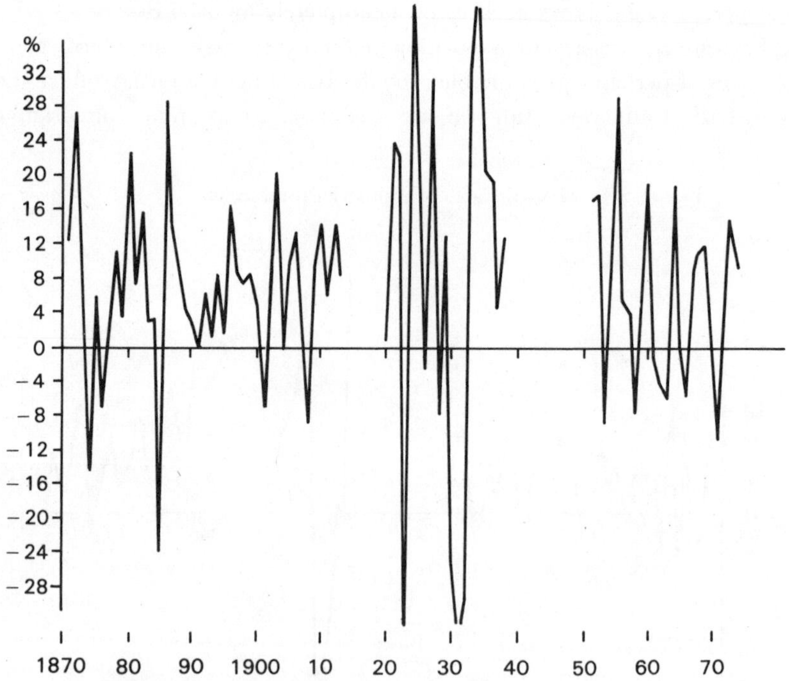

Sources:
1871–1913: W. G. Hoffmann, *Das Wachstum*, pp. 353f.
1920–74:   StatBA, *Bevölkerung und Wirtschaft 1872–1972*, pp. 181f;
StJb 1975, p. 247.
1871–1913: Mean growth rate = 6.3%
                   Variance = 97.8
                   Standard deviation = 1.6
1951–74:   Mean growth rate = 5.5%
                   Variance = 105
                   Standard deviation = 1.9

do find their expression in the series, but in general this is rather a 'growth cycle'. In passing, reference should again be made to the peculiarity of the fluctuations in the inter-war period. The characteristics of the business cycle in steel (figure 5.6) reveal an even more impressive 'growth cycle' in the pre-war period and a 'business cycle' in the post-war period. The figures show that the spread of growth rates in the post-war period was *greater* than in the pre-war period.[25]

Figure 5.6   Growth rates of steel production

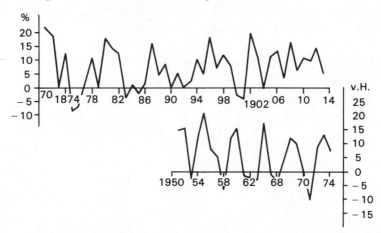

Sources:
1871–1913: W. G. Hoffmann, *Das Wachstum*, pp. 353f.
1920–74:   StatBA, *Bevölkerung und Wirtschaft 1872–1972*, p. 183;
StJb 1975, p. 247.
1871–1913: Mean growth rate = 6.8%
            Variance = 60.1
            Standard deviation = 1.2
1951–74: Mean growth rate = 5.7%
            Variance = 76.3
            Standard deviation = 1.5

III

Was there thus no 'classical business cycle' before 1914? Are those graphs in the textbooks, which contrast the 'former' and 'present' business cycle in a manner similar to that depicted in figure 5.1, wrong?[26] At any rate, the existence of the 'classical cycle' cannot be demonstrated in the way in which many economists assume. We cite Kurt W. Rothschild as being representative: 'In the classical cycle, the question of fluctuations was answered unambiguously: one made a clear distinction between periods of increasing and of decreasing production.'[27] That this statement of fact is open to question emerges from what we have already argued. But it can

also be shown that at that time no economist had undertaken the differentiation between the phases of the cycle in the fashion of Rothschild.[28] A
more careful reading of the literature before the 1940s shows that the
phenomenon of the business cycle was as a rule described differently.
Arthur Spiethoff certainly illustrated his *Musterkreislauf* (ideal cycle) in
the well-known manner, which bears a considerable resemblance to the
schematic graph at top left of figure 5.1 (see figure 5.7), but Spiethoff did
not draw any axes.[29] Certainly, it is fair to assume that time runs from left
to right; but Spiethoff leaves unclear what is to be read from bottom to
top. For him, this is an abstract, a vision of the concept 'business cycle',
which is put together out of numerous judgements.[30]

Figure 5.7   Spiethoff's 'Wechselstufen'

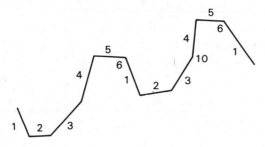

1 Downswing, 2 first rise, 3 second rise, 4 upswing, 5 capital scarcity, 6 crisis,
10 surpassing of previous peak

If anything in Spiethoff's work was to stand on a vertical axis, it was
certainly *not* production. As a researcher he concerned himself with the
time-series of production of various branches of the economy, but he came
to the conclusion that they did not fit in with his scheme of fluctuations
(*Wechsellagen*). So Spiethoff is possibly even more emphatic than the
position formulated above, when he says: 'Frequently the stagnation can
hardly or not at all be derived from figures on the German production of
goods.'[31] It would thus not be in the spirit of Spiethoff – or in that of
Joseph Schumpeter[32] – to impute to his picture of the cycle, especially in
the phase of decline, the later concept of fluctuations in the level of
production in the economy as a whole, or of production in the majority of
branches of industry.[33]

The earlier business cycle researchers[34] oriented themselves less towards
production and more towards prices, share prices, speculative waves,
foundation of new firms, issues of securities, shortages of credit, frequent
collapses, and interest rates. Standing in this tradition it is understandable

that the Harvard business cycle barometer, and that of the Berlin Institut
für Konjunkturforschung (Berlin Institute for Research into the business
cycles) included in the 1920s levels of interest, stock prices, and the prices
of goods among the outstanding business cycle indicators; even though the
purely symptomatic character of these movements in prices had already
been established by Spiethoff and others. Admittedly in his chronological
scheme Spiethoff did stress a regularly appearing 'over-production' which
was supposed to be the result of preceding speculative waves of investment. But the concept of 'over-production' must not be misunderstood as
depicting a situation that could only have been overcome through the
curtailment of production.[35]

It is very important to recognise that the authors who once spoke of a
business cycle drew on circumstances which could be directly observed, i.e.
which were experienced personally by economically active contemporaries. Interest on loans was paid, securities were issued, prices were
quoted, enterprises were founded, there clearly were bankruptcies – and all
these occurrences could relatively easily be recognised, counted, and
statistically condensed. There was hardly a disparity between the statistical
picture and the impression of the business world.

But, since the First World War, economic statistics and economic theory
have assumed a development of their own. Since at the latest the 1930s, the
attention of economic theorists and statisticians was directed towards quantitative presentations of aggregate quantities such as for example national
income, whose fictitious character is unmistakable.[36] So-called 'macro-
economic data' are after all produced only by economic theorists and economic statisticians. They do not exist outside the conceptual world of those
who calculate them according to given rules. That is not the case for a
single price, or for the interest on a loan, or the quotation of a share. Long
before economics as a science concerned itself with them, interest, prices,
and output of enterprises all belonged to the functioning of an economy.
On the other hand, the national product, the price level and similar quantities, with whose help today we describe movements of the economy and
whose interconnections are a subject of modern economic theory, cannot
be classed as existing at the functioning level of the economy itself: unless
of course one takes into account that the new economic concepts and
theories have since obtained an enormous historical force, which raises
them to the rank of real social facts. In the hands of those in government,
these numbers have grown to be a more and more important element in
their instruments of control. They are today decisive 'facts', which
influence state bureaucracies, corporate actions, and the opinion of the
electorate. Thus the mass media in reporting on the state of the economy

and its foreseeable development use concepts belonging to this economic and technical language. Undoubtedly the computed growth rate of the national product today plays a role in political decision-making processes and in the activities of private economic actors.

It is an open question whether the historian has the right to interpret earlier business cycles with the aid of present concepts and standards of analysis, and whether he is justified in applying to the present business cycle the notions of earlier trade cycle research. Because this question has not yet been examined, I shall attempt on the basis of the following figures to highlight characteristics, which were given more importance in the earlier treatment of business cycles than time-series of the production of the economy as a whole, or of aggregates of industrial or commercial activity.

Figure 5.8 shows rates of change in an index of raw material prices: that is a weighted average of the prices of coal, iron, textile raw materials,

Figure 5.8   Rates of change of raw material price index

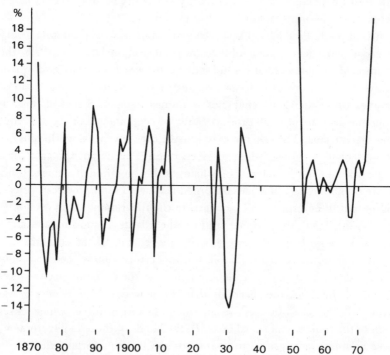

Sources:
StatBA, *Bevölkerung und Wirtschaft 1872–1972*, p. 247 and *WiSta*, various volumes.

wood, and similar materials. Here we find a picture of the pre-war business
cycle as having comparatively vigorous up- and down-turns. In the post-
war period there was a large disturbance in the Korean War boom, and the
year 1973 also presents a departure from the norm as a result of the oil
shock and world speculation in raw materials; but in the fifties and sixties
there were only relatively small fluctuations. That appears to be proof of
the 'classical business cycle' in the pre-war era.[37]

Figure 5.8 cannot, however, serve as proof that the widespread notions
about a rhythmic rise and fall of *the* prices have already been demonstrated
to be true. Rather, prices of raw materials then (as later) were particularly
volatile over the course of the business cycle. The same, however, is not
true of the cost of living index. Figure 5.9 shows Ashok Desai's cost of
living index,[38] which is the best available for the pre-war period, as well as
later official indices of consumer prices.[39] In the pre-war period, we are not
able to detect a regular sequence of rises and falls in the level of the cost of
living. Until the nineties there are frequently falls in the cost of living, in
accordance with the general trend of prices; and the phases in which prices

Figure 5.9   Rates of change of cost of living index

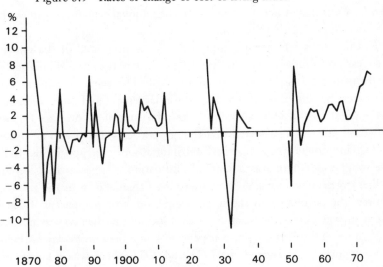

Sources:
A. Desai, *Real Wages in Germany 1871–1913*, Oxford 1968, p. 117.
StatBA, *Bevölkerung und Wirtschaft 1872–1972*, p. 250; *Lange Reihen
1974*, p. 133; StJb 1975, p. 448 (after 1950: 4 member household
with sole earning head of household of middle income). No measures of
distribution were calculated, because in the pre- and post-war periods
trends predominate in the growth rate series

rise are rarer. After the end of the nineties, we find no year, except 1913, in which the cost of living fell. Changes in the cost of living index scarcely reveal a business cycle – in contrast to the post-war period, in which, though the annual fluctuations are smaller overall, they are clearly cyclical.[40]

It needs to be stressed that earlier business cycle research did not claim that prices as such should fluctuate according to the phases of the business cycle. W. C. Mitchell and A. Spiethoff, for instance, agreed that, while raw material and capital goods prices show a fairly close correlation with the rhythm of the business cycle before the First World War, the prices of consumer goods did not. Spiethoff is admirably clear: 'To read the alternating phases from the overall movement of prices (general price level) in Germany is hardly possible.'[41]

Together with a few capital market indicators, *the* crucial business cycle indicator for Spiethoff was iron consumption, the sum of iron production and imports minus exports.[42] The assumption was ingenious, for using iron consumption, Spiethoff sought to describe what was in his opinion the critical determinant in the business cycle, namely fluctuations in investment activity, which were not directly measurable at that time.[43] Long after Spiethoff wrote, it has become possible to use W. G. Hoffmann's estimates of net investments in the national economy to show that Spiethoff's supposition was, on the whole, correct.[44]

In this way a long-term comparison can be presented of the relevant business cycle phenomenon in Spiethoff's sense of the term. The so-called investment ratio is presented in figure 5.10. The (net) investment ratio measures the sum of goods used for the enlargement and improvement of real capital measured as a share of the total sum of all produced goods. Spiethoff and others asserted that this proportion must rise in an upturn and fall in a downturn. Figure 5.10 substantiates these suppositions. In the pre-war period there was a marked alternation of phases of rising and falling investment ratios. Almost more even than shown in the previous figures, the peculiarity of the inter-war period is here apparent. Even in the years when investment activity was at its highest, the investment ratios did not reach those of the pre-war period[45] – and the minima lay far below those before 1914. Indeed, in 1931 and 1932, there was a substantial disinvestment. More was consumed than was produced.

In the post-war period, it is not only the very high average level of investment ratios which is striking. By comparison with the pre-war period, in the first instance we also find a certain confirmation of the view that there was less volatility. Both in absolute and in percentage terms, the spread of the annual values around an average or trend is smaller than

Figure 5.10   Net investment as share of NNP

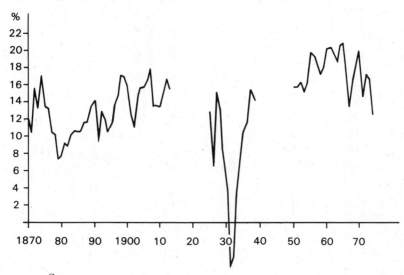

Sources:
1871–1913:   W. G. Hoffmann, *Das Wachstum*, pp. 825f.
1920–74:   StatBA, *Lange Reihen 1974*, pp. 144ff; StJb 1975,
             pp. 508 and 519
1871–1913:   Mean share = 12.9%
             Variance = 7.2
             Standard deviation = 0.2
1951–74:   Mean share = 17.5%
             Variance = 4.9
             Standard deviation = 0.1

before 1914. But after 1965 this changes! The falls in investment ratios from 1965 to 1967 and from 1972 to 1975 are comparable with those before 1914. In 1975 the net investment ratio sank to 9.6 per cent, that is to a low last reached for the period before the First World War in the early eighteen nineties.[46]

If more space were available, we should have to examine more precisely the central forces of the business cycle; and we would need to investigate further the growth rates of net investment (figure 5.11). For the moment it is enough to refer to the fact that, despite all preconceptions regarding the smoothing-out influences in the new circumstances of post-war business cycles which have often been described, after 1950 capital formation certainly did not fluctuate less rhythmically than before 1914. Both in the pre- *and* post-war periods, there are regular falls, though the first recession after 1950, in 1954, is an exception. In addition, the amplitudes of fluctuations after the Second World War are not noticeably smaller than

Figure 5.11   Growth rates of net investment at constant prices

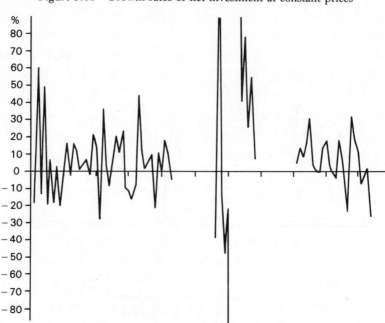

Sources:
1871–1913:   W. G. Hoffmann, *Das Wachstum*, pp. 827f.
1950–73:   SVR Jahresautachten 1974, pp. 229 and 233.
1974:   StJb 1975, pp. 508 and 519.
1871–1913:   Mean growth rate = 3.5%
             Variance = 364.7
             Standard deviation = 5.5
1951–74:   Mean growth rate = 4.7%
             Variance = 203.8
             Standard deviation = 3

before the First World War; it is the inter-war period which does not conform to the familiar pattern.

It is yet more important, for the purpose of comparative business cycle research, to examine the environment of investment activity which attracted the most attention of contemporaries before 1914 when they observed the periodic appearance of crises: the movement on the financial markets, and above all the volumes of financial capital formation through the issue of securities, the change in prices of securities, and the interest rates. In what follows, only a few indicators out of a wealth of information of relatively good quality available to us is presented.

Before the First World War, the level of share prices was held to be an important indicator of real economic development and of the mood of those demanding and those offering capital. Figure 5.12 affords a good impression of what we can imagine as the wave-like business cycles of the pre-war period, which we do not find so pronouncedly in production statistics. The rises and falls of share prices are unmistakable before 1914. No particular statistical method is required to depict it. In addition, it corresponds quite well with the course of the fluctuations of net investment ratios over time. After 1950, the picture is more complicated, especially as here business cycle and structural movement overlap. After the war it took some time before the share market was capable of functioning once more, so that we should exclude the early fifties from our enquiry. But after the late 1950s we observe fluctuations in the level of share prices of a kind otherwise found only twice in the last hundred years, namely in the *Gründerzeit* of the 1870s and the subsequent crisis, and in the Great Depression. It should be emphasised that nevertheless we do not hear of 'stock market panics' in the post-war period, as we did in the inter-war period and also in the pre-war period, despite price declines that were then usually rather less dramatic.

Figure 5.12 Share price index

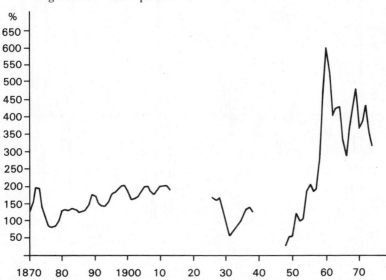

Sources:
StatBA, *Bevölkerung und Wirtschaft 1872–1972*, p. 214; various *StJb für die Bundesrepublik Deutschland*. No measures of distribution were calculated, because in the post-war period a trend predominates in the series

In the course of almost forty years between 1875 and 1913, share yields (yearly average dividends in percentages of the average price) changed only within a narrow 15 per cent band; whereas in the last twenty years in the Federal Republic, the yields of shares show fluctuations of 40 per cent around an average.[47] Using as indicators the level of share prices and share dividends, development proceeded far less steadily after the war than in the pre-war period.

The same phenomenon can be observed in an analysis of changes in the yields of fixed interest securities, that is of state loans and mortgage bonds (figure 5.13).[48] The regular but low amplitudes of changes in the so-called long-term rate of interest in the pre-war period stand in contrast to dramatic fluctuations in the post-war era: expressed in percentage points, they are three times as large as before 1914. Only in the inter-war period were the swings even bigger, but it has already become noticeable that only

Figure 5.13   Change in average yields of fixed interest securities

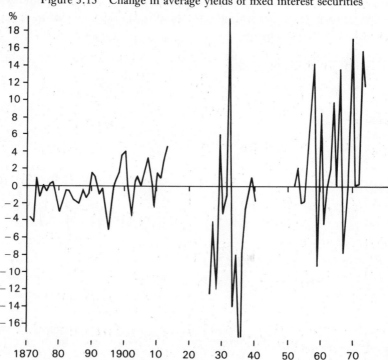

Sources:
StatBA, *Bevölkerung und Wirtschaft 1872–1972*, p. 214; DBBk, *Monatsbericht* 1975/11, p. 51. No measures of distribution were calculated, because the differences in variance are evident

comparing the post-war period with the inter-war yields neglects the highly interesting experiences of the 'free cycle' on financial markets before 1914, with their greater stability.

All in all in regard to the old style business cycle indicators, one cannot deny a decrease in the extent of post-war fluctuations with absolute certainty. The picture is more complicated. Examples of smoother development (e.g. in raw material prices) are balanced by others, in which development in the post-war period proceeded far less steadily and with visibly greater amplitudes of fluctuation (for instance in prices on financial markets).

IV

Even establishing such facts is important, but we should not avoid the question of how such data can be interpreted. As already announced, at this point only a few indications of a rather speculative nature shall be given.

We can above all hold economic policy responsible for the destabilisation of the credit markets emphasised at the end of the last section; in particular the monetary policy of the central bank plays a role. If monetary controllers wished to dampen an upturn in the post-war period, they attempted to raise interest rates above the level which tends to arise in an upturn anyway. If they wished to brake a downturn or encourage an upturn, they sought to reduce interest below the level provided by the market.[49] It is true that the central bank at first targeted the short-term market, but this, as a rule, also influenced the market for longer- and long-term securities. This resulted in pronounced fluctuations in security prices.

It is remarkable that a policy today is called 'stabilisation policy' – because of its goal regarding high employment and price stability – although it necessarily implies an increase in instability in another sector of the economy, in this case in the valuation of financial assets and their yields. Whereas before the First World War owners of state securities and mortgage bonds could be sure that the possible losses in prices of their securities almost never exceeded the annual yield of their securities (that is, after all, why such investments were held to be absolutely safe), this changed in the inter-war period. And in the post-war period no return to earlier conditions occurred.

But referring to the special role of economic policy, and above all monetary policy, cannot suffice as an answer to the question regarding the peculiar destabilisation of capital relations. The explanation would be too 'technical' and too superficial. The historian should ask why an economic system which is still characterised by numerous people as 'capitalist' tolerates such a considerable destabilisation of credit prices and asset values. It even seems to expect and support them. It is hard to imagine how people would have reacted before 1914 to changes in the value of monetary assets of the order repeatedly experienced in the post-war period. There was a broad stratum of 'capitalists' before 1914, i.e. owners of monetary assets, or 'Rentiers', who depended for their existence on proceeds from capital. The first and second inflations of the twentieth century in Germany certainly reduced the number of those interested in this kind of stability, and their wishes in the struggle over distribution was less pressing in view of their diminished power. But, in other western countries, in which there were no comparable devaluations of monetary assets through inflation, we can observe similar tendencies towards a post-war destabilisation of security prices and interest rates.

A more general answer must, it seems to me, be sought on the one hand in the fundamental structural change of western economic systems and on the other in the peculiar experience of risks in the inter-war period. Figure 5.14 illustrates this particularly well. It shows the movement of rates of unemployment, as far as they can be measured. Again, the series is not fully consistent as regards the source of the statistics. For example, the unemployment rates depicted from 1887 to 1931 rest on trade union data drawn from their members; from 1928 the source is official data of labour exchanges. But however large the possible scope for error may be, it is still indisputable that unemployment rates in the inter-war period were, with the exception of the inflationary years at the beginning of the Weimar Republic and the last years before the Second World War, far higher than in the pre-war period, and that unemployment rates in the post-war period after the removal of structural unemployment, the consequence of the devastations of the war and the inflow of expellees and refugees, remained not only far below that of the inter-war period, but on the whole probably also under the levels before 1914. Even if comparative statements are somewhat uncertain, the fact is relatively well established that before 1914 employment fluctuated more strongly according to the business cycle than in the post-war period.[50]

In view of the fact that we could not ascertain similarly clear differences in the fluctuations of total output, it appears tempting to attribute the stabilisation of employment in the post-war years to other circumstances rather than to a particularly successful policy of production stabilisation. So far this complex question has remained insufficiently examined to allow us to reach a definite answer.[51] The fact is that the general public – and this also means the electorate – thanks to a higher degree of suggestion on the part of the politicians and also of numerous economists, ascribes low unemployment largely to the consequences of economic policy. They do

Figure 5.14 Unemployment as share of employees

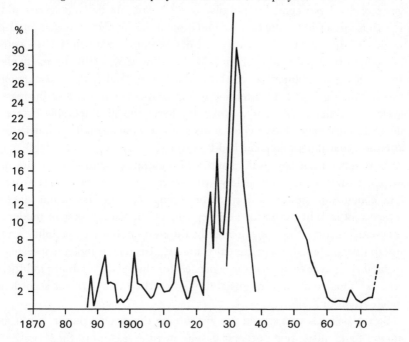

Sources:
1887–1938: B. R. Mitchell, *European Historical Statistics 1750–1970*, London 1975, pp. 167ff.
1950–71: StatBA, *Bevölkerung und Wirtschaft 1872–1972*, p. 148
1972–4: DBBk, *Statistische Beiheften zu den Monatsberichten*, Reihe 4 (own calculations from quarterly unemployment rates)

not explain it in terms of 'normalisation', in the sense of the removal of the restraints of the inter-war period and other automatically operating economic forces: for instance the coincidence of a general shortage of labour in relation to the possibilities of capital formation combined with substantial technical progress.

Whatever our conclusion, the shock of the Great Depression is one of the main points for interpreting post-war economic development. Since then, full employment became the undisputed major objective, whenever unemployment threatened to rise. In a society in which more than 70 per cent of those engaged in work are employed, and the vast majority are not engaged in agriculture but live in towns, employment risks are evaluated differently than in as yet underdeveloped societies, in which only a minority of the population is threatened by the risk of unemployment. That helps to explain why 1966/7 in the Federal Republic when unemployment rose to an annual average of rather over 2 per cent after a period of six years under 1 per cent, the political order seemed to be endangered and vigorous measures for the rapid stimulation of the economy were adopted – while far larger fluctuations in the rate of unemployment before 1914 were not felt to be a political problem. At that time it was still the relatively small changes on financial markets, the 'crises' and 'panics' occurring there, which gripped the attention of newspaper reports and of business cycle researchers. There is a symmetry here: the incomparably greater instability of financial assets now finds just the same negligible measure of attention that unemployment had before 1914.

A comparison of figures 5.13 and 5.14 illustrates significant changes in the German economy and society over the course of the last ninety years. The conclusion should be drawn from them that there is not one single measure of stability valid for every epoch. In the various eras of modern economic history there are evidently different notions of stability and instability and possibly a perpetual 'trade-off'. In an interdependent system instability in at least one sector is needed for the sake of stability in other sectors. This compensating instability is for the most part not accorded much attention.

So the belief is widespread not just among the general public, but also among economists, that post-war development at least until the seventies, proceeded considerably more steadily than formerly. That was the case until 1975 with regard to the goal of full employment, whose desirability had in the interim been upgraded. Concerning other important variables, it is not a valid conclusion, unless we reduce the comparison to a juxtaposition of inter- and post-war periods.

The surprising, or to put it more carefully problematical, aspect for the historian is the relatively short memory of all the interested parties. The development of the last decades appears to confirm that theories and policies as well as social norms orientate themselves as a rule towards recent experience; in consequence they run the risk of significant errors in evaluating the current situation. Thus in the Great Depression of 1929–33, the memory of the hyper-inflation and its terrible consequences still haunted the people in power in Germany, and contributed possibly to wrong reactions and to the heightening of the crisis. In the post-war period, theorists and politicians alike felt it their task above all to prevent a repetition of the ghastly events of the Great Depression and their political consequences. That the risks were probably exaggerated in the process and that sledgehammers were used to crack nuts became clear in the seventies: the weapons used, which led to a worldwide inflationary process, were no longer suitable, and the development of the inflationary process inescapably had to be stopped, even at the cost of a crisis. Had the economic policy makers in western industrialised countries limited themselves to removing the barriers to international trade installed in the inter-war period, and to putting through other structural reforms (though these did exist) for facilitating the 'self-regulatory forces', the fate of the business cycle would possibly have proceeded along the smoother tracks of the pre-, and not along those of the inter-war, period anyway.

A very recent suggestion expressed by Milton Friedman, Karl Brunner and others holds that it is not the private sector which is primarily responsible for the post-war fluctuations in the business cycle, but rather the policy of governments, doubtless aiming at stability but in reality achieving instability. Whether this thesis can derive support from the historical comparison is an urgent question, but it can only be posed here, and not answered.[52] Nevertheless, it deserves to be emphasised that the business cycle in Germany before 1914, largely uninfluenced by state activity, was also a growth cycle, whose up- and downturns certainly do not justify the view that former business cycles fluctuated more strongly than those after 1945. In some ways, development in the post-war period seems rather to have been more unsteady – and by and large, it progressed according to a cyclical pattern much more clearly after 1950 than it did before 1914.

6 TRENDS, CYCLES, STRUCTURAL BREAKS, CHANCE: WHAT DETERMINES TWENTIETH-CENTURY GERMAN ECONOMIC HISTORY?

As one of the four speakers on the general theme 'Historical Perspectives: Process and Plan, Event and Epoch?', I have the task of examining, on the basis of German economic historical sources for the twentieth century, the difficulties in approaching history correctly.* I hope to be able to show that considerable differences in judgement of specific historical phenomena and events depend on the different perspectives with which even the same material is examined. In the course of doing this, individual questions are also discussed, but in the main we are concerned here with problems in 'historical perspective', and not with the depiction of German economic history for its own sake.

I

At the outset, a quotation will illuminate the difficulties facing an historian who wishes to describe and interpret economic development in the twentieth century. One could find many similar quotations. The one chosen is from the impressive work of David Landes, *The Unbound Prometheus. Technological Change and Industrial Development in Western Europe from 1750 to the Present*. Landes says:

> It is not easy to write the economic history of the twentieth century. For one thing, it is too close to us; for another, it is messy by comparison with the halcyon nineteenth ... The story of each [European economy of the nineteenth century, K.B.], *mutatis mutandis*, fits closely to a kind of ideal model of modernisation; the leitmotiv is the process of industrial revolution. The twentieth century by contrast is a confusion of emergencies, disasters, improvisations and artificial expedients.[1]

Landes evidently sees the major difficulties of the historian as lying in the fact that while the nineteenth century had a leitmotiv, which can be used to organise material, there is no equivalent for the period after 1913.

Landes' claim for European economic history in general is all the more valid for Germany: the First World War, the post-war inflation, the brief recovery, the world depression, the Nazi peace-time economy, the Second World War, the collapse of the Reich, the occupation – the string of catastrophes and collapses makes the period from 1914 to 1949 incomparable with the preceding century. In addition, because of the territorial changes and the partition of 1945–9, we cannot be sure whether there is a single object of study called 'German economic history'. This partition was not just an opportunity for conducting a random test on the old German Empire with a segment which, according to the laws of probability, might have been more or less structurally the same as the previous whole. This question, which is certainly important, will not be dealt with more closely here. In common with other authors, I view the Federal Republic of Germany's economy as substantially the heir to that of the German Empire, with the consequence that long-term analyses should in principle be valid. Of course, they still demand the correction of original statistical data in order to establish comparability over time. And unavoidably, changes whose importance cannot as a rule be precisely measured are associated with this procedure.

We intend to use figure 6.1 to show why Landes found it so difficult to discover a leitmotiv for a twentieth-century economic development. With

Figure 6.1   Real per capita NNP in the territories of the German Empire and the Federal Republic

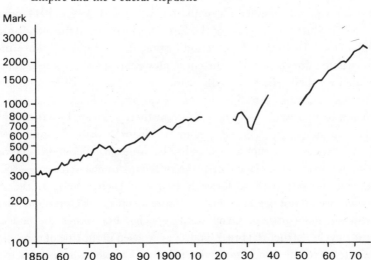

the help of numerous statistical operations – some rather dubious – we establish a comparison between time periods.[2] The graph shows the development of net national product (eliminating changes in price levels) per inhabitant for the respective territories. That is how we usually measure growth, whatever objections may be raised to the notion of 'national product' as a measure of prosperity.[3] Because the national product is divided by the population, a large part of those quantitative leaps which arose as a result of the territorial changes is corrected, although not all such effects are removed.[4] Because we wish to focus on rates of growth, a particular form of representation is selected. Instead of normal scale (with the same intervals between the numbers 100, 200, 300) the logarithmic scale is applied. In this multiples always stand at the same intervals, e.g. 100, 200, 400, 800, or 3, 6, 12, 24. Whenever numbers double, or treble, they have the same vertical distance from each other in the graph. In this way, it is easy to discern changes in the speed of growth: the flatter the curve is, the more slowly the economy grew; and the steeper the curve is, the faster economic growth.

After these preliminary remarks we can examine the graph. It shows that whatever we might say about the 'Great Depression' of the Bismarckian period or other crises before 1914, and however important they may appear in the specific context of pre-war problems, until 1913 economic development is dominated by relatively uninterrupted growth. There is a clear tendency in this era, and we are inclined to mark it using a straight line.

After 1913, the picture is quite different. Indeed, in the first instance, there is not even a picture at all. From 1914 to 1924, there is a gap, as there is no information comparable with that measured before 1914 on the national product for the years of the First World War and the inflation and stabilisation.[5] In 1925 a short period begins in which there is once more comparable information; but the curve now develops along a new course, to which we shall refer repeatedly. From the end of the 1930s until 1949, there is another big gap. The Federal Republic's official statistics begin with annual figures only in 1950. And now there seems to be a third phase in twentieth-century German economic history, with a rapid rise in national product per capita such as has been never experienced before.

The following remarks concern the problems of characterising each of these phases and their historical relation to each other. In the first instance, we do not need for this the four concepts of the principal theme of this section (process, plan, event, epoch), but rather the concepts 'trend', 'cycle', 'structural break' and 'chance' used in the title of this paper. In contrast to the concepts of the principal theme, which seem to be definable and interchangeable with a certain degree of arbitrariness, the concepts of the subsidiary theme are strictly related to one another, so that each individually can only be understood in its relation with the others. They denote different aspects, various levels of observation of the same historical (and here statistical) material, which may serve as a document of what in the principal theme was termed 'process'.

By a trend, we understand a continuous tendency in a time-series, which derives its force from an event operating over a longer term.[6] In figure 6.1, we can detect fairly clearly such a continuous tendency in the development from 1850 to 1914 and again after 1949 without requiring particular statistical methods of time-series analysis. As has already been mentioned, a smooth line, which we wish to characterise as a trend, can be laid through the values of the period 1850 to 1914. This is the trend of a growing economy.

The actual historical values for the most part do not lie precisely on this smooth curve, for a pure process of growth is of course a fiction: other influences also play their part. But if once we proceed from this fiction and calculate the year-by-year deviations in actual value from the trend values given and then express the deviations as percentages of the trend values, we may arrive at a time-series of relative deviations. This is illustrated in figure 6.2.[7] Here we have now another perspective: almost a history without growth. Here, 'cycle' and 'chance' dominate.

Figure 6.2 Deviations from trend of NNP (constant market prices)

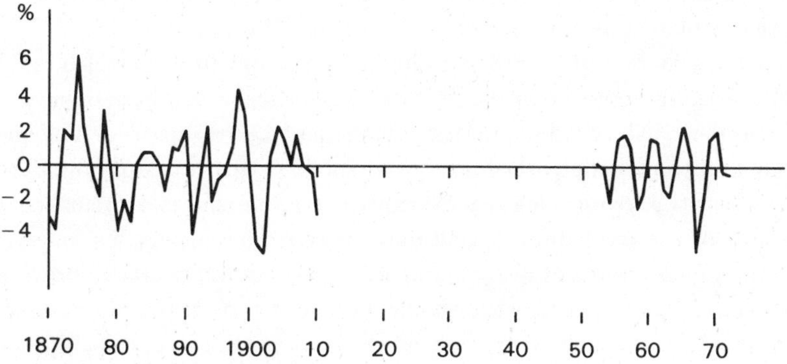

Sources:
1870–1910: W. G. Hoffmann, *Das Wachstum*, pp. 827f.
1952–1972: StatBA, *Lange Reihen 1974*, pp. 144f and StJb 1975 für die Bundesrepublik Deutschland, p. 508. Trend: 5 year moving average.
1870–1910: variance = 6.2
1952–72:   variance = 3.3

By cycles we understand those fluctuations which over the course of longer-term economic development may be identified as regular, and which repeat themselves according to a pattern, if not always in exactly the same way. We assume that the phases follow on from each other according to some sort of law, and not by chance.[8] As is well known, the view is widespread that capitalist development is necessarily cyclical. This has often been assessed negatively; but positive interpretations are also possible. Complex systems never show changes in levels without at least some oscillations. In the meantime, the economic policy attempts to dampen down the extent of swings in market economies; but if swings are part of the overall process of growth, they cannot be eliminated altogether.[9]

It is still an open question to what extent the deviations from the trend shown before 1914 and after 1949 can be divided into constituent components: regular business cycles, and what provisionally I still term 'chance'. Fundamentally, the term 'chance' is not really acceptable to the historian, because the concept suggests that nothing can be said as to causes. Often, however, causes are certainly discernible: wars, harvest failures, currency disorders, large strikes, domestic political crises, and the formation of large economic blocs, etc. In a strict sense these occurrences are not 'chance', but rather entirely explicable. In this context we mean that movements described as 'chance' can be explained neither by the pattern of the trend nor by a cyclical pattern; thus they cannot be explained in terms of *generalising* models of process. They are 'irregular' and therefore require specific explanations, in just the same way as their effects also need to be explained specifically. In addition, they are not predictable within the framework of the model used.

In this context, the word 'irregular' refers simply to a research strategy; of course it does not mean that we believe those manifestations to be improper. History is a mixture of regularities and irregularities. The question of the proportion of regular (i.e. amenable to general explanation) and irregular (i.e. requiring a specific explanation in each case) circumstances is one of the most difficult questions in economic history, as indeed in every sub-discipline of history. Furthermore, it is impossible to provide a definitive answer as to what should be counted as regularity and what irregularity; the answer depends on the framework of a specific question posed. In one perspective (in our case economic development) we may treat events as irregular, while in another perspective they represent part of a generalising explanation of process.

Much of course depends on how we distribute the weight of explanation in a specific context. At the Bochum conference on 'Industrial System and Political Development in the Weimar Republic', Alan S. Milward sum-

marised the historians' agreement about the developmental type of the
Weimar Republic: it was not of 'growth' but rather 'cycle'.[10] But the
problem does not consist only in determining two different kinds of regular
development in this period; we should also ask whether we can identify a
pattern of movement at all in the Weimar years. For not every upward or
downward movement constitutes a cycle. It may be that we should assign
the multiplicity of observed movements to irregular components; that we
should instead of explaining development in terms of patterns, find
numerous specific causes. This would then attribute to the political element a significance different from the one usually assumed in the context
of macro-economic analyses of trends and cycles.

If we again turn to figure 6.1, we find far more regularity in the pattern
after 1950 and before 1914 than we can between 1925 and 1938. Figure 6.2
provides us with further confirmation for the post-war period after 1950.
The turbulence of the years from 1914 to 1949 by contrast seems to allow
only the finely sliced kind of economic history which is expressed in the
chapter headings of our textbooks and handbooks: First World War, four
years; five to six years until the stabilisation of the Mark; a short era of the
'golden twenties', around five years; the depression, four years; six years'
National Socialist economic history before the war; six years' National
Socialist economic history in the war; three to four years' post-war
economy under the occupation … and then once more the historical longue
durée which allows at least a generation to appear as a single unit. Because,
however, trend, cycle and irregular components (chance) are only different
elements into which we divide up a concrete historical movement (here,
the movement of national income) in order to explain it in different ways,
the economic course of any period cannot be understood if any one element
is excluded. In order to be able to focus on the cycle, as Milward urges for
the Weimar period, the movement of the trend must be disregarded. But in
order to be able to disregard the trend, it must first be diagnosed! And in
order to be diagnosed, a picture of the historical process and its inter-
temporal connections is needed; we need to have a vision of more than just
one period. The thesis discussed below is that the period-specific characteristics of short periods of time cannot be understood without a vision of the
long-term course. Whoever speaks of the 'economic miracle after the
Second World War', or cites the period before 1914 as being one of 'happy
tranquility', whoever describes the 'golden twenties' or deals with the
'stagnation of the inter-war period', at least unconsciously brings into play
visions of an overall twentieth-century process. But in order to be scientific, we should not accept unconscious visions; we need to be able to
analyse them precisely.

II

In this section, three different possibilities of grasping the longer-term economic development of Germany in an overall vision are advanced. This is not done as a mere exercise, or in order to establish one idea or another as being correct. Rather we propose to demonstrate the multiplicity of possibilities of viewing long-term development and of dividing the explanatory burden between individual components – trend, cycle and irregularity.[11]

The material interpreted in all three cases is the time-series of net national product per capita, which is depicted in figure 6.1. Institutional factors, such as changes in the economic system, will be neglected. For it is our intention to vary the *vision* and not the fundamental material. Permanently altering the material of the base of the analysis would mean that it is likely that no consensus respecting an evaluation of longer-term processes can be found. However, even if we use the same evidence, there might be no natural consensus. Economic history, despite a background provided by an apparently well-developed science of economics, is not necessarily in possession of fundamentally better established findings than any other sub-discipline of history. Perhaps it does have an advantage in defining the multiplicity of possibilities more precisely, and emphasising the necessity for human judgement.[12]

Type 1. Figure 6.3 illustrates the first model for interpreting long-term economic development in Germany in the twentieth century.[13] It is based on three assumptions: (1) that it is possible to distinguish between 'normal movements' and 'disturbances of economic growth'; (2) that in the course of economic growth there is a tendency to return to 'normality' after disturbances; (3) that also in twentieth century Germany a long-term process of growth, similar to the one before 1913, is normal. The linear trend extending beyond 1913 is taken to mark the long-term developmental potentialities from which, as is evident, the reality departed for substantial periods. Some nineteenth-century economists, such as John Stuart Mill and William Stanley Jevons, asserted that disturbances in the developmental processes are digested, so that after some time the old type of movement is once more reproduced. Since the nineteenth century, there have been occasional allusions to this phenomenon. Above all, the Hungarian Ferenc Jánossy has recently elaborated such a model both for capitalist and socialist economies.[14] Because it is not possible to examine here the underlying economic theories, an analogy will be used. All parents and doctors know that babies who have lost weight during an illness as a

Figure 6.3   Real per capita NNP and logarithmic trend, German Empire and Federal Republic

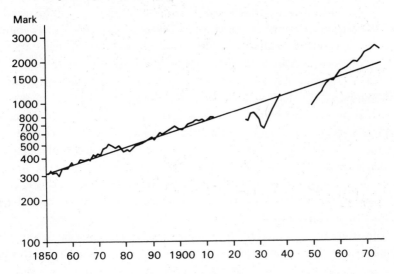

rule rapidly increase their weight once the illness is past. But rapid growth does not stop once the weight before the illness has been reached, but only once the growth *potential* in the interval has been made good. So it is possible to draw curves which extrapolate from the time before the illness and to find that the rapid growth after sickness only stops once weight moves near to the position on the extrapolated line. Not until then is what Janossy terms the 'period of reconstruction' brought to an end; the 'disturbance' has been completely digested and the period of 'normal development' recommences.

If this model is transferred to the economic development of Germany in the twentieth century, the following emerges. After the First World War, the line of actual development lay far below the phantom curve of 'possible development' in 1925. If one accepts the model, there was as a result a great opportunity for growth. Even after 1925, however, we cannot diagnose the high growth rates in GNP as typical of a 'period of reconstruction'. Only 1926 and 1927 stand out in this way. In 1929, national product per capita lay somewhat above that of 1913, but still around 15 per cent under the possible value as it emerges from the trend line of possibility. We shall later return in greater detail to the consequences of this observation for assessing Weimar development.[14a] But it is already now reasonable, if we accept the Type 1 model to seek specific reasons for the comparatively 'unsatisfactory growth' of Weimar even before the great depression. The slump then set the German economy a long way back again. The potential for growth, which the Nazis could find in 1933, was all the greater; for it was a question not just of overcoming a business cycle downturn, but also of eliminating an accumulated long-term backlog in growth. This would be the backdrop for what was already called at the time an 'economic miracle' (*Wirtschaftswunder*).[15] The extent to which the Second World War disturbed development cannot be assessed precisely with the aid of statistics for national income (as was the case after the First World War). Although, as M. Manz and W. Abelshauser in particular have shown,[16] national product per capita must have already increased before the currency reform of 1948, in 1950, the year for which the first official figures of the Federal Republic are available, it still lies far below the line of projected possibility. By contrast with development after the First World War, that which succeeded the Second World War does, however, correspond to the model of a period of reconstruction, for there was a long sequence of years with very high growth rates.

However, the potential for catching up was at last exhausted, and the curve should have swung back on to that of the extrapolated values. But in figure 6.3, the line of the actual values cuts through the trend line around 1960: this seems to strike a serious blow against the theory. But for the moment it is too soon to dispense with the theory of catching up. We have to remember that only minor changes in the gradient of the trend can easily alter the point of intersection, and that both our data and the assumption of the basic trend from the nineteenth century are not so securely established as to justify rejecting the whole concept simply because a particular year does not seem to fit. Furthermore, at present (1976) we are experiencing a period of on average lower growth rates; it could be that the general development of the economy is now falling back on to the trend from above, as was already the case after 1873. In any event, from what has already been said, it emerges that using the assumptions of Model 1, not only was the period 1914 to 1949 'abnormal', but also the above average growth of the period after the Second World War needs to be explained in terms of preceding disturbances.

As has already been indicated, it is not possible to examine here the theoretical problems underlying the concepts used.[16a] The critical core of the thesis is of course the assumption of a long-term 'normal' movement, the concept of a long-term trend of potentiality, taking the form of a logarithmic linear trend.[17]

Since at least for several important economies whose development can be described without gaps in the time-series, a logarithmic linear trend is a realistic hypothesis, we should not immediately reject such a concept for Germany. Figure 6.4 illustrates the economic development of Sweden,

Figure 6.4 Real per capita NNP, Sweden 1900–70

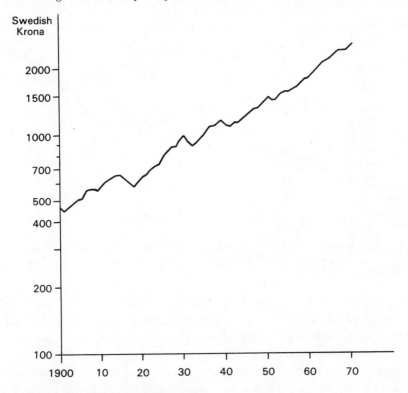

which can on the whole be described in terms of such a linear trend function. As we see, the strong downward movements in the First World War, in the world depression and (to some extent) at the beginning of the Second World War, were followed by phases of rapid catching-up.[18]

Type 2. Figure 6.5 shows a different concept for German economic development in the twentieth century. Here long-term development is illustrated in the form of a wave movement. Because the wave appears to fit the (fragmented) actual movement of the economy somewhat better, it might be supposed that it is less speculative than the trend line examined previously. But such a conclusion would be deceptive, for here too it is necessary to make numerous assumptions in order to accept a long-term movement of this kind.[19] In fact, it is also possible to draw on quite varied explanations for such a pattern of growth with a passing endogenous slowdown in development in the central section. We investigate only two of them below.

Figure 6.5   Real per capita NNP and trend-wave, German Empire and Federal Republic

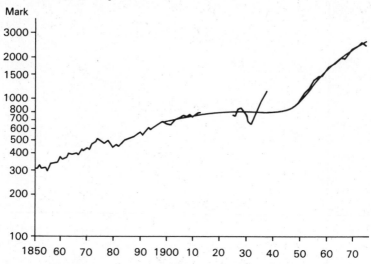

1   Joseph Schumpeter and Leon Dupriez are the economists who have most emphatically insisted on not presenting long-term economic development as a linear growth path, but interpret long-term development as cyclical – though naturally with cycles of far longer duration than business cycles.[20] They believed that innovation, investment activity, the extension of credit and similar impulses come in pushes, so that there was always and will always be an alternation of phases of rapid growth with periods of slower growth. As far as the chronology is concerned, it is not certain whether in Germany the coincidence of the beginning of the First World War with the beginning of a period of slower growth was just a chance; we must leave this question. The end of the slower growth period is variously described by the two authors. Schumpeter accepts the worldwide date as 1932, Dupriez as 1945.[21] Again, the problem is how to distinguish between 'disturbances' and 'regularity' in interpreting a concrete issue. For our purposes, an important point about the wave explanation is that its proponents presuppose, in addition to the disturbances they see, a continuous regular movement in explaining the different growth rates during the course of the twentieth century. To this extent they base their arguments on nineteenth-century experience.

2   This is somewhat different in the case of the following hypothesis about waves. Marxist and non-Marxist authors already after the First World War asserted that the force of capitalist development was slackening,

and that there was a threat of stagnation.[22] The Great Depression appeared to several stagnation theorists to be only a part of the process of the downfall of capitalism, though the different authors gave varying explanations. Of course, stagnation theories can only be used to explain the retardation phase, and not the wave movement. In fact, stagnation was not the last word, as we know now. How did the supersession of tendencies to stagnation through new stimuli come about? It would be possible to assume that the experience of stagnation, even of deep crisis, was 'digested' by the system, with the result that an economic system altered by the crisis, and in particular with a changed role of the state, was able to produce growth anew. Just as in a normal business cycle it is a widely held view that the crisis lays the conditions for a new impetus and thus for continued growth, so the 'secular crisis' can be understood as a condition for the internal change of the system, and thus for the continuation of (secular) growth. To be sure, it is only permissible to integrate such a concept in the wave form of figure 6.5 once the 'change in system' is built into the causal complex, and once institutional change is not ascribed to the components 'chance' or 'irregularity' by themselves. However, if the changed role of the state is seen as a completely new phenomenon, and not endogenously explicable through the system of hypotheses, it will be necessary to speak rather of a structural break. In this case a model of Type 3 will be used; this is the subject of the following discussion.

First we should indicate what consequences arise from the hypothesis of the regularity of waves for the interpretation of individual periods after 1913; especially by comparison with Model 1. In the second case, less explanatory weight would be given to the First World War and the political and economic post-war order as a 'disturbance factor' in the process of economic growth. Correspondingly, of course, the scope for successful political action would also have been smaller. With regard to the National Socialist period, it would in particular be of significance whether one dates the turning-point to 1932 (with Schumpeter) or to 1945 (with Dupriez). In the first case the National Socialists would have derived an advantage from trend factors; in the second case, the actual rise in national product would have been the more surprising, i.e. an explanation would have to draw still more power from the domain of cycle and irregularity.

Type 3. We now turn to the third model (see figure 6.6). It bears a certain similarity to the second, but the principle is different. We see no continuous trend, whether a straight line or a wave form. Rather, there are three different trends with distinct breaks, sharply dividing certain epochs from each other. According to the underlying concept, it is impossible to

Figure 6.6   Real per capita NNP and broken logarithmic trend, German Empire and Federal Republic

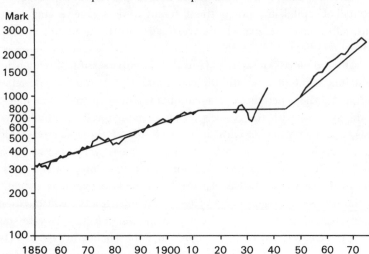

develop a common theoretical explanation for the longer-term develop-ment of the entire period. Each phase is conceived as being of a develop-mental type peculiar to itself and governed by its own laws. It would need neither to fit at specific corners nor to show the same type of linear development (though in our case, we have depicted three straight lines).

This is the moment to speak about the concept of 'structural break'. It does appear in the theme of the paper, but has not yet been referred to specifically. It necessarily belongs with the three other themes because – as may now be seen – decisions regarding the utility of trend forms are only possible with the aid of structural concepts.[23] What is here to be under-stood by 'structure'?[24]

In economics, growth paths and business cycles are often described with the aid of systems of mathematical equations, in which independent and dependent variables appear. Structure refers to an equation system. It represents the constant framework in the analysis of the period at issue, while the values of the variables of course change. But naturally structures are not unalterable over all ages. They never describe economic laws valid at any and every time. It may be that a particular formalised description system, a model, which describes development in a particular period well, does not fit development in another time. In the event that a model which satisfactorily describes both phases together cannot be successfully deployed, we speak of a 'structural break' and, for the various phases, we have to develop particular models with their own structures.

Whether we decide to interpret a discrepancy between actual observations and those described in the model as a sign of a structural break or only as a coincidence, i.e. an individually explicable deviation which does not in principle alter the pattern of the process, depends on what is to be explained, and on the extent of the deviations which may be accepted. This is why three different types of long-term model for twentieth-century development, which are hard to choose between, can be depicted here. Of course, in economic life, radical breaks rarely occur because the changes which go deepest still leave numerous factors unaltered or alter them only slightly (geographical position, climate, system of soil usage, language, state of knowledge of the population, volume of invested capital – even after the big devastations of the century – socio-structural attitudes, communication systems, legal forms, etc, etc). Yet it is plausible to follow numerous other authors and describe both 1914 and 1945 as relatively important breaks: this is suggested in figure 6.6. Most economists after 1948 engaged in the question of whether economic development could be forecast on the basis of past experience refused directly to use the history of the inter-war period as a stock of experience for prognostic purposes in the post-war period, because the structure was no longer the same.[25] But I have already made reference to the fact that the Great Depression too is often seen as *the* structural break in the first half of the twentieth century, after which the mechanism of market economies was fundamentally altered.[26] There are of course contrary positions to all these assertions, simply because structural concepts do differ from one another.

Once we assume it to be impossible to provide a common interpretation for the whole development of the twentieth century, and develop trend concepts peculiar to individual phases, it is an open question whether the years between 1914 and 1949 should be described as a period without growth (figure 6.6) or in different terms. It would for instance be possible to mark the breaks in both wars more strongly, and in each case fix the levels for the following trend periods beneath that prevailing at the end of the previous period, resulting in a sawtooth shape. Such a model would, if the concept of a linear trend is retained at all, imply growth for the inter-war period.[27]

The time-series of the national product are unfortunately so short that they leave plenty of scope for the imagination. But, in order to give a certain plausibility to the method of illustration selected, and to show that the trend forms chosen can at least be supported by other sources, figures for the production of crude steel are used (figure 6.7).[28] These do not of course replace the time-series of national product, but they have the advantage of showing no gaps. We recognise the basic pattern, which also

Figure 6.7   Steel production, German Empire and Federal Republic

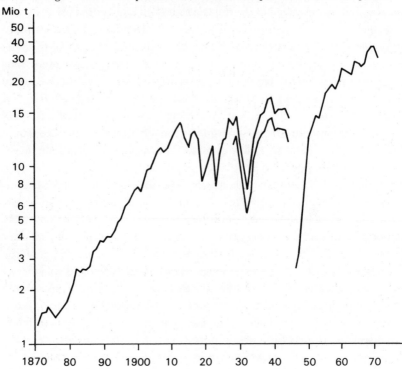

underlay figure 6.6. A phase of relatively constant growth up to 1913 is followed by a period in which, although production fluctuated wildly, the level of 1913 was never exceeded for any substantial period of time. The peak in the Second World War would then be the result of a special situation, which we could classify as irregular, as we could correspondingly describe the interruption of 1944/5. After a renewed structural break, a period of long-term sustained average growth followed, with admittedly decreasing rates of increase.

As far as the period after 1950 is concerned, if Model 3 is accepted, a peculiar explanation is required. Numerous experts have attempted to offer one by referring to a supposed acceleration of technical progress or to the effectiveness of special institutional factors. D. Petzina as well as others believes that after the Second World War the Federal Republic did more than just adapt to a secular trend (corresponding to Model 1).[29]

For the historical interpretation, it would be of great importance if we were able to identify separate periods of development marked by structural breaks, each requiring their own particular explanation, as in Model 3. In the first place there is a greater degree of freedom to explain developments; and particular circumstances specific to the period, including even biographical details of leading personalities, may enter the argumentation. It may also be presumed that the interpretation of phenomena given by contemporaries is substantially shaped by whether or not they themselves accept the concept of a break; and whether their concept is shared by historical analysts is a further interesting problem.

If we look back over the three models or images of the development of the economy as a whole in the twentieth century, we may conclude:

1   The same (incomplete) material – in this case the time-series of national product per capita – may be interpreted in various ways as a step on the way to characterising the long-term development of Germany in the twentieth century. Because we were concerned above all with depicting different visions, the models were developed in an extremely abstract form. We cannot decide between the alternatives. Within the framework of the limited space available, we are unable to deploy the arguments that would be needed for a choice.[30] In addition, it should be examined whether combinations of different trend-concepts should be used to explain development more appropriately. For example, a wave between 1913 and the 1950s might be drawn underneath the curve of the extrapolated linear trend of Type 1, but not as deep as or as flat as in figure 6.6. For the period after the Second World War, a possible explanation might connect the concept of a reconstruction period with the hypothesis of a secular structural change, etc.

2   Different interpretations of long-term development necessarily imply different opinions concerning the characteristics and the causes of development in shorter time-frames: hitherto above all historians have been interested in such explanations. This will be demonstrated in a crude way in the following section, examining an historically and politically explosive topic, developments in the National Socialist period and their connection to previous history. With this we return to our remark at the opening, that the period-specific individuality of an historically short epoch cannot be grasped without a picture of the totality of the historical process in a larger time-period.

III

In his book *Thesen eur deutschen Sozial- und Wirtschaftsgeschichte 1933 bis 1938*, E. Hennig writes:

> The Third Reich is to be understood as a class society, which was
> characterised by a concentration of capital, the increase of
> entrepreneurial and managerial remuneration, of net profits, of
> shares of industrial self-finance, etc. In short, there was a struc-
> tural advantage of big industry, while the rise in the average
> weekly wage of the workers between 1933 and 1939 remained, at
> 2.8%, far behind the growth of the national product, which grew
> at an average of 8.2%, and behind the rise in labour productivity,
> which grew at 10% over the period 1933 to 1937.[31]

It is a matter of a 'structural advantage', which it is supposed may be
derived from the figures presented and from subsequent evidence. What is
meant is evidently an advantaging that was quite specific to this political
system. Is the case really proven? At first the proof seems to be plausible,
but the matter is rather more complicated. We will not in the first instance
call into question the validity of the material.[32] If we accept it, we still have
an issue as to whether it is really possible to arrive at a 'structural bias'
from the straightforward numerical references given in the quotation. A
closer study of German and international economic history quickly shows
that the phenomena described can be encountered in *every* normal cyclical
upturn; after a depression of the kind represented by the world slump,
these phenomena should surely be expected to a greater measure than in
other cases. They represent to a considerable degree nothing more than the
return of development after a preceding downturn, in which profits for
instance shrank far more than the total of national income or wages.

A reference to the cyclical normality of the general direction of movement does not yet disprove Hennig's thesis, because it depends not on the
direction of movement, but on the extent of the changes. Proving the
special bias of the National Socialist system to the advantage of Big Business, however, assumes that it is possible successfully to isolate the components trend, cycle and irregularity (and thus the specific political factor)
in the observed variables. Hennig recognises this problem at least insofar
as it concerns the cycle, for he explicitly says that developments in the
National Socialist period should not be compared only with the previous
severe depression. This would make the period from 1933 onwards appear
in too favourable a light; instead one should go back to the so-called
Weimar boom of 1924 to 1929.[33] After numerous comparisons, he draws
the conclusion: 'If one compares the years 1928/9, the outstanding boom
years of the Weimar Republic, with 1938/9, the last years before the
Second World War, then the result of the comparison, in as far as the social
status and the standard of living of workers is concerned, is unfavourable to

National Socialism, that is German Fascism in power.'[34] By comparing one cyclical peak with another (as he suggests), the comparison really seems to exclude the cyclical element, and allows the trend, and what is meant by the concept 'structural bias', to appear.

But is the comparison with 1928/9 as a reference period really capable of demonstrating the theses? Figure 6.8 illustrates data which are used by Hennig at another point to identify the condition of class forces: the relation of income derived from work to the national income. The figure shows not only the period 1928 to 1939, but also a much longer perspective.[35] Income derived from work here includes not only the wage and salary income of employees, but also an arithmetically derived entrepreneurial wage for those active as self-employed, as farmers, artisans, or other entrepreneurs. This kind of income, which can only be estimated, needs to be included in income from labour in order to be able to distinguish it from income derived from wealth, but above all in order to eliminate longer-term changes in the structure of employment which may affect the wage share. Figure 6.8 shows that the relation of income from labour to national income fell sharply from the trough of the Great Depression until the end of the statistical series, in the National Socialist period, and that correspondingly the share of income from wealth increased rapidly. Before this is taken as a proof, the question of how justified the choice of the year 1928/9 is as the point of reference for a comparison must be examined. Was 1928/9 a 'normal situation'? The graph demonstrates

Figure 6.8   Labour's share of national income, German Empire and Federal Republic (from W. G. Hoffmann)

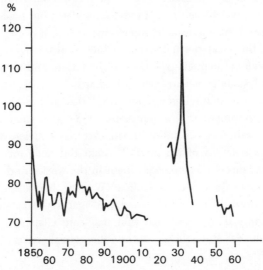

immediately that during the Weimar period the share of non-property income lay completely outside all historical comparisons! Not only the depression was 'abnormal'; the distribution of income *before* the crisis also was very unusual. This becomes clear from the long-term comparison. The recognisable peculiarity of the distribution of income may be linked to another, likewise exceptional circumstance, depicted in figure 6.9: in the so-called 'golden twenties' average annual unemployment among trade union members (for which statistics are available) only once fell below 7 per cent. Such a level was very unusual for the period up to 1914, and also for the period of the inflation.[36] It would be possible to show yet more unusual features in the period of reference chosen. The development of investment ratios, that is the proportion of net investments to the net national product, a critical quantity in determining growth and the course of the business cycle, is very striking (figure 6.10).[37] Again a long-term comparison reveals the peculiarity of the position during the Weimar 'boom'. Investment ratios were not only weak compared with the period after 1950, but they were also below those of the pre-war years, in both average and peak times.

If figures 6.8 to 6.10 were presented to an observer, expert in economics but who was not aware that this was a matter of twentieth-century German economic history and specifically of the National Socialist era, he would probably come to the conclusion that after 1933 a 'process of normalisation' had taken place. He would believe that, as a result of reasons which would require closer examination, disturbances which had previously hindered development had successfully been removed. His judgement would be substantially influenced by the picture derived from experience of the trend in the period before 1914 and after 1949; but he could also base his argument on international comparisons.

Of course, the word 'normalisation', which appears in our mental game, cannot be taken as the final opinion of the historian; and the model builder cannot afford such cynicism either. Perhaps, however, it does help to understand why even intelligent contemporaries, and foreigners, followed economic development in Germany after 1933 with such approval, and expected normalisation to follow from extreme policies. After all, the economic constellation of pre-crisis Weimar did not function properly! The crisis was surely no chance accident in the works, and its origins are already recognisable in the so-called 'Weimar boom'. The economic development until 1939 should be measured against the constellation of the year 1928/9 only if it is assumed that that constellation was capable of being continued. But there is no theoretical basis for such an assumption.[37a]

Of course it is not insignificant that the recovery from the crisis in Germany took place under the rule of the dictatorial party, which destroyed trade unions, prevented free wage bargaining (although this had already been distorted to the point of caricature before 1933), and allowed a state-run business cycle to develop into an armaments cycle. There are many characteristics of this period, which justify a moral condemnation. But the rise in the rate of profit, and the lagging of wages behind the development of productivity (see the quotation above) might be regarded as a condition for restoring full employment, a dream since 1923, and a goal which cannot only be said to have been held by capitalists. In any case, such a development occurred in almost every country after 1933 which managed to recover relatively rapidly from the trough of the depression, including countries where free trade unions continued to exist.[38]

Figure 6.9   Unemployed as percentage of employees

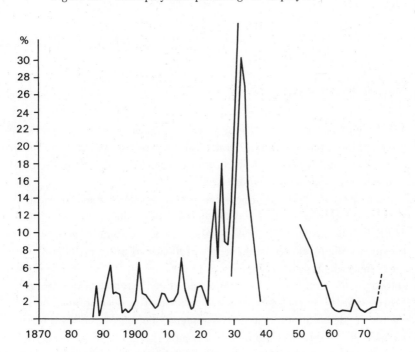

Sources:
1887–1938: B. R. Mitchell, *European Historical Statistics 1750–1970*, London 1975, p. 167ff.
1950–71:   StatBA, *Bevölkerung und Wirtschaft 1872–1972*, p. 148
1972–4:   DBBk; *Statistische Beiheften zu den Monatsberichten*, Reihe 4 (own calculations from quarterly unemployment rates)

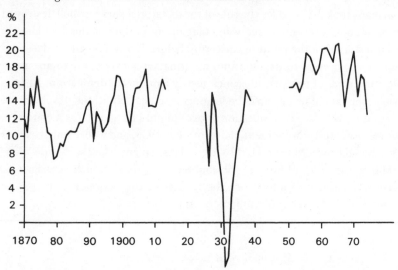

Figure 6.10   Net investment as share of NNP

Sources:
1871–1913: W. G. Hoffmann, *Das Wachstum*, pp. 825f.
1920–74:   StatBA, *Lange Reihen 1974*, pp. 144ff; StJb 1975,
pp. 508 and 519

IV

Finally, the relations between trend, cycle and irregular components, including structural breaks, will be presented once more on the
basis of different material. This offers an instructive example of the possibility of testing different hypotheses.

In figure 6.11 the heavy line shows five year averages for births in the
German Empire after 1900 and the Federal Republic until the end of the
1970s.[39] The structural break in development around 1900, when a
previously slight tendency for births to fall turned into a rapid downward
movement which stabilised at a much lower level after a few decades, is not
shown in the graph. As Köllmann has already pointed out, the graph
proves that an interpretation which ascribes the development of birth
figures to demoralisation as a consequence of the Versailles Treaty is
misguided.[40] The trend ignores this event.

Continuing our reflections on the relationship between trend, cycle and
irregular components, there is a problem in the evaluation of the period
1930 to 1939. Interpretation of the course after 1925 evidently creates
some difficulties. What determined further developments in Germany?
Somewhere here there appears to be an irregularity with regard to the

Figure 6.11   Birth rates in eleven European countries

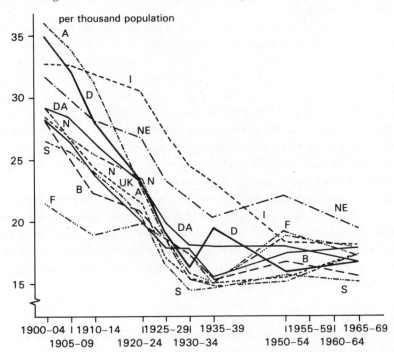

trend, but we do not yet know where. There are two possibilities of explanation: (a) 1930–4 is a downward deviation from the trend because for economic and other reasons the willingness to give birth decreased particularly severely in the great depression; (b) the movement of 1935–9 is an upward deviation from the trend, and is the result of National Socialist population policy and/or a change in values in the population in the phase of Nazi peacetime successes. The issue at stake is whether the trend should run further up or down, and whether the values in 1935–9 or those in 1930–4 correspond more to the trend line. Both explanations are plausible, but they cannot both be right at the same time.

It may be seen from this example that an historical mode of analysis does not always first identify the trend, then the cycle, and finally, in the conclusion, the irregular components as a residual. Here indeed it is the other way round: the shape of the trend emerges in the conclusion, according to whether more weight is given to National Socialist policy on the one hand or to the great depression on the other as irregular components in development. But – and this is after all what the whole paper is concerned with – *one* genre of decisions about a complex of problems always determines the remaining possibilities. The degrees of freedom to make choices are limited.

In order to decide the question of what the trend, and what the irregularity, in the development of natality can be, we can fortunately use international comparison. Such comparison is too rarely applied in German history. Figure 6.11 shows a surprisingly parallel movement in almost all of the states covered. It precludes referring only to national factors influencing the normal course of development. We now also recognise that in Germany it is not the value for 1930–4 which presents a peculiarity. It is close to the values of other countries and continues a common international movement. Rather the value for 1935–9 is exceptional, and falls quite outside the narrow band of development in other states.[41] Among the countries covered, there is no other case of so dramatic a rise in the birth figures, whether we look at countries with relatively good or relatively poor economic performance. Thus it appears justified to see the trend in Germany as lying below the actual values, and to characterise the movement in 1935–9 as an 'irregularity' which requires special explanation.[42]

V

Finally, we should remember that our observations stood under the general heading of the section in the conference: 'Historical Perspective: Process and Plan, Event and Epoch?' Because it was to be presumed that the majority of historians were in any case not inclined to interpret the question mark in the general heading in the sense of an 'either or', but to accept pluralism in approaching the question as a matter of course, I did not intend either to ceremoniously confirm previous preconceptions, or harden them by virtue of banal examples.

Who would be opposed to a multiplicity of possible approaches in any case? Certainly no economic historian, who has long been familiar with trend, cycle and chance. Given this fact, it was more important to show that the demand for a multi-level approach must not degenerate into arbitrariness, and that the problems are anything but banal. Here there should be a convergence of research interests. I have not been able to supply convenient recipes, and I have not even been able to make a decision between the three model types describing Germany's long-term development. But I did not wish to suggest hasty interpretations; above all it was my purpose to show how open our field of research still is if we wish to be serious about a conscious theoretical application of interrelated perspectives of historical analysis in the 'historical perspective' taken as the theme of this conference. Even in economic history, the importance of long- and medium-term regularities in comparison with specific explanatory factors of individual events may still be judged in very different ways. It may be an advance that methodological consciousness at least leads to a naming of the alternatives, and to a clearer characterisation of the inevitable subjective moments of judgement.[43]

7 THE FEDERAL REPUBLIC OF GERMANY IN THE SECULAR TREND OF ECONOMIC DEVELOPMENT

I Diagnosis of an unparalleled process

1   Never before in German economic history have there been twenty-five years of such rapid economic development as after 1947/8. By economic development, we understand two aspects: first, the growth of real national product per capita; secondly, the change in economic structures, especially the structures of production and use of GNP. From 1950 to 1975 real national product per capita rose threefold in the Federal Republic. In the same period, to give two examples of structural change, the proportion of those engaged in agriculture fell from around 34 per cent to a mere 7 per cent, and the proportion of hard coal in primary energy consumption fell from over 70 per cent to around 20 per cent.[1]

The circumstance that between 1950 and 1975 the economy produced no central conflict of political forces either at home or abroad must be considered highly exceptional in the long-term context. Indeed, it is possible to say, without offering specific proofs, that rapid economic development has contributed to the stability of the political order in the Federal Republic. The 'economic miracle' appears to be an important element in the de facto constitution of this part of divided Germany.

2   When the Federal Republic was founded, it was already felt that rapid growth might solve the politically explosive potentials for conflict in the post-war era (such as the refugee and expellee problem). Characteristically, it was the date of the currency and economic reform of June 1948 which was celebrated in the Federal Republic as the first new anniversary, and surely for a long time also the most important one. In contrast to the Weimar Republic, the Federal Republic might thus ceremonially base itself on an act of liquidation of the financial consequences of war. It was a massive expropriation and a quasi-revolutionary act, but it was largely

accepted. By contrast, the inflation of the First World War and its effects on production and employment first made the Weimar Republic possible, but in the longer term placed on to the democratic system, whose social and economic situation was already unstable, a heavy burden.[1a]

Even if it would be going too far to state that there was no major conflict between 1950 and 1975, it should still be stressed that the consensus democracy was not burdened by those disputes over the distribution of income and wealth characteristic of the inter-war period.[1b] That is true not only for the functional distribution of income to various kinds of income, but also for the distribution between various branches of the economy. In particular, the share of agriculture had been a major problem for political stability until the National Socialist period.

It is an historically unparalleled fact that two-thirds of those engaged in agriculture disappeared between 1950 and 1975, without any impact on party politics! It was due above all to the circumstance that the adjustment of the structure of production did not follow merely in the wake of strong external pressure, but emerged equally or perhaps even more from the speed of growth in other parts of the economy. Thus in this phase of 'relative depression' of agriculture, its real gross output still increased by 60 per cent, and income per person engaged in agriculture actually increased fivefold. This is why such enormous structural change could take place so peacefully: the relative losers were also able to gain a great deal in absolute terms because of the general process of economic growth.

3   The same pattern was repeated in many sectors. Rapid growth also made possible a relatively conflict-free transfer to the advantage of investment, but did so at the same time as real private per capita consumption expanded more than threefold. In the same way a rapid growth of state expenditure was possible, without the rivalry of private and public sectors appearing as a central political problem, as they had in the 1920s during the Weimar Republic. In particular, the extension of the so-called social net and the growth of the state's transfer activity proceeded relatively uncontroversially while national product grew at high rates. The considerable change in the geographical structure of the economy of the Federal Republic did not lead to conflicts threatening the political stability of a federal system. To be sure, the partition of Germany already freed the western territories from the legacy of historical regional conflicts. Even relatively disadvantaged regions of the Federal Republic were on the one hand assisted by new conditions in energy and in communications; on the other hand, disadvantaged regions could receive compensation payments when they threatened to become politically explosive.

4   The harnessing of distributional struggles domestically meant that the Federal Republic had to deal with fewer foreign trade conflicts following from a resistance (motivated by domestic politics) to foreign competitors in the German market. The Federal Republic was able to force through the programme of European integration and a worldwide economic liberalisation, without pushing important domestic political groups into a dangerous opposition.

This picture, it is true, would be incomplete without a reference to the fact that a speedy pace of development was not only a characteristic of the Federal Republic's economy, but that a worldwide prosperity without a previous historical parallel set in after the end of the Second World War. As a consequence, competing states involved themselves less in explicit struggles over distribution. Germany's partners accepted the Federal Republic's exports without much complaint. In consequence, the export ratio rose to more than a quarter of GDP by the 1970s. For the first time since accurate historical records were available, a German state had a balance of trade surplus for an extended period (after 1951). After 1950, currency reserves accumulated as never before in German history at the central bank; thus the Bundesbank was not obliged to operate with limited reserves as the Reichsbank had done in the Empire, in the Weimar Republic and in the Third Reich. From the 1950s until the middle of the 1970s there was the opposite problem: how to prevent too great an inflow of gold and foreign currency.

5   However we should not interpret the argument as demonstrating only that rapid economic growth made an unprecedentedly rapid change of structures of production politically acceptable. In economic terms, the causal direction is the opposite one. The rapid change in structures of production was an important prerequisite for growth. A rapid change in the structures of occupation, in sectoral and geographic production and in the structure of capital equipment belong to the attributes of high rates of growth. Where such changes are obstructed, development stops. Therefore it was crucial to growth in the Federal Republic that the social and political system tolerated such structural shifts and occasionally promoted them politically (for instance by keeping borders open to immigrants). In any case, these shifts were not systematically or permanently obstructed. This was the result in part of the fact that a constantly growing national income and state revenues made sums available to compensate for structural disadvantaging – if political conflicts over distribution became acute. It also followed from innovations in political and social variables (organisations, norms, power structure), which are examined in other contributions.[1c]

We should reflect on the fact that since the beginning of the 1970s lower growth rates have corresponded with an increase in distributional conflicts. The distribution of income and wealth has become more disputed. At the same time occupational and production structures are more resistant to adaptation. Once more there are massive problems in financing public expenditures described as unavoidable; once more there is a greater resistance to taxation; and once more increasing indebtedness appears as the way out. Private capital formation does not proceed as vigorously as previously since the beginning of the 1970s. And in addition international struggles over distribution have increased in significance since the first oil shock (1973). In the meantime (1980) the balance of payments causes anxieties previously encountered only in the first two years of the Federal Republic's existence.

6   It is conceivable that a future history will discern a crucial turning-point in the Federal Republic's economic and political history in the 1970s: not just because of the first oil shock.

This raises all the more a question as to what are the salient features of the history of the 'economic miracle' in the overall context of German economic history. Specifically, we need to ask whether the word 'unparalleled', at first used without hesitation, implies that it was a case of a development that departed from previous history, which could not be constructed out of the historical preconditions.

The economic history of the era after 1945 has frequently been described in these terms, even if one should not take references to a 'Stunde Null' in 1945 too literally. But, in general, observers diagnosed a break, and the economic history of 1945/8 was sharply distinguished from that of preceding periods. Only since the seventies has an attempt been made to see the indisputably peculiar development of the Federal Republic in the context of the long-term history of the German economy.[2]

Of course it is easier to make such a demand than it is to realise it, for there are considerable obstacles lying in the way of setting recent history in such a context. It is directly a consequence of the problematic of continuity and discontinuity that economic development in the Federal Republic appears on the one hand as something completely new, but on the other hand as a continuation of developments in the first half of the century. But matters become even more complicated when the possibility is considered that it may be the peculiarities which should be integrated into long-term perspective and that they even appear to demonstrate a continuity of secular trends. These are the issues discussed below. With this, references to continuity or discontinuity are naturally relativised. On no account should one stop at the superficial level of appearances.[3]

II   Reconstruction of secular growth trends?

1   Until now there have been only a few explicit analyses of long-term German economic development which examine the movement from the Empire to the Federal Republic from a standardised vision and specifically pursue the issue of whether the peculiar post-war development can in any way be fitted into a long-term pattern.[4]

The time-series of real national product per capita (see figure 7.1, and also figures 6.1 and 6.3)[5] allows various interpretations, or to put it more precisely, it does not exclude fairly diverse forms of explanation.[6] That there are three different fundamental patterns for explaining the remarkably long period of high average growth rates of GNP after the Second World War has been described above.[7] The first pattern, which may be abbreviated here as the 'hypothesis of a structural break', makes no connection between post-1945 development and preceding changes, except in that previous devastations perhaps left a special mark on the following reconstruction period. This interpretation emphasises the necessities of reconstruction: this was in any case already a classical explanation for temporary periods of faster growth. The very high growth rates of the years after the actual period of reconstruction are explained with reference to the specific constellations of this period alone.[8]

Those authors who wish to interpret the high growth of the period after the Second World War with the aid of a concept of 'long waves' of economic development originally developed by Kondratieff argue differently. There are now more adherents to this theory of the developmental dynamic, which is particularly associated with Joseph Schumpeter,[9] even if it should be said that rather different and even contradictory statements may be found under the common label 'wave hypothesis'.[10] I personally for the present am sceptical of these attempts, because in my opinion there has been no successful proof of the existence of waves in the strict sense in Germany (not all changes of growth rates are waves); and in addition I am not convinced by the existing contributions to the theory of endogenous cyclicality in the case of Germany. In contrast, it seems to be more plausible to emphasise the third model, may be in connection with a hypothesis of a structural break. I now turn to this, without substantiating further the somewhat apodictic verdicts on the wave hypothesis.[11]

2   Following Ferenc Jánossy,[12] we will term the third model that of the 'period of reconstruction'. For a more precise delineation I refer to the literature on the subject.[13] It is not necessary here to present and discuss all the economic and technical details. Assumptions regarding the long-term

Figure 7.1   Real per capita NNP in the territories of the German Empire and the Federal Republic

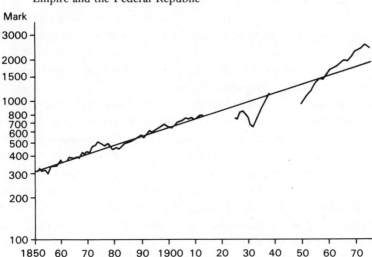

development of potential productivity are at the heart of Jánossy's work. In normal periods, he argues, this presented the limiting factor on the speed of economic growth. But there are also phases, in particular after extensive destruction, or after failures to reinvest or when there is only diminished investment activity, in which the usable resources and productive capital available can turn out to be the limiting factor. In such periods, he argues, there is a prospect of temporarily realising even very high growth rates of GNP in view of the surplus of usable technical qualifications.

Because the theoretical conception as well as the basis for an empirical scrutiny of Jánossy's theses are in many respects problematical, we apply the 'reconstruction hypothesis' in a somewhat freer and more speculative way. We take from Jánossy the notion of a trend curve, derived from a phase of so-called 'normal economic development' and extend it by extrapolation to the following periods.[14] As an experiment, we define the period from 1850 to 1913 as a phase of normal economic development. Thus figure 7.1 shows the trend curve extrapolated beyond 1913, on the assumption that the pre-1914 growth rate could have been maintained in the absence of external interference. Now the critical issue becomes apparent: from 1914, the development of real national product per capita lagged behind the long-term developmental potential for a substantial period of time. The gap between what was realised and what was possible was both in 1932 and in 1950 very substantial – and the growth rate in the subsequent periods are respectively correspondingly high.

This explanation is of course not complete. In the first instance, if any significance is accorded to the trend beyond 1913, it is only a possibility. That possibility did not need to be realised, as the development of the inter-war period showed. In order to explain why developmental potential was utilised differently after the Second World War than after the First would require further explanation. It is possible that such an explanation could be integrated into a long-term historical model. After all, patterns of argumentation which use learning variables already use such notions of historical fundamentals in order to explain decisions: ('Weimar taught us, therefore we have to ...'; 'The Nazi period taught us, therefore we have to ...'). In addition, it has often been correctly pointed out that the democratic society of the Federal Republic owes much to the actual process of modernisation in the National Socialist years. This may also have been crucial for economic development in the post-war period. Nevertheless, for the time being we shall answer the question of why the developmental potential was actually used so impressively after the Second World War when it had not been used after the First World War, by means of period-specific causal complexes. That is to say, we will use the 'hypothesis of the structural break'.

3   The model of the 'period of reconstruction' stands or falls with the hypothesis of a virtual trend describing the potential path. At present, the theory developed to explain this is still fairly primitive, and it leaves many questions open. There certainly exists a series of empirical facts which may substantiate the plausibility of the hypothesis. Among these is the observation of the growth paths of those countries not affected by wars and disturbances in the inter-war period. Where development was smoother overall, there were no economic miracles either.

A certain confirmation of the thesis that technical progress (together with changes in the qualification structure of employees) – a crucial determinant of growth – continued despite the devastation and the reduction in production 1943–7 may be found in the production functions for the period 1925 to 1938 and 1950 to 1957 published by members of the Ifo-Institute for Economic Research (Munich 1963).[15]

This work is in itself a provocation to historians! The authors intended at the beginning of the 1960s to project future growth of the Federal Republic's domestic product. For this they proposed to use an econometric production function, which was to show the effect of the combination of changes of utilised capital, quantity of labour, volume of imports, and technical progress. However, the authors considered an estimate resting solely on the relatively limited time-series available in the Federal Republic to that date too uncertain. The result was that they decided to include statistical information for the German Empire from 1925 to 1938! With that, of course, they needed to assume that both the structure of the equation and the parameters of the production function of the German economy remained completely untouched by the dramatic political and economic changes between 1925 and 1950. This hypothesis seems shocking. But the functions estimated did provide fairly accurate forecasts for a longer period after 1957 and 1961.[16] That need not fully confirm that it is correct to assume a structural constancy between Weimar, the National Socialist period, and the Federal Republic, but it nevertheless does suggest caution in the use of the concept of discontinuity.

The production function used by the authors is of particular interest in the context of the hypothesis of a 'reconstruction period'. I am not going to examine the details: it is enough to mention that the function includes a factor for technical progress, e^{dt}, in which e is a natural logarithmic base, d a parameter value to be estimated econometrically, and t a time index. In various experiments it proved unsatisfactory to continue the time index t, which has started with 1 for 1925 and had risen to 14 in 1938, with 15 in 1950 (although this was the next time point for which data were available). Although 1950 would have been the fifteenth year of the values presented in the series, the time index t was given the value of 26 (i.e. including the missing years). Together with a parameter value for d, this meant a potential technical progress of 23 per cent between 1938 and 1950. If, despite this, national product was lower in 1950, this was the result of capital reductions, and of the reduced quantity of labour and import volumes. In any event, this work also supports the assumption that a virtual progress-trend had existed right through the disturbances; even if the statistical values are not completely persuasive.

Finally one other procedure might support the basic thesis of a progress-ive trend dependent on the development of the structures of qualifications running straight through all disturbances. In 1967, W. Krug attempted to estimate the development of 'human capital' in the German Empire and in the Federal Republic.[16a] The author interprets a graph of a time-series on a semilogarithmic scale (figure 7.2) which 'shows that the course of the curve of human capital is relatively close to being a straight line'.[16b] It is true that Krug did not correct the statistics with regard to territorial changes, so that in reality the values did not lie on a straight line after all. If however the procedure repeatedly used here of converting the respective values for the German Empire and the Federal Republic by reference to the size of population is followed, it is possible to obtain a log linear trend. In 1950, the resources of human capital per head stood at 1378 Marks

(1913 prices) according to these calculations, while it amounted to 1062 Marks in 1938. On the whole, the annual rate of increase corresponded with that of the entire period 1870 to 1959. In a graph using a semilogarithmic scale there is no break in the upward development: there is certainly nothing corresponding with the devastation found in the curve for material capital (see figure 7.2).

Figure 7.2   Real per capita human capital, German Empire in the boundaries of 1871 and 1937 and Federal Republic 1870–1959 (from W. Krug)

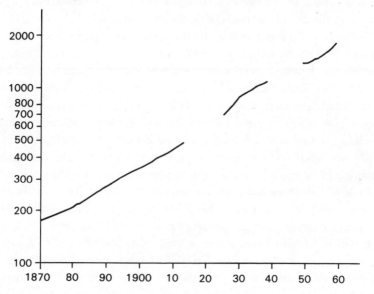

4   Figure 7.3 demonstrates that the production possibilities after 1945 were determined, to begin with, by a shortage of usable resources of productive capital, which could have converted the potential technology (which is also embodied in the non-material capital of the population) into actual technology. The figure also shows the possibility for making up the losses. The graph shows the development of that element of material capital stock most significant for growth, that is the reproducible assets (per capita in order to take into consideration territorial changes) at constant prices from 1850 to 1970.

Methodologically, this depiction is vulnerable; indeed it is rather bold both in respect of the conceptual problems and with regard to the difficulties in measurement.[17] Here it is only intended to provide an aid for orientation.

Again we recognise the inter-war period as being peculiar. The development seen before 1913 is interrupted. Even though the level of the value of

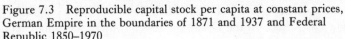

Figure 7.3 Reproducible capital stock per capita at constant prices, German Empire in the boundaries of 1871 and 1937 and Federal Republic 1850–1970

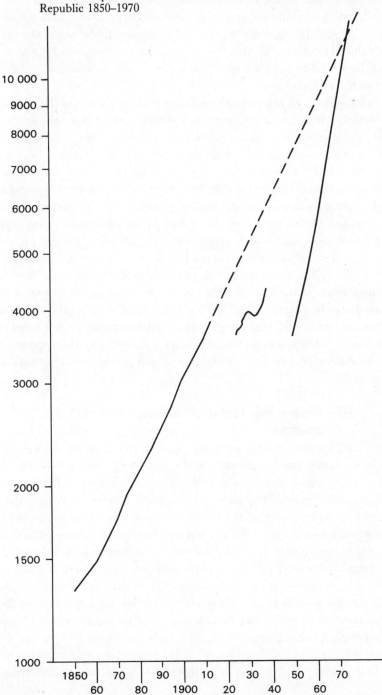

capital stock per capita in 1925 did lie below the 1913 value, there was only a slow correction. In the Great Depression, there was a new reduction of capital, which was followed (naturally) by a short period of rapid increase. But in 1949/50, the capital resources per inhabitant lie far below the pre-war value. However, the loss relative to 1938 is already made good by 1955. Nevertheless the pace of capital accumulation remained also there-after at a very high level.

If we dare to draw in a virtual trend after 1913 for the size of the stock of reproducible investment resources in a similar way to that followed for GNP, the inter-war period, even including the National Socialist recovery, appears as a phase of unutilised development potential. The gap between 'possibility' and 'actuality' is far greater still after the Second World War. This makes it comprehensible that there must have existed big opportuni-ties for investors in the post-war period. Considerably diminished capital risk was one of the typical characteristics of the process of substantial capital formation and high investment rates. In figure 7.3, the curve of the reproducible investment resources reaches the line of the virtual trend once more in the 1970s. This may give us pause for thought, but it may also be a consequence of the chance factor in the estimations, and thus be of reduced significance. Nevertheless, it is a part of the hypothesis of the 'reconstruction period' that the pace of capital accumulation at the end of such a period is supposed to ease off once the growth potential (presented as the difference between virtual trend and actual development) is exhausted.

III   Continuity and discontinuity of structural change

1   In this section we shall examine the question of whether similar processes can be detected in the pattern of structural change as well, which might suggest a 'developmental block' before 1949 and a 'reconstruction period' thereafter. A complete treatment of long-term changes in the structure of the German economy is for understandable reasons not possible here – but nor is it necessary. Our question, which is directed toward continuity and discontinuity in economic development, only requires the use of selected examples of the secular pattern of develop-ment. We propose to show that it is possible to diagnose *Entwicklungs-staus* (developmental block) and thus to generalise the hypothesis of the 'reconstruction period' – but this pattern is by no means universal and cannot explain everything.

2   This emerges immediately from figure 7.4.[18] The statistical relation-

Figure 7.4   Ratio of money (cash in circulation) to NNP in German Empire and Federal Republic within then existing boundaries 1880–1972 (per cent)

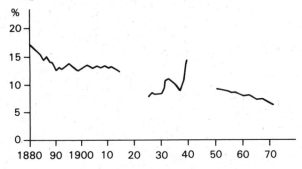

ship over time of the amount of cash in circulation to net national product can be interpreted as a measure of the 'modernity' of modes of payment. All over the world over the course of time more efficient kinds of money (such as deposits in banks) superseded cash, with a result that relatively less cash was used in transactions. Of course it takes time for the habits of large numbers of people to change, and thus the process is fairly protracted. In addition, it is partly determined by political factors, for those responsible for cash creation are in general (leaving aside some relatively unimportant anomalies) the central bank and/or the state.

As far as Germany is concerned, the graph shows a rather surprising development. The values for 1880 to 1913 and 1950 to 1972 even allow a linear trend to be constructed; with the result that 1950 appears to be linked logically through a continuous tendency to the value of 1913. In the inter-war period, completely different conditions prevailed. They were not continued after the Second World War. Rather, as we have already stated, from 1950 to 1970, the pattern of movement from 1880 to 1913 was reproduced, with the fortunate coincidence that in the currency reform of 1948 the connection had been made at the right level.

3   Figure 7.5 shows that there have been rather different patterns of long-term movement even within a single structural complex.[19] The figure represents the division of those in gainful employment according to different social categories (occupational position). From 1882 censuses, unfortunately taken at relatively long intervals, are included; in the post-war period it is possible to use yearly values. In order to make clear the change of pace in the evolution of structural shares, a logarithmic measure was chosen for the vertical axis. (There is a possible objection that the employment structure of the German Reich in 1939 should not be com-

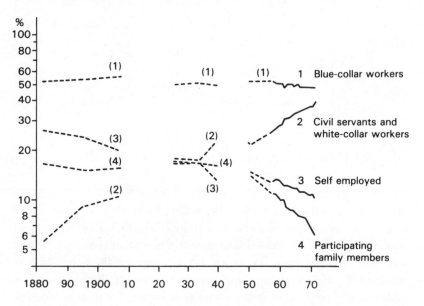

Figure 7.5   Gainfully employed population by social category,
German Empire and Federal Republic within then existing boundaries
1882–1972

pared directly with that of the Federal Republic; it can be dismissed in view
of the great similarity of the relative structures for the territory of the
Federal Republic in 1939 with those of the actual territory of the Reich.)[20]

For the moment, let us disregard once more the inter-war period and
look only at the periods up to the First and after the Second World War.
There is a continuously uniform direction of change (shrinkage or increase
in share) in only two categories: for independents (contraction) and for civil
servants and white-collar workers (expansion). To that extent, an already
classical pattern of change continued in the Federal Republic. It is true
that in 1950 the movement did not (as it did in figure 7.3) join up directly
with that before 1907 (the last census before the First World War). If we
linked the respective values of the curves in 1882 and 1972 with a straight
line (indicating constant rate of change), we would see that the pace of
development was somewhat different, evidently because in 1950 there was
a certain backlog of modernisation in the Federal Republic. Even extra-
polating the movement before the First World War, the share of
independents in 1950 seems somewhat too large (and thus it should be
corrected afterwards by means of faster change), and that of civil servants
and white-collar employees rather too small (and should likewise be corrected by a faster change). The adjustment speeds, which were indeed higher

after 1950, thus also fit into the model of a 'reconstruction period': even though there had been an unmistakable modernisation between 1907 and 1950.

The line for participating family members shows a quite different course. Different census procedures mean that great care is required here, but on the whole the share scarcely seems to have altered significantly until the period after the Second World War. Only then did a change which might be interpreted as a massive break occur. From then on, the share in the labour force fell rapidly at a more or less constant rate.

It is particularly difficult to analyse trends in the inter-war period because economic conditions were so different in the three census years for which data are available. The year 1933 was still one of deep depression. This at the least delayed structural change; possibly it reversed it. It is true that linking the results of the years 1925 and 1939 concerning the share of independents, and of civil servants and white-collar workers, the inter-war period appears as a phase of rapid modernisation. In 1939, the shares of these two groups lie quite distinctly respectively above and below the previously indicated 'secular trend' from the Empire to the Federal Republic. If a developmental block with a backlog of development is diagnosed for 1950, then it had not accumulated over a long period, but was a consequence of the war and its outcome. This is in contrast to the picture previously discussed for capital formation. Only among participating family members had there been a long-term accumulation of a modern-isation backlog.

4   The long-term patterns of the development of the social structures of occupation described above are closely connected causally with the patterns of development in the structure of production in the economy, i.e. the distribution of those occupied or employed among the various sectors of the economy. Since here we are interested not in the precise analysis of structural change for its own sake, but in the question of continuity or discontinuity of patterns of change, we will examine only four sectors of the economy.

In order to make clear rates of change, a logarithmic standard on the vertical axis was chosen. (In addition, for 1939 the difference between employment shares in the German Empire and in the territory of the future Federal Republic was relatively so slight as not to preclude a longer-term comparison.)

In figure 7.6[21] there is no curve which might over the entire period approximate to a straight line representing a secular movement. That is true especially for the periods before the First and after the Second World

Figure 7.6   Gainfully employed population by sector 1882–1972

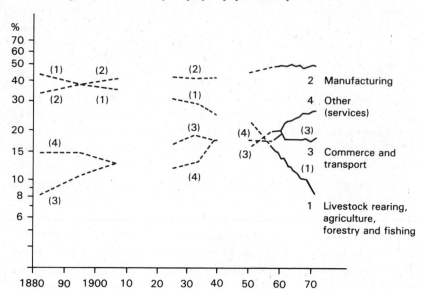

War. In three cases, the directions of movement even go into reverse. And in the one case in which the direction of movement is the same (shrinkage in the shares of agriculture and forestry), a straight line would conceal a feature of great historical interest, the quickening process of decline after the Second World War.

Let us concentrate on the long-term pattern of the declining share of agriculture. It is not a coincidence that it bears some resemblance to the pattern of change in the share of participating family members examined earlier. In this case also, it appears reasonable to speak of a developmental block up to 1950 as a modernisation potential. After the removal of obstacles, the potential could be utilised and produced rapid change. Whether and to what extent political measures, such as agrarian protectionism, or the destruction of international economic relations, or the general slowdown of economic growth in the inter-war period, or specifically German technical/economic conditions of production and marketing, caused the developmental block is hard to determine.[22] If the development of sectoral employment structures in Great Britain is taken as a guideline, where the structural change was not correspondingly influenced by politics, one might expect that the share of agriculture should already have declined appreciably before 1914, but by how much? I should like to offer a rather adventurous hypothesis, which can only be justified in the light of the speculative character of all the observations here.

Let us suppose that from the late nineteenth century to 1970 there had been a hidden potential trend of continuous decline of the agricultural share of employment, i.e. a decline at constant rate. Let us assume that this trend can be characterised by a line which in our graph connects the actual values of 1882 (when the structural effect of protectionism was not yet strongly felt) with those of 1970 (where adjustment had largely been completed). For 1907, instead of an actual share of 35 per cent (9.88 million employed), there would be a 'potential share' of 28 per cent (7.87 million employed). In other words, this would have required, with reference to the levels of 1882 and 1895, an absolute decline in the numbers of those employed in agriculture in imperial Germany. This would have led to quite a different kind of German history!

In fact the Federal Republic inherited a structure of production which provided both a chance and a necessity to adjust to long-term patterns established elsewhere. Without doubt, the rapid structural change of the 1950s and the 1960s, and especially the freeing of labour previously engaged in agriculture, represents one of the most important reasons for the high growth rates of domestic product in this period.[23] In this sense, the accumulated problems built up over previous history may really be counted among the opportunities that the Federal Republic possessed.

5   The picture regarding the continuity or discontinuity of Germany's links with the world economy is complex; particularly as the division of German territory inevitably has considerable effects here.

After the Second World War there was a great and unparalleled process of rapid increases in import and export shares. This may be understood to a substantial degree as a phenomenon of reconstruction: in the inter-war period Germany's links with external economies, represented in 1925/9 by an average export share (exports in relation to net national product at market prices) of 14.9 per cent, was below that of 1910/13 (17.5 per cent). After the 1920s the figure fell still further: to 12 per cent in 1930/4 and 6 per cent in 1935/8. The fall was worldwide. In 1950/4 the export share of the Federal Republic already was above that of the 1930s (13.3 per cent); and in the 1960s it rose to over 20 per cent and in the early 1970s continually lay above 25 per cent.[24]

Thus exports rose considerably more quickly than national product. This appears to demonstrate that the level of integration of the Federal Republic measured in this way exceeded that of the inter-war period, and thus constituted a novelty. But whether the Federal Republic is more closely integrated in the world economy than was the Empire before the First World War cannot be directly determined on the basis of a numerical comparison alone. After all, the territory of the Federal Republic is considerably smaller than that of the German Empire, which means that other things being equal, export shares should rise. Of course, the extent of so-called 'institutional integration' in the European Community exceeds anything previously existing between independent sovereign states. Previously, however, the barriers to integration, which institutional integration was designed to counter, had not existed either. Thus it cannot be excluded from consideration that the rapidly growing involvement of the Federal Republic with a (predominantly western) world economy was nothing new, but rather a reconstruction phenomenon, which gave strong developmental impulses to the economy after 1949.

On the other hand, there are numerous indications that the possibility of structural change in the pattern of Germany's economic relations with other countries should be considered. One of the most obvious signs of a break in the secular trend, rather than of a reconstruction, is in the structure of goods traded by Germany, and especially in imports. In the ten years after 1950, the structure of Germany's imports changed more radically than in the preceding fifty years, and this movement continued until the 1970s. In 1950, foods and raw materials together constituted almost the same share of imports (73.7 per cent) as they had in 1913 (73.1 per cent) and in the entire inter-war period. The structure of imports was typical since the nineteenth century for an industrial country. Among imported goods, finished products played a subordinate role. But that changed quite dramatically after the Second World War. From 1950 to 1970, the share of foods and raw materials in imports fell from 73.7 per cent to 31.7 per cent (for foods alone from 44.1 per cent to 16.7 per cent). By contrast, the share of finished products rose from 12.6 per cent to 52 per cent.[25] This is certainly not a phenomenon which can be explained within the framework of the reconstruction period hypothesis. It was something new in the secular history of the world economy. Since the Second World War, the international division of labour means something wholly different than in imperial Germany: a close involvement of industrialised countries with each other, and an expansion of trade in manufactured goods.

There was one more significant break after the Second World War in the historical pattern of German economic history. Germany ceased to be largely self-sufficient in energy. Previously an exporter of energy, Germany now faced a decline in its hard coal production, which could no longer meet the pressure of international competition, and relied more and more on imported oil. In 1950 only around 5 per cent of the primary energy consumption of the Federal Republic (measured in calorific value) was imported, while in 1975 imports accounted for almost two-thirds.[26] That is a truly revolutionary alteration of the economic constellation: at first it seemed relatively uncontroversial, and its potential for conflict has only now become clear. It appears similar to the controversies over agrarian versus industrial state that were fought before the First World War, when it was a matter of dependence on food imports.

6   It would be possible to cite a considerable amount of further evidence for the hypothesis that there was a developmental break in the long-term course of economic history in Germany in the middle of this century; but the reconstruction phenomenon could also be supported by further material. The observation of E. von Knorring and H. Schmucker that the structure of private consumption (that is, the distribution of expenditure on consumption among various categories) remained relatively stable from the end of the nineteenth century until after the Second World War (above all for the more substantial expenditures, and ignoring business cycle fluctuations) is especially impressive.[27] After 1950, a rapid change then followed, which might be described as unparalleled (table 7.1).[28]

The two traditional items of consumption (food and clothing) which still figured most prominently in 1950 as well as in the inter-war period and involved around 60 per cent of consumers' budgets fell by 1977 to one-third. At the same time expenditure on transport and communications increased, with the largest role being taken by the acquisition and main-tenance of motor vehicles and fuel. The erratic increase in the share of rents may in the first instance be ascribed to the abolition of rent control, and thus represented a political phenomenon associated with the

Table 7.1. *Consumers' expenditure 1950–77 (per cent)*

	1950	1960	1970	1977
Foodstuffs	43,0	38,6	30,6	27,5
Clothing and shoes	15,4	12,5	10,6	9,8
Rent	7,2	7,6	12,5	12,5
Electricity, gas and fuel	3,0	3,9	3,7	4,5
Other household costs (furniture, equipment etc.)	12,1	13,5	12,3	11,8
Transport and communications	5,7	7,8	13,6	15,5
Health and hygiene	3,2	3,6	4,6	4,9
Entertainment and education (including radio, television, books, theatre and cinema)	6,6	7,6	7,3	7,4
Personal spending (including hotels and inclusive tours)	3,8	4,9	4,8	5,9

Source: Sachverständigenrat, *Jahresgutachten 1980/1*.

reconstruction of free markets. The tendency is thus for the share of housing expenditure prevalent before the First World War to be re-established.

After the Second World War, the Federal Republic entered the 'age of mass consumption' of durable goods and services which W. W. Rostow describes as the last stage in his scheme of development.[29] The most important new consumer goods which helped to carry the expansion of consumption after 1950 were already developed in the inter-war period and to some extent even before the First World War. In the United States they already provided an engine for growth in the 1920s. Thus it is possible to speak of latent demand which had grown in Germany in the inter-war period, with the result that the forces of development prevailing after 1945 were not completely new. We do see a break in the statistical time-series of shares in consumption; but again it may be explained not through new circumstances, but by circumstances which had already taken effect elsewhere and needed to wait for such an opportunity in Germany.

7   To conclude this section: in the case of structural change, we frequently encounter the same difficulties in interpreting the character of the secular trend as we encountered when we examined growth in general. Certainly the statistical data offer many pointers indicating that the Federal Republic's development is something special and new. The pace of structural change strikes us particularly in the present case.

But this does not need to be seen as a proof of a fundamentally new pattern of development, since the remarkably rapid structural changes could also be the consequence of a preceding blockage. These blockages of long-standing movements resulted from the political constellation of the war and inter-war periods, and from the generally slower economic development after 1913.

Of course, we also see that in many cases in Germany, there was an erratic catch-up and 'modernisation' in the wake of the Great Depression, so that it seems plausible to locate some of the structural breaks, though by no means all of them, in the Great Depression. This is also the case in long-term analysis of the USA or Great Britain. But alongside those developments which show structural breaks, there are also others which indicate an initially perplexing measure of long-term continuity and development.

The necessarily brief outline presented here certainly cannot provide satisfactory explanations. Often only rather generalised explanations are at present available, which do not give sufficiently concrete answers to the questions thrown up by the course of German history.

IV   Old or new patterns of the economic system?

1   The reader will have noted that Germany's economic development has up to now been described without referring to political or institutional variables. The observed secular tendencies may be connected to the
political system and its changes, but in the first instance they have
appeared as elements of a relatively autonomous economy and especially of
trends before 1914 and after 1950. In economics this is not an unusual
procedure; but in Germany's case it may be inappropriate, since the
economic system is usually seen as having experienced violent changes in
direction over the course of the twentieth century.

Unfortunately, there is as yet no procedure to measure or describe in a
reasonably consistent and condensed form changes in the economic system.
Only a few partial aspects of the more general concept of an economic
system show long-term changes which can be described with relatively
easily measurable variables. Among these, for example, is the share of
public expenditure in GNP as an indicator of the supposedly growing
activity of the state; or statistics showing the concentration of enterprise as
an indicator of economic power and monopolisation. But even the signifi-
ca..ice of these fundamental figures for statements about the economic
system is hotly disputed; and in addition such figures are rarely available
for longer-term analyses. It is therefore necessary to rely on various kinds
of casual observation in order to depict change in an economic system.[30]

2   The received opinion is that, until the middle of the twentieth century,
German economic history was characterised by a tendency towards more
state and bigger private bureaucracies (in interest associations and similar
bodies). The wars and the world depression stimulated this process, while
in the Weimar period there was at least initially a certain dismantling of the
war economy (but never, of course, a reconstruction of the pre-1914
system). Bureaucratisation reached a peak indisputably with the economic
system for total war; but it was very important for the future of the Federal
Republic that the National Socialist regime permitted institutions to
survive with which a non-state economy could operate. Enterprises, and
commodity and factor markets still existed, however much they were subject to control.

3   The basic tendency which had dominated until the advent of total war
did not continue after the Second World War, with the exception of the
first years of occupation. In significant areas, there was actually a retreat.
This was true not only of the dismantling of the actual war economy – that

might have been expected in any event in a demilitarised and democratised state. It also held good for the reconstructions of institutions which had been in part already in place for a long time, but had been destroyed in the inter-war period, of instruments and former goals in state planning in the disposition of goods, ownership, and factors of production. Both the domestic and the external economic systems were affected. To a large extent it was a question of returning to earlier patterns of market economies.

If one attempts to give a more precise indication of a period in which a system similar to that of the Federal Republic after 1950 might have prevailed, we find an insuperable difficulty in transposing the model of a secular trend to the history of the German economy. In the first place, the economic system of the Federal Republic did not in reality remain unaltered for any considerable period of time. The process of liberalisation itself took several years, even decades, and coincided with a process of extending or reconstructing mechanisms of state intervention. Secondly, the reversion of the trend, or the reconstruction of earlier organisational forms, took place in such a complex way that it cannot easily be determined whether the old or the new was predominant. We can give three examples:

(a)   When in 1958 the DM became fully convertible at fixed rates of exchange, this was a recreation of the situation before 1914 or between 1924 and 1931. But the DM was now a paper currency, like the Mark and RM between 1914 and 1923 and after 1933. But there is some evidence to suggest that the currency system after 1948 or 1958 was generically new, despite significant characteristics, including the institutionalised cooperation of central banks, which appeared to be a reconstruction of an older pattern.

(b)   After the Second World War, wage formation was once more left to a free labour market with negotiations and agreements between organised parties. There was no longer compulsory state arbitration – that is, the organisation of the labour market which had held sway from 1923 to 1933 was not resumed. Thus both the patterns previously existing (one from the National Socialist dictatorship, and one from the Weimar period) were rejected; fundamentally there was a return to a system which had existed only for a very short time after the First World War. There was also a completely new structure of the trade union movement, and a rather different relationship between parties in the labour market. Thus there was a mixture of reversion to the old (reconstruction) and of the new.

(c)   In the organisation of housing, completely different historical layers may be detected after 1949. In part, the housing market was liberalised and to that extent a condition which had not existed since the

First World War was brought back. On the other hand, there had never before been such a degree of state direction of house construction and utilisation, and the instruments were of a new kind. This is particularly true of the massive changes in the civil law autonomy of rent contracts. Legislation established as a norm the social limitation of private property. How then can we characterise the new order: as a resurrection of the free market (reconstruction), or as a far-reaching change in the character of the legal relationships prevailing in such markets (new development)?

4 Whatever the concept of the market economy and of dismantling state intervention that prevailed after 1948, and whatever results the model of the market may have produced, it is after all true that the state plays a significantly greater role in the economy after the Second World War than it did in the Weimar period. This is true both with regard to withdrawals from the national product (public consumption and investment) and with regard to transfer payments. But why was there until the 1970s nothing to parallel the bitter complaints from industry or the massive conflicts over the high fiscal burden on private activity that had gripped the Weimar Republic?

It is possible to give many answers to this question. But it seems to me to be important to refer to historical patterns formed in the consciousness of the participants. In the Federal Republic, in the 1950s and 1960s, there was a reduction of state influence, not only by comparison with the war, but also with the preceding period before 1939, which was still characterised as peacetime. In the Weimar Republic, however, things were altogether different. The enormously increased role of the state represented an extraordinary provocation, because it offended a firmly held notion of normal conditions in the pre-war era.[31] It would have taken an astonishing degree of adaptability to deal with such discrepancy between notions of normality on the one hand and the reality on the other hand without massive conflict. Such adaptability would certainly have been facilitated by rapid economic development, but in Weimar this failed to be realised.

5 This view still remains biassed in the sort of traditional discussion of the tasks of the state which occurred in the Empire and in the 1920s. However, the economic role of the state has been shaped subsequently by what is at least qualitatively a wholly new kind of task. To this end, new instruments and new institutions were also developed. Since the Second World War, so-called macro-economic management has been among the most important tasks of the state. The instrument developed for this purpose, and used intensively in many states, was the fiscal management of

demand – amounting to a state guarantee of aggregate demand in the economy, and the guarantee of full employment.

The caesura here is of course not to be located at the end of the Second World War, but in the Great Depression. At that time, the notion that the private sector could direct itself broke down. The economic and political risks apparent in this crisis led to a revaluation of political and economic values in all capitalist states. Full employment became the dominant goal of economic policy simply because, for a long time, it was believed that Keynes' theory and the instruments developed on the basis of it supplied the appropriate means of direction.

It remains debatable whether it was really this policy after the Second World War which gave to the western world comparatively uninterrupted growth at high levels. Many economists believe that they can assume this. Others argue against this view and believe that politicians and their advisers ascribe to themselves a merit which they do not deserve. In fact in the Federal Republic, with the exception of 1950, demand management with explicit reference to employment came relatively late. In 1967 the Law on Stability and Growth, which indeed contains a description of the goals of state financial policy hitherto not expressed in legal form, was passed. The goals listed in Paragraph 1, however, had already in practice been accepted long before.

The increasing difficulties in fulfilling the goals set and the expectations awakened may perhaps indicate that in the 1950s and 1960s particularly advantageous circumstances were more responsible for the high growth rates than was macro-economic management. We can speak of a break with traditional developments within the norms for economic policy, although it is not easy to distinguish between rhetoric and real change in norms. After 1980 continuous high rates of unemployment were accepted in relative silence. But this structural break, if it is one, presumably cannot explain the described phenomenon of high post-war growth rates. In that case the hypothesis of a period of reconstruction discussed earlier would remain valid; and we would not need an hypothesis of a structural break, associated with a developmental break in basic ideas concerning economic policy.

V   Concluding remarks

The present paper is intended to be an essay on methodology. Particular solutions are not suggested here. Inevitably, however, the time approaches at which German twentieth-century history will no longer be describable preeminently in terms of a series of periods dramatically distinguished one from the other, in which 1945 marks a practically total caesura. Even the most radical political, military and economic turning-point changes only a relatively small part of those resources previously accumulated within a society. Previously accumulated assets always continue to influence the new era, and history continues to take effect. Existing resources on the one hand facilitate the overcoming of an interruption in the flow; but on the other hand through their existence they also limit the mobility of historical processes.

However correct such general observations may be, the goal behind this essay was to show how complex the 'resources' which served as the historical foundation for following development in the case of the Federal Republic actually are. Previous patterns of development were (or may have been) of considerable influence on the sometimes quite different developmental patterns of the Federal Republic.

8 GERMANY'S EXPERIENCE OF INFLATION

In Germany after the Second World War, examining the problem of creeping inflation, or the continual rise in price levels, awakened memories of the terrible past of the years 1914 to 1923 and 1934 to 1948. Often it was stated that no nation had inflationary experiences as bad as those of Germany; and in consequence no other country was so sensitive to threats to the value of money, or ran economic policy in accordance with these fears.

Of course, with the passage of time, this memory became less and less a highly personal one. For instance, as early as 1972, when the rate of inflation in the Federal Republic began to increase, only those over 65 still had adult memories of the inflation after the First World War – and they formed less than 13 per cent of the population. Almost half of those living in the Federal territory in 1972 had in 1948, the year of the currency reform, not yet reached eighteen years of age, and thus had no personal impression of the suppressed inflation of the National Socialist and immediate post-war periods. By 1980, the proportion of those who had themselves experienced inflations had already fallen to less than a third.

But politics is of course determined by older people and their experiences. Younger people too are included in the stream of historical tradition and in the permanent social indoctrination, the result of which we may call inflation-consciousness.

It is still therefore widely known in Germany that in this century two great inflationary processes occurred, and that in connection with them on the one hand millions of people lost their savings and on the other immense new fortunes could be made.[1] Some historians draw a direct connection between the rise of the National Socialists and the triumph of Hitler in the year 1933, and the inflation of 1923: according to them, the inflation had proletarianised broad sections of the middle classes and rendered them politically unreliable. Other historians recognise at least an indirect connection between the inflation of 1923 and the catastrophic end of the Weimar Republic: according to them, a fear of inflation derived from very recent experiences restrained the government, a few years later in the world depression, from pursuing the only correct policy for combating unemployment: that is a devaluation of the Mark and the financing of additional state expenditure with paper credit. Heinrich Brüning, the Reich Chancellor responsible for the deflationary policies in 1930–2, did in fact see his room for manoeuvre as defined in this way. As he explained to the British Prime Minister, Ramsay MacDonald, in June 1931: 'One must either go along with deflation or devalue the currency. For us [the German government, K.B.] only the first could be considered, since, six years after experiencing unparalleled inflation, new inflation, even in careful doses, is not possible. The Mark would immediately sink to bottomless depths.'[2] Today we know that the assumptions underlying such a supposition are debatable. To be sure, it is an illusion to assume that in Germany, under the conditions prevailing in the years 1929 to 1933, mass unemployment could have been altogether avoided. The depression affected the whole world. Even the USA had over twelve million unemployed at its trough. But the extent of the German crisis might presumably still have been limited. The people who were then in power, and those advising them, made a counter-cyclical policy impossible for themselves by describing any such measure under the shocking name of 'inflation'. In this way experiences, or even the conjuring up of shadows from the past, may cloud people's vision in the present. It is all the more important, since inflation and its consequences are talked about again today, to know the history of this phenomenon in Germany.

Oddly enough, the originally American word 'inflation', which has since been on everyone's lips, was known scarcely to anyone in Germany before the First World War. It did not occur even in academic work. None of the great textbooks and none of the encyclopaedias of economics even contained it in their subject index. But not only the term was absent. When the first inflationary process of the century was already under way, that is to say during the course of the First World War, understanding of the occurrence was largely lacking. Germany was not an exception here. In almost all of the belligerent states, the governments failed to restrict private demand to the same extent that they raised their claims to national income: the result was that demand was greater than the supply of goods available at current prices.

Superficially it was just a problem of financing. The state needed money for the payment of soldiers and for weapons and other war materials. In Germany this money was, to put it in a simplified way, advanced by the

Reichsbank after the alteration of its statutes. From time to time the enormous additional purchasing power, which had thus come into circulation, was then taken from the public once more by means of war loans. Almost a hundred thousand million Marks accumulated in this way; this was the extent to which creditors temporarily refrained from the satisfaction of their consumption and investment wishes, and gave precedence to the state in consuming GNP. But this voluntary renunciation of consumption sufficed less and less over the course of the war, once the initial enthusiasm had evaporated.

Theoretically it would have been possible to reduce consumption by taxing citizens. But though such a course succeeded, at least in part in several belligerent states, it was less possible in Germany. On the one hand, the government did not wish to impose this 'sacrifice' on its subjects, especially as it hoped to make the defeated opponents pay the war debts. On the other hand, with an outdated taxation system the government simply could not effect a vigorous increase in tax rates in order to finance expenditure on the war effort. Financially, the German Reich created by Bismarck was hopelessly backward. Because loans no longer provided enough money, and because taxation as a definitive means of reducing consumption was not implemented, the consolidation of short-term bank credits could not be accomplished, with the result that additional purchasing power entered circulation. That was the beginning of the inflation.

Inflation is nothing more than the creation of *additional* purchasing power, permitting certain consumers to satisfy themselves without others voluntarily renouncing their share of GNP. But because – or to put it more accurately, the extent to which – GNP does not grow, not everyone can get on to the bandwagon. *Who* gets on and *who* is forced to stand back is, in the case of so-called 'open inflation', the result of the process of price increases. Those with only a fixed nominal budget for purchases must stand back. With increased goods prices, in real terms they can afford less. That is the real 'meaning' of all inflation. The cause of inflation lies in a redistributive process, desired by the state or by social groups, under conditions of varying access to monetary means.

Until the end of the war in 1918, in the wake of inflation, currency depreciation in the German Empire measured by the wholesale price index already amounted to around 50 per cent. The exchange rate of the mark against the former gold value had fallen by around 30 per cent. Then the end of the war not only failed to bring any change for the better, it immediately made an inflation-free financing of the national budget more difficult. Whereas, a few years earlier, it had still been possible to obtain contributions of thousands of millions for war loans in the giddiness of a hoped-for victory, the defeat, which was not accepted by many sections of the population, rapidly dried up such a source of finance. In addition, there was an enormous backlog of demand from a population that had suffered deprivation during the war, and which could scarcely be induced to voluntary saving without very high interest rates. But such rates could scarcely have been expected from the Socialists in power, since their position was insecure, and the national budget was already burdened to the extent of almost 60 per cent with payments for debt service. The demobilisation of the armed forces, the transition of the economy from war to peace production, the payment of bereavement and invalidity pensions, not to mention the reparation payments threatened – the size of which as yet was completely unknown – all required further enormous sums from the national and local budgets.

There was still no more or less adequate taxation system. The constitution of the new state, which might supply a basis for such a system, was not passed until August 1919. Tax laws corresponding to the new constitutional principles were passed within a year, a considerable achievement when one compares it with the fate of the far less comprehensive tax reforms of today. But for the time being there were no efficient central state taxes, and so there remained no alternative but to finance state expenditure in much the same way as the wartime governments had done: through recourse to the bank of issue's power to create money.

Whatever critical comments wise economists later made regarding this period, and however much they castigated the incomprehension of monetary theory displayed by these governments, we should admit that no theory could be useful which did not also take into account political conditions. Just as in the years 1789 to 1796 in France the inflationary assignat economy first made the bourgeois revolutionary governments possible at all, so also was it only the inflationary financing of deficits in public budgets which made in the years after 1918 the beginning of the Weimar experiment possible. In the wild political turbulence, with revolutionary threats from the left and threats of *putsches* from the right, a policy of balancing the budget threatened the existence of the state. Not even the victorious powers trusted themselves to stabilise their finances immediately after the war. As the League of Nations study once stated, inflation is the kind of taxation which even the weakest governments can implement, when they no longer have any other political means of enforcement. We should add that this is the case when a 'taxation' of this sort hits the politically weakest groups, those least capable of offering resistance to the withdrawal of their purchasing power. The Weimar state rested on a coalition of employers and trade unions, which had in the immediate aftermath of the war agreed on a kind of truce, in order to prevent a radical revolution. These groups retained their political influence, with the consequence that they could hardly be drastically burdened. On the contrary, wages were now heavily increased, and at the same time unemployment, which posed the main threat to the stability of the state, needed to be avoided. For the first time in German history, full employment became the declared primary goal of politics. As things lay, in income terms it was above all the employers who profited from this; so also did the workers, although to a lesser extent.

I do not by any means wish to link my claim that inflation in the years 1918 to 1920 was politically necessary to a comprehensive condonement of inflation. I only wish to make it understandable how a process which was later repeatedly described to us as plain madness came into being, and into what a tragic ensnarement those responsible for policy fell. It was one of the paradoxes of the Weimar Republic that even the Social Democratic government could follow no other economic policy than one which gave immense advantages to capitalists who had previously been described as class enemies. The success of the government depended on the economic ignorance of the masses and on the fact that so many had no means of resisting the expropriation of their property.

For the time being, it was necessary to reduce unemployment and increase production. That happened in a surprising way. Germany did indeed have extremely low unemployment, between 1 per cent and 4 per cent, in comparison with other European countries in the post-war period. Britain, France and the USA were noticeably worse off. Whatever the justice of distribution, a climate of continuous excess demand and easy financing of investment from growing entrepreneurial profits and from inflationary credit contributed to the rapid formation of real capital in the form of new plant as well as reconstruction of old plant. Within a few years the loss of the merchant navy, for instance, which had been decreed by the Treaty of Versailles, had largely been made good. It is true that it was repeatedly objected that some of the investments made in the period of booming inflation were not particularly pressing in a longer-term view. In addition, the productivity of the almost fully employed labour force was certainly unsatisfactory. But as long as they continued the positive effects of the inflation on the economy as a whole should not be overlooked, although in the interval they have all but totally vanished from our collective memories.

For a moment, in the years 1920 and 1921, it looked as if the inflationary cycle could be stopped: prices remained stable for a while, and real wages increased measurably. But it was not possible to set state finances straight without the danger of a domestic political radicalisation; and the victorious powers did not wish to cooperate in the stabilisation. The London Ultimatum of May 1921 with its horrendous reparation demands necessarily led the ruling constellation to new inflationary measures. The turmoil rapidly became worse. While the value of the Mark had, by mid-1921, sunk to around 7 per cent of its value of 1913, it had declined to 1 per cent by mid-1922 and by the beginning of 1923 to less than 0.0004 per cent. Mortgage bonds worth 10,000 Marks in pre-war currency were now worth only four gold Marks.

In the interim, many people began to understand what was happening. Index clauses began to appear in contracts. The public only held money for a few hours, and tried to obtain goods as soon as possible. Wages had to be paid at ever shorter intervals, and eventually wage agreements took future price rises into account. The more inflation progressed, the less was the success in balancing public budgets, because every tax, even ones which were apparently confiscatory, was by the time it was actually paid only worth a fraction in real terms of the original value.

The end of this witches' sabbath did not come immediately. Stabilisation only succeeded after the money economy reached the verge of total collapse in 1923, and *no one* could any longer gain advantage from the situation: not the government or the employers, and not the organised and employed workers. In November 1923, the Mark was worth only $\frac{1}{10}^{12}$ of the old gold Mark. But the real expropriation of monetary assets lay further back, and had nothing to do with the occupation of the Ruhr in 1923, which had merely further accelerated the inflationary cycle. It is surely insignificant whether one retains a thousandth of one's assets, or only a millionth millionth.

There is no doubt that in some respects the inflation must be seen as a revolutionary change in social structure. It is not true, as one reads occasionally, that the whole of the middle class was ruined. Large sections of the middle class, as debtors and producers of goods, derived advantages: this was the case for agriculture and for sections of manufacturing industry. But the so-called 'Rentier capitalists' were badly hit, and all provision for the future in the shape of savings was affected. Of course it was not just a matter of total depreciation. In several revaluation decrees, old claims of mortgagees, owners of mortgage bonds, and investors in savings accounts were revalued with sums between 25 per cent and 12.5 per cent. The state creditors came off worst, with revaluation of between 2 per cent and 8 per cent. But here it was possible to refer to the fact that it was largely assets formed only during the war that were expropriated; and that in addition, the removal of this debt in later years in theory would correspond to a lower tax rate, since state debt which had been written off no longer needed to be serviced. No government, even a monarchy if it had remained in Germany, could have avoided the radical reduction of the immense state debt after the lost war, and in the absence of reparations from Germany's enemies.

We can see in conclusion that the inflation of 1914 to 1923 was not an accident in the works of a capitalist economy. On the contrary, it was primarily a political phenomenon. It resulted from the conditions in which the war was fought and from the military collapse; and it represented one of the possible techniques for liquidating the republic's political inheritance. That it brought with it indescribable suffering for many people is the view still prevalent today. But, as an historian, one is obliged to consider in addition what other possibilities were available. Recently economists have once more argued about their assessment of these events; and there are authors who even hold the view that the process observed can still be called mild compared with all other thinkable realistic alternatives. They hold that the majority of the population, at least until 1922, was better off as a consequence of that policy than it would have been from any other. It is part of the tragedy of the Weimar Republic that its critics have always measured it against different, but always ideal, conditions, often with Utopian characteristics.

We now move forward in time and come to the second great inflation of our recent past, the inflation of the Hitler-State. Its external course was quite different from the Weimar inflation. For the government had learnt from the past and possessed quite different tools of power. But fundamentally the problem was similar: what was at issue was the securing by the state of substantially larger portions of GNP than citizens were willing voluntarily to accord it in a market order, or than should have been forced through by means of open, and unpopular, taxation.

The inflation began in 1933 in the first instance with extended measures of work creation. These showed that the Brüning government's fears regarding the inflationary consequence of such expenditure were apparently groundless. As yet prices hardly rose. It is true that it took considerable isolation from the world market by means of foreign exchange control in order not to expose the isolated German reflation to a balance of payments danger. The government used various tricks to disguise from the public the extent of the fast-growing budget deficits. This became all the more important when the goal of rearmament came to the fore after 1935, at a time when many still believed in the peaceful intentions of their Führer. From 1936 to 1938 the economic boom was, however, already a side product of a quite different set of goals on the part of the state, which took ever larger slices from an increasing social product in order to prepare for a war of aggression. Over the six years of peace between 1933 and 1939, the state debt already rose threefold, financed partly by inflation, and partly through long-term credits.

When it proved that competing claims on the real national product despite all precautions exceeded the available volume of goods, a general wage and price freeze was enacted in 1936. With that, the path to open inflation was barred. The following period until 1948 is termed that of 'suppressed inflation', because an enormous potential demand swelled up, but the price regulator was put out of action. The allocation of produce took its place, and here the state authorities were able to award themselves the highest priority, without having to pay higher prices in the process. At the same time, the state attempted to reduce the pressure of demand it had itself created through printing money, by means of indirect and direct borrowing rather than through taxation. A large fortune in debt claims, which lacked any real backing, once again accumulated in the hands of investors.

Looked at solely from the financial point of view, the system for increasing the state's share which had been created as a provisional measure stood the test of war. Immense military achievements were financed without apparent strain. In the first instance, a part of state spending was financed with the assistance of the Reichsbank. A rigorous control of the capital market meant that the increased liquidity of industry and credit institutions was drained off again through new Reich issues of loans. Of course, the reduction in liquidity did not succeed entirely, and growing sums remained in the hands of the public. But there were no opportunities to purchase. In view of the threat of draconian punishments, before the end of the war there was no substantial black market parallel to the official market.

It is not important to describe the individual characteristics of this process of inflation here. In any event it is clear that in concrete terms a substantial redistribution of national income resulted. Its consequences were once more concealed through the build-up of an enormous stock of debt claims, which gave the illusion of wealth. At the end of the war, the total Reich debt amounted to a sum of four hundred thousand million RM. That was almost five times greater than the entire national income for 1938. Since the greater part of government securities was not held by the public at all, but by the banking system, and the public held its assets in the form of savings accounts and other liquid assets, at the end of the war the grotesque sum of approximately three hundred million RM in liquidity (cash, savings deposits, and deposits in banks) was held by Germans.

If the controls and the price freeze had been abandoned now, an immense flood of purchasing power would have resulted. The suppressed inflation would have become an open one. However, for the time being, the victorious allied powers adhered to controls. But, because punishments for circumventing regulations were now applied more mildly, a black market, with which every citizen somehow came into contact, could now develop. On this market, a cigarette cost between 3 and 5 RM and butter 150 to 300 RM a pound. More and more however, goods were bartered, because often it was impossible to obtain the bare necessities for money at all. Many people had money to excess. Once more, as after 1918, there was no problem of unemployment. In view of the monetary surplus, it was not difficult to pay people, however little they were actually capable of doing. But in contrast to the period after 1918, public budgets were now also balanced, so that no new inflationary pressure could emanate from that quarter. Tax receipts in comparison to national income at this time were astronomical. Yet, to a substantial extent, they were not paid out of incomes at all, but rather out of liquid assets and out of the so-called 'money overhang'. That such an economy was corrupt and desolate is too well known to require further elaboration.

It was three years before the Second World War was financially liquidated through a currency reform. Once more, this question was associated with major political problems: this time the division of Germany among other things. It was the allied military governments who took over the responsibility for the currency reform. It was they who determined the method by which the money overhang might be removed. They enacted a forced reduction of monetary assets, an expropriation of the greater part of the debt claims (for the moment without compensation), and the simultaneous issue of new currency, the Deutsche Mark (DM). The expropriation was massive and controversial to its extent and with regard to its attendant social costs. But from an economic viewpoint it was successful. Since at more or less the same time the work of reconstruction also showed its first visible successes, and an eventual equalisation of burdens was envisaged (it is true that this offered only very limited help to those harmed by inflation), the expropriation was far less politically explosive on this occasion than that which had take place after 1918. Politically also, the population was in a different frame of mind: it perceived a much more direct need, for instance on the part of refugees and expellees; and this time people realised that the war had been brought on by Germany. Thus Germans were more prepared to assume the consequences. In addition, in 1948 it could not yet clearly be seen to what extent the owners of material assets had once more done better than those with money.

The outcome of the National Socialist inflation and its liquidation through the currency reform also favoured debtors and harmed creditors. For the mass of the population it reduced nominal prosperity and levelled wealth; but at the same time it favoured the owners of real assets.

As yet there are no remotely adequate figures enabling us to determine with precision the development of wealth and the distribution of wealth in Germany over the past decades. But there are several indicators to the process of private impoverishment linked to inflationary processes. Whereas, according to one set of tax statistics, there were 221 out of every 10,000 inhabitants declaring wealth of over 26,400 Marks before the First World War, in 1928 only 74 of every 10,000 declared the equivalent wealth in purchasing power terms (40,000 RM or over). In 1953 after the Second World War, the equivalent figure had fallen to 19 (for a comparable wealth in constant purchasing power of 32,400 DM). Private wealth according to tax statistics had thus been reduced in relative terms to one tenth of the amount of 1913.[3]

Of course, this cannot be explained by inflation alone. And even if inflation itself is held responsible for the process (in the case of monetary and debt claim assets), it is not valid to conclude that inflation itself was the cause of the expropriation. Lost wars did lead and would have led to a loss of income and wealth in any case. The inflationary processes were the particular forms taken by politically motivated redistributive processes. If people approved and supported the political goals preceding inflations, that is, for example, rearmament, war or full employment – such were the German goals – then wanting to avoid the consequences amounted to schizophrenia. Had those harmed by inflation not been the victims, then *other* individuals, or the same individuals, would have had to make sacrifices in another way, for example by paying higher taxes. The liquidation of wars could not occur without losses. After 1945 this was widely recognised. After 1923, it was less accepted, in the first place because the inflation of 1920 to 1923 overstepped the 'necessary mark' for regulating post-war problems and all too obviously also became the instrument of private inflationary interests. In addition, it was connected with the question of reparations. After all, the sole blame for inflation was laid at the door of the reparations demands of the victors.

Can anything of relevance to the present be learnt from these historical events? I think they can. An example might be this conclusion: that inflations are not primarily economic problems with secondary social problems, but are instead primarily struggles over distribution with monetary conditions and consequences. In consequence, abstract models of monetary theory provide little help in explaining them.[4] In particular, we can learn much regarding the mechanics of such processes as hyperinflation or suppressed inflation. For instance, it can be seen that a suppressed inflation with a wage and prices freeze may only be manipulated if the political pressure of the government grows, and if it has sufficient instruments at its disposal to prevent participants in the social process from using their collective purchasing power – that is to say, if the controlled economy is extended ever further, with the exercise eventually of political terror. But it would certainly be misleading fully to equate the processes today termed 'inflationary' with historical events dealt with here simply because they bear the same name.

9 CONSTRAINTS AND ROOM FOR MANOEUVRE IN THE GREAT DEPRESSION OF THE EARLY THIRTIES: TOWARDS A REVISION OF THE RECEIVED HISTORICAL PICTURE

I

The great depression of the early thirties is one of the most important turning points in the history of the twentieth century. It has to date been a unique phenomenon in the history of economic crises as regards its length, its depth and its spread to practically all the countries forming part of the world economy.[1] In many states it led to sharp political crises in whose wake there followed shifts in the structure of party politics, and radical changes of course in domestic and foreign policy as well as formal or informal constitutional changes.

With the depression begins a new epoch in the history of capitalist or market economies. From this point so-called *Globalsteuerung* (macro economic policy) became the duty of the state. In particular, the goal of a high level of employment, not to say full employment, received practically the status of a constitutional requirement. This is one of the most important consequences of the great depression – throughout the whole world. But for the Germans, the consequences went even further. In their country there was something additional that allowed the economic crisis to become an event of exceptional historical significance: the collapse of the Weimar Republic and the rise to power of National Socialism. Among the answers to the question, 'How was this possible? How was Hitler possible?', it is usual to refer to the great depression.[2]

In this regard, it is easy to see that the question has often been posed as to whether the crisis could have been avoided if only politicians had had more insight or more competence. Already during the crisis, several contemporaries thought that this could have been the case.[3] The affirmative answer became more common as, later in the 1930s, people were able to observe the evident success of an expansionist economic policy.[4] After the Second World War this became the general view.[5] At that time, in the fifties and sixties, as is well-known, relatively major economic crises did not occur. Did this not prove that it was possible to steer the cyclical development close to an ideal path? And if it was possible to do so now – why could one not have also done so earlier? Why not, indeed, as early as the great depression? Against the background of considerable optimism regarding the possibility of controlling the business cycle in the present and also in the future, what we can call a 'retrospective optimism' about the solubility of the problems of the past became widespread.

In the meantime, it is true, our world has once more altered. Since at the latest 1973/4 we no longer hold the firm conviction that the business cycle can be controlled relatively arbitrarily and easily.[6] This gives history a new perspective when examining in a manner at once less self-assured and less critical those who held positions of responsibility during the world depression.[7] After all, it is not the case that one can only learn lessons from the past for the present – one also learns lessons from the present for the past. The mutual interaction here indicated gives our subject, the world depression, both its topicality and its fascination.

The aim of what follows will be to examine why, in the Great Crisis of the early thirties, no expansionary policy was pursued until the summer of 1932, when the Papen government for the first time announced (rather than actually implemented)[8] a relatively large programme of stimulating the economy through fiscal policy.[9] In pursuing this investigation, I shall first examine the question of *when* such an anticyclical policy could and should have been implemented. Next, it must be asked whether *appropriate means* were available. This is a complex question. We must therefore divide it into: (1) the question of the technical availability of such means; (2) the question of the political availability of the means – that is, of the domestic and foreign political circumstances which shaped the room for manoeuvre for an active counter-cyclical policy; and (3) the question of the effects which may have been expected to follow from the application of such economic policy instruments.

All in all, we are concerned with the fundamental question as to whether a lack of insight and competence on the part of those in government must really bear the explanatory load for such a terrible event, or whether there are not, after all, causes – which we have to impute to the world of objective circumstance – which were not under the control of those in government at the time.[10]

II

I shall start with the question as to the point in time at which a completely new economic strategy might, at the earliest, realistically have

been expected. It is remarkable that this question has not hitherto sufficiently been taken into account in the historical literature which is sharply
critical of the policy of that time. If we attune ourselves to the state of
knowledge of contemporaries during the crisis – rather than to our own
which is of course much more complete since we already know the consequences[11] – then we must first observe that, for the German policy-
makers, and indeed for all others throughout the world, until early 1931
there was no compelling motive to handle the crisis in any other way than
the path actually taken. The situation did not look so severe from the
outset as to make one fear the worst. And even fearing the worst – who
could then know that things would get so bad, or that, for instance, in 1932
the annual average unemployment of workers would be 30 per cent?

All previous depressions had taken a different course. The one under
discussion had not even begun particularly dramatically, judged by the
standards of preceding crises. In the first 'world depression' after the First
World War,[12] i.e. in the crisis of the years 1920/1 which had badly shaken
Western Europe, the United States and Japan, and from which Germany
was only spared because until 1923 an inflation raged – in this crisis the
countries affected plummeted into the abyss far more sharply than in
1929/30.[13] But the fall lasted just one year. And on the basis of the purged
situation a new upturn resulted. In Germany too there had already been a
profound setback in the economic cycle once before during the Weimar
Republic, in 1925/6, when the production of capital goods and consumer
goods both collapsed within a short space of each other by nearly one-third
over eight months.[14] But here too a recovery rapidly set in, and the steep
decline was followed by all the more vigorous growth.

Thus it was not possible for contemporaries to learn from these or other
previous experiences that lesson which has become theoretically virtually a
platitude subsequently: that is, that a vicious downward circle gains
momentum and must be therefore combated from a very early stage.[15]
Naturally, as the crisis developed,[16] from 1929 to 1930 and from 1930 to
1931, it was disturbing that the tendencies towards recovery, familiar from
earlier crises, and which also periodically manifested themselves even in
this downturn, were unable to sustain themselves with any real vigour. In
fact, something ran more and more counter to that model which had been
developed by observers on the basis of earlier experiences.[17]

It is true that this resulted from a whole series of circumstances, which
nobody could have foreseen at the time because they bore the character of
historical accidents.[18] In Germany, there were above all the sudden disturbances coming from politics, which erupted on to the economic sphere:
there were especially the repeated threats to the stability of the Brüning

government.[19] When, for example, on 14 September 1930, the NSDAP was able to raise the number of its seats from 12 to 107, the sensational success of a party, which had fanatically promised domestic and foreign political confrontation, had a shock-effect on the economy. And this exogenous shock pushed the German crisis on to an altogether new course.[20] A great deal of credit was called in, new credit was not given, a large amount of money left the Reich as capital flight because people were no longer sure what course a future German government might follow. The Reichsbank, in order to protect its meagre currency reserves, had to raise interest rates dramatically – and that in the middle of a depression in which interest rates otherwise normally fall. Not until four years later did the interest rate for short-term credit in Germany return to the level prevailing before the September elections in 1930.[21]

But even after September 1930, there was, in the general downward movement of the cycle, another worldwide phase in which it was possible to hope that the crisis might take a gentler course – that was from January to the beginning of April 1931.[22] Several important indicators of the course of the business cycle again point upward at that time. We can show a situation that forecasters and politicians observed in figure 9.1, which illustrates the production of consumer goods subject to so-called elastic demand, i.e. textiles, clothing, shoes, household goods and furniture.[23] In the dashed curve seasonal influences in production have been eliminated. We can take this opportunity to cast another glance at the sharp downturn of 1925/6 and compare it with the process of decline after 1929. In addition, we may observe that for this indicator the peak before the crisis was not 1929 but 1927. But we should, above all, discern that, in the spring of 1931, the downward movement was interrupted by a quite vigorous upturn, which was interpreted even by contemporaries as a sign of a fundamental alteration of direction in the cycle.[24]

We still do not know exactly what caused the end of the short-term upswing in mid-April in Germany as well as in other countries, and what produced the renewed downward movement. In any event, highly unusual occurrences led to a dramatic and critical turn. In Austria, the largest bank became insolvent in May. In Germany, several big enterprises went bankrupt or were on the verge of doing so. Caused partly by the governmental crisis of the beginning of June, in which the Brüning government only barely survived an attempt to overthrow it, a run on the banks began. It was associated with considerable withdrawals of gold from the Reichsbank. In July the banks closed their doors and the Reich suspended the obligation to convert the Reichsmark into gold or foreign currency.[25] A short while later, in September, after heavy outflows of gold, the Bank of

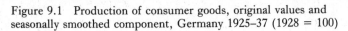

Figure 9.1   Production of consumer goods, original values and
seasonally smoothed component, Germany 1925–37 (1928 = 100)

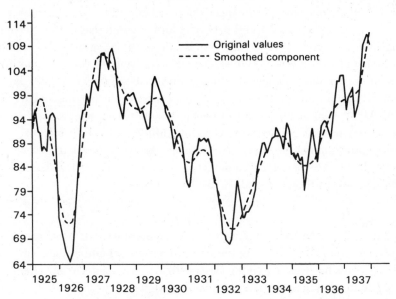

England became practically internationally insolvent and Britain freed the
pound's exchange rate from the gold standard. The international currency
system had collapsed.[26]

With the national and international financial crisis of the summer of
1931, a new phase of the world economic crisis set in.[27] Now, in the
summer of 1931, it proved that what happened was a structural crisis of the
national and international economic order. Only now did people widely
begin to feel that the crisis would not lead automatically to a new upswing.
And only now, in the spring or summer of 1931, did plans to deal with the
crisis through an active policy gradually emerge from the most diverse
corners of the political spectrum. In contrast to the emergency measures
practised both at that time and earlier, these new policy proposals showed
entirely new characteristics.[28] Thus, the proposal was now made that the
state ought to create greater demand, even if it did not have adequate
current income at its disposal, and in that case to finance the additional
demand through further indebtedness.[29]

But with this, the answer is also at hand with regard to our first question, that is, the question as to the 'when' of the application of new
instruments for fighting the crisis. If we do not expect governments to
have prophetic talents, and in particular a knowledge which only subsequent generations can possibly have; if, rather, we expect of them at

best the realisation of the most advanced knowledge currently available, then, before the summer of 1931, a fundamental change in economic policy could not have been expected.

If *this* is accepted, then it is necessary also to admit that prompt actions against the slump were already impossible on time grounds. For in the summer of 1931 it was objectively too late to prevent the rise of unemployment to 6 million people for that winter, the winter of 1931/2. Even massive policy measures never affect the course of the business cycle *that* quickly.[30] At most, the trough of the depression, which was reached in the summer of 1932,[31] could have been shifted forward by some months, and the upturn might have set in somewhat sooner and somewhat more vigorously. Whether *that* would have been possible is of course dependent on what measures could and should have been applied.

III

With that, we come to the second question: what means could have been applied? When, in the second half of 1931 and in the course of 1932, plans for overcoming the crisis with active measures really emerged in public, they usually had one major weakness. They required instruments which were not at all available and which could not be created simply through national legislation. That is true above all for plans for financing increased state expenditure through the Reichsbank. For due to the earlier experience of inflation, the Reichsbank had in 1922 and 1924 been substantially removed from the purview of government influence. Above and beyond that, it was prohibited by law from giving the state any substantial amount of credit.[32] It might be asked why, in this situation, the Reichsbank Law was not simply changed. First, for reasons we have yet to go into, people did not want to do that. Secondly, they would not have been able to accomplish this without major complications because, since the regulation of reparations in the settlement of 1924, the Reichsbank Law had become part of the system of international contracts, finally negotiated in the Young Plan of 1929 and ceremoniously ratified in 1930. In addition, the exchange rate of the Reichsmark was subject to the same constraints.[33]

Governments which did not wish to pursue an adventurist course in foreign policy were still not in a position simply to disregard these international constraints – certainly in 1931 and probably also in 1932.[33a] And negotiations on these matters might touch off waves of speculation which would damage Germany. It is not surprising that it was above all those authors who strove for a fundamental realignment of German politics who at the time showed themselves to be decidedly in favour of experimentation in respect of Reichsbank credit or the exchange rate.[34] But it was precisely this circumstance – that economic policy was intended to be a Trojan horse for many other purposes, or even simply that it might possibly serve as one – which naturally alarmed the political centre and foreigners.

German policy was caught up in many additional dilemmas. This already became clear when, in May 1931, a first plan was published recommending state expenses financed through credit as a way of increasing employment – the so-called Brauns Memorandum.[35] Of course, the authors were adamant in rejecting the idea that the state might turn to the domestic capital market. Here it would have had to have driven interest rates up to yet more fantastic heights and thus crowded out private investors altogether. The Brauns committee also rejected any central bank credit: that is to say that they took notice of the political constraints. In these circumstances, only a single possibility for action remained, which the committee then really suggested: the taking up of foreign credit.[36] But the recommendation to overcome the financial worries of the government by resorting to the foreign capital market came out just at the moment at which the Reich government found itself in sharp conflict with France and her former allies on a number of fronts. At issue at the time were the plans for a German–Austrian customs union which had been published shortly before, as well as rearmament questions and the announcement of renewed revisionist desires regarding reparations and the German eastern frontier in the Corridor and in Upper Silesia.[37] Brüning may have always thought about revising the Versailles Treaty[38] – but at this time, his foreign policy offensive was designed to accommodate the opposition on the right which had become manifestly dangerous in the wake of the September 1930 election. He had to demonstrate that the government had not lost sight of Germany's national interest. But whatever his domestic political motives were, it is no wonder that France, whose currency reserves were still enormous, did not, in the light of such a domestic German situation, wish to appear as the disinterested monetary rescuer of a German government: her security interests had already been too persistently violated by Germany, but also by France's former allies.[39]

There is much to be said for the view formulated in July 1931 by Otto von Zwiedineck-Südenhorst that the central problem affecting the German labour market lay in the European foreign policy. Numerous advisers agreed with Zwiedineck that it was precisely for economic reasons that it was necessary to do anything – absolutely anything – to maintain international confidence in Germany.[40] But was the 'foreign policy capitulation', which had become so pressing in the summer of 1931, really still politically thinkable? The very consideration of asking for French credit in order to remedy the acute and highly dangerous currency crisis of July 1931, credit which France understandably wanted to link with political conditions,[41] induced the leaders of the so-called 'National Opposition' to protest publicly. They declared that, if they were in power, they would not fulfil such conditions.[42] And Reich President von Hindenburg threatened to resign in the event that the government accepted such credit.[43] That would surely have meant the end of the Weimar Republic in the summer of 1931 – so narrow was the German government's room for manoeuvre in respect of an internationally coordinated rescue action in the middle of the 1931 financial crisis.[44] Thereafter, foreign credit remained just a distant hope and no longer a reality. An expansionary policy of public expenditure to fill the demand-gap could now have been financed only through domestic money creation by the Reichsbank.

But it was not only the legal contractual reasons mentioned earlier that stood in the way of domestic credit creation through the Reichsbank – a credit creation which represented the only possibility of financing a budget deficit. At the time, Brüning and his advisors, partly publicly but also partly confidentially, cited two major political reasons. The first was understandably not discussed publicly and so it did not appear until the publication of source material and memoirs: it concerned Brüning's intention to remove reparations permanently by demonstrating Germany's insolvency.[45] In the light of such a goal it was impossible to finance any public programme which foreign governments could not have afforded either.

The second reason, which dominated the public discussion of this subject, concerned the fear that a public spending policy financed with new money would once more lead to inflation. The means of such policy were already well known. From 1918 to 1923 it had been implemented for the purpose of work creation, and great successes had been achieved: by international standards, Germany had one of the lowest unemployment rates after the First World War.[46] But at that time inflation had however got completely out of control, and the experiment ended in a disaster from which Germany had not yet, even in the crisis, fully recovered. The experience did not tempt people to embark on similar adventures.[47]

In the economic and historical literature on the depression, the inflation argument is usually held to be of considerable psychological importance because of Germany's special experiences; but at the same time it is thought to be wrong since it is well known that, in situations when there are high rates of unemployment, additional purchasing power is not likely to have an inflationary effect.[48] Today we would not hold such a view so unconditionally – and, in the circumstances then prevailing in Germany, a genuinely inflationary development does not seem to have been so very improbable in the event that effective actions had been undertaken in the policy sphere.[49]

But quite apart from how economists now evaluate the arguments of that time, a fact remains of the utmost importance for the historian: Brüning could not, until the spring of 1932, have obtained the slightest political support from any politically relevant group for a policy that increased state expenditure financed by the Reichsbank. Whatever objections may be advanced by economic theorists against the actual economic policy followed by Brüning – it was a policy which was not in principle put into question by an alternative strategy either by one of the parties close to the government or tolerating it, or by any employers' organisation[50] or the trade unions.[51] Social forces which otherwise were profoundly antagonistic towards one another still shared this one of all convictions.[52] In particular the leadership of the SPD, on whose toleration the Brüning cabinet was crucially dependent in the aftermath of the September elections, was – like the Labour Party in Britain for that matter[53] – opposed to any currency experiment and constantly conjured up the danger of inflation, which they believed necessarily would follow from additional state spending.[54]

In situations such as the one we observe here, the crucial point is not the intellectual achievements, thoughts, plans, or insights of outsiders. An alternative would have had to be proposed by a political force. Up to mid-1932, there was no such force. Under these circumstances, whoever expects Brüning to have pursued a different economic policy (for which there was, in addition, no model in any other country in 1931/2 either)[55] is ascribing to him a power over the objective conditions which he surely did not possess.[56]

Because of foreign and domestic political influences, the room for action in economic policy was, at least during Brüning's period in government – that is, up to May 1932 – far narrower than is realised by a later criticism concentrating exclusively on economic theory.[57]

IV

But with that we have not yet reached the end. Because even if one is prepared to accept that at that time there was no wide choice of policy options available, some questions remain. One may perhaps already have developed an understanding for or even a sympathy with the people who were then in positions of responsibility. But setting aside the certainly serious political complications, were there not nevertheless objective possibilities for intervening at that time? Even if there may be much to be said against the creation of money in order to finance budget deficits, would such a creation not have been helpful? And even if there was a good deal of objection to a devaluation of the Reichsmark – would such a step not nevertheless have brought success?[58]

If, in the first instance, we examine those few pieces of advice published until mid-1932 and illustrated with numerical data, produced mainly by outsiders, we arrive at the view that none of the plans of this period could significantly have affected the course of the economy.[59] For even plans described by contemporaries as adventurously inflationary were far too small in scale. In 1932, the deficit in demand ran to over 30 thousand million RM. However, the most extreme from among the more precisely worked-out plans for increasing public expenditure in 1932 still only provided for an expenditure of around two thousand million RM. At the time, that appeared to be an immense amount which, after all, corresponded to about one-third of the 1931 Reich budget and could – as has already been pointed out – have been financed only after a major alteration of the then valid Reichsbank Law. But two thousand million RM comprised only approximately 2.3 per cent of the Gross National Product of 1929, that is, only 2.3 per cent of the total goods and services available in the year in which the crisis is usually held to have begun.[60] Can we really expect that the economy would have changed direction in consequence of such a relatively small sum? In 1975, the net public sector borrowing requirement in the Federal Republic amounted to 5.2 per cent of GNP:[61] and even such a sum did not appreciably lower the rate of unemployment. What, then, can justify the optimistic view that in 1931/2 relatively small sums would have achieved a much greater effect? No, there existed no wonder weapons of economic policy against Hitler in any political arsenal at that time.[62]

V

Do we, at least *today*, have a valid solution to the problems of that time? No one has yet presented anything other than merely negative criticism of the policy of budget balancing and of administrative lowering of cost that was actually practised then.[63] I have no solution either. But I hope to be able to give reasons why, at that time, there could have been no solution at all, in today's sense of a solution to an economic problem. The truth is that the issues at that time were far, far more difficult.

In order to understand this, we must now go into the pre-history of the crisis. For it is not just the case that the slump was something terrible that had no parallel before or after in our history. The *preceding* economic development, between the inflation and the great depression, is also without parallel in German economic history.[64] In order to see the Weimar Republic in a proper perspective, an overview of the growth of the German economy since 1850 is presented in figure 9.2. It shows the development of the annual Net National Product per capita in Germany (in the respective borders of the time).[65] The curve begins in 1850 and it continues until the gap, occasioned by the war, between 1914 and 1924. It then continues from 1925 until 1938, when there is another gap, which cannot be filled, from 1939 to 1949. For the Federal Republic, figures have been used from 1950 until 1975. The scale used on the vertical axis to measure the annual flow of goods and services is a peculiar one: it is logarithmic. Its purpose is to show immediately the rate of growth in the respective periods. When the gradient of the curve is steep, we see high growth rates; when the curve is flatter, the growth rates are slower.

From 1850 to 1913, we observe by and large a stable growth with several cyclical deviations around a linear trend. The extended straight line shows how the flow of goods would have developed after 1913 had the per capita growth rates of the national product remained the same as in the preceding decades. At first glance, the relatively sustained, and on average very high, growth rates in the Federal Republic are impressive. The Weimar Republic is entirely peculiar. We notice the severity of the slump from 1929 to 1932, but it is also clear that no enduring or vigorous growth preceded it. From 1925 to 1926, there is a decline, followed by a jump from 1926 to 1927 – but then a marked levelling off and rapidly a decline. Only in 1928, ten years after the war, did national product per capita exceed the 1913 level, and then only by a little.

Figure 9.2   Real per capita NNP in the territories of the German Empire and the Federal Republic

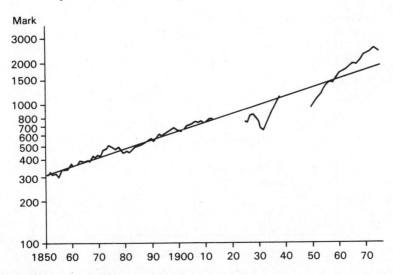

No, there was no strong upturn before the crisis.[66] Between 1925 and 1929 investment activity, i.e. the supply of new means of production, factories, machines, houses and means of transport actually remained far below the sums regularly devoted to these ends before 1914.[67] On the other hand, private per capita consumption in 1928 did stand 16 per cent above that of the pre-war period, and public current expenditure (per capita) actually stood at 34 per cent higher.[68] These figures show a fundamental weakness of the Weimar situation, for which we will provide further evidence. Weimar did not have those characteristic features of a strongly growing economy, but rather those of an economy caught up in severe struggles over distribution of income. We will substantiate this analysis with reference to the following figures.

Figure 9.3 illustrates the long-term development of productivity in the German economy.[69] By productivity or, more precisely, labour pro-

Figure 9.3   Productivity of labour (NNP at market prices of 1913 per employed person), Germany and Federal Republic within then existing boundaries 1880–1975

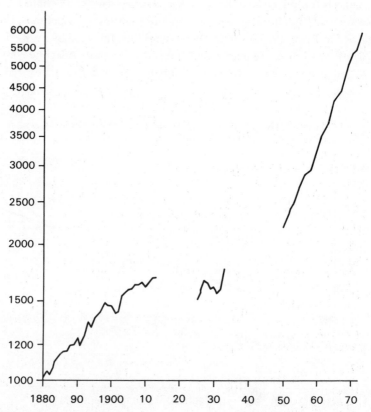

ductivity, we understand the average quantity of goods and services per member of the labour force, per annum. Whereas productivity increased relatively rapidly in imperial Germany, and rose breathtakingly after the Second World War, in the twenties it did not even reach the pre-war level! So weak were the forces of growth at this time.

What is especially interesting in this connection is the circumstance that, from 1925 to 1929, the rise of average wage earnings apparently occurred regardless of the development of productivity just illustrated. Shortly after 1924, average real hourly earnings exceeded clearly those which had pertained before 1914, and average weekly earnings – as an average of all employees – rose strongly as well.[70] In an international comparison of the development of earnings from the pre-war period to 1930/1, Germany comes off surprisingly well by comparison with the victor-states of the First World War – with the United States, France or Great Britain.[71]

How substantially the development of earnings exceeded the limits set by the development of productivity, and thus directly affected income distribution, is shown in figure 9.4.[72] The curve of the so-called 'cumulated position of real wages' is a somewhat complicated construction: but it is enough to understand that the curve runs parallel to the zero axis as long as average real wages change approximately in the same proportion as changes in productivity. From 1950 to 1970, this was the case in the Federal Republic. It is noteworthy that a rise after 1970 coincides strikingly with the decline in investment rates since that time. But the upward

Figure 9.4 Cumulated real wage position of employed, Germany and Federal Republic within then existing boundaries 1925–77

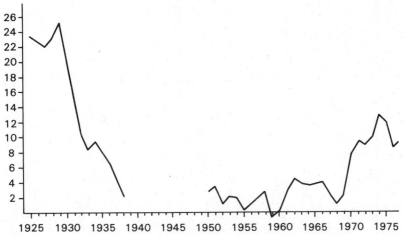

deviation after 1970 was still not nearly as great as that which may be calculated for the years 1925 to 1929, that is for the years prior to the great depression.

What does so great a distance between the position of real wages and the zero axis mean? Put simply: in the Weimar Republic, labour was on average so expensive that incomes from entrepreneurial activity and property were relatively reduced. In view of the international development of prices, in a system of fixed exchange rates, in which the central bank had to pursue a restrictive policy in order to protect its currency reserves, higher costs of labour could not completely be passed on to the consumer through higher prices.[73] In conjunction with the rise of other costs, the result was a squeeze of those kinds of income from which normally investments were financed.[74]

Today, economists point to the fact that wages which considerably exceed the boundaries given by the rise in productivity are likely to increase unemployment. We frequently incur criticisms as a result: that the science of economics, a science which often calls the undoable by its correct name, has had to put up with such criticism from the start. But the Weimar period can teach us that matters were such as theoreticians now describe: for after 1925 unemployment was already higher than ever before in Germany – not only after 1929. That is illustrated by figure 9.5.[75] On the

Figure 9.5   Unemployed as percentage of employees

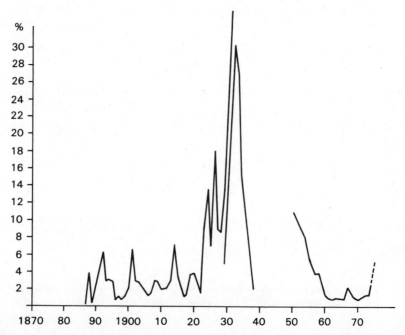

vertical axis are unemployment rates since 1887. In order once more to make long-term comparisons, the chart continues into the very recent past. In respect of unemployment the Weimar Republic deviates from the historical norm as well. And this is not just the case in the depression when unemployment rates rose to an officially recorded figure of 30 per cent. Since the end of the inflation there had already been hitherto unparalleled rates of unemployment. Even in the best year in the business cycle (1927), the unemployment rate did not fall below a level higher than that of the worst years before 1914.

In summarising the results of these charts, we should state that:

(1) The graphs show the economy from 1925 to 1929 as abnormal, even as a 'sick' economy.[76]
(2) It is hard to imagine how such a process could have continued in that fashion for much longer.
(3) After 1929, once the crisis had openly broken out, it could not just be a matter of returning to a previous state of affairs.
(4) Thus the task would now have to be to combine a 'cleansing' associated with normal business cycle depressions with a structural purge.

A truly gigantic programme!

VI

But why had matters been permitted to come to such a pass and why had they not already been tackled decisively before 1929, or even cured – and the later crisis thus reduced in extent?[77] There is no purely economic explanation for this. Politics must once more come into play.

From the end of the First World War the new Weimar state, unstable both internally and externally, depended on buying the agreement of elites and voting masses in order to stabilise itself. It obtained their assent with the tools of economic and social policy; far more than any previous German state had done, it became a state of subvention and redistribution. Without doubt, wonderful things happened – but equally without doubt, these wonderful things also imposed a considerable burden on the country's economy. The state, for whatever political reasons, lived beyond its economic means.

Wage determination also was, from the outset, in large measure politically determined. This already began at the end of the First World War when employers, together with trade union leaders, founded the so-called 'Central Working Community' (Zentralarbeitsgemeinschaft). This was one, if not the most, important prop of the parliamentarisation of the republic in a defensive war against ongoing revolutionary demands.[78] At the time, the employers complied with old trade union demands almost completely. They offered among other things, an eight-hour day, and wage settlement by negotiating parties on the basis of mutual recognition.[79] Wages rose by leaps and bounds. It is a slight exaggeration, but not fundamentally wrong, to say that at this time a revolutionary movement was transformed into a movement of wages. And in fact, at the beginning of the Weimar Republic, there is a kind of 'concerted action' towards the overcoming of a problem which was perceived as pressing by virtually all members of the various elites; in order to prevent anarchy, they supported the foundation of parliamentary democracy.

In the wake of the inflation, which became increasingly rapid, what part of these gains could really be genuine or long-term remained an open question. But by the end of 1923 at the latest, when stabilisation of the currency came and the sham blessing of constantly financeable demand – whatever the cost – stopped suddenly, hard economic facts made their appearance. In particular, the relation of costs to prices was highly unfavourable. The employers now tried to correct the consequences of the wage, social and financial policy of the preceding phase: for example, they tried to raise the hours of work while maintaining constant nominal wages, or at least they tried to dampen the upward movement of wages while holding the hours of work constant.[80] But this involved more than just economics. The employers' endeavour to reverse many of those concessions they themselves had offered in the face of the revolution must now have looked to their employees, and above all to the leaders of the trade unions, like a betrayal of the political fundamentals of Weimar.

So the consensus of employers and trade unions which had once carried the state broke down rapidly, and the conflict grew ever more severe. Factually, the turn of events after this was such that the parties to negotiations arrived increasingly rarely at agreements by themselves, and that the state's provision for compulsory arbitration drove wage rates to ever greater heights, for the state authorities were perfectly conscious of the political dimensions of the question. When necessary, they replaced the compromise of the early Weimar period with what the employers increasingly called a 'wage dictatorship'.[81] Our charts have shown that to a certain extent the employers were right in terms of economic rationality.[82] But with affairs such as they were, it was not a question of individual skill or insight to solve economic seminar problems that were at stake, but fundamentally political questions. What was at issue was the material constitution of Weimar.

Who could have solved the problems of the abnormal, 'sick' economy in time? The weak state, which had already been unable to find a majority consensus over much smaller problems and which itself unflinchingly cooperated in attempting to preserve domestic political peace, but constantly through its short-term solutions multiplied the long-term burdens on the economy?[83] The parties to the wage agreements, which had grown more and more hostile to one another? – for instance, was there to be a renewed 'concerted action'?[84] Where was the great common goal to be found, at a time in which nobody spoke of growth politics (which even today scarcely inspire big political compromises)?

Let us avoid the ahistorical accusation that the historical actors should have been united in the face of the threat of Hitler. That was not a goal that could be universally recognised and to which everything else could have been subordinated. Nor was it as politically unifying as had been the goal of the prevention of revolution at the beginning of the Weimar Republic. No, constraints had developed which were so terrible that even today we still cannot present any real solutions. For even if one were able to agree now that it would, at that time, have been correct in the light of the economic situation to downplay the urgency of struggles over distribution in favour of an economic and social policy more strongly oriented towards criteria of efficiency and growth, then one would still not hold in one's hand the key to the historical secret. Would renunciation by labour in the struggle over distribution – for instance a wage freeze after 1925, or even the reduction of wages in favour of higher entrepreneurial profits – not have broken the trade unions and thus have prepared the way for truly radical forces?[85] Only on a very high level of abstraction, in a blackboard exercise far removed from political reality, could one sketch certain solutions: however, the conclusion would still be unavoidable that these solutions would not have worked. No one had – and has – an answer.

If we look more closely at these truly fateful entanglements we may perhaps better understand that a substantial number of those holding positions of responsibility did not diagnose the outbreak of the great depression as a catastrophe, but even saw it as an opportunity for purgation in an otherwise unsolvable situation.[86] For now the facts seemed to allow a legitimacy for the revision of the economic, financial and social policies of the state: this was the *Stimmrecht der Sachen* (vote of objective reality).[87] The parties to wage agreements also might, so some people hoped, now obtain a legitimacy in order to revise wages policy and avoid yet higher unemployment. Many people had such hopes. They believed that a new constellation of economic facts would result from the crisis they had lived through, and this new constellation might not only reduce unemployment below, say the 8.4 per cent annual average for 1928, but also guarantee enduring growth. Such a correction did indeed occur during the depression. But the man who inherited the correction so heroically implemented by Brüning and by the forces around him, was called . . . Adolf Hitler.[88]

VII

I tried bit by bit and cumulatively, to demonstrate those constraints which ensured that no policy of the sort later demanded of them was actually pursued by those in positions of responsibility in Germany at the time. In addition, I attempted to show that those proposals for a new economic policy discussed at the time very probably could not have helped in any case. That an expansionary economic policy actually did assist the subsequent upturn after 1932 is explicable in part because a readjustment, and especially a massive lowering of costs, actually did occur during the depression. Previously, there had been no such solution to Germany's economic problem. For in Germany the real problem of the Great Depression was its pre-history, and the subsequent economic constraints that followed from that pre-history. The pre-history reveals an economic system that was not capable of functioning in the long-term. It was embedded in a political system scarcely capable of functioning either. This was the worst of all conceivable combinations. We can only study this tragedy, and we should abstain from engaging in over-presumptuous criticism.

10 ECONOMIC CAUSES OF THE COLLAPSE OF THE WEIMAR REPUBLIC

I Introductory remarks

1   After an overview by Hagen Schulze on the state of research concerning 'The Collapse of the Weimar Republic', eleven speakers at a symposium of the Fritz Thyssen Stiftung examined various causes of the collapse.[1] The structure of this common task is given by the following formula:

$$CR = f(X)$$

The 'collapse of the Republic' (CR) is explained by causes denoted by the symbol X. In the first instance this symbol represents a complex of still unknown causes. Its elements need to be elaborated. How and whether these elements actually caused CR follows from theoretical connections (f), which equally need to be considered.

What role can an economic historian play in this effort? He is not a particular expert on the phenomenon described here as the 'collapse of the Republic' and which, as such, requires more precise definition. In addition, the economic historian has no particular competence to investigate the whole complex of problems comprehended in X. And he finds it hard to make statements about f, the functional connection of all the elements of X in relation to CR. Without investigating f, even the impact of single causal elements cannot be fully assessed. In order to deal with the problem of imputation, as we call the determination of the explanatory impact of the single elements, a generalist is evidently required who should furnish a total explanation. The specialist can only advance and discuss facts which he believes might be relevant in particular explanatory contexts. Whether the facts referred to are really functional or causal in the sense described here can only emerge from the as yet unavailable precise description of the collapse, and from the theories which are used to explain the collapse.

2   Yet every contributor to the collective undertaking must tentatively arrive at some decision in order to be able to speak at all about specific causes of the collapse of the Weimar Republic. He has to establish in the first place what is meant by the notion of 'collapse'. I agree with Hagen Schulze in *not* identifying the collapse of the Weimar Republic with Hitler's rise to power. Without going into further detail, I claim that there might have been other kinds of regime following a parliamentary democracy which had already collapsed well before 30 January 1933. If, however, we accept that 30 January 1933 is not the date of the collapse, we need to give another and earlier point in time. I understand the decision of Andreas Hillgruber and others to date the collapse of the Weimar Republic to the winter of 1929/30.[2]

3   Such a conclusion, which cannot be arrived at by economic historians alone, has considerable consequences for the selection of the economic causes which require discussion. If the collapse of the Republic is dated as early as the winter of 1929/30, the role of the great depression in explaining the collapse of the Weimar experiment no longer requires attention. The depression would then only have played a part in selecting which of the various possible regimes followed something that had already collapsed.[3]

4   Hagen Schulze put together three statements which relate to the contribution of economic circumstances in explaining the collapse of the Republic. They concern:

(1) an argument regarding the economic system. It is claimed that the absence of a redistribution of economic power, say through the socialisation of banks, big business or big agricultural units, was crucial;

(2) the role of the inflation and the great depression, especially with regard to the economic situation of relevant social groups and the legitimacy of the rule of those groups whose support was crucial to the Republic;

(3) the influence of economic interest groups on political decisions, an influence which may have destroyed the Republic.

In all three cases Schulze finds good grounds at least to doubt that these contributions amount to an explanation: in each case he refers to imprecisions and vagueness or even to insufficient evidence. I substantially subscribe to his criticism – though this does not preclude differences of detail in our argumentation.

But we should point to a danger of such critical objections. If we wish to explain a complex historical phenomenon and for this purpose put a multiplicity of influential factors to isolated tests, it is likely that we will be able to identify no one factor as crucial. Economic historians know that from the long-standing discussion of the causes of industrialisation. Whenever a comparatively important group of causal factors was described, strong evidence was also presented that challenged the influence of those factors. In the end perhaps we were surprised that the event had occurred at all. In considering the collapse of the Weimar Republic, we therefore should ask whether the problem did not lie in the accumulation of causal factors, each of which may not on its own have been decisive, but which when put together proved disruptive. The critical point would be then the *accumulation* of causes.[4] Individual causes in Germany which can be isolated frequently correspond to developments in other countries, where there was no collapse of the democratic order. Such explanations can therefore never be held to be exclusively responsible for the collapse of Weimar – but they could form part of an explanation.

5 Thus economic questions may have played a greater role than merely augmenting what Hagen Schulze termed 'the primary stress factors'. Political thought in Weimar, and the behaviour of the parties, may be understood as representing more important destabilising factors, but it still needs to be asked whether such dysfunctional ideologies might not have proved themselves more malleable under better economic circumstances; or whether the parties might more readily have been able to accept the compromises necessary for the preservation of the system. In other circumstances it might have been possible that no compromises of the sort repeatedly demanded of the Weimar parties might have been needed at all. Perhaps these parties were not especially 'frightened of responsibility' if the responsibility had been for normal business in a normal environment: but they were overstrained through gigantic responsibilities even before 1930.

In his contribution, Ernst Friesenhahn points to the fact that the Federal Republic has not so far had to endure the 'crucial test', 'that is, how government and parliament would, by constitutional means, deal with a situation of economic stagnation in which the Federal Republic might have something like the 6 million unemployed of Weimar'.[5] He has thematised the central role of the economic situation for the functioning of the constitutional apparatus; and he has indicated that the 'economic miracle' might be counted among the most important constitutive elements in the Federal Republic of Germany. Correspondingly, we ought to seek to identify in Weimar powerful factors of economic stress which endangered the system, and even caused it to collapse. For Friesenhahn the test came in the great depression; but if we accept the argument advanced above, the depression only delivered to Hitler a republic which had already collapsed.

This is the range of problems which is the subject of the subsequent analysis. It is certainly not the only way of discussing the end of Weimar, but it is a particularly important one. Its importance emerges in the historiographical tradition. The role of the economic crisis, as well as that of the inflation, in the destabilisation of the Weimar political system has frequently been discussed; and these factual complexes are part of the repertoire in explaining Weimar's collapse. Yet the middle years, which are considered to have passed in relative normality, and are usually described as the 'golden twenties', have largely been ignored. In fact, however, the collapse of the Republic in 1929/30 emerges precisely from the accumulation of economic problems, for which the political system no longer had any possible solutions.

II A general framework for an economic explanation

1   For the question 'How and why can politics be ruined by the economy – when and under what preconditions do economic developments lead to irreversible processes of political destabilisation?', there are as yet no well developed theoretical models.[6] Therefore the attempt at developing an explanatory pattern for the specific case of the Weimar Republic is bound up with considerable risks. I take these risks for the sake of stimulating discussion.

2   I proceed from the following thesis: rapid economic growth can blunt or even completely suppress political conflicts, especially conflicts over distribution. That is to say, in rapidly growing economies over a long time all politically important groups can be better off in absolute terms – even those which over that long term are relatively worse off in respect of distribution of wealth.[7] In a slowly growing or in a stagnating or perhaps a shrinking economy, however, an improvement for some necessarily always implies an absolute worsening for others. And in general this gives rise to more resistance, which has to be broken and, to the extent that it has broken, causes disappointment.

3   If, in such phases of slower economic growth, those disadvantaged economically either absolutely or relatively fear that they may, or do actually suffer, a loss of political position, a sharpening of conflicts over

the distribution of political power is likely. The political conflicts become the vehicle for losers who aspire to compensate for the economic losses via political means.

4   The conflicts over distribution addressed under 2 above might still mean comparatively little to the state and thus to the cause of political stability if they were acted out in a social sub-system of a (private) market economy, with only weak links with the sphere of the state. That would be the case if the conflicts over distribution developed exclusively in goods and factors markets and also found their solutions in them. The largely anonymous market mechanisms do, it is true, also permit economic conflicts to arise; but at the same time they determine the outcome of such conflicts, without responsibilities being directly apportionable to specific groups or individuals. One becomes either a victim or a beneficiary of the anonymous market. As a rule, this decentralises conflicts.

On the other hand, all economic conflicts mediated via the state tend to work themselves out quite openly; they are even, in the framework of a democratic constitution, dramatised according to the requirements of the system.[8] It is possible directly to distinguish opponents and allies in the struggle over distribution, and to ascribe to them success or failure. If this imputation to rival groups is not successful, there always remains the possibility of ascribing losses (or the absence of gains) to the incompetence or viciousness of the very machinery for resolving conflicts. In this case it becomes tempting to renounce loyalty, or to bring new rules into the political game.

5   That many conflicts (and thus necessarily many failures to achieve expectations) are bundled in the same institution – as opposed to the decentralisation prevailing in a market economy – is particularly dangerous in this connection. When the bundling becomes altogether too massive, there arise Gordian Knots which are no longer soluble. In consequence, under some circumstances, the situation may result in which even problems which are held by all parties to be urgent can no longer find a political solution, because rival groups are not prepared to treat these problems in isolation, and because a general alteration of the political arrangement thus cannot come about.

6   Of course, the fact that the state, through the instruments of redistribution at its disposal, can also defuse social conflicts must not be overlooked. Such defusion depends largely on whether the burdens of state policy can be made to be felt less than the beneficial manifestations. This is

where there is an irresoluble contradiction: it is precisely in situations in which redistribution is particularly urgent that distributive margins are narrow, that is to say that the burdening effects are acutely felt.

There are, it is true, two ways out of this, which do indeed allow the short-term goal of reducing conflict to be attained, but only at the price of a probable long-term endangering of political stability: (i) inflation and (ii) the limitation of the forces of economic growth.

Inflation is a specific form of resolution of conflicts over distribution in politically weak states, which cannot risk letting real distribution become apparent through a simultaneous nominal redistribution. State spending financed through the creation of currency appears in the first instance to contribute to the satisfaction of numerous needs. Nominally, many more demands are satisfied than there is real product available. As long as the currency illusion dominates, even those who are in fact carrying real burdens feel themselves to a large extent to be beneficiaries. By contrast, financing state expenditure exclusively through taxation (or choking off the growth of money supply that might make an aggressive wage or price policy feasible) will immediately bring out the real burdens and would provoke a resistance, which might not be politically tolerable. But it is clear that inflation is not an instrument that may be applied to pacifying conflicts over distribution for an indefinite period of time. As the currency illusion diminishes, the pacifying effect turns to the opposite. Inflation can end in the crisis of the system.[9]

Another way to blunt conflict over distribution through state measures of redistribution, which however in so doing simultaneously reduces the long-term possibilities of resolving the problem, would be to support private and public consumption at the cost of private and public investment (which do not directly enter the calculations of individual utility). In the long run this operates dysfunctionally. Yet such a policy can be desirable if future economic development is on the whole judged optimistically, and if future development is not primarily dependent on the size of the investment quota. But then the risks in the event of a failure of such preconditions to come about become all the greater.

III   Specific theses on the state of the problem before the collapse of Weimar

From the model of the significance of economic elements in the crisis of political systems sketched out above, I shall now derive some specific theses on the economic fate of the Weimar Republic.

1   At the end of the inflationary process in 1923, the dramatic changes in

the absolute and relative wealth of the population (its real and financial means) became obvious. Losses appear to have predominated, although they were very unevenly distributed.[10] After that in 1924 it became apparent that also incomes were substantially below those of the pre-war period; here too significant differences between social groups emerged. To that extent, a demand for either an absolute or a relative improvement of income and distribution of income and property now existed, with powerful claims to legitimacy. Yet the conflicts associated with the attempt to restore the pre-war position, a position felt to have been 'normal', were not the only ones that racked the Weimar system. Frequently demands were raised claiming larger shares of GNP in order to realise claims already made long before the war, as well as for the redemption of promises made during the revolutionary phase. Such claims now coincided with the typical 'post-war claims' of a phase of purgation and rebuilding. Out of this there emerged a potential for severe conflicts over distribution, conflicts which came to characterise the later twenties.

2   Unhappily, these were made at the time of an objectively relatively adverse general economic situation. The phase between the inflation and the great depression was not a period of sustained growth in which struggles over distribution might have been moderated through an actual allocation to all claimants. Certainly there were temporary reliefs and short phases of stabilisation: but it is precisely in these moments that the longer-term damaging conjunction of problems arose, problems each of which could, politically, no longer be solved in isolation. At the same time, those factors which could have promoted long-term growth were weakened.

3   Distributional conflicts were, as a consequence of the specific institutions for resolving conflict in Germany, transferred to the level of the state and/or at least the negative results of the conflicts were loaded upon the state. In this connection, the state's arbitration in wage conflicts, which increasingly liberated the partners in wage negotiations from the pressure to compromise and allowed the burden of making wage policy to fall on to the state, played a quite outstanding role.

The political rejection of a particular German responsibility for the First World War (and the exoneration of the politics of the Kaiserreich) corresponded in economic discussions with a heaping of the burdens of the post-war period on to the Weimar Republic. These burdens were not understood as being the (inevitable) heritage of the war. Of course, in addition to this came the fact that the state had to fulfil far more economic and socio-political control functions after the war than before. This resulted inevitably from the post-war situation – quite independently of all the wishful thinking that took place regarding a new economic and social order. Beyond this, there was a German peculiarity, which had already begun to emerge before the war. The state participated to a very considerable extent in the allocation and the distribution of economic opportunities and rewards already before the war.[11] There was thus a tradition of politicising conflicts over distribution, and of deploying political instruments in order to moderate such conflicts.

4   In this connection it was of considerable importance that the parties which mainly carried politically the beginnings of Weimar democracy, the SPD and the Centre, were '*Weltanschauungsparteien*', parties with a philosophical world view who ascribed to themselves a universal competence at least to interpret but then also to regulate social processes. Because, at the root of their political understanding, these parties were anti-capitalist in orientation, they trusted less in the anonymous forces of the market (and thus the decentralisation of economic conflicts). They had no chance of unburdening themselves through a rapid 'liberalisation' of regulatory functions. The guiding maxim of '*Sozialstaatlichkeit*' (Welfare State) often even demanded the opposite, that is, the inclusion of markets which had until then still functioned autonomously within the regulatory competence of the state. Certainly, this extension of control frequently failed to correspond with a corresponding ability to provide for the necessary decisions in real terms. Where the state could do this, it was often at the expense of other goals and to the detriment of the interests of others, who became in consequence politically mobilised. To put it more simply, conflict resolution also took place at the cost of the chances of being able to meet such demands in the future.

5   The Republic derived a certain relief from the burden of domestic conflicts from the fact that it was – at least partly – successful in diverting public opinion as to the cause of the perceived economic problems. It re-addressed the disappointments, and the massive failure of claims, to the outside world. That was the role which the burden of reparations played throughout the course of the Weimar Republic. Certainly, the price paid for this was a high one: the strategy shackled German domestic and foreign policy. The generally held view that it was above all reparations which were to blame for so many socio-economic ills made the German government especially responsible for economic recovery which did take place. It did not want to share the credit for this. The government needed to look for solutions to the reparation problem, since such an outcome would leave a

greater national income for Germany which might be distributed in order to lessen domestic social conflict.

6   What do we have in mind, when we speak of conflicts of distribution? If we look first at the expenditure side of GNP, then it was a matter of sharing the cake between private and state use. Then the apportionment between consumption and investment was at issue. In addition, the necessity of achieving an export surplus played a large role. A major problem was that the public sector had considerably increased in size by comparison with the pre-war period. At the end of the twenties it confronted serious structural difficulties in financing its requirements, in spite of the relatively increased burden of taxes and social insurance contributions. It was already repeatedly in cash difficulties, which could only be overcome through lowering expenditure (decreased fulfilment of those duties the state had either inherited or assumed) or increasing income (raising the burdens on the economy), unless faster economic growth with an unaltered relative tax burden could bring help from the revenue side. But precisely such a financial policy came to be an obstacle to faster growth. The German balance of payments situation was desperate; and the possibilities for solving it were highly controversial. In the absence of a continuing inflow of foreign capital, an increase of around 40 or 50 per cent in German exports would have been needed to meet all of Germany's obligations. This could not be expected either with regard to foreseeable trends in the world market or to the development of domestic costs. And what if the inflow of foreign credit were not only to stop, but if a reversal of the net flows set in?[12]

Associated with the conflicts over the use of the national product was a basic conflict over the distribution of national income. It was above all here that politically accentuated demands clashed. On the one hand, such demands rested on norms of social justice and on the goal of a rapid raising of living standards; on the other, such aspirations referred to the necessity in the first instance to supply a potential of productive forces, and particularly to facilitate capital formation. Of course it was not the case that trade union wage policy can be described as being oriented solely towards a distributive goal. The 'purchasing power theory' of the trade unions certainly seemed to trade unionists as more than a policy furthering their particular interests. But to the opposing side, to the German employers, the argument that it was necessary to ensure greater mass purchasing power by means of wage increases in order to increase the market (and thus also profits) appeared only as an alibi in view of the cost returns of businesses and their particular external financial dependence. In matters of

fundamentals, there could be no consensus about an economically viable
wage policy – and at the same time state authorities had a major responsibility for wage formation.

7   It was not least the problems of economic and social policy developing
or accumulating in the course of the 1920s which, even before 1929,
brought so many of those in positions of responsibility to look for alternative political arrangements, and especially for more authoritarian control
by uninterested experts. And it was this clue of problems which, at the
beginning of the great depression, actually encouraged the opinion that the
economic crisis could be used to achieve the very restoration of healthy
conditions which the political system was held no longer to be capable of
achieving on its own. So the crisis was at first interpreted as being a helpful
process, which would make the voice of objective facts tell – until it
emerged that the process became far more dangerous because of the completely novel quality of the crisis.

The concrete conditions of economic development will be considered
below, in order to substantiate the assertions already made regarding the
possible economic causes of the systemic crisis. It is true that I shall not be
able fully to live up to the requirements listed by Karl Dietrich Bracher:
'Here too, of course, the difficulties commence at the moment when one
turns one's gaze from the general world economic context and from the
deterministically accepted columns of production, price, sales, export and
import figures and toward the domestic, and again organisationally and
politically determined, causational and motivational chains'.[13] But nevertheless even the demonstration of weighty economic and social problems at
the end of the twenties may be justified in the context of the overall task
sketched out in the introduction. The economic historian should in any
case concern himself in the first instance with the 'columns'. In a final
section, some thoughts on 'causational and motivational chains' will then
follow.

IV   The formation of the need to solve complex distributional problems

1   Proceeding from the assertion that the scope for distribution,
on which the intensity of social conflicts largely depends, is partly
determined by the pace of economic progress, some facts concerning the
growth process in the Weimar Republic before the great depression will
now be presented. Even if it is now recognised in the literature that
economic growth in Germany – as well as in other European countries
though not in the United States – was relatively weak until 1929,[14] it is not

superfluous, in the present context, to examine these weaknesses once more.

It is certainly far more difficult to name the causes of the 'relative stagnation'. Many rival hypotheses exist. Their spectrum ranges from global models of long wave development in capitalist countries (according to which the Weimar Republic would, so to speak by accident, have chanced upon a particularly unhappy phase of economic development) all the way to explanations which draw on very specific German circumstances, and which then of course immediately raise the question of why there was no similar trend in other countries. Wolfram Fischer has rightly pointed out that, with regard to certain indicators of economic progress, Germany actually came off better before 1929 than Britain.[15] But then in many respects Britain was, after all, economically and politically not as endangered as Germany.

It should explicitly be emphasised that I cannot imagine that it is possible with the aid of scientific methods to reduce the multiplicity of explanations of the causes of the general weakness of growth in the 1920s.[16] But this is surely not a problem specific to economic history. In the end, this symposium too is an example of how difficult it is to select out of an excessive supply of plausible arguments, that one which might carry the explanatory burden on its own.

2   If we speak here of a weakness in growth, this does not mean that there was no economic growth. There was indeed such growth. But it worked out to amount less in total than one might (theoretically) have anticipated after the considerable deficits in growth during and in the immediate aftermath of the war. If reconstruction of the German economy and a return to a long-term trend had been as rapid after the First World War as after the Second, then the real per capita national income would in 1929 have exceeded that of 1913 by around 25 per cent. But in fact the per capita national income in 1929 was only around 6 per cent above the pre-war level.[17] With that it was clear that the relatively improved position of certain groups must have been linked to an absolutely worsened position for others.

If, before 1929, there was ever a reconstruction phase with high growth rates and lasting for a number of years, then it was from 1919 to 1922. Of course, we cannot ascertain this on the basis of directly established statistics for GNP (NNP), but only by using other indicators, above all, industrial and agricultural production.[18] From 1919 industrial production (then 37 per cent of the 1913 level) advanced rapidly during the inflation and was able to make up the large part of the wartime loss: by 1922 production was 70 per cent of 1913. Then in 1923 came a major collapse (46 per cent of 1913 levels), which was not fully made good in 1924 (69 per cent). In 1924 there was thus still a great 'need for reconstruction' and as yet unmet 'need to catch up' with the progress of production in other countries, above all in the USA.

And it is of the greatest importance to recognise that this need (and the opportunity for growth that it provided) could by no means fully be satisfied during the following years. From 1924 to 1925 a large increase in industrial production (from 69 per cent to 81 per cent of the 1913 level) did ensue, but, as early as 1926, the business cycle turned with a drastic shrinkage of industrial production. This fell by 11 per cent (seasonally adjusted) over the space of nine months; production of investment goods fell still further.[19] From the trough in 1926 to the peak at the end of 1927, what could be regarded as an explosion in production then took place: from 1926 to 1927 industrial production rose again by 25 per cent, and returned for the first time to the level of 1913. Real GNP per capita grew by 8.2 per cent from 1926 to 1927, but this movement did not proceed unimpeded. From 1927 to 1928 the growth rate was 3.8 per cent, and from 1928 to 1929 GNP was already in decline (−1.0 per cent).[20]

It is hard to establish a precise upper turning-point of the business cycle in Germany, since the individual business cycle indicators reached their respective peaks at points scattered within a period between 1927 and 1929. The only established fact is that the turning-point had certainly occurred before the summer of 1929 and definitely long before the collapse of the New York Stock Exchange boom in October 1929, with which the popular literature on the subject often begins. As early as mid-1927, the level of industrial production ceased to rise – though it is true that this is only valid for an average of all branches of industry. Production in mining, metal-work and the chemical industry continued to rise until the end of 1928, whereas building had already declined since 1927. And production of those branches of consumer goods of so-called elastic demand, that is in the textile industry, in leather working and production, and in clothing, there was still more dramatic shrinkage. Had matters been 'normal', there would still have been above average growth rates for a reasonable period after the stabilisation in 1923/4 in view of the potential scope for growth after the wartime and post-war losses, and the recessions should (as comparison with the period after 1948 shows) have proved milder.[21]

3   From 1926 to 1929, the average unemployment figure which, for the inflation years 1921 and 1922 is estimated at only 350,000 and 210,000 respectively, did not fall below 1.3 million in any year – not even in 1927,

the peak year for production increases.[22] It is true that information on unemployment levels is, for several reasons, unreliable – and not methodologically precisely comparable with those figures used today either; but from the longer-term information available it can be concluded that, in the second half of the 1920s, the unemployment rate did not fall below 6.7 per cent (for 1925) of trade union members. In 1927, the strongest year in terms of growth, the unemployment rate stood at an average of 8.8 per cent. Unemployment rates were thus not only far higher than in the immediate inflationary post-war period, but also than in the decades before 1914![23]

In the winter of 1928/9, the unemployment rate rose to over 20 per cent of trade union members – although it is true that this rise was partly caused by the extreme cold. In February 1929, 3 million unemployed were already registered with the labour offices, 1.3 million remained unemployed in the following season.

In the late 1920s a situation which today we would characterise as a sort of 'stagflation' resulted, since generally unsatisfactory rates of production increase and substantial long-term unemployment coincided with a continuing rise in prices. Thus consumer prices rose by 2.6 per cent from 1927 to 1928. All in all there was no (positive) economic miracle in the twenties.

4 But we must now analyse the situation somewhat more precisely, especially with regard to those problems which were the subject of political conflicts. It was asserted above that conflicts about distribution are accentuated by relatively weak growth. And in fact, by comparison with the pre-war period, what were in many respects exciting new diversions of GNP to new uses and to new social groups did indeed occur. These changes could scarcely be accepted in silence by those who lost relatively, especially as a relative loss, because of the negligible growth, meant a perpetuation of what was, in comparison with the pre-war period, an absolute loss.

Let us begin with the structure of expenditure. Here, it is striking that public consumption (current expenditure) per capita (at constant prices) was greater in the twenties than before the war, despite a lower GNP. Thus, the proportion of total GNP taken up by public consumption had risen enormously, in spite of the fact that armaments were no longer a significant part of state spending. Added to this was the fact that the public sector (the Reich, and regional and local authorities) pursued the redistribution of income by means of so-called transfers to a far greater extent than had been done before the war: in consequence the tax burden on national income in the Weimar Republic lay markedly above that during the Empire. While the state's share (state expenditure as a share of net national product) stood at approximately 15 per cent in 1913, it amounted to approximately 26 per cent in the later twenties.[24] No wonder that the extent of state activity was heavily controversial, especially as it also in part competed with private activity, and above all because state activity had to be paid for through deductions in expenditure for other kinds of use.

It is not possible to ascertain exactly to what extent increased state consumption and state redistribution of income in favour of private consumption impaired capital formation. But it is indisputable that in the twenties the investment quota (even with private and public investments combined) was lower than before the war.[25] While, according to W. G. Hoffmann's calculations, the average (real) net investment share in the German Reich had stood at 16 per cent in 1910/13, in the so-called 'Weimar boom' from 1925/9 it amounted to only 10.5 per cent. True, this is an aggregate figure for all kinds of investment (inclusive of house-building and agriculture), but business (*Gewerbe*) appears to have come off only a little better than other sectors, since in 1925/9 investments in manufacturing remained considerably behind those of 1905/13. In addition, the capital intensity of the economy as a whole, that is the relation of the capital stock to labour, in the twenties still remained below the level before the war, thus there existed a significant potential for replenishment (and for further progress).

Since in developed economies the level of accumulation critically affects the rate of growth, the weak investment activity of Weimar was significant. In the short term, accumulation constitutes a major element of demand (especially for the investment goods industry); and in the medium and long term it is decisive for productivity increases. It might be said that poor accumulation leads to poor economic growth; even if the relationship is not completely constant, as is clear from cross-sectional comparison of various countries.

5   In this connection it is of particular importance that the relatively low real capital formation described above was financed by what was, in the long-term context, a most unusual structure of savings formation. Investigating the extent to which net investments between 1925 and 1929 were financed through the savings of individual domestic and foreign sectors, the following results emerge: 41 per cent of investments were financed through public sector savings (surpluses of current receipts over current expenditure), 9 per cent through undistributed profits of corporations (self-financing), 14 per cent through private savings on the part of households and private companies or individual employers, and 36 per cent through

the transfer of capital across national frontiers, i.e. through the net import of capital![26] Germany, which had been a capital exporting country before the war, became now – to a massive extent – a capital importing country. The influx of foreign capital assumed a key role in the investment process. Beside foreign capital, only government directly or indirectly played a predominant role in the process of capital formation. This role went far beyond that known before the war.

The 'heart of capitalism', the process of accumulation, in the twenties followed completely different rules to those applying previously. The private disposition of capital on the part of the domestic population represented only one quarter of domestic investment. Here it becomes clear to what an extent economic development had become dependent on political factors. Disturbances of the international capital movements on the one hand, and changes in the position of public authority budgets on the other, necessarily had dramatic consequences for investment, as became apparent as early as 1928/9.[27]

6   What happened here? In spite of various attempts at an explanation, it seems to me that as yet no satisfactory interpretation is available. In particular, neither economic theory nor empirical work appears to me to have delivered clear criteria for answering the question of whether the continuing unemployment of the late 1920s, coupled with growth rates relatively low for a period of reconstruction, were primarily the results of weaknesses in demand, or whether this was a classical case of real-wage unemployment, or perhaps both factors played a role.

It is indisputable that in the twenties exports no longer played the role they had done before the war. Although German territory had diminished in size, the export quota (exports in relation to net national product of market prices) in the twenties was lower than before 1914 – even though the figure includes exports paid as reparations. One could conclude from this that the weak recovery of the twenties followed from an unsatisfactory level of foreign demand. On the other hand, however, export is not simply exogenous, and it is not dependent on world demand alone, but also on domestic prices and costs. In this case, the domestic economic situation in the course of the 1920s probably produced consequences for Germany's performance on the world markets.

In contrast to the case of the British pound in 1925, it is hardly possible to assert for Germany that the exchange rate of the Reichsmark was fundamentally incorrectly set in 1923/4, and that in consequence exports were impeded from the outset by unfavourable costs.[28] Following E. H. Phelps Brown and M. H. Browne's calculations, wage price-costs in German industry in 1925 stood at 48 per cent above those of 1913; while in the same period they had risen by 67 per cent in Britain and by 64 per cent in the United States. At the exchange rates of 1914, Germany could – at least with regard to the wage piece-costs – still command a comparative advantage in 1925.[29] But this advantage seems to have disappeared rapidly. Whereas up to 1929 the wage piece-rates fell in the USA and Britain (that is, progress in productivity was relatively greater than wage increases), they rose in the German case. In 1929, wage piece-costs in German industry stood at 65 per cent above those of 1913, whereas in Britain they stood at 54 per cent higher and in the USA at 48 per cent higher. Thus Germany's possible comparative advantage with respect to wages had disappeared, or had even turned into a disadvantage (if one uses 1913 as the 'norm'). Therefore it is at least unsatisfactory to infer from a slower expansion of world trade an exogenous brake on growth for Germany.

In 1929, John Maynard Keynes dealt with the German reparations problem, and in this connection with the German wage level as well, in the course of a fictitious interview with Irving Fisher. Keynes' answer to Fisher is interesting:

> For after all, what is the reason why Germany's exports are no larger than they are at the moment? It is certainly not that her export industries cannot get the necessary labour, for there is a surplus of labour in nearly all the leading export industries. Undoubtedly, the reason why she has no more exports is because her costs of production do not enable her manufacturers to compete on international markets on a large scale. She can only export more if she cuts down her costs of production, and it is roughly true to say that she can only cut down her costs of production materially if her wages are reduced. Now, it has been calculated that in order to produce an adequate export surplus she would have to increase her export of finished goods by at least 40%. By how much would she have to reduce her wages in order to produce this result? I do not know. But the amount of reduction of wages which would be necessary is the measure of the difficulty of the transfer problem.[30]

7   There is no space here to pursue the history of wage policies in the 1920s more closely, or to discuss their economic consequences within the framework of theoretical concepts. Everyone knows that a lively discussion of this theme already took place in the twenties. But recently Hartmut Soell in describing the 'failure of the economic and social power-elites' and

of the Weimar Republic has taken up a position on this problem which runs as follows: 'Industry in particular showed itself incompetent to accept the offer of cooperation made by the trades unions in 1918, or to adopt a dynamic strategy of growth, which would have above all presumed an increase in domestic purchasing power through the expansion of real wages!'[31] Such a conclusion begs the question whether real wages in industry did indeed rise so little, and whether a more rapid rise could really be imagined under the circumstances then prevailing. The truth is that a policy of increasing real wages and strengthening domestic demand certainly existed during the twenties, as has already been indicated above. We will now argue this in greater detail.

Calculating the development of real wages is difficult, and subject to various uncertainties. Following the official statistics on average gross weekly earnings and on gross hourly earnings of industrial workers divided by the cost of living index, there was an increase of 8.2 per cent in weekly earnings and of 24 per cent in hourly earnings (due to the introduction of shorter working weeks) between 1913/14 and 1928.[32] In contrast, the real income of those engaged in agriculture remained far below the position of 1913 right until 1929: the unfavourable distribution had thus altered yet further to the disadvantage of agriculture.[33]

Domestic purchasing power may have been generally too weak – but I would see the weakness as lying rather in a demand for investment goods than in consumption. If one follows W. G. Hoffmann's calculations, then (real) private per capita consumption in 1928 already stood at a level 16 per cent above that of the pre-war period, and public consumption per capita at 34 per cent.[34] Everyone knows that it was extensive public consumption which, at the time, was so extensively criticised – not just by the Agent-General for Reparations Payments. There was certainly no lack of demand in the economy as a whole here.

8   In the context of the altogether slow growth of real GNP, it is important that the described rise in real wages was associated with a considerable change in the distribution of incomes that benefited employees. If an 'adjusted wage share' is used as a basis for measuring distribution, then from 1913 to 1928 an increase in the wage share from 46.4 per cent to 57.5 per cent, or from 52.5 per cent to 65.2 per cent resulted.[35]

A similar tendential change emerges from the calculations of W. G. Hoffmann's so-called labour income share. Hoffmann does not correct an actual time-series of wage shares in order to compensate for changes in employment structure, but calculates a fictitious income from work for self-employed and gainfully employed family members. This is added to

wage income, and compared with national income. According to Hoffmann, the labour share established in this way rose from between 70 per
cent and 72 per cent over the period 1901 to 1913 to 87 per cent in the
period 1925 to 1929.[36] A reduction of the shares of capital income (interest,
profits) directly follows from this. The reduction is certainly a consequence
of the loss of a substantial part of monetary assets, and of the state's policy
in stabilising rents, but not exclusively.[37] In any event, the average income
of all those in employment never came so close to the average income of
the working population as a whole before 1914 or after 1950 as it did in the
period 1925 to 1929.[38]

9   All in all, it seems to me that it is not possible to draw the conclusion
from the statistical evidence in the 1920s that a (yet) more rapid raising of
real wages, as Hartmut Soell suggests, would have been a useful strategy in
order to increase growth rates. It is hard to imagine how this could have
been achieved in an open economy at fixed exchange rates, especially as the
international economy was already plagued by scarcely soluble problems.

So far it has been shown that the economy of the late twenties was
anything other than 'healthy'. The growth rates in real national product
per capita were relatively low when measured in terms of the relative
backwardness of the German economy, which was a consequence of the
war. Unemployment was a constant problem. Capital formation remained
highly deficient. Foreign economic relations were in disarray. In the struggle over the distribution of a GNP that was only slowly increasing, government authorities and workers were relatively successful, but their success
appears to have overburdened the economy, so that on the one hand the
forces of growth were not sufficiently strengthened and, on the other, risks
in the spheres of money and credit accumulated. This boded ill for the
future. Undoubtedly it was the considerable imports of capital which
prevented many a conflict over distribution from manifesting itself so
clearly in Germany; otherwise these conflicts would have emerged earlier.
Without such large imports of capital, neither the state nor employers
would have been able to finance even such expansion of incomes as may be
observed – certainly they would not have been able to do this within the
framework of the gold standard at fixed exchange rates.

I would draw the following somewhat dramatic conclusion: things could
not continue in the way they had done.[39] This was a conclusion which
became clear to most contemporaries. From 1928, the streams of capital
from abroad already lagged far behind the sums necessary to solve Germany's balance of payments problems. The budgets of public authorities,
and especially unemployment insurance, came into increasing difficulties.

Wage conflicts reached such a degree of severity that they called into question the whole system of collective industrial agreements, and even the organisation of the labour market. Agricultural policy became irresolubly inconsistent with other areas of state policy. From all sides, there came demands for fundamental reforms. The Reparations Agent was, so to speak, the permanent critic of German economic and social policy, as was the President of the Reichsbank Hjalmar Schacht. But also the interest associations and the political parties believed structural changes to be necessary. The 'guidelines for a readjustment of German economic policy', which the executive board of the Reich Association of German Industry proposed in a paper of December 1929, looked particularly radical.[40]

10 If the problem is posed in this way, the question also arises why it was not resolved earlier – or at the latest by the end of the 1920s. Dietmar Petzina, comparing the world depression with the recession of the years 1974/5, recently examined the years before the depression as well, and summed up his verdict as follows: 'It was surely a decisive structural problem of the Weimar Republic that the governments were not successful in correcting this overburdening of the economic system.'[41] Why did governments not succeed? And what might their solutions have looked like in concrete terms? Nobody has yet described this. I would like to venture the personal judgement that, under the given circumstances, there was no chance of easing the distributional conflicts by means of a successful growth policy, and so maintaining the loyalties of all the important political groups. In the following section, this conclusion will be substantiated with several statements in the form of theses.

V The material basis of the Weimar Republic in the systemic crisis

1 Even if it would be all too simplistic to assert that the Weimar Republic was characterised primarily by struggles over distribution, and that a consensual long-term economic policy oriented towards reconstruction and growth was never followed, the alternatives of 'distribution politics versus production politics' do nevertheless characterise the substantial part of Weimar's structural problematic. On 3 November 1925, during a discussion by party leaders on coalition alternatives, Adam Stegerwald suggested to Reich Chancellor Luther that: 'It was, furthermore, also true that it was hard to put through an economic policy with the Social Democrats, because they did not pursue the politics of production, but only of distribution'.[42] We must leave aside the question of whether, in this concrete case, the verdict was justified, and of what

intentions underpinned it. At this point it is important simply to demonstrate that the alternatives between the politics of distribution and the politics of production have not just been formulated with the benefit of hindsight. In 1929, the Reich Labour Ministry actually explicitly confirmed the primacy of the distributional goal in wage policy with regard to the previous period.[43] In academic publications, the dominance of distributive politics was already frequently lamented during the twenties. As an example, we cite the Bonn economist Herbert von Beckerath. In a 'programmatic critique of the German economy today', he characterised the position of the public administration and of the masses in the country as follows:

> As a result of the European states' tradition, they have adopted the belief in the miraculous economic capacity of a centralised institutional management of the economy; they combine this belief with economic and social theories which are geared less toward the degree of efficiency in creating the national product than toward justice regarding its distribution. There is inadequate general insight into elementary economic necessities, which are independent of the social constitution of the economy . . . in consequence in our case economic struggles are not decided or settled by arbitration in the manner demanded by an economic interest in productivity, namely according to the principle of least *economic* resistance, but according to the principle of the least *political* resistance.[44]

2. If Herbert von Beckerath was right, the obvious reason seems to be that there was above all a lack of insight and of competence on the part of those in positions of responsibility. In contrast with him, I should prefer to emphasise rather the complexity of the problems they had to face. Basically, in each individual case, powerful reasons for an increased share of GNP could be put forward. But, due to the limitation of the material base, such demands could only partially be met. Claims that were highly legitimate remained unfulfilled – and this gradually delegitimised the institutions for resolving conflicts, since those who were disappointed simply arrived at the view that 'the system' which ignored the justice of their claims must be fundamentally wrong.

3   There were, in my opinion, few alternative possibilities, because those expectations which were disappointed could only have been satisfied at the expense of the claims of others: would such an outcome have been enforce-

able and would the results really have increased political stability? It would be possible to dispute the particulars – whether this or that measure of subsidy, of social security, of provision of public services, of the securing of incomes through tariff protection, or many other policies, really made a contribution to Weimar's political stability. Yet this was the ambitious goal for the sake of which such policies were implemented: for the Weimar state, so unstable domestically and externally, was from the first dependent on buying itself political endorsement with such achievements. It could hardly refer to any other major successes – for instance in foreign policy.

During the inflationary period, it was possible to leave open the options for a number of years, and many of the most pressing claims appeared to find consideration – at least on paper. But more and more it became apparent that this was not a lasting or real solution. When the illusion of money vanished altogether, not only did the currency system fall apart, but a great crisis of the state broke out. The political order remained threatened even after the stabilisation of the currency so that it is difficult to imagine that much greater chances now existed of denying those claims whose justice had already been recognised before. The dispute about the revaluation of old debts showed that even the inflationary method of redistributing burdens could not, in the long run, be completely effective. Here too there were considerations of justice which demanded that the state assumed at least a part of the old debts, even if this assumption placed a heavy burden on future financial policy.[45] How could the state set itself against similarly pressing demands for justice? It is beyond doubt that the state faced a dilemma. In the long run, the distribution of burdens was assuredly indefensible, but in the short term a change in the distribution of burdens was surely just as indefensible. Only an 'economic miracle' could have brought a way out of the dilemma. But in light of the prevailing conditions, this would surely have also had to have been an even greater miracle than that after 1947.

4   Likewise I would be inclined to exclude the possibility of an economically supportable 'solution of the wage conflict'. To be sure, we can use economic models to show that a less rapid rise in real wages would have made domestic capital formation and exports, and thus monetary policy and much else, easier. But could something of this sort have been put through, and would it even have been unquestionably desirable with regard to the political stability of the Republic?

As is well known, from November 1918 wage settlements were highly politicised. At that time, employers not only accepted the old demands of the labour movement concerning the shortening of working hours and wage settlements through mutually recognised autonomous associations, they indeed even suggested them in order to counter the danger of revolution. The trade unions and employers' organisations formed, in the 'Central Working Community' (Zentralarbeitsgemeinschaft), a force for order of the highest importance at the beginning of the Republic, and which carried the process of parliamentarisation. At that time, through the agreement of the trade union leaders and the employers, all those labour market arrangements were created which were later seemingly to produce such economically unreasonable results. In short, all in all, the revolution was diverted into a great movement of wages.[46] On this front too, it remained uncertain what would prove durable from the gains of 1918/19. But already by the end of the inflation, and particularly after the stabilisation of the currency, completely different economic conditions emerged, in which those achievements which had once been agreed upon now became the problem.[47]

In this new phase, in which employers sought with all the means at their disposal to lower wage rates or to prevent their rise, I do not deny that old class positions also assumed a new weight, and the destruction of the trade unions periodically appeared to become for the employers a goal in its own right – and a mortal danger to the Republic.[48] But I believe equally that we cannot overlook the fact that there were very reasonable grounds for the employers' demands not to allow production costs, and especially wage costs, to grow too rapidly from their low level. For employers also, the room for manoeuvre was not as great as they might have wished; in many areas it was indeed pretty narrow.[49] This was recognised by Eugen Varga, the theoretician of the Comintern, who interpreted the attempts of employers to stop the rise in wages not as an expression of a traditional patriarchal point of view, but as the consequence of the laws of the capitalist (or market economic) system.[50]

But for the labour unions and their leaders, the issue was not solely one of economic policy. When, after the inflation the desire for revision on the part of the employers grew ever stronger, the unions appeared to have been expelled from the Weimar compromise. They felt this as a betrayal of the fundamental precepts of the Weimar Republic. Now, once the revolutionary danger was over, ought most of Weimar's long-term achievements to be no longer valid? No one who understood the political problems could expect trade unions to vacate positions which had been won previously or to guarantee extensive material concessions to the employers. The split in the labour movement meant that a radical left opposition of the Communist party limited the trade union wing's ability to act. Would a policy of wage freeze not, under certain circumstances, have split the trade unions and thus left the way open for what might have been truly radical forces? But no one who saw through the *economic* problems could follow calmly the development of costs. Here, mutual exigencies had come into being which, over the course of time, exceeded the capacity on the part of the interested parties to compromise.

On this front the transition of 1923/4 was finally accomplished by means of the deployment of the new institution of compulsory state arbitration. In the long-term perspective, this proved counter-productive. For a while, it is true, it guaranteed the solution of conflicts, but in the end it relieved the contractual partners of all responsibility, since they no longer stood under pressure to reach an agreement.[51] With the transference of the burden of wage formation to state arbitration authorities, important fundaments of the Weimar Republic were removed. I hold this to be a central element in the collapse of the Weimar Republic. Once the settlement of wages had become an affair of the state, it also became immediately important for the opponents in conflicts over wages to exert direct influence on those who occupied political positions. If this result could not be achieved by parliamentary means, then it became tempting to use extra-parliamentary forces.

It is part of the tragedy of the collapse of the Weimar Republic that, as in other areas, precisely those arrangements and decisions which were intended to secure the material constitution of the Republic contributed in the longer term to its undermining. In this fashion, conflicts were at first pacified, but the capacity to resolve those conflicts which accumulated was reduced.

5   I come to a conclusion which is certainly pessimistic, and opens up a tragic dimension. While on a very high level of abstraction, in blackboard exercises far removed from political reality, it might be possible to sketch out certain solutions to the economic impasse, those were, for good reasons in each case, politically unrealisable. Too much would have had to have been altered at the same time – and that surely was not feasible. An economic miracle on the world market might still have helped. In its absence, the situation was no longer controllable – and this represented at least *one* element in the collapse of the Republic, an element which came into effect well before the great depression.

11 GERMANY'S EXCHANGE RATE OPTIONS DURING THE GREAT DEPRESSION

I

1 Judgement on German economic policy during the great depression has been passed long ago. It is true that there have been repeated attempts to excuse the behaviour of those responsible by explaining it in terms of circumstances or of honourable motives. But the conclusion itself – that the policy represented a series of major mistakes – has as yet scarcely been challenged.[1] This is especially true in the case of German monetary policy, and above all for the sequence of decisions to maintain the gold parity and thus also the parity against the dollar and the French franc.[1a] The decision not to alter the old Reichsmark parity against gold after Britain left gold on 20/21 September 1931 ushered in the last and most radical round of Brüning's deflationary policy. It led to the fourth emergency decree of 8 December 1931. The Reich government in any event regarded the enormous effort of the decreed lowering of costs as the German reply to the British measure.[2]

Nevertheless, for the purpose of a critical analysis, it is useful to free oneself from the impression that the decision to adhere to parity virtually and of necessity led to all the subsequent and unsuccessful measures, and in particular to the failure to adopt a more active economic policy. Would, for instance, an expansionary monetary and fiscal policy have presupposed the change in the parity in light of the fact that the rigid minimum gold cover of notes had already been removed after July 1931, and that exchange controls could in principle have prevented the loss of currency reserves? As is generally known, the 'reformers' who after the summer of 1931 pleaded for a counter-cyclical fiscal and monetary policy, with few exceptions, demanded no change in the exchange rate and least of all a change in the existing system of (fixed) exchange rates.[3] On the other hand, Great Britain demonstrated to the world that a floating exchange rate did not necessarily mean safeguarding an expansionary fiscal policy with an exchange policy. The British Government's declaration of 20 September 1931 even explicitly disclaimed such an intention:

> His Majesty's Government are securing a balanced budget and the internal position of the country is sound. This position must be maintained. It is one thing to go off the gold standard with an unbalanced budget and uncontrolled inflation; it is quite another thing to take this measure, not because of internal financial difficulties, but because of excessive withdrawals of borrowed capital.[4]

However, not only fiscal policy, but also Great Britain's monetary policy, remained positively restrictive after the floating of sterling. Not until spring 1932 was the new situation used for a new strategy in combating deflation.[5] This kind of experience suggests that we should not consider as excessively self-evident the key role of the parities question when it comes to the discussion of possibilities for a more rapid ending of the German crisis.

2   It might still of course be the case that German exchange rate policy emerges as the central error of the years 1931/2. But plausible as some of the arguments do sound, proof of this has not yet been furnished. Judgements of this kind, which are to be found throughout the literature on the subject, rest not on scrupulous investigations of the question, but, for the most part, on fragmentary material and relatively vague suppositions. Even the sequence of the most important policy decisions in Germany after the floating of the pound has not as yet been accurately described; and there has been no systematic analysis of the motives of the actors and no examination of the paths which were (at least in theory) open to them. Indeed, this is perhaps the most important desideratum of research up to now. Irrespective of the fact that there is so great a degree of unanimity in condemning the German path of monetary policy, the historical analyses contain little information as to what – in the opinion of the critics – those responsible at the time should have done.[6]

3   But whoever considers monetary policy, and in particular exchange rate policy, between 1931 and 1933, to have been wrong or even catastrophic, must bring forward reasoned conjectures to the effect that another sequence of decisions – whether or not the decisions could have been put into effect – would in all probability have brought about a more favourable development. This presupposes naming the other possible paths in order to establish and evaluate the pros and cons with regard to

economic and other policy objectives. Contrary to the impression that one gains from reading some of the critical studies, it was not a matter of a simple yes/no decision on the gold standard, but rather of a very complex cluster of decisions. This will be demonstrated in greater detail below.

II

1   The assertion that the critical historical literature on the subject has not as yet satisfactorily explained what the Reich government or what the Reichsbank could have done must sound surprising since, after all, there have been enough complaints about the German failure to devalue or to follow the pound sterling. Such observations appear to contain precise references. Unfortunately, this is not the case. In the case of those who recommend 'Abwertung' (devaluation), the very concept is unclear. For it is not evident whether the authors are implying it in today's meaning, or whether they are using the language of the early thirties. Today, we understand by an 'Abwertung' (devaluation) in the system of fixed exchange rates, as a re-fixing of the exchange rate against other currencies but at a lower level (that is, less foreign currency for one's own currency), which is precisely how the rate of devaluation is described. At that time, what was understood by 'Abwertung' was the more or less free fall in exchange rates after the parity of the Reichsmark against gold or the dollar had been abandoned. A diminution of the legal foreign value of the currency was called 'Devalvation', and the general overall concept was 'currency depreciation'.[7]

During the fourth quarter of 1931, some voices were raised in Germany demanding Devalvation (devaluation) while others wanted the Reichsmark to float, at least against the dollar. Which proposals do the present critics, who believe that Germany should have 'devalued', favour? And if it is to be Devalvation – what rates are the respective authors thinking in terms of? For, after all, the results would depend on the measure of the devaluation.[7a]

The recommendation that Germany should have followed the pound is not unambiguous either. Should the exchange rate of the Reichsmark have been floated, as was the case with sterling, or should Germany have gone over to a sterling standard and linked the mark to the pound? If one decides in favour of the latter alternative it would still of course be necessary to determine whether Germany should join the sterling bloc at the old exchange rate of the Reichsmark against the pound (20.492 RM) or at a new one: Canada, for instance, took the latter course.

It is not only the critical literature which fails to give a precise account of the various possibilities for action. The same is true of most of the contemporary calls to deviate from the previous path of policy. What could

Carl Krämer, for example, have had in mind when on 25 December 1931 he recommended 'painstakingly copying the Bank of England's measures' and, three weeks later, suggested a 'Devalvation corresponding to the depreciation of the pound against the dollar'?[8] In the light of the ambiguities of the historical and critical literature, as well as of the contemporary sources, it is important to present an overview of all the possible paths which might have been followed in order finally to determine, as concretely as possible, what was actually suggested at the time, and what should have been done.

2   To this end it is convenient to begin with an important assumption. We should not at the outset too narrowly limit the possible solutions we propose by regarding the Bank Laws of 1924 and 1930 and the Young Plan Law as unalterable or inviolable.[9] As is generally known, the commitment to maintain mint parity included in Article 31 of the Bank Law was a cornerstone of the New or Young Plan alongside the removal of the foreign control of the Reichsbank and the reiteration of the guarantee of the Reichsbank's independence. No one can today ignore the serious objections to altering or violating those binding agreements.[10] For the purposes of analysis, however, these scruples may for the moment be deferred.[11] It would be possible to imagine situations in which the German government would even have taken on the expected costs of a violation of the law, if only the overall expected benefits might have justified such a step. In this case it becomes necessary to add to the economic cost-benefit calculation an assessment of the political risks and an evaluation of the conceivable political damage.[11a]

We need not speculate whether France would have stood in the way of an internationally agreed suspension of Article 31. There is concrete evidence that France's representatives, as early as the London Conference of July 1931, had lodged a massive objection to proposals suggested by Chancellor Brüning and supported by the British and Americans for altering Articles 29 and 31 of the Bank Law.[12]

3   In this connection, I may be permitted one aside relating to the speech given by John Maynard Keynes in the Überseeclub in Hamburg on 8 January 1932. In this speech, as Wilhelm Grotkropp notes, Keynes put out an invitation to the Germans to join the Sterling Club, but later – in the course of conversation – it emerged that the German obligations under the Young Plan had 'not been known' to him.[13] Heinrich Brüning reported a similar conversation with Keynes on 11 January 1932 in his memoirs. Asked by Brüning how he thought to circumvent the stipulations of the

Young Plan regarding the German currency, Keynes, it appeared, had not taken these laws into account at all.[14] We now know, however, that Keynes not only knew of the legal ties, but that he explicitly referred to them in a memorandum for the British Prime Minister's Advisory Committee.[15] Is it possible that he misled his German audience? A more precise reading of the speech, however, shows that even in Hamburg Keynes certainly did take into account the narrow room for manoeuvre available for the German government. Among other things, Keynes said (assuming the newspaper quoted him correctly): 'I recognise the psychological and high political reasons which necessitate the present unbearable pressure on the life of the German economy; but the continuation of the existing deflationary pressure would represent a disastrous error *once the need for an impressive demonstration of this sort has passed*' (emphasis K.B).[16]

III

1   Table 11.1 summarises the available possibilities for action – or the necessities for decisions. Using this table, we can both characterise the various contemporary recommendations more precisely, and discern those concrete decisions which determined the course actually followed. In addition, on the basis of this overview, we can also consider what might practically have been done in Germany – though for this we need to make assumptions regarding the efficacy of the measures, assumptions which we shall describe in greater detail below.

The core is provided by *fundamental decisions on exchange rate policy*, i.e. decisions on the system of exchange rates within which the Reichsmark should in future be managed. A decision in favour of stable exchange rates necessitated a further decision as to whether the old or whether new parities should be in effect.

In addition to these fundamental decisions, *supplementary decisions* were needed: (i) If one wished to decide in favour of floating the exchange rate of the Reichsmark (against whichever other currencies), it was necessary to determine whether the float should be free or whether it should be a 'dirty float' in the context of a 'managed currency' with the goal of either *de facto* stability or of politically motivated changes in the exchange rate. (ii) As Germany had already had exchange controls since 19 July 1931, it was inevitably also necessary to decide whether these exchange controls could or should be lifted in the future – or whether they should remain in place or even be augmented. In this connection, it was also necessary to decide whether the external sale of gold was to be banned entirely (a gold embargo), whether only the central bank should undertake gold sales, or whether they should remain altogether free. (iii) On 19 August 1931, a

Table 11.1. *Possible choices in exchange rate policy in Germany 1931/32*

	RM rate against			Flexible rates: managed floating?	Gold embargo?	Exchange control?	Standstill agreement?	Moratorium?
	Gold	$, French franc	£ and sterling bloc					
I	stable altered	stable unaltered	stable unaltered		yes/ no	yes/ no	yes/ no	yes/ no
II	stable altered	stable altered	stable altered	—	yes/ no	yes/ no	yes/ no	yes/ no
III	stable unaltered	stable unaltered	stable unaltered	—	yes/ no	yes/ no	yes/ no	yes/ no
IV	stable unaltered	stable unaltered	flexible	—	yes/ no	yes/ no	yes/ no	yes/ no
V	stable altered	stable altered	flexible	yes/ no	yes/ no	yes/ no	yes/ no	yes/ no
VI	flexible	flexible	stable unaltered	yes/ no	yes/ no	yes/ no	yes/ no	yes/ no
VII	flexible	flexible	stable altered	yes/ no	yes/ no	yes/ no	yes/ no	yes/ no
VIII	flexible	flexible	flexible	yes/ no	yes/ no	yes/ no	yes/ no	yes/ no

IX Substitute and/or supplementary devaluation through tariff and tax policy in combination with I–VIII standstill agreement on short-term German liabilities and bankers' credit lines created an organised market which provided a certain protection for debtors, a postponement of amortisation and interest payments, and the retention of certain credit lines. A decision now had to be taken on how the standstill (which was thought to be in operation for only a limited period) was to be operated in the future. If the agreement were not to be renewed (though in fact such a renewal did take place with a credit agreement in 1932), a moratorium would have had to be imposed. In any case, there was always the question of a moratorium for those loans not included in the standstill agreement.

2   The construction of the cases starts from a base in September 1931, and includes a range of expectations which were found in contemporary sources. As a result, Cases I to III differ from Cases IV to VIII. Whereas Cases IV to VIII describe the decisions which were dependent exclusively on German decisions (and reflected German expectations), Cases I to III include either a concerted action on the part of the major currencies (Case I) or another form of a return of sterling to gold (Cases II and III).

With the exception of the just-mentioned possible changes in Britain's exchange rate policy and of the concerted action referred to in Case I, the possibilities for action to be discussed are based on the assumption that the United States and France as well as other similar gold countries, on the one hand, and Great Britain and those currencies floating either on their own or in the sterling bloc on the other, would not change their fundamental exchange policies. This assumption corresponds to the contemporary reality. But in September to October 1931, a return to the gold standard on the part of Great Britain was still widely anticipated, while it was held to be unlikely that France or the United States would abandon gold parities.[17]

3   The possibility of a concerted action, described in the table as Case I, in which Germany also could have participated, does not on the face of it appear to have been likely in the concrete situation following the floating of the pound in September 1931; but here reality plays a trick on us. In fact, even after sterling floated, suggestions in line with this case were discussed at the highest levels. All gold currencies were supposed to alter the price of gold by the same proportions (a 50 per cent devaluation) so that the inter-currency relations could remain unchanged and Britain might then rejoin the gold standard system (at the old rate against the dollar?).

The most prominent exponent of this plan was the General Manager of the B.I.S. in Basel, Pierre Quesnay, who expanded on it on various occasions in late September, and at the time stimulated a certain amount of attention, and created a certain amount of confusion. At first it was thought that the plan had either been agreed with the French government and the Bank of France, or that it represented the official view of the B.I.S. Neither, as rapidly became apparent, was the case. On 26 September 1931, Reichsbank President Hans Luther reported on this idea to the Reich Cabinet and explained its intentions: increased prices as a result of increased note issue, above all in those countries which had fixed minimum reserve ratios. The cabinet discussed this plan at a meeting called to prepare the visit of the French Premier and Foreign Minister the following day, since at the time it was still assumed that the French backed Quesnay's ideas. It is true that the minutes of the cabinet meeting of 27 September contain no reference to this point of the debate.[18] For the discussion, we need to rely on the diaries of the Secretary of State in the Finance Ministry, Hans Schäffer. After giving an account of Luther's report, Schäffer continues:

> He himself [Luther] then said he characterised the matter as 'Gallic magic' and refused to pursue the matter further. I [Schäffer] hold the affair to be very significant, particularly as it rests on long-considered plans. By these means it would be possible to make good the British pound devaluation. Trendelenburg [Secretary of State in the Reich Ministry of Economic Affairs and Acting Minister] expresses himself to the same effect.[19]

The matter can then be pursued somewhat further, as the Reichsbank delegate to the B.I.S., Reichsbank Director Franz Hülse, still expressed himself strongly in favour of the Quesnay plan in a letter to Luther dated 30 September 1931. Wilhelm Vocke, a member of the Reichsbank Directorate, presented his thoughts on the plan in a wide-ranging paper which was sent both to Karl Blessing (also active on behalf of the Reichsbank in Basel) and to the Secretary of State in the Reich Chancellory, Hermann Pünder. Vocke, weighing up the pros and cons, decided against (and we will agree with him in this).[20]

In the German camp, Wladimir Woytinsky argued in favour of a concerted international reflationary plan by means of an increase in the gold price, even before the pound had left the gold standard; but he saw no scope for autonomous German action to raise domestic prices.[21] Robert Dalberg also, on 3 October 1931, described the possibility of a coordinated international devaluation against gold in a memorandum delivered to Reich Chancellor Brüning, to the President of the Reichsbank, and to the responsible Reich ministers.[22] I call this proposal the 'Dalberg Plan A' in order to distinguish it from two other proposals he put forward. This plan, put forward after the sterling crisis, amounted to a proposal that all countries should first seek a firm parity against the pound and that sterling, which was at that time devalued by around 20 per cent relative to gold, should then be stabilised. Dalberg anticipated that such a devaluation would bring about price rises of around 20 per cent, and if it were possible to keep nominal wages stable, this should bring about an international upturn. With an eye to practicality, however, Dalberg added in an appendix to Plan A another proposal (which we shall call Dalberg Plan B): this corresponds to Case VI in our table.[23]

4   Case II looks like a normal case of devaluation within a system of fixed exchange rates. For that reason it could not exist in such a form after the pound had floated. But this is an opportunity to discuss the remark found in Brüning's memoirs. He reports on different considerations made as early as the initial weeks of September (that is, *before* the floating of the pound), and in this context he notes 'that I had a secret agreement with Luther to undertake a 20% devaluation of the Mark after the cancellation of Reparations'.[24] This puzzles me. We find no kind of matching report on Luther's part, and no references in the available primary sources. The logic of all of Brüning's other statements really runs counter to the possibility that he could have entertained such an idea *before* the pound had floated.

5   Case II can also be made to correspond with the reality of a floating pound if it is interpreted not as an initial, but as a consequential, step. The sort of constellation denoted here would have emerged after the devaluation of the Reichsmark against gold and the gold currencies (Case V) if the British pound had once more been stabilised: assuming that the exchange rate of the RM against the pound would have been altered from that prevailing before 21 September 1931. Today we know that the pound was not stabilised, but between September and December 1931 there were many different experts' opinions regarding the future of the pound. Many expected the pound soon to revert to the gold standard (albeit at a lower rate of exchange). The (anonymous) proposal for Devalvation of 11 December 1931 published by R. Dalberg and W. Grävell (I call it Dalberg Plan C) corresponds to Case V, with the expectation of transition to Case II.[25]

In his article of 2 December, Ernst Wagemann critically discussed the proposals outlined as models in Cases II and V, and drew the conclusion that devaluation (Devalvation) could not be recommended. Some of his arguments could also be applied to Cases VI to VIII, but it appears that Wagemann held the possibility of allowing the RM's exchange rate to fluctuate freely to be so remote that he did not include it in any of his own deliberations. He refers to it only in the introduction in order to give a more precise definition of the concept of Devalvation.[26]

6   Case III should not be omitted from any comprehensive overview of the possibilities of action in exchange rate policy in the autumn of 1931, although in retrospect it appears to be of little importance. At the time, many experts took very seriously the possibility that the floating of the pound would come to an end soon with a stabilisation (at a lower level), and that the other currencies would stay on the gold standard at the old exchange rate. Such expectations could be built on the British government's press release of 20 September 1931 on the suspension of Subsection 2 of the Gold Standard Act, which ended with the following formulation: '... and there is no doubt that the present exchange difficulties will prove only temporary'.[27] In their interpretations, the major British ambassadors abroad likewise conveyed to their host governments the impression that it was only a matter of a temporary floating. Under these circumstances, people everywhere had good grounds to consider *what* the eventual rate of devaluation would be. In September and October people still reckoned on a maximum of 10 to 15 per cent,[28] a correction which was held not to have been too dangerous.

7   As far as regards exchange rate policy (without the additional decisions of the final columns of the table, which remain still to be discussed), Case IV was the path actually taken: since the mark's gold parity was not changed, the dollar, franc and other gold currencies stayed at par (until 1933) and the pound, with other currencies, continued to float. It is true that in Germany there were at least plans, and even some modest attempts at carrying them out, for a combination of Case IV and Case IX in the spirit of an *Ersatz-Abwertung* (substitute-devaluation). We shall return to this below.

8   Reference has already been made above to the fact that in his memorandum of 3 October 1931 Dalberg described something corresponding to Case VI as a second (and surely also more realistic) path (Dalberg Plan B). Going over to a sterling standard was, at that time, also characterised by others as useful and necessary (if this is what was meant when people recommended 'following the pound' – if not, it would have been a case of Path VIII). In recommending that the Reichsmark rate against the (floating) British pound should be fixed, the general assumption was that

the old RM rate of 20.429 was to remain in effect; it would then have had to be maintained by the Reichsbank in a manner similar to that in which the dollar exchange rate actually was maintained.

R. E. Lüke has, however, stated that at that time Britain was in principle in favour of 'Germany's going it alone', and had desired a German 'devaluation', but 'not in the same ratio as Britain'.[29] For Germany this would have meant: (i) Germany's abandoning the gold-dollar standard and going over to the pound (that is, a stabilised exchange rate with the pound), but combined with a simultaneous upward revaluation of the Reichsmark relative to the exchange rate before 21 September; or (ii) by floating the Reichsmark but intervening if necessary with a view to maintaining a certain rate of revaluation against the pound (Case VIII with the additional assumption about the character of the mark float). One can exclude the second possibility (i.e. VII with interventions) from the beginning, because the Reichsbank did not have the means to manipulate the exchange rate in this fashion.[29a] But possibility (i) also seems to be artificial, although Canada indeed opted for this path in order to manoeuvre between the two superpowers, between the dollar and the pound. Germany would have fallen between two stools and would have enjoyed the advantages of neither decision; but at the same time she would have assumed all the political risks and she would have had to have made herself to a great extent dependent on Britain. It could not be ruled out that the pound might rise again (as it actually did in Spring 1932) and that, in the end, an upward revaluation of the Reichsmark against the dollar and the franc – or only a minimal degree of revaluation – might actually be the result of such a policy.

9   Cases VI and VII respectively are of greater interest to the historian since it was evidently along these paths that Britain invited Germany to accompany her – if the sources are to be believed. Without a detailed knowledge of the British sources, it is of course at present not yet possible to estimate how seriously such invitations were meant. In the nature of things, the British interest in Germany's joining the pound (even at the old exchange rate) should not be exaggerated. If there had been such an invitation, it cannot have been a very warm one. I think it significant, for instance, that the Deputy Governor of the Bank of England, Sir Ernest Harvey (who took charge of the bank in the absence of Montagu Norman during the decisive phase of leaving the gold standard), had already discussed the decision on 19 September 1931 with the Governor of the Federal Reserve Bank in New York, but only informed the German Reichsbank on the morning of (Sunday) 20 September. On that day, however, Harry A.

Siepmann (an advisor to the Governor of the Bank of England), really does appear to have asked the Vice-President of the Reichsbank Dreyse (Luther was on a short holiday and only returned to the bank in the afternoon) 'whether it was not thought desirable to link the German Mark to the pound'.[30]

This more or less tentative enquiry was presumably also conveyed to the American Embassy by Schäffer. Schäffer's diary entry for 23 September 1931 simply contains a reference to a response to an enquiry from the US Embassy regarding the question of a German float: Schäffer had explained 'that the Reichsbank and Reich government had the will to keep a firm grip on the Mark and to combat commercial competition through other means'.[31] But a telegram of the US Ambassador Sackett to the US Secretary of State on 23 September, which because of its importance was passed on to the White House, states: 'For your confidential information. I learn from a high government treasury official that on Sunday morning September 20th the Bank of England requested the Reichsbank to join England in foresaking the gold standard. This request caused the Reichsbank to consider the matter with the result as indicated above.'[32]

There is as yet no evidence for the conjecture that the British Government had, through some channel or other, declared itself in favour of a change in the German exchange rate regime. In view of Britain's interests, this would have been a fairly surprising attitude. Much more plausible is the position adopted by Sir Frederick Leith Ross of the British Treasury on 30 September 1931 in a memorandum to the Central Europe director of the Foreign Office, Orme Sargent: 'I do not think that we need urge Germany to follow us; they will probably have to do it in the long run but the longer they can keep themselves on the gold standard so much the better for our exports.'[33] In the published diplomatic correspondence between the British Embassy in Berlin and Whitehall there is, rather, an indication that German policy was indeed regarded with scepticism, and that no one sought to steer her currency policy in a different direction. It is true that in *February 1932* the Vice President of the Reichsbank, Dreyse, in a letter to the Undersecretary in the Foreign Ministry, Dr Dieckhoff, explained the earlier interpretation by Leith Ross of Reichsbank policy in this way: 'Perhaps there was more behind the statements of Leith Ross – who in consequence of his relationship with the Bank of England does stand fairly close intellectually to the matters outlined above – than his words appear to say. I have in mind a concealed canvassing for entry into the "Sterling Club".'[33a] But this seems too insubstantial a base of evidence to derive a thesis of a British invitation, even a belated British invitation.

Nor do we stand on firmer ground respecting the recommendation of the

B.I.S. alluded to by Luther in his autobiography, according to which, in opposition to the German government's decision not to follow the pound, 'the opposed viewpoint' had been 'very forcefully represented'.[34] It is true that there are indications that the Reichsbank directors, delegated to Basel, F. Hülse and K. Blessing, declared themselves to be in favour of following the pound,[35] but these were not official statements at the B.I.S. What emerges from Hans Schäffer's diaries concerning the mood at the B.I.S. conflicts with such an interpretation. On 23 September, F. Hülse had a telephone conversation with the official responsible for reparations in the Reich Finance Ministry, Berger, who reported to Schäffer: 'Hülse told Berger that the people in Basel were convinced that we must not go along with England, because stability was our only support'.[36] In the general context, given a knowledge of other accounts from Basel, this appears to me to be far more credible than Luther's account. It is true that one does have to take account of the fact that there were on the staff of the Basel bank experts whose estimation of the situation differed from that of those in executive authority. But it is on the latter that policy depended. And they still defended the gold standard through the whole of 1932!

It is not possible here to examine further the remaining serious or tentative, and frequently surely only suspected or imagined, attempts by foreign, and especially British, quarters to canvas the Germans on behalf of the Sterling Club. The only matter still to be discussed here is the account, which is also contained in the standard literature on the subject, that the Governor of the Bank of England, Montagu Norman, had himself recommended devaluation (did this mean joining the pound?) to Germany. To be sure, during the London Conference after the July crisis, Montagu Norman did also discuss the question of suspending the legal convertibility of the mark to gold and the minimum gold reserve regulations of the Reichsbank with the Germans; he even held a moratorium on foreign debts to be possible and necessary. Schäffer and Luther (on the basis of a telephone conversation with Vocke, a member of the London delegation) agree in their reports on this. From Luther we learn, in addition: 'A possible suspension of convertibility in the case of bank notes was also said to have been discussed. Sprague [an American advisor to the Bank of England, K.B.] stated that a certain devaluation of the mark abroad, perhaps by 10%, could come about in such a case'. Schäffer's diary reads as follows: 'The alternative, if foreign countries continue to make withdrawals, would be an external moratorium. And that was the only thing which Sprague had advised as an emergency measure; but that would destroy our foreign credit for a long time'.[37] Was that supposed to have been a recommendation to devalue on the part of Sprague?

In the decisive days after sterling began to float, Norman can have presented no advice to the Germans, because he was at sea on the return journey from a vacation and only took up his official business again on 28 September 1931.[38] On 11/12 October, Norman met Luther at the B.I.S. in Basel. Here – rather belatedly – he could have made recommendations to Luther, about which it must be said that we have no other evidence. In a detailed note by Hilger van Scherpenberg (a counsellor with the German Embassy in London) regarding a conversation with Montagu Norman on 19 October 1931 in London, it emerges that at this point Norman still believed that Germany would have to give up gold parity within a few weeks:

> Herr Reichsbankpräsident Luther was said to have discussed this question in detail with him in Basel, and even while he did admit that in consequence of the disciplined posture of the German population, things were possible in Germany which elsewhere would be out of the question, he had still not succeeded in recognising the factual basis for the Reichsbank's relative optimism.[39]

This would still not prove that Norman had given (albeit relatively late) advice, but it would not contradict such a supposition either. However, a later note by the Reichsbank Director W. Vocke regarding a conversation with Norman on 3 December does contradict it after all. Vocke describes the discussion about the probability of a stabilisation of the pound (Norman did not want to stabilise) and then writes: 'Norman emphasised in passing *afresh* [K.B.'s emphasis] that it had, quite as a matter of course, been correct of the Reichsbank at all costs to maintain the Reichsmark at its full value, and he wished us to use all our strength, and hoped that we should succeed in this in the future too.'[40]

With that, however, we are not yet quite at the end of our discussion of Cases VI and VII, that is, of the transition of the Mark to a sterling standard. For a mysterious and hitherto undescribed occurrence still remains to be discussed. On 15 January 1932, the British Ambassador in Berlin, Sir Horace Rumbold, sent to London a report of a conversation with Brüning:

> Finally, I referred to a lecture which Mr Keynes had delivered at Hamburg in which he had spoken of the United Kingdom having gone off the gold standard and had invited Germany to join what he called the 'Sterling Club'. Dr. Brüning said that this was out of the question. I understood him to say that if the pound sterling appre-

ciated considerably in terms of Marks, perhaps to 18, there might
be a possibility of linking the German currency to sterling, but
this was conjecture, and he was merely expressing a personal
opinion. I said, speaking personally, that it seemed to me that it
would be difficult to stabilise the pound anyhow before there had
been a settlement of our fiscal policy and of the reparations and
war debts question.[40a]

If Sir Horace had understood Brüning correctly, then this statement would
be highly interesting, for it would take the ground away from many dog-
matic statements and would allow Brüning to emerge as a much more
pragmatic politician in matters of currency policy. Unfortunately, to the
present date, we have no similar expressions from other sources; and it is
possible that Brüning had here only made an attempt to find out something
from the British Ambassador about the planned future exchange rate of
sterling.

10   In the historical and critical literature, Case VIII has received a
certain upgrading, above all in connection with a reassessment of the
achievements of a system of flexible exchange rates. It is important to
distinguish two variants here: (i) all currencies, and especially the dollar,
leave the gold standard and go over to a general system of flexible exchange
rates; (ii) the Reichsmark, with the pound and other currencies, leaves the
gold parity while the dollar, franc and some other currencies stay on the
gold standard. G. Haberler claims that the first variant could have brought
about a more rapid and more effective end to the crisis.[41] In the contemporary sources, I find no reference to this having seriously been proposed in
Germany at the time (although one cannot exclude the possibility that a
system of flexible exchange rates might have developed from a step-wise
abandonment of the gold standard). The second path may have been meant
when it was recommended that Germany should follow Great Britain's
example without this leading to a firm exchange rate link with the pound
sterling. Most of the countries of the so-called Sterling Club did not
actually enter into a formally fixed link with the pound. In this case also, it
is hard to establish who in Germany clearly, uncompromisingly, and con-
sistently argued in favour of this path. The circumstance that Case VIII
was often brought up as a bogy by those who defended the actual policy of
the government and the Reichsbank is, however, all the more noteworthy.
Nothing other than Case VIII could have been implied when people feared
a 'fall in the exchange rate to bottomless depths',[42] which certainly could
not have been assumed in the case of any of Paths I to VII. And many of

those who feared inflation developing out of the experiment appear to have had this case in mind.

In any event, Case VII is the one which had a relatively strong – negative – propaganda impact, and thus also dominated the discussions of alternative paths. The first public announcements by the Reich Chancellor and the Reichsbank President after the floating of the pound made a comparison with the great inflation in order to allow this extreme possibility to appear as the actual alternative to an adherence to the current system (Case IV).[43] Of course, for a more precise analysis of the probable results of Path VIII, it would be particularly important to explain what additional regulations (presented in the last columns of table 1) should have been put into effect.

11   In Germany, Path IX was really developed only after the National Socialist seizure of power. We shall not go into that here. But it was already discussed earlier, with the intention of preventing an undesired change in the Reichsmark's exchange rate by means of measures which were supposed, at least in part, to have a similar effect to an alteration of the exchange rate.[44] In the Reich Cabinet there was a discussion in January 1932 as to whether it would not be possible to correct upward revaluations of the RM by means of a tariff policy. While the cabinet deliberated the 'Presidential Decree Respecting Exceptional Tariff Measures', the departments differed in their opinions, and the question of possible retaliatory measures played a big part.[45] Nevertheless, the decree was voted through by the cabinet and signed by the Reich President on 18 January 1932. It empowered the government of the Reich 'in the case of pressing economic need: (1) to impose compensatory surcharges on individual goods or groups of goods originating in countries whose currencies have sunk below the gold parity ...' Such tariffs compensating for exchange rate alterations came into force in the case of butter as early as 23 January 1932. While on the import side certain substitute measures for devaluation were already taken, and others envisaged, the government took a passive stance respecting corresponding measures to compensate exporters. Even the highest echelons of the Reichsverband der Deutschen Industrie (Reich Association of German Industry) who supported the encouragement of exports *per se*, found it difficult to suggest measures which might immediately awaken a suspicion of dumping abroad, such as a system of import certificates.[46]

However, in a brilliant note, B. Josephy sketched a way in which, with the help of measures belonging to Path IX and affecting foreign trade, the problem of an increase in the burden of foreign and domestic debts in gold and dollars, which would follow from a devaluation, could be circumvented. It would have been possible to 'maintain a stable gold exchange rate and to combine a tax on the purchase of foreign currency with a corresponding premium on foreign currency obtained from exports'.[47] This is an early case of 'substitute-devaluations' seeking to unite the incompatible – similar to the way in which the Federal Republic of Germany acted in the case of its upward substitute-revaluation of 1968.

12   With that, our survey of the possibilities of action in exchange rate policy, that is, of the contents of table 11.1, is complete. Of course, it has already been noted that the cases mentioned cannot be evaluated unless one examines additional decisions on the right-hand edge of the table in every case; yet up to now we have avoided a systematic treatment of the problem. This we shall now, very briefly, undertake.

Measures which have up to now been characterised as additional decisions, and which might in specific cases have been genuinely complementary, frequently represented in these deliberations a substitute for the alteration of exchange rates. After all, for Great Britain, the floating of the pound explicitly represented an alternative to foreign exchange controls and an external moratorium. Germany's particular problem was that in September it already had both (although the moratorium only affected reparations debts and there was a standstill agreement for commercial short-term loans – a superficially more amicable form of a moratorium). Because as early as the autumn of 1931 the Reichsmark was no longer fully convertible, there was no 'state of emergency' of the sort that everyone saw in the British case.[48] In the subsequent period foreign exchange controls and the standstill or moratorium remained determinants of policy, and always reduced the pressure on the government and the Reichsbank to arrive at a decision. Since an alteration in exchange rates policy would have appeared a voluntary and not an emergency action, it was subject to a specific constraint of legitimacy. It is noteworthy that the introduction of foreign exchange control in July 1931 already had the legitimation of an unquestionably acute emergency. But beyond that, it was legitimised by the consent, and even the recommendation of the Americans and British, especially as it was still thought that Germany's main problem was that of capital flight.[49]

There was not one voice in Germany that believed a fully convertible RM was possible – whatever exchange rate policy might be envisaged. The continuation of exchange control also accompanied as a flanking measure all the proposals of devaluation, and it was even to be extended in some respects. Admittedly, one can only speculate fairly vaguely as to what concrete shape such control might have taken in each individual case. For the major problem was that short-term foreign debts were for the most part payable in foreign exchange, so that a devaluation in isolation could scarcely have checked credit withdrawals; in contrast, in Britain, it was usually a question of loans denominated in sterling. In Britain, a heavy devaluation of the pound meant the punishment of an excessive degree of distrust on the part of investors.

Whether limiting convertibility in Germany was needed only in order to prevent capital flight or an excessively rapid withdrawal of credit, or whether exchange control might also have been used to regulate the balance of trade, cannot be determined without a discussion of the various paths open in exchange rate policy, and of the concrete goals of alternative policies on the part of the government or the Reichsbank. It is well known that, within the system of unchanged gold parity in 1931/2, exchange control did not constrain importers – partly in consequence of the generally deflationary policy. On the whole, their foreign exchange requirements could always be satisfied until 1933. It is not possible, however, to conclude from this that, after a measure of devaluation of the Reichsmark, there would have been even fewer grounds for a limitation of mark convertibility on balance of trade grounds. If, simultaneously, a domestic recovery had set in, and if (as in other cases) the proceeds from exports had failed to rise in proportion to the domestic recovery, a foreign exchange problem would have arisen or have been exacerbated as a result of an increasingly unfavourable trade balance. On the whole, it seems sensible to assume that all exchange rate policy paths in Germany would have had to continue to be combined with foreign exchange controls.[50] Under these circumstances, one can only offer statements of *probable* effects in changes in the German exchange rate policy in 1931/2 if one gives fairly precise information on how the limitations on convertibility could and should have looked in detail.[50a]

Similarly, we surely have to assume that, whatever the decision on exchange rate policy, it would still have been necessary to strive to pacify organised short-term foreign creditors, or to declare a *de facto* moratorium on foreign debts. With this, however, we have already established that flexible exchange rates could not have achieved in Germany a similar effect to that in Britain: the automatic adjustment of the balance of payments (while the effect on the balance of trade in Britain was, after all, remarkably slight). Nobody in Germany who thought about exchange rate policy alternatives believed the loosening of the standstill or a relaxation of the moratorium (or threat of moratorium) to have been a realistic alternative. On the contrary, Carl Krämer indeed actually suggested linking devaluation to the declaration of a general moratorium on foreign debts.[51] The purpose of this measure was supposed, in the first place, to counteract the growth in the Reichsmark debt, which otherwise would have followed from a Mark devaluation. This might have presented a (theoretical) possibility to counter the argument, taken very seriously at the time, against devaluing the Reichsmark – even though it would have meant further risks to the German position. This example shows how important it is to take note of the surrounding conditions when considering the individual paths proposed.

Under the circumstances already described, can one even imagine that there might have been a free floating of the Reichsmark? Certainly, in the autumn of 1931, Germany possessed no reserves of any kind that might have allowed an intervention on foreign exchange markets. Whether it might later have possessed such means (as they streamed into Great Britain in the course of 1932) is very much open to doubt. But it can be assumed that in all probability, in the event of a floating, the Reichsbank would have behaved in exactly the same way as did those central banks whose currencies were freed from gold exchange parities. It would, like the other central banks, presumably first have pursued a sharply restrictive monetary policy with crisis discount rates in order to prevent too severe a fall in the exchange rate (from which everywhere an inflationary effect was anticipated).[52] This would perhaps also have been the only possibility for Germany to exert an influence on capital movements – movements which are not entirely controllable by the central bank. But control would have prevented precisely what could and should have been the objective of the float: the freeing of monetary and credit policy from balance of payments considerations. This was the function which had already been partly fulfilled by limiting convertibility; thus, in December 1931, we may observe the beginning of a policy of step-by-step lowering of the German discount rate, while Britain (with a free exchange rate) still clung to the high interest rates of September 1931!

It would be interesting to consider what effect the deregulation of the exchange rate in the context of a free float would really have had for Germany, focusing on the possibility sketched out above of influencing exchange rates by means of interest policy (and taking into account variations in assumptions about foreign exchange controls or moratoriums). Scenarios of this sort have not as yet been developed, but I believe that we lack any possibility of estimating the probable development of the Reichsmark's exchange rate after a float.

IV

The function of these models was not fully to describe and discuss the actors' motives in arriving at their decisions. And still less was there space here for a comprehensive evaluation, especially since a closer analysis of the comparative advantages of all the imaginable paths would be necessary for such a purpose. It proved necessary in the first place actually to prepare the ground for systematic work of that kind, and to give a sufficiently clear description of the various currency policy options.

In conclusion, reference should at least be made to the fact that the government would have been unable to base itself on any major political group, or on any group of academic opinion, had it taken any other course than the one actually chosen (Case IV with the possibility of Case III). It was a wholly different case in Britain where, from 1925, there had not only been academics who doubted the wisdom of a seemingly over-valued exchange rate, but also influential politicians and men engaged in practical business life, especially in industry, and finally even within the Bank of England, with the result that not even the City offered a united resistance to what Carl Melchior described in a conversation with Hans Schäffer on 23 September 1931 as the 'industrial party'.[53] There were no such constellations in Germany where even industry had, through its interest organisation, declared itself clearly in favour of the maintenance of Mark parity.[54] In the absence of any pressure at all in the opposite direction, it can scarcely be seen from where Brüning might have drawn the political legitimation for a heretical step.[55]

Of course, this does not absolve the historian from pursuing the question of whether things might not still have been done better, even if we recognise that Brüning could not actually have done it. That is an issue which has often apparently been examined, but which no one has yet tackled properly. It is true that we have knowledge not available to contemporaries, even if few of these erred as greatly as did one group of American experts, who wrote at the beginning of 1933: 'When all these factors are balanced against each other, the conclusion may be drawn that without the burden of reparation payments Germany may be regarded as a solvent and going concern ...'[56]

NOTES

1 Protectionism in historical perspective

1 A. W. Coats, 'Political Economy and the Tariff Reform Campaign of 1903', *Journal of Law and Economics*, 11 (1968), pp. 181–229. D. Winch, *Economics and Policy. A Historical Study* (London 1969), pp. 47ff.
2 F. Schneider, W. Pommerehne, B. Frey, 'Relata referimus: Ergebnisse und Analyse einer Befragung deutscher Ökonomen', *ZfgS*, 139 (1983), pp. 19–68.
3 See also W. M. Curtiss, 'Restrictions on International Trade. Why do they persist?' *Toward Liberty. Essays in Honor of Ludwig von Mises on the Occasion of his 90th Birthday, Vol. 2* (Menlo Park 1973), pp. 108–17.
4 *Stenographische Berichte über die Verhandlungen des Deutschen Reichstags*, 2. May 1897, p. 932.
5 The terms 'normative' and 'positive' theories are used here in the meaning of recent writing on political economy. See also C. C. v. Weizsäcker, 'Staatliche Regulierung – positive und normative Theorie', *Schweizerische Zeitschrift für Volkswirtschaft und Statistik*, 118 (1982), pp. 325–43.
6 Basic contributions to the positive theory of protection and its application to historical cases: C. Kindleberger, 'Group Behavior and International Trade', *JPE*, 59 (1951), pp. 30–47 – reprinted in C. Kindleberger, *Economic Response* (Cambridge, Mass. 1978), pp. 19–83; B. D. Baack and E. J. Ray, 'Tariff Policy and Comparative Advantage in the Iron and Steel Industry: 1870–1929', *EEH*, 6 (1973), pp. 3–23; J. J. Pincus, 'Pressure Groups and the Pattern of Tariffs', *JPE*, 83 (1975), pp. 757–78; R. E. Caves, 'Economic Models of Political Choice: Canada's Tariff Structure', *Canadian Journal of Economics*, 9 (1976), pp. 278–300; J. J. Pincus, *Pressure Groups and Politics in Antebellum Tariffs* (New York 1977); C. Kindleberger, 'The Rise of Free Trade in Western Europe, 1820–1875', *JEH*, 35 (1975), pp. 20–55 – reprinted in C. Kindleberger, *Economic Response*, pp. 39–65; M. A. Yeager, 'Trade Protection as an International Commodity: The Case of Steel', *JEH*, 40 (1980), pp. 33ff.; H. Glismann, 'Einige politische Determinanten der Protektion – Eine Fallstudie', in O. Issing (ed.), *Zukunftsprobleme der Marktwirtschaft* (Berlin 1981), pp. 615–32; K. Anderson and R. E. Baldwin, 'The Political Market for Protection in Industrial Countries: Empirical Evidence', *World Bank, Staff Working Paper*, No. 492, October 1981; B. D. Baack and J. Ray, 'The Political Economy of Tariff Policy: A Case Study of the U.S.', *EEH*, 20 (1983), pp. 73–93.
7 Customs tariffs as revenue have been examined in particular by P. Langen, *Das*

Zollsystem und die Zollpolitik in Deutschland seit der Reichsgründung von 1871 in ihrer Bedeutung für die öffentliche Mittelbeschaffung (Diss. Bonn 1957).

8 C. Brinckmann, *Die preussische Handelspolitik vor dem Zollverein und der Wiederaufbau vor hundert Jahren* (Berlin/Leipzig 1922); W. Treue, *Wirtschaftszustände und die Wirtschaftspolitik in Preussen 1815 bis 1825* (Stuttgart 1937); T. Ohnishi, 'Zolltarifpolitik Preussens bis zur Gründung des Deutschen Zollvereins', *Ein Beitrag zur Finanz- und Aussenhandelspolitik Preussens* (Göttingen 1972).

9 W. O. Henderson, *The Zollverein*, 3rd edn (London 1968).

10 See H. Best, *Interesssenpolitik und nationale Integration 1848/49, Handelspolitische Konflikte im frühindustriellen Deutschland* (Göttingen 1980); H.-W. Hahn, 'Wirtschaftliche Integration im 19. Jahrhundert', *Die hessischen Staaten und der Deutsche Zollverein* (Göttingen 1982), pp. 181ff.

11 Bismarck, *Die gesammelten Werke, Vol. 15: Erinnerung und Gedanke*. Kritische Neuausgabe aufgrund des gesamten schriftlichen Nachlasses, G. Ritter and R. Stadelmann (eds.) (Berlin 1932), p. 28.

12 The distinction between 'necessary' and 'possible' is made by D. C. Moore, 'The Corn Laws and High Farming', *Economic History Review, 2nd Series*, 18 (1965), pp. 544–61. See also on the repeal of the Corn Laws S. Fairlie, 'The Nineteenth Century Corn Law Reconsidered', *Economic History Review, 2nd Series*, 18 (1965), pp. 562ff.; S. Fairlie, 'The Corn Laws and British Wheat Production', *Economic History Review, 2nd Series*, 22 (1969), pp. 89ff. C. Kindleberger, 'The Rise of Free Trade' (see footnote 6); W. Vamplew, 'The Protection of English Cereal Producers: The Corn Laws Reassessed', *Economic History Review, 2nd Series*, 33 (1980), pp. 382ff.; D. McCloskey, 'Magnanimous Albion: Free Trade and British National Income 1841–1881', *Explorations in Economic History*, 17 (1980), pp. 303ff.

13 For an economic analysis of this process see M. Olson and C. C. Harris Jr, 'Free Trade in "Corn": a Statistical Study of the Prices and Production of Wheat in Great Britain from 1873 to 1914', *Quarterly Journal of Economics*, 73 (1959), pp. 145ff.

14 C. Kindleberger, 'The Rise of Free Trade', p. 36, attributes an important role to the intellectual triumph of political economy.

15 B.-J. Wendt, 'Freihandel und Friedenssicherung. Zur Bedeutung des Cobden-Vertrages von 1860 zwischen England und Frankreich', *Vierteljahrschrift für Sozial- und Wirtschaftsgeschichte*, 61 (1974), pp. 29–64; see also A. L. Dunham, 'The Anglo-French Treaty of Commerce of 1860 and the Progress of the Industrial Revolution in France' (Ann Arbor 1930 – new edition, New York 1971); M. Rist, 'Une expérience française de libération des échanges au XIX siècle. Le Traité de 1860', *Revue d'Economie Politique*, 66 (1956), pp. 908–61.

16 K. Graf, *Die zollpolitischen Zielsetzungen im Wandel der Geschichte* (Zurich 1970), p. 197.

17 W. Lotz, 'Die Ideen der deutschen Handelspolitik von 1860–1891', *Die Handelspolitik der wichtigeren Kulturstaaten in den letzten Jahrzehnten*, Vol. II (*Schriften des Vereins für Socialpolitik*, Vol. 50) (Leipzig 1982), p. 28.

18 On Prussia – Germany, see W. Zorn, 'Wirtschafts- und sozialgeschichtliche Zusammenhänge der deutschen Reichsgründungszeit (1850–1879)', in H. Böhme (ed.), *Probleme der Reichsgründungszeit 1848–1879* (Cologne 1968), pp. 296–316.

19 See V. Hentschel, *Die deutschen Freihändler und der volkswirtschaftliche Kongress 1858–1885* (Stuttgart 1975).

20 Thus S. Pollard, *Peaceful Conquest. The Industrialization of Europe 1760–1970* (Oxford 1981), p. 260.

21 K. W. Hardach, 'Die Haltung der deutschen Landwirtschaft in der Getreidezoll-Diskussion 1878/79', *Zeitschrift für Agrargeschichte und Agrarsoziologie*, 15 (1967), pp. 33–48; K. W. Hardach, *Die Bedeutung wirtschaftlicher Faktoren bei der Wiedereinführung der Weizen- und Getreidezölle in Deutschland 1879* (Berlin 1967). See also I. N. Lambi, *Free Trade and Protection in Germany 1868–1879* (Wiesbaden 1963); H. Böhme, *Deutschlands Weg zu Grossmacht, Studien zum Verhältnis von Wirtschaft und Staat während der Reichsgründungszeit 1848–1879* (Cologne 1966).

22 P. Schöller, 'L'Évolution séculaire des taux de fret et d'assurance maritimes 1819–1940', *Bulletin de l'Institut des Recherches Economiques et Sociales Louvain*, No. 5, August 1951, pp. 519–47; D. C. North, 'Ocean Freight Rates and Economic Development 1750–1913', *Journal of Economic History*, 18 (1958), pp. 537ff.; C. K. Harley, 'Transportation, the World Wheat Trade, and the Kuznets Cycle, 1850–1913', *Explorations in Economic History*, 17 (1980), pp. 218–50.

23 J. Nadal, 'Der Fehlschlag der Industriellen Revolution in Spanien 1830–1913', in C. Cipolla and K. Borchardt (eds.), *Die Entwicklung der industriellen Gesellschaften* (*Europäische Wirtschaftsgeschichte*, Vol. 5) (Stuttgart 1977), p. 358.

24 See on this above all A. Zimmermann, *Die Handelspolitik des Deutschen Reichs vom Frankfurter Frieden bis zur Gegenwart* (Berlin 1899); W. Gerloff, *Die Finanz- und Zollpolitik des Deutschen Reiches nebst ihren Beziehungen zu Landes- und Gemeindefinanzen von der Gründung des Norddeutschen Bundes bis zur Gegenwart* (Jena 1913); M. Stürmer, *Regierung und Reichstag im Bismarckstaat 1871 bis 1880, Cäsarismus oder Parlamentarismus* (Düsseldorf 1974); O. Pflanze, *Bismarcks Herrschaftstechnik als Problem der gegenwärtigen Historiographie* (Munich 1982), pp. 14ff.

25 At this point it must be left open whether another thesis is correct, that Bismarck intended at the time to unite the two most powerful interest groups in German society, the owners of large estates and the leaders of industry, in a new state-supporting coalition and thus exclude the liberals. This thesis has been challenged on good grounds. But even in this case it would be necessary to stress the supply side in the market for protection.

26 A. Lohren, *Das System des Schutzes nationaler Arbeit* (Potsdam 1880); K. W. Hardach, 'Beschäftigungspolitische Aspekte der deutschen Aussenhandelspolitik ausgangs der 1870er Jahre', *Schmollers Jahrbuch*, 86, II (1966), pp. 641–54.

27 Cited in O. Pflanze, *Bismarcks Herrschaftstechnik*, p. 19.

28 S. B. Webb, 'Agricultural Protection in Wilhelminian Germany: Forging an Empire with Pork and Rye', *Journal of Economic History*, 42 (1982), p. 314.

29 On the following, see W. Lotz, 'Die Handelspolitik des Deutschen Reiches unter Graf Caprivi und Fürst Hohenlohe (1890–1900)', *Beiträge zur neuesten Handelspolitik*, Vol. III (*Schriften des Vereins für Socialpolitik*, Vol. 92) (Leipzig 1901), pp. 47–218; R. Weitowitz, *Deutsche Politik und Handelspolitik unter Reichskanzler Leo von Caprivi 1890–1894* (Düsseldorf 1978); Helmut Böhme: '"Grenzen des Wachstums", aussenwirtschaftliche Beziehungen und gesellschaftliche Systemstabilisierung', Bemerkungen zum deutsch-russischen Verhältnis 1886–1894, in D. Stegmann, B.-W. Wendt and P.-C. Witt (eds.), *Industrielle Gesellschaft und politisches System: Beiträge zur politischen Sozialgeschichte* (Bonn 1978), pp. 175–92).

30 M. Stürmer, *Das ruhelose Reich, Deutschland 1866–1918* (Berlin 1983), pp. 270ff.

31 Among the measures which can be described as a support for agrarian interests are: (1) the provision of settlement credits under the Law for the

Encouragement of the Creation of Farm Leases; (2) subsidies for rural elementary schools and land improvement; (3) cancellation of the necessity to demonstrate the origin of grain in the case of re-imports (1894); (4) amendment of the Animal contagious diseases act (1894); (5) in Prussia the Miquel tax reforms, which lightened the tax burden on agriculture.

32 G. Franz, *Quellen zur Geschichte des deutschen Bauernstandes in der Neuzeit* (Darmstadt 1963), p. 501. On the representations of agrarian interests, see H.-J. Puhle, *Agrarische Interessenpolitik und preussischer Konservatismus im Wilhelminischen Reich (1893–1914), Ein Beitrag zur Analyse des Nationalismus in Deutschland am Beispiel des Bundes der Landwirte und der Deutsch-Konservativen Partei* (Hanover 1966).

33 Weitowitz is correct in distancing himself from the occasionally over-rash conclusions in the literature on the economic significance of trade treaties. R. Weitowitz, *Deutsche Politik*, pp. 300ff.

34 Thus C. Kindleberger, *Power and Money* (London 1970), p. 122.

35 M. Corden, *The Theory of Protection* (Oxford 1971); J. C. Hunt: 'Peasant, Grain Tariffs, and Meat Quotas: Imperial German Protectionism Reexamined', *Central European History*, 7 (1974), pp. 311–31; S. B. Webb, 'Agricultural Protection' (see note 28).

36 On methods of export promotion, see H.-P. Ullmann, 'Staatliche Exportförderung und private Exportinitiative. Probleme des Staatsinterventionismus im Deutschen Kaiserreich am Beispiel der staatlichen Aussenhandelsförderung (1880–1919)', *Vierteljahrschrift für Sozial- und Wirtschaftsgeschichte*, 65 (1978), pp. 157–216.

37 See on this H. Dietzel, 'Agrar-Industriestaat oder Industriestaat?' *Handwörterbuch der Staatswissenschaften*, 4th edn, Vol. 1 (Jena 1923), pp. 62–72; K. D. Barkin, *The Controversy over German Industrialization 1890–1902* (Chicago 1970).

38 A similar debate was conducted substantially earlier in England. See E. Nolte, *Marxismus und Industrielle Revolution* (Stuttgart 1983).

39 The term 'General Compensation' was used by C. C. von Weizsäcker in his contribution 'Was leistet die Konzeption der "Property Rights" für aktuelle wirtschaftspolitische Probleme?' at the Basel meeting of the Verein für Socialpolitik, September 1983.

40 T. Nipperdey, 'Interessenverbände und Parteien in Deutschland vor dem Ersten Weltkrieg', *Politische Vierteljahrschrift*, 2 (1961), pp. 262–80; H. Kaelble, 'Industrielle Interessenverbände vor 1941', in W. Ruegg and O. Neuloh (eds.), *Zur soziologischen Theorie und Analyse des 19. Jahrhunderts* (Göttingen 1971), pp. 180–92; D. Stegmann, 'Die Erben Bismarcks', *Parteien und Verbände in der Spätphase des Wilhelminischen Deutschland, Sammlungspolitik 1879–1918* (Cologne 1970); 'Linksliberale Bankiers, Kaufleute und Industrielle 1880–1900. Ein Beitrag zur Vorgeschichte des Handelsvertragsvereins', *Tradition*, 21 (1976), pp. 4–36; P. Ullmann, *Der 'Bund der Industriellen' 1895–1914* (Göttingen 1976); S. Mielke, *Der Hansa-Bund für Gewerbe, Handel und Industrie 1909–1914* (Göttingen 1976).

41 S. Pollard, *Peaceful Conquest*, p. 268.

42 See recently on this M. Olson, *The Rise and Decline of Nations: Economic Growth, Stagflation, and Social Rigidities* (New Haven 1982), pp. 137, 140ff.; D. C. Mueller (ed.), *The Political Economy of Growth* (New Haven 1983), with contributions from M. C. Olson and some of his critics.

43 P. Bairoch, *Commerce extérieur et développement économique de l'Europe au XIXᵉ siècle* (Paris 1976), pp. 288ff. See also 'Commerce extérieur et développement économique. Quelques enseignements de l'expérience libre-

échangiste de la France au XIXe siècle', *Revue Economique*, 21 (1970), pp. 1–33.

44 J. M. Keynes: Lecture Notes for 'What Should the Conference Do Now?', 28 June 1933, in *The Collected Writings of John Maynard Keynes, Vol. 21: Activities 1931–1939. World Crisis and Policies in Britain and America* (London 1982), p. 269.

45 R. E. Baldwin, 'Protectionist Pressures in the United States', in R. C. Amacher, G. Haberler and D. Willett (eds.), *Challenges to a Liberal International Economic Order* (AEI-symposia; 79C) (Washington 1979), p. 235. Similarly B. Ohlin, 'Some Aspects of Policies for Freer Trade', in R. E. Baldwin, *et al.*, *Trade, Growth, and the Balance of Payments* (Festschrift for G. Haberler) (Chicago 1966), pp. 82–92.

46 R. E. Baldwin also recommends such compensations for the current situation. See R. E. Baldwin, 'Protectionist Pressures', p. 237.

47 Compare on these events C. Kindleberger, *Die Weltwirtschaftskrise 1929–1939* (Munich 1973), pp. 227ff.

48 'Mr Roosevelt is Magnificently Right', Article in Daily Mail, 4 July 1933, printed in *Collected Writings of John Maynard Keynes, Vol. 21: Activities 1931– 1939. World Crisis and Policies in Britain and America* (London 1982), pp. 273–7.

49 Compare H. J. Schröder: *Deutschland und die Vereinigten Staaten 1933–1939, Wirtschaft und Politik in der Entwicklung des deutsch-amerikanischen Gegensatzes* (Wiesbaden 1970); C. Kindleberger, *Die Weltwirtschaftskrise* (see footnote 47); D. Junker, *Der unteilbare Weltmarkt. Das ökonomische Interesse in der Aussenpolitik der USA 1933–1941* (Stuttgart 1975); J. S. Davis, *The World Between the Wars, 1919–1939: An Economist's View* (Baltimore 1975); B. M. Rowland, 'Preparing the American Ascendancy: The Transfer of Economic Power from Britain to the United States, 1933–1944', in B. M. Rowland (ed.), *Balance of Power or Hegemony: The Interwar Monetary System* (New York 1976), pp. 195–228; C. Kindleberger, 'U.S. Foreign Economic Policy, 1776–1976', *Foreign Affairs* 55 (1976/7), pp. 395–417.

50 Thus a title in D. Junker, *Der unteilbare Weltmarkt*, p. 81. For the deeper logic of American growth policy as a national and international peace strategy, see Ch. S. Maier, 'The Politics of Productivity: Foundations of American International Economic Policy After World War II', *International Organization*, 31 (1977), pp. 607–33, reprinted in P. Katzenstein (ed.), *Between Power and Plenty: Foreign Economic Policies of Advanced Industrial States* (Madison 1978).

51 T. Ferguson, 'Von Versailles zum New Deal: Der Triumph des multinationalen Liberalismus in Amerika', *Amerika – Traum und Depression, 1920–40*. Katalog einer Ausstellung, Berlin 1980, pp. 436–59, based on his unpublished Ph.D. Thesis, 'Critical Alignment: The Fall of the House of Morgan and the Origins of the New Deal', Massachusetts Institute of Technology.

52 The considerable reduction of barriers to trade did not, it is true, occur quickly, and there was constantly a threat of relapse. But in 1936 the 'Tripartite Monetary Agreement' was concluded between the USA, Great Britain and France. After a series of commercial treaties mostly with raw material producers (with a corresponding opening of their markets to American exports) in 1938 a commercial treaty was concluded between Great Britain and the USA.

2 Was there a capital shortage in the first half of the nineteenth century in Germany?

1 By Germany, the area of the German Reich within the borders of 1871 without Alsace–Lorraine is understood here.

2 The importance of the mid-century period is also given prominence *inter alia* by Sombart, Sartorius v. Waltershausen, Pohle. W. W. Rostow, *Stages of Economic Growth* (Cambridge 1960), dates the 'take-off' of Germany to the years 1850–73, although in a more recent publication, Rostow has undertaken a different periodisation, see Rostow, *The World Economy. History and Prospect* (London 1978), p. 407: 'Take-off 1840–1870'.

3 In preference to many other references: J. H. Clapham, *The Economic Development of France and Germany 1815–1914* (Cambridge 1936[4]), p. 88; J. Kulischer, *Allgemeine Wirtschaftsgeschichte des Mittelalters und der Neuzeit*, Vol. 2 (new edition, Darmstadt 1958), p. 475; F. Schnabel, *Deutsche Geschichte im Neunzehnten Jahrhundert*, Vol. 3 (Freiburg 1950), pp. 262ff.; W. O. Henderson, *The State and the Industrial Revolution in Prussia 1740–1870* (Liverpool 1958), p. 21; W. Treue, 'Wirtschafts- und Sozialgeschichte Deutschlands', in *Gebhardt's Handbuch der deutschen Geschichte*, Vol. 3 (Stuttgart 1960[8]), pp. 363, 367, 376, 379, etc. According to A. L. Dunham, *The Industrial Revolution in France 1815–1848* (New York 1955), p. 213, the majority of authors dealing with France maintain the same thesis.

4 J. Kahn, *Geschichte des Zinsfußes in Deutschland seit 1815* (Stuttgart 1884), pp. 70, 97; B. Brockhage, *Zur Entwicklung des preußisch-deutschen Kapitalexports, 1. Teil: Der Berliner Markt für ausländische Staatspapiere 1816 bis um 1840* (Leipzig 1910), pp. 182, 215; J. Riesser, *Zur Entwicklungsgeschichte der deutschen Großbanken mit besonderer Rücksicht auf Konzentrationsbestrebungen* (Jena 1905), p. 29; A. Sartorius v. Waltershausen, *Deutsche Wirtschaftsgeschichte 1815–1914* (Jena 1923[2]), pp. 31, 55; F. Lütge, *Deutsche Sozial- und Wirtschaftsgeschichte* (Berlin 1960[2]), p. 400, but, see also pp. 405f.; H. Mottek, 'Zum Verlauf und zu einigen Hauptproblemen der industriellen Revolution in Deutschland', H. Mottek, H. Blumberg, H. Wutzmer and W. Becker, *Studien zur Geschichte der Industriellen Revolution in Deutschland* (Berlin 1960), p. 27. To substantiate their view, most of these authors refer to the development of the interest rates for securities.

5 Because this concerns a problem of factoral proportionality, this approach is omitted from further consideration. In the literature on economic development, the lack of means of production is a characteristic of underdevelopment, and therefore cannot explain it.

6 See W. A. Lewis, *The Theory of Economic Growth* (London 1955), pp. 213ff.

7 For Prussia, there is a little-substantiated estimate by L. Krug at the beginning of the century, in L. Krug, *Betrachtungen über den National-Reichtum des Preußischen Staates und über den Wohlstand seiner Bewohner*, Part 1 (Berlin 1805), p. 286. He assumes precious metals resources of 90 million Rthl., of which only 30 million is supposed to have been demonetarised. A. Soetbeer indeed refused to supply estimates about the extent of non-monetary resources even for later periods, see his, *Materialien zur Erläuterung und Beurteilung der wirtschaftlichen Edelmetallverhältnisse und der Währungsfrage* (Berlin 1886[2]), p. 32. R. Tilly has recently estimated the circulation of money in Germany in 1845 at 185 million Taler, the circulation of money-substitutes at 240 million, see his, *Kapital, Staat und sozialer Protest in der deutschen Industrialisierung* (Göttingen 1980), p. 43.

8 With E. Salin, 'Unterentwickelte Länder. Begriff und Wirklichkeit', *Kyklos*, 12 (1959), pp. 416f., one would have to view Germany as a country with an active population and hoards.

8a The statement that consumption could have been decreased has been criticised by F.-W. Henning, 'Kapitalbildungsmöglichkeiten der bäuerlichen Bevölkerung in Deutschland am Anfang des 19. Jahrhunderts', in W. Fischer (ed.), *Beiträge zu Wirtschaftswachstum und Wirtschaftsstruktur, SchVfSp N.F.*, 63 (Berlin 1971), p. 81. In clarification, it should be admitted that my statement does not refer to all individuals. Pre-industrial poverty was, as is well known, considerable. But here it is a matter of aggregates, as the word 'average' signals. The facts supplied indicate that it would have been conceivable (relatively) to decrease consumption (in the economy as a whole) further, even if it cannot be maintained that this would have been easy. Furthermore, the argument under '2' does not stand for itself alone and, as one recognises under '4', carries only a very small burden of proof.

9 Of the total consumption in Prussia in the years 1806 to 1849 a share – interestingly showing a downward trend – of 5 to 8 per cent fell to spirits, beer, wine, tobacco, herbs, imported fruit, if we can trust E. Engel and Dieterici's material, see their 'Zur statistischen Ermittlung der Consumption pro Kopf der Bevölkerung im preußischen Staate', *ZPStB*, 4 (1864), pp. 128ff. But, of course, this amount naturally does not include luxury goods alone – and neither does it comprehend all luxury goods. The indication that very considerable sums were paid out for the importation of groceries may also be of significance. On this, see M. Kutz, *Deutschlands Außenhandel von der französischen Revolution bis zur Gründung des Zollvereins* (Wiesbaden 1974), p. 365. According to his calculations, in 1830 the total value of German imports of groceries amounted to 44.6 million Talers.

9a For complementary estimates of the national income and the average per capita income in Prussia in the first half of the nineteenth century, see now G. Hohorst, *Wirtschaftswachstum und Bevölkerungsentwicklung in Preußen 1816 bis 1914* (New York 1977), pp. 273ff. E. Schremmer, 'Agrareinkommen und Kapitalbildung im 19. Jahrhundert in Südwestdeutschland', *JNSt*, 176 (1964), pp. 196ff, rightly draws our attention to the importance of the concept of 'disposable income'. Really, there must have been a fairly considerable *forced saving*.

10 On concealed unemployment and its significance for the economy as a whole, see also Mottek, 'Zum Verlauf'. On such possibilities of the extension of land, of house-building and on building up livestock Henning, 'Kapitalbildungs-möglichkeiten', is also informative.

11 'Statistische Übersicht der Fabrikations- und gewerblichen Zustände in den verschiedenen Staaten des Dt. Zollvereins im Jahre 1846', *Mittteilungen des statistischen Bureaus in Berlin*, 4 (1851), pp. 252ff.; see also G. Neuhaus, 'Die berufliche und soziale Gliederung der Bevölkerung im Zeitalter des Kapitalismus', GdS, IX/1 (Tübingen 1926), pp. 363ff. A recent summary with many references to sources: K. H. Kaufhold, 'Handwerk und Industrie 1800–1850', *HdWSG*, 2 (Stuttgart 1976), pp. 321ff.

12 This estimate was (in 1961) based on very rough clues and was not intended to claim to provide a quotable statement about the actual level of the fixed and liquid assets of the textile industry. The intention was only to state the *order of magnitude* of capital resources, in order to be able to draw conclusions about the conceivable outlay of investment. A more precisely broken down estimate for the years 1846, 1861 and 1875 has since appeared which, while it, too, has to work with assumptions, draws on far more sources. Taken as a whole, it

confirms the order of magnitude of the old estimate. See H. Blumberg, *Die deutsche Textilindustrie in der industriellen Revolution* (Berlin 1965), pp. 43–52. Blumberg estimates the sum total of the fixed assets and inventory of the German textile industry (factory industry, especially in spinning and handweaving as the main profession) for 1846 at 156 million Talers and for 1861 at 250 million Talers. G. Kirchhain, 'Das Wachstum der deutschen Baumwollindustrie im 19. Jahrhundert. Eine historische Modellstudie zur empirischen Wachstumsforschung' (Thesis, Münster 1973), p. 113 estimates the average assets of cotton-spinning, that is of the most mechanised branch of the textile industry, for the period 1846/8 at 26.9 million Marks (ca. 9 million Talers).

13 W. G. Hoffmann and J. H. Müller, *Das deutsche Volkseinkommen 1851–1957* (Tübingen 1959), p. 14. It is true that we, unlike Hoffmann/Müller, did not extrapolate the calculation from Prussia to the area of the German Empire within the borders of 1871, but only to the area of the Zollverein, for which the data above for the assets of the textile industry are valid.

13a Hoffmann/Müller put the figures of national income for the years 1851/5 at, on average, 9.6 thousand million Marks. By contrast, W. G. Hoffmann, F. Grumbach and H. Hesse, *Das Wachstum der deutschen Wirtschaft seit der Mitte des 19. Jahrhunderts* (Berlin 1965), pp. 506f. estimate the national income in the same period at 5.2 thousand million Marks on average. It is not necessary to go into the reasons for the large divergencies and to decide in favour of one figure here – but the uncertainty of all data for estimates should be brought to mind.

13b If one follows the new estimates by R. Tilly, 'Capital Formation in Germany in the Nineteenth Century', *CEHE*, VII/1 (Cambridge 1978), p. 427 then, out of the net investment of the economy in general, the following portions fell to the net investment of 'industry' in Prussia (in constant prices) in the periods: 1816–22: 2.2 per cent; 1822–31: 5.0 per cent; 1830/1–1840: 3.0 per cent; 1840–49: 3.3 per cent. Thus, it may be taken as proven that the funds required for industrial investments could hardly have been in any way limited by the macro-economic savings-capacity even in the event of a decisive extension in comparison to what we have observed.

14 Here, too, only very rough estimates are possible. But the order of magnitude can be approximately gauged from 'Kammerrede des Staatsministers Fürst Oettingen-Wallerstein v. 4. 9. 1839', printed in *Beiträge zur Statistik des Königreichs Bayern*, Vol. 86 (Munich 1914), pp. 267f. From this emerges an upper limit in the value of livestock in Bavaria at the end of the thirties of 200 million Talers. For Prussia, a figure of ca. 380 million Talers is given for the middle of the century, see 'Die Viehhaltung im Preußischen Staate in der Zeit von 1816 bis 1858', *ZPStB*, 1 (1861), pp. 229f. Krug (see footnote 7) names livestock assets of 180 million Talers for Prussia in 1805. For a new summary, Tilly, *Capital Formation* (see footnote 13b), p. 393. He puts the value of livestock in Prussia, 1816, at 707 million Marks, 1849 at 1.19 thousand million Marks. The total reproducible material wealth of agriculture in Prussia (capital stock without land values) was estimated by Tilly at 2.7 thousand million Marks in 1816, at 4.1 thousand million Marks in 1849.

15 F. Engel, *ZPStB*, 1 (1861), pp. 31f. mentions agricultural fixed assets totalling 4.5 thousand million Talers (= 13.5 thousand million Marks), Krug (1803), assets of 2 thousand million Talers. The change in value could be traced back to many factors, if it seems numerically reliable at all.

16 For Germany, beside Krug's work and occasional similar estimates of regional significance, there are only statistics for national wealth again from the end of

the nineteenth century and partly reaching into the twentieth century from Helfferich, Jastrow, Schmoller, Weyermann, *inter alia*.

17 On fire insurance values F. W. Reden, *Deutschland und das übrige Europa* (Wiesbaden 1854), p. 236. This information was compared with that of E. Engel for Saxony (*Das Königreich Sachsen in statistischer und staatswissenschaftlicher Beziehung*, Vol. 1 (1853), p. 240) and correspondingly corrected. An important older source for methodology is v. Hülsen, 'Geschichte, Umfang und Bedeutung des öffentlichen Feuerversicherungswesens', *ZPStB*, 7 (1867), pp. 320ff. On the scientific value of fire insurance statistics basically, K. Maywald, 'Fire Insurance and the Capital Coefficient in Great Britain 1866–1952', *EHR*, 2nd Series, 9 (1956/7), pp. 89ff.

17a Our estimate of the net investment (1961) is below the average annual figure for the net investment in buildings given by Hoffmann, *Wachstum* (see footnote 13a), pp. 218ff., for the period 1851–5 (there, 347 million Marks) but is probably closer to the order of magnitude at the end of the forties. Moreover, our estimate did not refer to Germany in the borders of 1871. Tilly, *Capital Formation* (see footnote 13b), pp. 399ff., it is true, finds net investments in buildings for Prussia 1843–9 of only 69 million Marks on average, which (calculated on the basis of population quotas) would give only 153 million Marks for Germany. Of course, these were relatively bad years, whereas considerably more is supposed to have been invested in 1840–3 (calculated for Germany, an average annual sum of 225 million Marks), which again fits into the order of magnitude of our own estimate (1961).

17b Supplementarily, reference could also be made to the now available estimates of public infrastructural investments in K. Borchard, 'Staatsverbrauch und öffentliche Investitionen in Deutschland 1780–1850' (Thesis, Göttingen 1968), pp. 225ff.

18 'I think it is fair to say that on the whole the demand side has not attracted anything like the attention that the supply side has commanded in historical enquiry.' G. Ohlin, 'Balanced Economic Growth in History', *AER*, 49 (1959), Pap. a. Proc. p. 345.

19 This could, however, be said for France with a certain degree of justice, see R. Cameron, 'Profit, croissance et stagnation en France au XIXe siècle', *Economie Appliquée*, 10 (1957), pp. 409ff.

20 On this, instead of the out-of-date work of G. Bondi, *Deutschlands Außenhandel 1815 bis 1870* (Berlin 1958), see the more recent works, Kutz, *Deutschlands Außenhandel*; B. v. Borries, *Deutschlands Außenhandel 1836 bis 1856. Eine statistische Untersuchung zur Frühindustrialisierung* (Stuttgart 1970); R. H. Dumke, 'Anglo-deutscher Handel und Frühindustrialisierung in Deutschland 1822–1865', *GuG*, 5 (1979), pp. 175ff.

21 E. Richter, *Das Preußische Staatsschuldwesen und die Preußischen Staatspapiere* (1869); W. Gerloff, 'Der Staatshaushalt und das Finanzwesen Deutschlands', *HdFW*, 1st Edn, Vol. 3, p. 6. Of course, Prussia appears to have been an exception in its lasting tendency to consolidate the budget (Borchard, *Staatsverbrauch*). There, the total sum of the debts of the individual German states in 1850 is given at 603.6 million Talers (p. 106).

22 In 1961, I wrote that 'agricultural export' had sunk to 14 per cent, and gave as my reference for it a report from Jacobs to the British Privy Council, communicated in a paper by Avenarius, which M. Weyermann, *Zur Geschichte des Immobiliarkreditwesens in Preußen mit besonderer Nutzanwendung auf der Theorie der Bodenverschuldung* (Karlsruhe 1910), p. 164 had quoted, and characterised this information as being presumably not very reliable. In fact, it cannot be sustained with regard to the total *agricultural* export, as Kutz (see

footnote 9), p. 296 shows. Wool actually balanced the really substantial decline in the export of cereals and wood at this time. For the export of *cereals*, Jacobs' information agrees almost completely with Kutz's estimate.

23 E. Baumstark, *Staatswirtschaftliche Versuche über Staatskredit, Staatsschulden und Staatspapiere* (Heidelberg 1833), p. 381.

24 On the underlying model, see W. Abel, *Agrarkrisen und Agrarkonjunktur in Mitteleuropa vom 13. bis zum 19. Jahrhundert* (Hamburg 1966[2]); W. Abel, *Massenarmut und Hungerkrisen im vorindustriellen Europa* (Hamburg 1974).

25 According to E. Gothein, *Verfassungs- und Wirtschaftsgeschichte der Stadt Cöln vom Untergange der Reichsfreiheit bis zur Errichtung des Deutschen Reiches* (Cologne 1916), p. 367.

26 'During the heyday of sales to America in the years 1845 to 1853, and even to 1860, most of the larger wealths were accumulated . . .' in the Aachen cloth industry, see A. Thun, *Die Industrie am Niederrhein und ihre Arbeiter*, Part 1 (Leipzig 1879), p. 73. One firm earned 60,000 Talers annually, another, in a few years, 250,000 (Ibid. p. 26).

27 The thesis advocated by J. Kulischer, 'Der Kapitalgewinn im 19. Jahrhundert', *JNSt*, 3/25 (1903), pp. 145–92 and 289–322 that there were high extra profits when new techniques were introduced is assuredly not correct in this generalised form.

28 On the development of interest rates, above all of public loans, but also of other credits, see Kahn, *Geschichte des Zinsfußes*; E. Voye, *über die Höhe der verschiedenen Zinssätze und ihre wechselseitige Abhängigkeit. Die Entwicklung des Zinsfußes in Preußen von 1807 bis 1900* (Jena 1912); S. Homer, *A History of Interest Rates* (New Brunswick 1963), pp. 254ff. There is valuable information on the international comparison. A. Spiethoff, *Die wirtschaftlichen Wechsellagen*, Vol. 1(Tübingen 1955), p. 113 and Mottek, 'Zum Verlauf', p. 27, base their surely correct view of the relative excess of capital even in the thirties on the observation of low interest rates. But here one must take note of several things: (1) When the credit markets are not interconnected or at any rate arbitrage only arises to a limited extent, the fall of interest rates in one market indicated nothing about the situation in another. From the same time, we know of credits with more than 20 per cent interest! (2) With regard to interest on mortgages, it should be noted that the legal upper limit on interest was often exceeded through manipulations of the value of loans. (On the significance of the legislation on usury in our period see F. Blaich, 'Zinsfreiheit als Problem der deutschen Wirtschaftspolitik zwischen 1857 und 1871', *SchJb*, 91 (1971), pp. 269ff.) (3) Bank interest often did not show the market condition since, after all, a rationing of credit ensued in periods of strain without the rates being increased. So, 'on higher decree', the Bavarian Credit and Exchange Bank left its rate unchanged, although by no means all those in search of credit were satisfied (see *Festschrift* for the fiftieth anniversary of the Bank (1885), p. 22). Of the same bank, it is reported from Nürnberg in 1840 that at 4 per cent (the legal interest rate for it) no business could be done, as money was to be had at 3.5 per cent on this market. (A. Jegel, *Die wirtschaftliche Entwicklung von Nürnberg, Fürth, Stein und des Nürnberger Raumes seit 1806* (Nürnberg undated), p. 21).

29 *Verhandlungen der Stände des Kgr. Bayern im Jahre 1819*, No. 10, pp. 427ff.

30 A very few figures should illustrate this: in 1833 the production of iron in Prussia amounted to only 37 per cent of the production of 1828 – according to M. Sering, *Geschichte der preußisch-deutschen Eisenzölle von 1818 bis zur Gegenwart* (Leipzig 1882), p. 275. – The production of cotton goods in 1847

amounted to only 60 per cent of that of 1846. If one ranks the individual years according to the extent of production, then the following order results, going from the years of the lowest to those of the highest production: 1837–9, 1847, 1841, 1844, 1840, 1842, 1848, 1843, 1845, 1850, 1849, 1846 – according to Spiethoff, *Die wirtschaftlichen Wechsellagen*, Vol. II, table 13; see the recent work by Kirchhain, 'Das Wachstum', pp. 29ff.

31 For an inquiry into the structure of costs in the Saxon cotton industry, 1856, see *Zeitschrift des Statistischen Bureaus d. Königl. Sächsischen Ministeriums d. Innern* 8 (1856), pp. 117–52. There, it is stated that 66.86 per cent of the value of production is of raw materials. According to relatively recent investigations by Kirchhain, 'Das Wachstum', pp. 146ff., this does appear to be more or less applicable to spinning and weaving for this period, but not for the whole foregoing period, for which we can, in part, observe considerable fluctuations in the structure of costs. But, in any case, the share of materials in the gross production values of the cotton industry was considerable. Therewith the producers also bore a considerable trading risk. It is no coincidence that, in the early phase of the German textile industry, the mercantile entrepreneurs, the traders, dominate; on this, see W. Zorn, 'Typen und Entwicklungskräfte deutschen Unternehmertums im 19. Jahrhundert', *VSWG*, 49 (1957), pp. 57ff.; H. Wutzmer, 'Die Herkunft der industriellen Bourgeoisie in den vierziger Jahren des 19. Jahrhunderts', in Mottek, *et al.* (eds.), *Studien*, pp. 145ff. Recently: J. Kocka, *Unternehmer in der deutschen Industrialisierung* (Göttingen 1975), pp. 42ff.

32 That this is true not only of the pre-industrial site of Munich and its environs becomes clear from numerous other reports. Thus, in 1839, it is likewise said in Basle that 'it is not business that lacks capital, but capital that lacks business' – according to H. Mauersberg, *Wirtschafts- und Sozialgeschichte zentral-europäischer Städte in neuerer Zeit* (Göttingen 1969), pp. 353f. From Berlin, O. Wiedfeldt, *Statistische Studien zur Entwicklungsgeschichte der Berliner Industrie von 1720 bis 1890* (Leipzig 1898), p. 77 reports: 'Of course, industry, newly and carefully grown from small beginnings after all, scarcely felt a need for big capital.' However, see also L. Baar, *Die Berliner Industrie in der industriellen Revolution* (Berlin 1966), pp. 140ff.

33 For instance Krug, *Betrachtungen*, p. 282: 'The saying that he who pays his debts improves his property, is so correct that no state would be better helped than if all people in the same could pay their debts . . .' For England, much the same is reported by Sayers, *Lloyds Bank in the History of English Banking* (Oxford 1957), p. 89.

34 G. Schmoller, *Zur Geschichte der deutschen Kleingewerbe im 19. Jahrhundert* (Halle 1870). Schmoller even calls the time from 1838 till 1843 the 'bloom of the small business' (pp. 59ff.). On crafts and their fate in the early phase of industrialisation otherwise, see W. Fischer, *Wirtschaft und Gesellschaft im Zeitalter der Industrialisierung* (Göttingen 1972), pp. 315ff.; Kaufhold, 'Handwerk'.

35 K. Neidlinger, *Studien zur Geschichte der deutschen Effektenspekulation von ihren Anfängen bis zum Beginn der Eisenbahnaktienspekulation* (Jena 1930).

36 *Ibid.*, p. 51.

37 At estimated fixed assets of 4.5 thousand million Talers (inclusive of land values), the level of real estate loan in agriculture was given at 2.5 thousand million Talers, see *ZPStB*, 1 (1861), p. 45. On development of real estate indebtedness see Weyermann, *Zur Geschichte des Immobiliarkreditwesens*.

38 Brockhage, *Zur Entwicklung*. But, see also v. Borries, *Deutschlands Außenhandel*, pp. 235ff.

38a One must distinguish carefully between the question as to whether (and when)

Germany was a net capital importing country and the question as to which role (gross) capital imports can have played. Even a net capital *exporting* country does, as a rule, have capital *imports*. On the basis of his estimates of the balance of trade and other positions of the balance of payments, v. Borries, *ibid.*, comes to the conclusion that in the forties there must have been a *net* capital *import* by Germany. The figure given as the balance, of an annual average of 17.4 million Talers in the period 1836–56, of course throws up new questions, especially as v. Borries himself refers to the almost technical character of the calculations. All the possible errors of assessment of the previously given figures thus enter the estimate of capital import for which v. Borries does not give any independent proofs. In fact, the statistics for the international movement of capital for the first half of the century are very unsatisfactory. On this, L. H. Jenks, *The Migration of British Capital to 1875* (New York 1927), p. 178; nevertheless, Jenks (p. 189) does say: 'Industrially self-sufficient, the Rhinelands were already exporting capital'! On this, see also a memorandum by David Hansemann from the year 1846, in which it is said: 'In Prussia, by contrast, English money was not used for the railway undertakings; for Anglo-Prussian railway companies do not exist, and furthermore the English have acquired next to no Prussian railway shares. It deserves simultaneously to be observed here that for other industrial enterprises, too, the entrepreneurial spirit of the English capitalists turns far more to other countries than to Prussia. It requires no demonstration that in Prussian monetary and financial conditions, the lack of an influx of English funds into Prussian railways and other industrial enterprises works all the more disadvantageously since the Western neighbouring countries enjoy the advantage of such an influx, . . .' Printed in W. Steitz (ed.), *Quellen zur deutschen Wirtschafts- und Sozialgeschichte im 19. Jahrhundert bis zur Reichsgründung* (Darmstadt 1980), p. 220. – R. E. Cameron demonstrates that, between 1816 and 1851, only some 2 per cent of the total capital exports of France, too, can have gone to Germany.

39 The view of H. Haussherr, *Wirtschaftsgeschichte der Neuzeit* (Cologne 1960³), p. 397 is surely exaggerated: 'Most [entrepreneurs, K.B.] were dependent on foreign capital in their rise . . .' For limited companies, foreign capital may have been of greater importance in the early fifties, see H. Blumberg, 'Die Finanzierung der Neugründungen und Erweiterungen von Industriebetrieben in Form der Aktiengesellschaften während der fünfziger Jahre des neunzehnten Jahrhunderts in Deutschland, am Beispiel der preußischen Verhältnisse erläutert', in Mottek, *et al.* (eds.), *Geschichte der Industriellen Revolution*, pp. 191ff. On the question of foreign participation in companies in Germany J. Legge, *Kapital- und Verwaltungsüberfremdung bei der Industrie und den Verkehrsanstalten Deutschlands von 1800 bis 1923/4* (Halberstadt 1924), is still indispensable. The respective tendency of industries lying in border regions to have capital links with the neighbouring country is characteristic. This is shown for industry in Baden by W. Fischer, 'Ansätze zur Industrialisierung in Baden 1770 bis 1870', *VSWG*, 47 (1960), pp. 214ff.

40 Report of Rother and Count Alvensleben to the Prussian King, 3 December 1839: 'Capitalists are not inclined here properly to appreciate industrial enterprises: even the most solid plans for share companies generally find little resonance, everyone prefers, instead of turning his assets to industry, to put them into mortgages or state securities, in order quietly to enjoy the fruits of the same as safely as possible, and a few individuals have become inclined, with the present low interest rate, only to the purchase of landed estates.' – Cited, according to Blumberg, 'Die Finanzierung', p. 167.

41 'Even capital, however much it may have declined and, like very much else,

appears for the present to have reverted to a dangerous immobility, is not yet entirely lacking, for only recently, the few capitalists we have complained about the difficulty in finding a place for it even at moderate interest and knew of no other way out than to put it into public securities.' E. D. Friedländer, 'Ostpreußens Handel' cited, according to W. Treue, 'Wirtschaftszustände und Wirtschaftspolitik in Preußen 1815–1825', *VSWG*, 31 (Beiheft 1937), p. 161.

42 For that reason too, far less of the immense discharge sums from the agricultural reforms flowed into the process of industrialisation than one might have thought. H. Winkel has more closely described the institutional linkages for the investment of 'free capital' in the process of the discharge of land debts, see H. Winkel, *Die Ablösungskapitalien aus der Bauernbefreiung in West- und Süddeutschland. Höhe und Verwendung bei Stands- und Grundherren* (Stuttgart 1968). On the transferred discharge sums, see also Steitz, *Quellen*, pp. 379–86.

43 Only in the forties did the interest differentials of the mortgage-debentures of the Prussian districts dwindle; only in the thirties did the short-term deviations of interest rates of most forms of credit lessen. See Kahn, *Geschichte des Zinsfußes*, pp. 49f. and 228, and also Voye, *Über die Höhe*.

44 If reference is repeatedly made to the financial emergencies of the early industrialists, as for instance of Krupps, it is often overlooked that many of them sought not fixed interest bearing credits, but risk-capital, to be given them without the control of the donor. That was not attractive to investors. For such contributions there remained only the family, which then provided further means in cases of emergency to avoid the 'shame' of bankruptcy. (On this, see also J. Kocka, 'Familie, Unternehmer und Kapitalismus. An Beispielen aus der frühen deutschen Industrialisierung', *ZUG*, 24 (1979), pp. 99ff.) If risk capital had to be acquired outside the family, the providers of money were, as a rule, to be taken into the business as partners. This is not a problem of the capital market in the strict sense, but of the mobility of the capitalists, and thus of new legal forms of enterprise. On the financing of industry, see also E. Klein, 'Zur Frage der Industriefinanzierung im frühen 19. Jahrhundert', in H. Kellenbenz (ed.), *Öffentliche Finanzen und privates Kapital im späten Mittelalter und in der ersten Hälfte des 19. Jahrhunderts* (Stuttgart 1971), pp. 118ff.; A. Brusatti, 'Das Problem der Unternehmensfinanzierung in der Habsburger Monarchie 1815–1848', in *Ibid.*, pp. 129ff.; P. C. Martin, 'Frühindustrielles Gewerbe in der Rechtsform der AG', in Fischer (ed.), *Beiträge*, pp. 195ff.; P. Coym, 'Unternehmensfinanzierung im frühen 19. Jahrhundert, dargestellt am Beispiel der Rheinprovinz und Westphalens' (Thesis, Hamburg 1971); Kocka, *Unternehmer*, pp. 65ff.

45 With regard to England, E. Hamilton, 'Profit Inflation and the Industrial Revolution 1715–1800', *QJE*, 56 (1942), pp. 256ff., is of the opinion that the banking system is not a cause but a consequence of industrialisation.

46 It is a good idea of R. Tilly that a more highly developed capital market would not necessarily have been to the advantage of industry. Possibly even the capital devoted – for whatever reason – to business, would then have found its way more easily into other investment possibilities. See Tilly, *Kapital*, p. 224.

47 See *inter alia* E. Klein, 'Die Königlich Württembergische Hofbank und ihre Bedeutung für die Industriefinanzierung in der ersten Hälfte des 19. Jahrhunderts', *JNSt*, 179 (1966), pp. 324ff.; R. Tilly, *Financial Institutions and Industrialization in the Rhineland, 1815–1870* (Madison 1966); R. Tilly, 'Banken und Industrialisierung in Deutschland, 1850–1870: Ein Überblick', Tilly, *Kapital*, pp. 29ff. The caution of the banks at the beginning of the fifties

is widely documented. In the statutes both of the Darmstädter Bank für Handel und Industrie (Section 10, para. 1) and of the Schaaffhausensche Bankverein (Section 20) is to be found the regulation: 'The bank is authorised to pursue all kinds of banking business, consequently including such businesses as it can easily withdraw its moneys from as soon as it needs them, at any time.' Cited in Riesser, *Zur Entwicklungsgeschichte*, p. 40.

48 The part played by limited companies in early industrialisation is certainly exaggerated in general. For instance, W. Treue in *Gebhardts Hdb. der deutschen Geschichte*, in the section 'Finanzierung der Industrie', deals almost exclusively with the development of limited companies, credit banks and cartels. The industrial limited company of the early period can, moreover, frequently still be understood as a kind of partnership on an extended basis (with facilitated membership fluctuation). It still rarely turns to the open market, and even seeks to emphasise the commitment of shareholders to the enterprise.

49 Further to this, only a few figures will be named by way of example, which W. Zorn, *Handels- und Industriegeschichte Bayerisch-Schwabens 1648–1870* (Augsburg 1961), gives for wealth in Augsburg: 1808 annual earnings Schaezler 167,220 fl. wealth of the same 1813 1 million fl., 1820, 1.7 million fl., estate 2 million fl. Süsskind assets 1806 100,000 fl. Profits in the following years 1807 66,353 fl, 1808 96,042 fl, 1809 126,019 fl, 1814 189,854 fl. Süsskind himself calculated a profit of 2.7 million up to 1825. These profits accrued from trade in securities and money.

50 Hamilton, *Profit Inflation*; E. Hamilton, 'Prices and Progress', *JEH*, 12 (1952), pp. 325ff. Of course, Hamilton's thesis has frequently been criticised, on this, see in summary G. M. Meyer and R. E. Baldwin, *Economic Development. Theory, History, Policy* (New York 1957), pp. 172ff.

50a In a critique of these reflections, P. C. Martin has rightly drawn attention to the fact that, in the monetary system dominant at the time, a 'low inflation' of this sort could by no means have been brought about in the form known today. In distinction to other states, state paper money and bank notes were, after all, unknown as a source of inflationary financing in the German States, or strictly limited in their issue. It would thus have required a considerable alteration of the institutional conditions even to render possible the experiment carried out intellectually here. In the *given* institutional framework, a low inflationary trend could only have appeared in connection with an export surplus, in consequence of which precious metal would have streamed into the country. Anything of the kind was too far removed from reality to waste further thought on its conditions. On the critique, see P. C. Martin, 'Monetäre Probleme der Frühindustrialisierung am Beispiel der Rheinprovinz (1860–1848)', *JNSt*, 181 (1967/8), p. 140.

51 On this, M. M. Postan, 'Recent Trends in the Accumulation of Capital', *EHR*, 6 (1935/6), pp. 1ff.; see also H. J. Habakkuk, 'Economic Functions of Landowners in the Seventeenth and Eighteenth Centuries', *EEH*, 6 (1953), pp. 92–101; D. Felix, 'Profit Inflation and Industrial Growth, the Historic Record and Contemporary Analogies', *QEH*, 70 (1956), pp. 441ff.

52 Mottek, 'Zum Verlauf', p. 27 recognises, with Marx, the question of the motivation for the conversion of monetary funds, but is of the opinion that, for capitalists, no economic or extra-economic compulsion for a transformation into industrial capitalists existed. In order to prove whether this is correct, one would have to know what Mottek understands by 'compulsion'. I hold the expression 'pressure' to be justified. But here it is similar to the dynamic of bodies of liquid or gas: they only develop into a current if there is a lower pressure at other points, and one could also see negative pressure (the incentive)

as the origin of the current, which then stimulates the 'flow'. What is then action, what reaction, one may evaluate differently.

53 On the comparison of trading and industrial capital, *inter alia* T. S. Ashton, *The Industrial Revolution 1760–1870* (London 1848), p. 99; Fischer, *Ansätze*, p. 224; see also the titles named in notes 12, 31, 44 and 47.

54 On the elimination of commerce through the directly exporting producers of England, see A. Sartorius v. Walterhausen, *Die Entstehung der Weltwirtschaft* (Jena 1931), p. 162, footnote 1.

55 On the conversions, see W. Stempel, 'Zinsherabsetzungen der preußischen Staatsschulden im 19. Jahrhundert', *FA*, 13 (1896), pp. 176ff.

56 That is certainly not true of the 'small rentier', who is not very mobile, but passes on his capital without entrepreneurial activity of his own. For him, the most important form of investment remains mortgages, debentures, state papers and then railway shares.

57 The importance of the sinking effective rates of interest of securities for the founding of new enterprises in the thirties is also stressed by J. Grassmann, *Die Entwicklung der Augsburger Industrie im Neunzehnten Jahrhundert* (Augsburg 1894). A different view is taken by K. Bösselmann, *Die Entwicklung des deutschen Aktienwesens im 19. Jahrhundert. Ein Beitrag zur Frage der Finanzierung gemeinwirtschaftlicher Unternehmungen und zu den Reformen des Aktienrechts* (Berlin 1939), p. 12, who does not see the search for profit on the part of the capitalists as a motive, but the intention 'to equip a backward economic system with the necessary means of production'. That is less reasonable, and surely indebted rather to the anti-capitalist current of the time in which the author wrote the book.

58 In a report of the Bavarian Minister of the Interior of 13 March 1837, the following was named as the purpose of mechanical cotton-spinning and weaving: 'Evidently, Augsburg can only reach renewed prosperity and a rejuvenated importance if the aforementioned, given the evident migration of the exchange business to Munich, throws itself into factory enterprises . . .' Zorn, *Handels- und Industriegeschichte*, p. 145.

59 Regarding the small use for big aggregates generally, A. O. Hirschman, *The Strategy of Economic Development* (New Haven 1958), pp. 32f. This also as a plea for regional disaggregation in S. Pollard, 'Industrialization and the European Economy', *EHR*, 24 (1975), pp. 638ff.; S. Pollard, 'Industrialization and Integration of the European Economy', O. Büsch, W. Fischer and H. Herzfeld (eds.), *Industrialisierung und die europäische Wirtschaft im 19. Jahrhundert* (Berlin 1975), pp. 3ff.

3 Regional variations in growth in Germany in the nineteenth century with particular reference to the west–east developmental gradient

1 'Uncorrected incomes' emerge directly from tax statistics: assessed incomes + incomes below the tax-free limit. Not included are the incomes of natural persons not included in taxation, the income of government agencies, the undistributed profits of corporations.

2 See *inter alia* the following sources: 'Average prices in Prussian provinces 1816–1870', ZPStB, 2 (1871), pp. 235–43; market price of foodstuffs in towns of the German Reich respectively in *Statistisches Jahrbuch für das Deutsche Reich*; W. Eggert, 'Die Bewegung der Holzpreise und Tagelohnsätze in den preußischen Staatsforsten von 1800 bis 1879', *ZPStB*, 23 (1883), pp. 1ff.; grain

prices in Germany since 1792 in *VjhStDR*, 1 (1935). Summaries: J. Kuczynski, 'Zwei Studien über Handels- und Marktprobleme', *JWG* (1960/II), pp. 113–41; J. Kúczynski, 'Hilfsmittel, Voraussetzungen, Parameter und Gesetzmäßigkeiten bei der Herausbildung des nationalen Marktes im Kapitalismus', *JWG* (1973/III). On the question of the adjustment of rye prices, however, see the recent work by R. Fremdling and G. Hohorst, 'Marktintegration der preußischen Wirtschaft des 19. Jahrhunderts. Skizze eines Forschungsansatzes zur Fluktuation der Roggenpreise zwischen 1821 und 1865', in R. Fremdling and R. Tilly (eds.), *Industrialisierung und Raum. Studien zur regionalen Differenzierung im Deutschland des 19. Jahrhunderts* (Stuttgart 1979), pp. 56ff.

3 For the period of the late twenties in the twentieth century it was estimated that, in the countryside, $\frac{4}{5}$ of nominal town income gives the same standard of living! See *Das deutsche Volkseinkommen vor und nach dem Kriege. Einzelschriften zur Statistik des Deutschen Reiches No. 2* (Berlin 1932), p. 72. Further material on inter-regional price comparisons in Germany and a discussion of the index problematic arising here in *VKf*, 10/2B (1935), pp. 185ff.

4 A great deal of material on wages in the nineteenth century in J. Kuczynski, *Die Geschichte der Lage der Arbeiter unter dem Kapitalismus, Teil 1*, Vols. 1–3 (Berlin 1961–2). Very important is R. Kuczynski, *Die Entwicklung der gewerblichen Löhne seit der Begründung des Deutschen Reiches* (Berlin 1909). G. Bry, *Wages in Germany 1871–1945* (Princeton 1960), pp. 371 and 106ff. works with this material. F. Grumbach and H. König, 'Beschäftigung und Löhne der deutschen Industriewirtschaft 1888–1954', *WA*, 79 (1957), pp. 125ff. use material from accident insurance statistics.

5 Regularly published in the 'Centralblatt für das Deutsche Reich. Auszüge für größere Städte', *Stat. Jb. dt. Städte*, especially 19 (1913), pp. 823ff., with an overview. A rough map of the regional wage differentiation in *Handbuch der Wirtschaftskunde Deutschlands*, Vol. 1 (Leipzig 1901), pp. 328f.

6 Sources, e.g. E. Engel, 'Die Klassen- und qualifizierte Einkommensteuer und die Einkommensverteilung in preußischen Staaten in den Jahren 1852 bis 1875', *ZPStB*, 15 (1875), pp. 105ff.; 'Die Wohlstandsverteilung in Preußen nach den Ergebnissen der Einkommensteuerveranlagung', *ZPStB*, 34 (1894), p. 33; G. Evert, 'Socialstatistische Streifzüge durch die Materialien der Veranlagung zur Staatseinkommensteuer in Preußen von 1892 bis 1901', *ZPStB*, 42 (1902), pp. 245–72.

6a With conclusions from time-series which process results of tax statistics caution is indeed always required, because *inter alia* the changes in tax law can have a big influence. Therefore one will not, for the time being, be permitted to draw any firm conclusions from the circumstance of a strong convergence of the distribution of income tax paid per capita in the Prussian provinces communicated by H. Hesse. See H. Hesse, 'Die Entwicklung der regionalen Einkommensdifferenzen im Wachstumsprozess der deutschen Wirtschaft vor 1913', in W. Fischer (ed.), *Beiträge zu Wirtschaftswachstum und Wirtschaftsstruktur im 16. und 19. Jh.*, *SchVfSp N.F.*, 63 (Berlin 1971), pp. 261ff.

7 *Stat. Handbuch für den Preußischen Staat*, III (1898), p. 396; *Statistisches Jahrbuch für den Preußischen Staat* 1 (1903), *et seq*. See also E. v. Massenbach, 'Die Verbreitung der Ärzte und Apotheken im preußischen Staate im Jahre 1871', *ZPStB*, 12 (1872), pp. 351ff. The statistics are not comparable between the individual years since the statistical criteria were repeatedly altered. It is assumed that the indicator function was not affected by this.

7a The positions of Hanover and Schleswig-Holstein have to be assessed with care. According to G. Hohorst, *Wirschaftswachstum und Bevölkerungsentwicklung in Preußen 1816 bis 1914* (New York 1977), p. 345, particular circumstances could have led to a distortion here – as indeed both provinces in figure 3.2 still showed a higher density of doctors than their income position would have indicated. According to Hohorst's income figures, Hanover and Schleswig-Holstein still belonged to the poor regions into the eighties.

8 The sources for pupil numbers are E. Engel, 'Beiträge zur Geschichte und Statistik des Unterrichts, insbesondere des Volksschulunterrichts im preußischen Staate', *ZPStB*, 9 (1869), pp. 99ff and 153ff. Further contributions – by other authors too – in later volumes as also in *Stat. Handbuch für den Preußischen Staat* and *Stat. Jahrbuch für den Preußischen Staat*, various volumes.

8a Appropriately, see footnote 7a.

9 A very interesting study, rich in information, on this: H. Kisch, 'The Textile Industry in the Rhineland: A Comparative Study in Industrialization', *JEH*, 19 (1959), pp. 541ff.

10 See W. Abel, *Geschichte der deutschen Landwirtschaft* (Stuttgart 1962), p. 155.

11 See O. Schlier, *Der deutsche Industriekörper seit 1860* (Tübingen 1922); W. Zorn, 'Binnenwirtschaftliche Verflechtungen um 1800', in F. Lütge (ed.), *Die wirtschafliche Situation in Deutschland und Österreich um die Wende vom 18. zum 19. Jahrhundert* (Stuttgart 1964), pp. 99ff.; W. Zorn, 'Schwerpunkte der deutschen Ausfuhrindustrie im 18. Jahrhundert', *JNSt*, 173 (1961), pp. 422ff. See the recent work by P. Kriedte, H. Medick and J. Schlumbohm, *Industrialisierung vor der Industrialisierung. Gewerbliche Warenproduktion auf dem Lande in der Formationsperiode des Kapitalismus* (Göttingen 1977). Also E. Schremmer, 'Das 18. Jahrhundert, das Kontinuitätsproblem und die Geschichte der Industrialisierung: Erfahrungen für die Entwicklungsländer?', *ZAA*, 29 (1981), pp. 58ff.

12 See especially Kisch (see footnote 9).

13 D. C. North, 'Location Theory and Regional Economic Growth', *Journal of Political Economy*, 63 (1955), pp. 243–58.

14 J. G. Williamson, 'Regional Inequality and the Process of National Development: A Description of the Patterns', *EDCC*, 13 (1965), Part II, pp. 1ff.

15 In W. Abel, K. Borchardt, H. Kellenbenz and W. Zorn (eds.), *Wirtschaft, Geschichte und Wirtschaftsgeschichte. Festschrift zum 65 Geburtstag von Friedrich Lütge* (Stuttgart 1966), pp. 325ff.

16 In F. Lütge (ed.), *Wirtschaftliche und soziale Probleme der gewerblichen Entwicklung im 15.–16. und im 19. Jahrhundert* (Stuttgart 1968), pp. 115ff.

17 Th. J. Orsagh, 'The Probable Geographical Distribution of German Income, 1882–1964', *ZfGS*, 124 (1968), pp. 280ff.

18 *Ibid.*, p. 281.

19 Hesse, 'Die Entwicklung'.

20 F. B. Tipton Jr, *Regional Variations in the Economic Development of Germany During the Nineteenth Century* (Middletown, Conn., 1976).

21 Hohorst, *Wirtschaftswachstum*. A summary is now available in G. Hohorst, 'Regionale Entwicklungsunterschiede im Industrialisierungsprozess Preußens – ein auf Ungleichgewichten basierendes Entwicklungsmodell', in S. Pollard (ed.), *Region und Industrialisierung. Studien zur Rolle der Region in der Wirtschaftsgeschichte der letzten zwei Jahrhunderte* (Göttingen 1980), pp. 215ff. See also G. Hohorst, 'Nationale und regionale Konjunkturen – Probleme

der Aggregation', in W. H. Schröder and R. Spree (eds.), *Historische Konjunkturforschung* (Stuttgart 1981), pp. 234ff.

22 S. Pollard, 'Industrialization and Integration of the European Economy', in O. Büsch, W. Fischer and H. Herzfeld (eds.), *Industrialisierung und 'Europäische Wirtschaft' im 19. Jahrhundert* (Berlin 1976) – there, see also the printed contributions to the discussion.

23 R. Fremdling, T. Pierenkemper and R. Tilly, 'Regionale Differenzierung in Deutschland als Schwerpunkt wirtschaftshistorischer Forschung', in Fremdling and Tilly (eds.), *Industrialisierung*, pp. 9ff.

24 H. Kiesewetter, 'Erklärungshypothesen zur regionalen Industrialisierung in Deutschland im 19. Jahrhundert', *VSWG*, 67 (1980), pp. 305ff.

25 W. Abelshauser, 'Staat, Infrastruktur und regionaler Wohlstandsausgleich im Preußen der Hochindustrialisierung', in F. Blaich (ed.), *Staatliche Umverteilungspolitik in historischer Perspektive. Beiträge zur Entwicklung des Staatsinterventionismus in Deutschland und Österreich*, SchVfSp N. F., 109 (Berlin 1980), pp. 9ff.

26 Fremdling and Tilly, *Industrialisierung*, p. 11.

4 Investment in education and instruction in the nineteenth century

1 'Correspondingly an unknown fraction of what we call wages . . . even "production workers' wages", no doubt constitutes a rent on that human capital.' R. M. Solow, 'A Sceptical Note on the Constancy of Relative Shares', *AER*, 48 (1958), p. 630.

2 E. van den Haag, *Education as an Industry* (New York 1956).

3 T. W. Schultz, 'Capital Formation by Education', *JPE*, 68 (1960), pp. 571ff.; T. W. Schultz, 'Investment in Human Capital', *AER*, 51 (1961), pp. 1ff.; E. F. Denison, *The Sources of Economic Growth in the United States* (Committee for Economic Development, Suppl. Paper No. 13, 1962); F. Machlup, *The Production and Distribution of Knowledge in the United States* (Princeton 1962). In Germany: W. G. Hoffmann, 'Erziehungs- und Forschungsausgaben im wirtschaftlichen Wachstumsprozeß', in G. Hess (ed.), *Eine Freundesgabe der Wissenschaft für Ernst Hellmut Vits* (Braunschweig 1963), pp. 101ff.; E. Liefmann-Keil, 'Erwerbstätigkeit, Ausbildung und wirtschaftliches Wachstum', in F. Neumark (ed.), *Strukturwandlungen einer wachsenden Wirtschaft*, SchVfSp N. F., 30/1 (Berlin 1964), pp. 378ff.; G. Bombach, *Bildungswesen und wirtschaftliche Entwicklung* (Heidelberg 1964).

4 A. Smith, *Wealth of Nations: An Inquiry into the Nature and Causes of the Wealth of Nations*, Vol. 1, chapter 10, section 1; see also M. Blaug, 'The Economics of Education in English Classical Political Economy: A Reexamination', in A. Skinner and T. Wilson (eds.), *Essays on Adam Smith* (Oxford 1975), pp. 568ff.

5 E. A. J. Johnson, 'The Place of Science, Vocational Training, and "Art" in Pre-Smithian Economic Thought', *JEH*, 24 (1964), pp. 129ff.

6 J. B. Say, *Handbuch der practischen Nationalökonomie oder der gesamten Staatswirtschaft*, Vol. 4, part 5, chapter 9.

7 J. H. von Thünen, *Der isolierte Staat*, Vol. 2, Section 2 and Section 12, Ausgabe Waentig (Jena 1921^2), pp. 440ff. and 512. On the history of the concepts of human capital in educational politics, see J. R. Walsh, 'Capital Concept Applied to Man', *QJE*, 49 (1935), pp. 255ff.; B. F. Kiker, 'The Historical Roots of the Concept of Human Capital', *JPE*, 74 (1966), pp. 481ff.;

K. Hüfner, 'Die Entwicklung des Humankapitalkonzepts', in K. Hüfner (ed.), *Bildungsinvestitionen und Wirtschaftswachstum. Ausgewählte Beiträge zur Bildungsökonomie* (Stuttgart 1970), pp. 11ff.

8 In 1965 several newer publications escaped me, too, above all I. Meyer, 'Der Geldwert des Menschenlebens und seine Beziehungen zur Versicherung', (Thesis, Handelshochschule Berlin 1930), which, in its historical overview, dealt primarily with Wittstein, Lüdtge and Engel. In the tradition of science of insurance literature, also L. Zeitlein, *Life's Value in Cash* (London 1962). In the social policy tradition, see E. Liefmann-Keil, Ökonomische Theorie der Sozialpolitik (Berlin 1961), pp. 74f.

9 A comparatively early summary in Ottiker Démarais, 'Die wirtschaftliche Wertbestimmung von Leben und Gesundheit, Krankheit und Tod', *Assekuranz-Jahrbuch*, 8 (1887), part 2, pp. 20ff. An evidently interesting report by E. Chadwick to the Hygiene Congress in Paris 1878 must have been stimulating.

10 The following works by E. Engel are important in our connection and hereafter are cited in abbreviated form only with the date of publication: (1) 'Der Wohltätigkeits-Congreß in Brüssel im September 1853 und die Bekämpfung des Pauperismus', in *Zeitschrift des Statistischen Bureaus des Königlichen Sächsischen Ministeriums des Innern*, 2 (1856), pp. 153–72; (2) *Der Preis der Arbeit* (Berlin 1866/72^2); (3) 'Der Preis der Arbeit bei den deutschen Eisenbahnen in den Jahren 1850, 1859, und 1869', *ZPStB*, 14 (1874), pp. 93–128; (4) 'Der Preis der Arbeit im preußischen Staatsdienste im Jahre 1875', *ZPStB*, 16 (1876), pp. 417–91; (5) *Der Werth des Menschen, Teil 1. Der Kostenwerth des Menschen* (Berlin 1883).

11 T. Wittstein, *Mathematische Statistik und deren Anwendung auf Nationalökonomie und Versicherungs-Wissenschaft* (Hanover 1867), Section III, 'Der Capitalwerth des Menschen' pp. 49–55.

12 R. Lüdtge, 'Über den Goldwerth des Menschen', *Deutsche Versicherungszeitung*, 14 (1873), No. 56, 20 July 1873; R. Lüdtge, 'Über den Versicherungswerth des Menschen', Ibid., No. 62, 10 August 1873.

13 *Statistisches Handbuch für den Preußischen Staat*, 1 (Berlin 1888).

14 *Ibid.*, p. 425. See also P. Lundgreen, *Bildung und Wirtschaftswachstum im Industrialisierungsprozeß des 19. Jahrhunderts* (Berlin 1973), p. 111.

15 *Ibid.*, pp. 454f./pp. 460f.

15a For other years and also other countries, see the share of national income for expenditure for training and education in Lundgreen, *Bildung*, p. 77.

15b On this problem, see the postscript.

16 In 1871, 9.5 per cent of the male and 14.73 per cent of the female population of Prussia were illiterate – in Posen even 31.8 and 41.04 per cent respectively. Of course, the extent of illiteracy is substantially a question of the age structure. In 1864/5, 'only' 17 per cent of the recruits from the province of Posen were illiterate, see *ZPStB*, 14 (1874), pp. 147ff. On statistics for school attendance in Prussia from 1800 to 1911, see Lundgreen, *Bildung*, p. 92; on illiteracy in Prussia, see also G. Hohorst, J. Kocka and G. A. Ritter, *Sozialgeschichtliches Arbeitsbuch. Materialen zur Statistik des Kaiserreichs 1870–1914* (Munich 1975), pp. 165ff.

17 Figures for Prussia in E. Engel, 'Beiträge zur Geschichte und Statistik des Unterrichts, insbesondere des Volksschul-Unterrichts, im preußischem Staate', *ZPStB*, 9 (1869), pp. 99ff. and 153ff. For the territory of the German Reich from 1830/1, F. Edding, *Internationale Tendenzen in der Entwicklung der Ausgaben für Schulen und Hochschulen* (Kiel 1958), tabular appendix, p. 54*.

17a On the crisis on the labour market of academics, particularly of the state service, see the contributions in U. Hermann, *Studien zur historischen*

Bildungsökonomie und zur Wissenschaftsgeschichte der Pädagogik . . .
(Zeitschrift für Pädagogik, Beiheft 14) (Weinheim 1977), pp. 13–130: 'Die Krise des Qualifikations- und Berechtigungswesens im deutschen Kaiserreich 1870–1914'; further H. G. Herrlitz and H. Titze, 'Überfüllung als bildungspolitische Strategie. Zur administrativen Steuerung der Lehrerarbeitslosigkeit in Preußen 1870–1914', *Die deutsche Schule*, 68 (1976), pp. 348ff., reprinted in U. Herrmann (ed.), *Schule und Gesellschaft im 19. Jahrhundert. Sozialgeschichte der Schule im Übergang zur Industriegesellschaft* (Weinheim 1977), pp. 348ff. There also interesting tables of the subject choices of Abitur candidates and of the examinations for the teaching profession in the higher schools.

17b Today, I would no longer advance the theory of external effects for the justification of state activity in the education system in the same way. For the reasons, see M. Blaug, *An Introduction to the Economics of Education* (London 1970), pp. 105ff., and C. C. von Weizsäcker, 'Lenkungsprobleme der Hochschulpolitik', in H. Arndt and S. Swatek, *Grundfragen der Infrastrukturplanung für wachsende Wirtschaften*, SchVfSp N.F., 58 (Berlin 1971), pp. 535ff.

17c A calculation in educational economic terms would not focus on the direct costs of the continuation of the training process beyond the period of compulsory schooling, but on the income eluding the individual who is to be trained, the opportunity costs of training. The pupil in further education does, after all, enter working life later and thus waives (for the sake of future higher incomes) an earlier earning possibility. Quantitative information on this is estimated in W. Krug, 'Erfassung des durch Ausbildung entgangenen Einkommens', *SchJb* 86 (1966), pp. 561ff.; W. Krug, 'Quantitative Beziehungen zwischen materiellem und immateriellem Kapital', *JNSt*, 180 (1967), pp. 50f.

18 See note 10.

19 Thünen, *Der isolierte Staat*, 2.

19a On this, see now K. H. Jarausch, 'Frequenz und Struktur. Zur Sozialgeschichte der Studenten im Kaiserreich', in P. Baumgart (ed.), *Bildungspolitik in Preußen zur Zeit des Kaiserreichs* (Stuttgart 1980), pp. 119ff.; P. Lundgreen, *Sozialgeschichte der deutschen Schule im Überblick, Teil 1: 1770–1918* (Göttingen 1980), pp. 83ff. and 108.

20 Engel, *Der Werth des Menschen*, p. 50.

21 Krug, *Erfassung*.

22 Krug, *Beziehungen*.

23 H. v. Laer, *Industrialisierung und Qualität der Arbeit. Eine Bildungsökonomische Untersuchung für das 19. Jahrhundert* (New York 1977).

24 Lundgreen, *Bildung*, pp. 75ff. Here Lundgreen refers to a then not yet published manuscript, in which A. P. Thirlwall described the corresponding educational economic calculations. This manuscript has been published in the interim, P. Lundgreen (with a Contribution by A. P. Thirlwall), 'Educational Expansion and Economic Growth in 19th Century Germany. A Quantitative Study', in L. Stone (ed.), *Schooling and Society. Studies in the History of Education* (Baltimore 1976), pp. 20ff.

25 P. Lundgreen, 'Historische Bildungsforschung', in R. Rürup (ed.), *Historische Sozialwissenschaft. Beiträge zur Einführung in die Forschungspraxis* (Göttingen 1977), pp. 96ff.

5　Changes in the phenomenon of the business cycle over the last hundred years

1　From the wealth of such remarks, I shall name, only from the German-speaking area, E. Salin, 'Stand und Aufgaben der Konjunkturforschung', introduction to A. Spiethoff, *Die wirtschaftlichen Wechsellagen Aufschwung, Krise und Stockung* (Tübingen 1955), pp. 1ff. E. Salin in an exhaustive contribution to discussion in H. Giersch and K. Borchardt (eds.), *Diagnose und Prognose als wirtschaftswissenschaftliche Methodenprobleme*, SchVfSp N.F., 25 (Berlin 1962), pp. 464ff. T. Pütz, 'Geschichtliche Wandlungen der Konjunkturschwankungen und Konjunkturpolitik', in F. Greiß and F. W. Meyer (eds.), *Wirtschaft, Gesellschaft und Kultur. Festgabe für Alfred Müller-Armack* (Berlin 1961), p. 176. W. Weber and H. Neiss, 'Einleitung. Entwicklung und Probleme der Konjunkturtheorie', in W. Weber and H. Neiss (eds.), *Konjunktur- und Beschäftigungstheorie* (Cologne 1967), p. 14.

2　The pre-history, papers and a summary of the discussions of the conference are published in M. Bronfenbrenner (ed.), *Is the Business Cycle Obsolete? Based on a Conference of the Social Science Research Council Committee on Economic Stability* (New York 1969).

3　For the Federal Republic – with a bibliography – A. Wagner, *Die Wachstumszyklen in der Bundesrepublik Deutschland* (Tübingen 1972). That the phaenotype of the cycles in the Federal Republic cannot be generalised with equanimity emerges from J. A. Licari and M. Gilbert, 'Is there a Postwar Growth Cycle?', *Kyklos*, 27 (1974), pp. 511ff. If one uses a test of cyclicity developed by W. A. Wallis and G. H. Moore, most of the time-series of the growth rates of national products of western countries (with the exception of the Federal Republic and of Canada) do not fulfil the condition of the regularity of the spread of growth rates which is customarily asserted.

4　A. E. Ott (ed.), *Wachstumszyklen. Über die neue Form der Konjunkturschwankungen. Theoretische und empirische Beiträge*, SchVfSp N.F., 71 (Berlin 1973). That the concept 'growth cycle' does not only (rightly) characterise the modern movement is already expressed in the title of the Thesis of R. Spree, 'Die Wachstumszyklen der deutschen Wirtschaft von 1840 bis 1880, mit einem konjunkturstatistischen Anhang' (Berlin 1977). But then see the title of his second book, *Wachstumstrends und Konjunkturzyklen in der deutschen Wirtschaft von 1820 bis 1913* (Göttingen 1978).

5　In the original place of publication, different figures were given. The disagreement arised from the fact that, at that time, it was only a matter of preliminary figures, whereas use has here been made of the opportunity of giving the actual values.

6　Beside the works named in notes 2 to 4, see E. Lundberg, *Instability and Economic Growth* (New Haven 1968); A. F. Burns, *The Business Cycle in a Changing World* (New York 1969), pp. 101ff.; G. H. Moore, 'Some Secular Changes in Business Cycles', *AER*, 64 (1974), Pap. a. Proc. pp. 133ff.

7　Substantially more differentiated, rating the role of governments less and that of other influences in the long term more highly, R. C. O. Matthews, 'Why has Britain had Full Employment Since the War?', *EJ*, 78 (1968), pp. 555ff.

8　A comparison is possible on the basis of the figures in B. R. Mitchell, *European Historical Statistics 1750–1970* (London 1975), pp. 166ff.

9　We find evidence of this in many of the aforementioned works. Of the remaining literature, we refer only to a selection, I. Mintz, *Dating Postwar Business Cycles, Methods and their Application to Western Germany, 1950–1967* (National Bureau of Economic Research, Occasional Paper No. 107) (New

York 1969), p. 1: 'Those who regard an absolute decline in the main economic activities as an essential feature of business cycles, see a deep gap between *earlier* and *recent* economic fluctuations.' J. Kromphardt, *Wachstum und Konjunktur. Grundlagen ihrer theoretischen Analyse und wirtschaftspolitischen Steuerung* (Göttingen 1972), p. 139: 'A striking difference between the *present* and the *earlier* business cycles lies in the fact that in the post-war period the national product does not recede even in the troughs of business cyclical development' (K.B.'s emphasis).

10 A noteworthy exception are R. C. O. Matthews, *The Trade Cycle* (Cambridge 1959); Matthews, 'Postwar Business Cycles in the United Kingdom', in Bronfenbrenner (ed.), *Is the Business Cycle Obsolete?*; Matthews, *Britain*.

11 A few exceptions aside, the present study is confined to Germany (the Reich in the respective borders until 1938, the Federal Republic of Germany since 1949). Thus the statements have no general validity for western industrial countries. Before that can be arrived at, numerous national studies are still needed. Attention should once more explicitly be drawn to the fact that the last hundred years are to be discussed. That the phenomenon of the business cycle also experienced changes in the course of the nineteenth century is shown by R. Spree, 'Veränderungen der Muster zyklischen Wachstums der deutschen Wirtschaft von der Früh- zur Hochindustrialisierung', *GuG*, 5 (1979), pp. 228ff.

12 Within the framework of this study, the fluctuation in each single series is observed. Because of the normal lag-structures, the ups and downs of different business cycle indicators do not necessarily cover the same time periods.

13 A conceptual distinction is drawn here between the unsteadiness or instability of a process and cyclicity. We call all processes with fluctuations of the rates of change of a variable unsteady or unstable. Measurements of spread give the degree of the deviations. We call a development cyclical only if the deviations of growth rates demonstrate a certain adherence to a rule of chronological sequence, in the ideal case, a sine fluctuation at a constant interval and constant amplitude as in figure 5.1. Because this ideal case has never existed in reality, whether one calls a development cyclical occasionally depends on the criteria of the observer.

14 I owe the calculations of the statistics in the following figures to R. Weichhardt.

15 Thus, the Sachverständigenrat zur Begutachtung der wirtschaflichen Entwicklung, in its annual report 1972/3 in Tz. 152 puts it as follows: the cyclical pivotal process 'expresses itself in the succession of speeding up and slowing down of production activity'. The recent attempts at comprehending growth cycles primarily as fluctuations in the degree of capacity utilisation is not addressed here, because this concept is not applicable for historical long-term comparison.

16 On this *et seq.*, see W. G. Hoffmann in collaboration with F. Grumbach and H. Hesse, *Das Wachstum der deutschen Wirtschaft seit der Mitte des 19. Jahrhunderts* (Berlin 1965).

17 A comprehensive international overview on the peculiarity of the inter-war period is to be found in Lundberg, *Instability*, pp. 22ff. See also K. Borchardt, 'Wachstum und Wechsellagen 1914 bis 1970', *HdWSG*, 2 (Stuttgart 1976), Chapter 15, Section a, with references to further literature.

18 According to Hoffmann's calculations (see note 16), the production of agriculture in 1891 receded by 6 per cent compared with the previous year. Its proportion of the total production of the national economy comprised still 32 per cent. The increase in the production of manufacturing industry and crafts

ran at 2.3 per cent in 1890/91. The time-series of the net domestic product at constant prices calculated by W. G. Hoffmann was not used for our historical analysis of the business cycle because it rests far more than that of the net national product on techniques of estimating, which lay stress on the trend.

19　C. H. Feinstein, *National Income, Expenditure and Output of the United Kingdom, 1855–1965* (Cambridge 1972). See also Mitchell, *Statistics*.

20　R. A. Gordon, 'The Stability of the U.S. Economy' in Bronfenbrenner (ed.), *Is the Business Cycle Obsolete?*, pp. 37ff. rightly refers to the comparatively mild pre-war contractions: 'But let me make one correction. When it is said serious depressions (in the post-war period, K.B.) are obsolete, the depressions that are meant are ones like 1920–1921 and 1929–1933. From the time that the regular cyclical movement began (somewhere around 1825) up to the beginning of the 1920s, there was not a single yearly downturn of industrial production in Great Britain of more than 10 per cent. In the history of the cycles in the United States this limit was exceeded only twice . . .'.

21　We will dispense with giving spread measures for the measurement of the instability of the growth rates of the net national product as R. Hopp, *Schwankungen des wirtschaftlichen Wachstums in Westdeutschland 1954–1967* (Meisenheim 1969), pp. 1f. did. The results depend heavily on the choice of the underlying trend. In the pre-war period, one could use a long-term average of growth rates. In the post-war period that would certainly be wrong. But which trend deserves preference is at the moment hardly to be said with any power of persuasion.

22　The chosen method for the calculation of trends is that of moving multi-annual averages. For the pre-war period, moving 7-year averages were selected, for the post-war period, moving 5-year averages. This method has the advantage that one does not have to commit oneself regarding the mathematical form of the trend. Its drawback consists in the fact that, at the beginning and end respectively, years are omitted (if one does not extrapolate them). For the inter-war period, so short a period is then left, that we refrained entirely from illustrating the fluctuations around the trend. Because of the losses of information through the use of moving multi-annual averages, the analysis of growth rates serves as a basis for the remainder of the course of the portrayal, whether or not it has some disadvantages in respect of deviations from the trend.

23　R. Wagenführ, *Die Industriewirtschaft. Entwicklungstendenzen der deutschen und internationalen Industrieproduktion 1860 bis 1932*, VKf Sonderheft, 31 (1933). See also StatBA, *Bevölkerung und Wirtschaft 1872–1972* (Stuttgart 1972), p. 176 (with printing errors, for the annual values for 1890 to 1900 are missing).

24　Were one to compare G. Hoffmann's and his collaborators' estimates of production of mining and salt works and also of industry and crafts up to 1913 with the production of manufacturing industry from 1950 onwards on the basis of official statistics, development in the post-war period would appear far more unstable than in the pre-war period. Unfortunately, Mitchell, *Statistics*, pp. 355ff. treated Hoffmann's figures, which related to industry and crafts, without additional comment as an index of industrial production and linked them up with the later official indices of industrial production.

25　As also in the spread dimensions, see note to figure 5.6.

26　See for instance A. Stobbe, *Gesamtwirtschaftliche Theorie* (Heidelberg 1975), p. 122; R. L. Frey, *Wirtschaft, Staat und Wohlfahrt. Eine Einführung in die Nationalökonomie* (Basle 1975), pp. 61f.

27　K. W. Rothschild, 'Bemerkungen zur konjunkturellen Entwicklung der österreichischen Wirtschaft 1954–1970', in Ott (ed.), *Wachstumszyklen*, pp. 213f. Of course, Rothschild too can base his work on such capacities as are used by G. Haberler in his *Prosperität und Depression. Eine theoretische Untersuchung der Konjunkturbewegungen* (Tübingen 1955), pp. 248f., 255, etc. The case is somewhat different with those authors (W. C. Mitchell among others) who define the business cycle as 'successive changes in activity', see *ESS*, 3 (1930), p. 92. Here it is precisely the indicator which is still openly problematised. G. Tichy has already indicated in the same volume, p. 143, that Rothschild's statement of the facts is open to question.

28 Kromphardt, *Wachstum und Konjunktur*, p. 139 also misreads the previous cycle research when he claims that 'earlier' it was usual to measure the phases or the cycle by rises and falls of national product.

29 Spiethoff, *Wechsellagen*, Vol. 1, p. 83. This illustration is not yet to be found in the article 'Krisen', *HdSt*, 6 (1925[4]), which the book otherwise follows.

30 This emerges from a thesis completed under Spiethoff's supervision: H. Kuschmann, *Die Untersuchungen des Berliner Instituts für Konjunkturforschung. Darstellung und Kritik* (Beiträge zur Erforschung der wirtschaftlichen Wechsellagen Aufschwung, Krise, Stockung, ed. A. Spiethoff Heft 7) (Jena 1933), pp. 52ff. Kuschmann writes of the ideal cycle as follows: 'Thus they (the earlier business cycle researchers), when they spoke of movement, certainly did not mean by that what is meant by it today with the help of the normal index. They did not mean that a given economic state of affairs "moves" in the sense that the individual components of a time-series at the moment C were larger than at the moment A, but rather that a certain economic manifestation at the moment C had a different general significance than the same manifestation at the moment A. That, at any rate, is how we see Spiethoff's "ideal cycle".' (p. 53).

31 Spiethoff, *Wechsellagen*, p. 73. One could cite further evidence from Spiethoff, but also from A. Aftalion and W. C. Mitchell. Just in passing, it should be noted that Spiethoff too saw how the production of producer goods was more likely to fluctuate cyclically than that of consumer goods, with which he attested to completely 'irregular' movements. To that extent, his observations agree with our experiences of the cyclicality of production in various branches of industry.

32 J. Schumpeter, *Business Cycles. A Theoretical, Historical, and Statistical Analysis of the Capitalist Process*, Vol. II (New York 1939), p. 500, *inter alia*.

33 We will only indicate the problematic, that in some circumstances the aggregation to macro-economic values could have a certain smoothing effect. Of course, the opposite can also be demonstrated. Matthews, *The Trade Cycle*, has described how the apparently regular fluctuations of the sum of gross investments within the country and foreign investments may, with a cycle of seven to ten years, be ascribed to the aggregation effect of two series, which did not run synchronously and, even by comparison with the income cycle, showed double the length of phases.

34 Before the First World War, Clément Juglar, Michael v. Tugan-Baranowsky, Mentor Bouniatian, Jean Lescure, Albert Aftalion, Wesley C. Mitchell.

35 The governing theoretical concept in Spiethoff is the 'creation of unequilibrium'. The means of overcoming it were: lowering prices, creation of reserves, curtailment of production, export of overproduction, 'decreasing cost of production'. In numerous dissertations, Spiethoff's students sought to demonstrate to what degree the various means of overcoming overproduction made their appearance in the branches.

36 As also in the case of Schumpeter, *Business Cycles*, p. 496.

37 E. Wagemann, *Konjunkturlehre, eine Grundlegung zur Lehre vom Rhythmus der Wirtschaft* (Berlin 1928), p. 174 believes that up to 1914 the price index of raw materials and semi-manufactured goods is to be regarded as a rather good reflection of the degree of activity. It is, however, important to recognise that this price index is significantly influenced in its course by the prices of goods traded internationally – which is why it is no coincidence that international comparisons between the business-cyclical movement before the First World War, which make use of an indicator afforded by raw material prices, arrived at synchronous business-cycle movement in the main trading countries.

38 A. Desai, *Real Wages in Germany, 1871–1913* (Oxford 1968).

39 We should here remind ourselves again of the fact that the use of different price index series in a long-term comparison is problematic, but that the attempt must nevertheless – if only as an experiment – be undertaken.

40 This is not the place to demonstrate on the basis of further illustrations of price movement that it is in any event not permissible to state that, in the business cycles of the nineteenth century, *the* prices usually rose in upturns and fell in downturns, which is how Pütz, 'Geschichtliche Wandlungen', among others, puts it.

41 Spiethoff, *Wechsellagen*, pp. 45f.; see also W. C. Mitchell, *Business Cycles, the Problem and its Setting* (New York 1913), p. 100.

42 This finds expression for instance in the following quotation: 'The downturn line of iron consumption is, alongside the occurrences in the capital market, the decisive manifestation of stagnation.' Spiethoff, *Wechsellagen*, p. 72.

43 As late as 1933, his student Kuschmann (*Die Untersuchungen*, p. 69) writes: 'Due to the comparatively incomplete statistical material which was available for the last century and because of the lack of suitable statistical methods, it was naturally not possible to determine with statistical precision the change in the *importance of capital goods* in the economic system. In any event, however, it must be attempted' (K.B.'s emphasis).

44 Between the time-series of iron consumption (according to Spiethoff) and the time-series of net investments in constant prices (according to Hoffmann) there is a high correlation ($r = 0.97$) between 1850 and 1913. It is true that here, as in all comparisons between time-series, the trend is all powerful. If only the growth rates are correlated, then a considerably worse correlation ($r = 0.11$) emerges, which is, however, substantially improved if moving triennial values of growth rates in iron consumption and net investments are taken, and if one restricts oneself to the period 1870–1913, in which the statistical material is more reliable ($r = 0.58$).

45 In this case it is particularly regrettable that we can record production and investment only from 1925 on. It may be conjectured that, directly after the First World War and under the influence of the inflation, the investment ratio was at first high. On this, see W. Abelshauser, 'Inflation und Stabilisierung. Zum Problem ihrer makroökonomischen Auswirkungen auf die Rekonstruktion der deutschen Wirtschaft nach dem Ersten Weltkrieg', in O. Büsch and G. Feldman (eds.), *Historische Prozesse der deutschen Inflation 1914 bis 1924* (Berlin 1978), pp. 161ff.; C.-L. Holtfrerich, *Die deutsche Inflation 1914–1923. Ursachen und Folgen in internationaler Perspektive* (Berlin 1980), pp. 200ff.

46 Calculated according to StatBA, *Lange Reihen zur Wirtschaftsentwicklung* (1980), pp. 167 and 173.

47 StatBA, *Bevölkerung*, p. 214; Deutsche Bundesbank, *Deutsches Geld- und Bankwesen in Zahlen 1876–1975* (Frankfurt 1976), p. 279. See also monthly reports of the Deutsche Bundesbank.

48 If one concerns oneself with interest rates and yields, one employs time-series

which have several advantages for historical comparison. They are, as a rule, better established through primary sources of high standing than other statistical quantities, and throw up no difficulties regarding the long-term comparability of the units of calculation because interest rates and yields are, after all, figures with no dimensions. So no changes in the value of money have to be considered in the longer-term comparison. Nevertheless, in this case too problems of long-term comparability do arise. The instruments of finance, for which the interest is paid have often altered their character in the course of history and, much more frequently still, their significance in the general system of all instruments of finance. In our connection, it is of great weight that, under the standing title 'long-term securities', considerable changes in the average life of securities are concealed, as is emphasised by P. Cagan, *Changes in the Cyclical Behaviour of Interest Rates* (National Bureau of Economic Research, Occasional Paper 100) (New York 1966) and *RES* (1966). See also K. Borchardt, 'Realkredit und Pfandbriefmarkt im Wandel von 100 Jahren', *100 Jahre Rheinische Hypothekenbank* (Frankfurt 1971), pp. 123ff., 137, 178ff.

49 The standard deviations of the average bank discount rates of the Reichsbank / the Bank deutscher Länder / Deutsche Bundesbank stood at 0.7 in 1876–1913 and 1.2 in 1948–1974, the variation coefficients at 0.17 and 0.28 respectively; StatBA, *Bevölkerung*, p. 219, also monthly reports of the Deutsche Bundesbank.

50 The average unemployment rate between 1887 and 1913 stood at 2.4 per cent – with an annual growth rate of the numbers of those in employment at 1.8 per cent. (The increase in employment was derived from an extrapolation from the numbers of salaried employees and workers in 1882 and 1907.)

51 On this, see Matthews, *Britain* (see footnote 7), pp. 555ff.

52 It has been examined more for the USA, see *inter alia* M. Friedman, 'Geldangebot, Preis- und Produktionsänderungen', *ORDO* 11 (1959), pp. 193ff. reprinted in E. Dürr (ed.), *Geld- und Bankpolitik* (Cologne 1969), pp. 115ff.; M. Friedman, *The Optimum Quantity of Money and other Essays* (Chicago 1969), chapter 3. H. Stein, 'Where Stands the New Fiscal Policy?', *JMCB*, 1 (1969), pp. 463ff.; K. Brunner, 'The Policy Discussions by Stein and Warswick, A Comment', *JMCB*, 1 (1969), p. 496ff.

6 Trends, cycles, structural breaks, chance: what determines twentieth-century German economic history?

* This was one of the general themes of the 31st German Historical Congress of 1976 in Mannheim.

1 D. Landes, *The Unbound Prometheus. Technological Change and Industrial Development in Western Europe from 1750 to the Present* (Cambridge 1969), p. 359.

2 For 1850–1950, the values are given from the information in W. G. Hoffmann, F. Grumbach and H. Hesse, *Das Wachstum der deutschen Wirtschaft seit der Mitte des 19. Jahrhunderts* (Berlin 1965). The following curve for the period after the Second World War was provided with the aid of the growth rates of the national product per inhabitant at constant prices of 1962 taken from StatBA, *Lange Reihen* (1974) as an extension of the value calculated by Hoffmann for 1950. The shortcomings of this procedure are familiar to everyone versed in the subject. In particular, the index problem of long time-series is not to be solved if one makes big demands of the method.

3 On this problem, see D. Usher, *The Measurement of Economic Growth* (Oxford 1980) and U.-P. Reich, Ph. Sonntag and H.-W. Holub, *Arbeit-Konsum-Rechnung. Axiomatische Kritik und Erweiterung der Volkswirtschaftlichen Gesamtrechnung* (Cologne 1977).

4 It is too early to estimate how large remnants of discontinuity are. One gains a certain point of departure from the attempt of the Federal Statistical Office both at giving national product figures for the period 1925–39 in the borders of the German Reich as the territory stood in 1937 and at estimating them in the borders of the Federal Republic (without the Saarland and Berlin). On this, see StatBA, *Bevölkerung und Wirtschaft 1872–1972* (Stuttgart 1972), pp. 260f. The deviations seem to be so minor as to become hardly visible in figure 6.1.

5 Several authors have, it is true, ventured estimates of national product for the years after 1914, but not only the weak data base speaks against use of this information in the present context. On the problem, see K. Borchardt, 'Wachstum und Wechsellagen 1914–1970', *HdWSG*, 2 (Stuttgart 1976), pp. 686 and 696.

6 See I. Esenwein-Rothe, *Die Methoden der Wirtschaftsstatistik*, Vol. 2 (Göttingen 1976), pp. 213ff. This definition was intended to preclude the misunderstanding that trends are so to speak general historical laws. Such an assumption is rightly criticised by K. R. Popper, *The Poverty of Historicism* (London 1957), pp. 115ff. On this, see S. Kuznets, *Wesen und Bedeutung des Trends. Zur Theorie der säkularen Bewegung* (Bonn 1930). No opposition in principle must therefore be seen between trend and event, for – as R. Koselleck puts it – 'continuance' too can become an event. See R. Koselleck, 'Darstellung, Ereignis und Struktur', in G. Schulze (ed.), *Geschichte heute. Positionen, Tendenzen, Probleme* (Göttingen 1973), p. 312.

7 What is at issue in the present context is not specifically to substantiate the choice of the method of calculation of the trend selected for figure 6.2 specially in order to underpin it with a theory of the trend. Precisely this is to be the subject of the later considerations. Therefore an empirical decision has been arrived at. For the determination of the trend up to 1914, moving 7 year averages were chosen, for the trend from 1950 on, moving 5 year averages. Calculations according to Hoffmann (see note 2) and StatBA, *Lange Reihen* (1974), pp. 144ff., and also *WiSta* (1977/2). The period from 1914–49 was left out, because the time-series available is too short for trend calculations in view of the enormous fluctuations.

8 We are here ignoring the seasonal fluctuations, which are also important for certain historical explanations. They do not appear in time-series of annual values.

9 That the business cycles were in some respects greater after 1950 than before 1914 is shown above, pp. 59ff.

10 A. S. Milward, 'Bericht', in H. Mommsen, D. Petzina and B. Weisbrod (eds.), *Industrielles System und politische Entwicklung in der Weimarer Republik. Verhandlungen des Internationalen Symposiums in Bochum vom 12.–17. Juni 1973* (Düsseldorf 1974), p. 52.

11 The basic uncertainty in the interpretation of the long-term development and the three pure types of illustrations are also addressed by G. Bombach in the discussion of the problem of long-term forecasts in H. Giersch and K. Borchardt (eds.), *Diagnose und Prognose als wirtschaftswissenschaftliche Methodenprobleme*, *SchVfSp N.F.*, 25 (Berlin 1962), p. 528. That, with one and the same material – in this case US industrial production – one can support very different mathematical trend formulas, is shown by E. Ames, 'Trend, Cycles and Stagnation in U.S. Manufacturing since 1860', *OEP*, 11 (1959), pp. 270ff.

12 That is expressed with desirable clarity in Kuznets, *Wesen*, p. 13: 'Before one calculates a mathematical curve as a trend for a given time-series, one has to answer three questions: 1. For which period should the adjusted curve be calculated? 2. What form should the calculated curve take? 3. According to which method do we wish to proceed? If one has answered these three questions, then one has already introduced just as many assumptions about the characteristics of the secular movements to be calculated.'

13 For the actual values in figure 6.3, see note 2. The linear trend curve was laid down through the beginning and end values of the time-series 1850–1913. That is an arbitrary decision, which has the advantage of clearness. A straight line trend constructed via the method of least squares, however, deviates only quite negligibly in respect of position and gradient from the one selected.

14 F. Jánossy, *Das Ende der Wirtschaftswunder. Erscheinung und Wesen der wirtschaftlichen Entwicklung* (Frankfurt 1969). It is true that Jánossy bases his argument on the time-series of industrial production so that, for this reason alone, his depiction does not completely conform to the method chosen here. On the discussion about the theory of the reconstruction period, see *inter alia* W. Abelshauser, *Wirtschaft in Westdeutschland 1945–1948. Rekonstruktion und Wachstumsbedingungen in der amerikanischen und britischen Zone* (Stuttgart 1975), pp. 23ff.

14a See also the contribution in chapter 7 of this volume.

15 See *inter alia* H. Priester, *Das deutsche Wirtschaftswunder* (Amsterdam 1936).

16 M. Manz, 'Stagnation und Aufschwung in der französischen Zone von 1945 bis 1948' (Thesis, Mannheim 1968); Abelshauser, *Wirtschaft*.

16a On this, see also the following contribution esp. p. 112ff.

17 Although the concept of a 'normal development' runs into many objections, it is nevertheless widespread. The references in qualitative and quantitative findings are innumerable. So, for instance, the President of the Statistical Office of the Reich wrote in the preface of the work, *Das deutsche Volkseinkommen vor und nach dem Kriege, Einzelschriften zur Statistik des Deutschen Reiches*, 24 (1932) that the pre-war span had been included in the investigation 'in order to gain a yard-stick for the evaluation of the present through the picture of development of a relatively long economic period'. D. C. Paige, F. T. Blackaby and S. Freund, 'Economic Growth, the Last Hundred Years, National Institute of Economic and Social Research, Economic Review' (July 1961) analyse growth since the end of the nineteenth century for the same reason. They call the inter-war period abnormal because the developments to be observed here can probably not be explained by long-term prognoses. Similar aims characterise the well-known studies by A. Maddison and S. Kuznets (see note 18).

18 Source for figure 4: O. Krantz and C.-A. Nilsson, *Swedish National Product 1861–1970. New Aspects on Methods and Measurement* (Lund 1975), p. 180. Sweden serves here only as an example; other countries could equally be chosen. E. Ames (note 11) favours a logarithmic-linear trend for US industrial production too. S. Kuznets, *Economic Growth of Nations. Total Output and Production Structure* (Cambridge Mass. 1971), pp. 41ff. summarises the picture of growth of numerous developed countries to the effect that either a relatively even average growth had been present, or that relatively high post-war growth rates had compensated for a preceding worse development. (Japan appears to be the major exception.) The international comparative figures provided by A. Maddison, *Economic Growth in the West* (London 1964) suggest a similar finding for most states.

19 The curve was drawn with a free hand, and thus no apparent precision of a mathematical form was pretended. Other waves could also be construed; in

particular one could undertake the attempt to render Kondratieff- or Kuznets-cycles visible before 1914, to vary the gradient in the inter-war period and to place the turning-points in different years.

20 J. Schumpeter, *Business Cycles*, 2 Vols. (New York and London 1939). L. Dupriez 'Der "Kondratieff" und die Konjunkturentwicklung seit 1945', *WA*, 93 (1963), pp. 262ff.; J. Schumpeter, '1945 bis 1971 als Aufschwungsphase eines Kondratieff-Zyklus?', *Ifo-Studien*, 18 (1972), pp. 503ff. Dupriez supports his view more comprehensively in *Mouvements économiques généraux* (Louvain 1947).

21 A (weak) long wave gained from the time-series of industrial production would, according to Ames' calculations (see note 11), have a low-point in 1942. Similarly, W. N. Parker, in W. C. Scoville and J. C. Laforce (eds.), *The Economic Development of Western Europe – From 1914 to the Present* (1970), p. 75. Because of disturbances, which are never out of the question, the exact dating of the wavy movement is always difficult. With reference to England, when in the inter-war period the more rapid progress, undisputed for the thirties, set in is, for example, continuously debated. On this, see D. H. Aldcroft and H. W. Richardson, *The British Economy, 1870–1939* (London 1969) and D. H. Aldcroft and P. Fearon (eds.), *Economic Growth in 20th-Century Britain* (London 1969). ˙

22 For references to literature, description and discussion, see D. Petzina and W. Abelshauser, 'Zum Problem der relativen Stagnation der deutschen Wirtschaft in den zwanziger Jahren', in Mommsen, *et al.* (eds.) (see footnote 10), pp. 57ff., and the report by A. S. Milward, in *Ibid.*, pp. 51ff. On the general stagnation problem, see B. Higgins, 'Concepts and Criteria of Secular Stagnation', in *Income, Employment, and Public Policy, Essays in Honour of A. H. Hansen* (New York 1948).

23 See S. Kuznets' statement cited in note 12.

24 'Structure' is an ambiguous concept, which is very variously used. See F. Machlup, 'Structure and Structural change: Weaselwords and Jargon', *ZfN*, 18 (1958), pp. 280ff., and G. Bombach, 'Der Strukturbegriff in der Ökonomie', in F. Neumark (ed.), *Strukturwandlungen einer wachsenden Wirtschaft, SchVfSp N.F.*, 30/1 (Berlin 1964), pp. 10ff. In the present context, what is at issue is not the 'statistician's concept of structure' but the 'econometrician's concept of structure', which J. Akerman, *Theory of Industrialisation. Causal Analysis and Economic Plans* (Lund 1960), p. 184 calls a 'macro-dynamic one'. The structure is here defined as the system of functional and stochastic relationships between exogenous and endogenous variables. Constancy of structure means the unalterability of the functional relationships as of the estimated parameters.

25 Differently from the authors of the Ifo Institute, whose task it was to estimate a production function for the Federal Republic of Germany, and who also made use of the empirical data of the inter-war period for this purpose in order to obtain the longer time-series necessary for econometric operations. See *Bestimmungsfaktoren der deutschen Produktion, Ifo-Studien*, 7 (1961). As a later examination showed, the parameters of these estimates were surprisingly well-established, see G. Gehrig and K. C. Kuhlo, 'Überprüfung der ökonometrischen Projektion von 1962', *Ifo-Studien*, 18 (1972), pp. 275ff. More on this in the following contribution pp. 132ff.

26 From a wide selection, A. Predöhl, 'Die Epochenbedeutung der Weltwirtschaftskrise von 1929–31', *VfZ*, 1 (1953), pp. 97ff.

27 At this point, reference should be made to the nonsense of deriving 'average growth rates' from the corner values of a period (in our case, therefore, 1950 and 1913), if the intermediate values run a long way distant from the

logarithmic-linear trend. What affords a meaning for the period 1850 to 1913, because the movement remains 'close to the trend', is stupid for the period after 1913 – but unfortunately widespread nevertheless.

28 Source, StatBA, *Bevölkerung*, pp. 182f., and *StJb* (1976), p. 255. Lower curve: 1928–44 production in the borders of the Federal Republic territory.

29 D. Petzina, 'Grundriß der deutschen Wirtschaftsgeschichte 1918 bis 1945', in Institut für Zeitgeschichte (ed.), *Deutsche Geschichte seit dem Ersten Weltkrieg*, Vol. 2 (Stuttgart 1973), p. 676. Reworked in Institut für Zeitgeschichte (ed.), *Die deutsche Wirtschaft in der Zwischenkriegszeit* (Wiesbaden 1977), p. 20.

30 In the discussion on the paper, information was especially asked for on this, as was to be expected, because it was considered unsatisfactory to see oneself exposed to such a multiplicity of interpretation. But all that can be done is repeatedly to ask for understanding of the fact that the intentionally emphasised uncertainty should not be negated through an act of simple decisionism. At any event, for deciding on the questions at issue, the developments on the 'actual periphery', that is in the present, are of the greatest interest. They will contribute in the decisions on which types are to be chosen. On this, see also the following contribution.

31 E. Hennig, *Thesen zur deutschen Sozial- und Wirtschaftsgeschichte 1933 bis 1938* (Frankfurt 1973), p. 22.

32 Of course, the short-comings cannot remain entirely unmentioned. In the quotation itself a very dubious position is already taken up, which could deceive the reader. There is no economic sense, given rapidly sinking unemployment figures, in counterposing the rates of increase in *rates* of pay to the rates of increase in national product (2.8 per cent by comparison with 8.2 per cent in the annual average). In fact, the rates of increase in the wage *total* remained behind those of the national product – but they would give the more correct relative figure. Furthermore, the author frequently uses material which has since been overtaken by more recent research; just as a certain arbitrariness in the evaluation of sources is in general to be regretted. Certain errors in interpretation are of weight. In order, for instance, to prove that, in the great depression 'the social position of the capital investors improved', Hennig uses figures for national income, and income from work (wages and salaries) from the well-known book by G. Kroll (*Von der Weltwirtschaftskrise zur Staatskonjunktur* (Berlin 1958), and also what Hennig simply calls 'capital income', although Kroll correctly states that it is a matter of 'incomes of private individuals from capital assets' (interest and dividend incomes from monetary assets): these are, however, only a relatively small part of the 'non-work incomes' = incomes from property. In 1929 this stood at 3.7 per cent of the national income! And because income from interest (not least due to increasing state debts) did not sink quite as quickly as the national income, Hennig infers 'the improvement in the social situation of the owners of capital', whereas the share of income from property did indeed recede in the world economic crisis (as it always does in crises) – see below, figure 6.8.

33 Hennig, *Thesen*, p. 18.

34 *Ibid.*, p. 103.

35 Figure 6.8 is taken directly from Hoffmann, *Das Wachstum*, p. 88. In order to exclude the effect of the structural change of employment (shares of self-employed and of employees), 'incomes from work' here also contain arithmetically calculated income from work of the self-employed (predominantly freelance professionals, peasants, artisans). The 'income from entrepreneurial activity and assets' of this group is, after all, not correctly identified by the concept 'profit'. The difference between the income from work estimated by Hoffmann and the

national income is the estimated 'income from property' in the narrower sense. Where the relation of income from work to national income exceeds 100 per cent, a net loss or decrease of assets would have to be construed or it would be indicated that the self-employed could earn no comparable incomes from labour.

36 For unemployment rates, there are various, not always completely concurring time-series. The one used here follows the representation by B. R. Mitchell, *European Historical Statistics 1750–1970* (London 1975), pp. 167ff., who in turn refers to the *Yearbook of Labour Statistics*. Up to 1929, the material refers to information from trade unions, after 1929 unemployment rates from official unemployment insurance statistics. The overlap in 1929 is intended to indicate the possible differences of dimension. Figures after 1950, StatBA, *Bevölkerung*, p. 148 supplemented by actual values from *StJb* (1976).

37a On this, see K. Borchardt, 'Economic causes of the collapse of the Weimar Republic', in this volume pp. 161ff.
StJb (1976), pp. 516 and 526.

37a On this, see K. Borchardt, 'Economic causes of the collapse of the Weimar Republic', in this volume p. 000ff.

38 If one follows relatively recent calculations by E. H. Phelps Brown ('Levels and Movements of Industrial Productivity and Real Wages Internationally Compared, 1860–1970', *EJ*, 83 (1973), pp. 58ff.), then it emerges that in Germany between 1933 and 1938 the increase in productivity in industry (productivity = output per person employed) amounted to 18.8 per cent, the increase in the real wage to 4 per cent; in Sweden productivity rose by 30 per cent in the same period, the real wage by 9.8 per cent; in Great Britain productivity rose by 15.5 per cent, the real wage by 0.8 per cent. In the USA, on the other hand, the increase in productivity up to 1937 amounted to 12.2 per cent (up to the following renewed crisis year 1938, only 2.2 per cent), while the increase in the real wage up to 1937 amounted to 14.6 per cent (up to 1938 even 23.8 per cent) – and the USA recuperated with great difficulty after the crisis, retained for a long time high mass unemployment, which could only be reduced rapidly after the entry into the War in 1941).

39 Calculated according to Mitchell, *European Historical Statistics*, pp. 116ff. Five annual averages are presented in order to allow the shape of the trend to stand out more clearly. An average value for Germany 1915–19 has not been calculated.

40 W. Köllmann, 'Bevölkerungsentwicklung in der Weimarer Republik', in Mommsen, *et al.* (eds.), *Industrielles System*, pp. 76ff. See also J. Reulecke, 'Zusammenfassung des Beitrags "Wirtschaft und Bevölkerung ausgewählter Städte im Ersten Weltkrieg"', *30. Versammlung deutscher Historiker Braunschweig. Beiheft zu GWU* (Stuttgart 1976), p. 50, and the discussion by W. Köllman there, p. 51.

41 This was already described in 1940 in a comprehensive analysis by D. V. Glass, *Population, Policies and Movements in Europe* (1940, reprinted London 1967), pp. 269–313. Glass begins the description of the German case as follows: 'One of the most striking phenomena of recent years is the change in the trend of marriage- and birth-rates in Germany since 1933.'

42 If one proceeds from the assumption that birth numbers are not determined by the birth behaviour of small minorities, but are rather mass phenomena, something might additionally be gained from observation of this circumstance for the recognition of the mood of these masses, much as the deformation of sensibility may be regretted.

43 The discussion has been continued in this spirit by W. Abelshauser and D. Petzina, 'Krise und Rekonstruktion. Zur Interpretation der

gesamtwirtschaftlichen Entwicklung Deutschlands im 20. Jh.', in W. H.
Schröder and R. Spree (eds.), *Historische Konjunkturforschung* (Stuttgart 1981),
pp. 75ff. (In this collection of essays there are also several contributions which
are concerned with the renaissance of the model of 'long waves'.) W. Fischer,
'Die Weltwirtschaft im 20. Jahrhundert. Beharrung und Wandel', *HZ*, 229
(1979), pp. 54ff. That the weakness of growth at the end of the seventies
enlivened concern with long-term trend-concepts is shown among others in H.
H. Glismann, H. Rodemer and H. Hesse, *Zur Natur der Wachstumsschwäche
in der Bundesrepublik Deutschland. Eine empirische Analyse langer Zyklen
wirtschaftlicher Entwicklung, Kieler Diskussionsbeiträge*, 55 (Institut für
Weltwirtschaft Kiel, June 1978).

7 The Federal Republic of Germany in the secular trend of economic development

1 Statistical information is not substantiated in each individual case in order not to
extend the scope of the manuscript too far. Those interested can easily find the
references through official statistics and summaries of economic history. In
particular, reference should be made to Statistisches Bundesamt, *Bevölkerung
und Wirtschaft 1872–1972* (Wiesbaden 1972); Deutsche Bundesbank, *Deutsches
Geld- und Bankwesen in Zahlen 1876–1975* (Frankfurt 1976); Statistisches
Bundesamt, *Lange Reihen zur Wirtschaftsentwicklung* (1978).

1a See K. Borchardt, 'Germany's experience of inflation' in this volume,
pp. 132ff.

1b See the present volume, pp. 144ff. and 162ff.

1c In its content, this essay is coordinated with other contributions in the
collection: W. Conze and M. R. Lepsius (eds.), *Sozialgeschichte der
Bundesrepublik Deutschland. Beiträge zum Kontinuitätsproblem* (Stuttgart
1983).

2 See K. Borchardt, 'Trend, cycle, structural breaks, chance: what determines
twentieth-century German economic history?' in this volume, pp. 84ff. New
work on the same theme on a broader basis, W. Abelshauser and D. Petzina,
'Krise und Rekonstruktion. Zur Interpretation der gesamtwirtschaftlichen
Entwicklung Deutschlands im 20. Jh.', in W. H. Schröder and R. Spree (eds.),
Historische Konjunkturforschung (Stuttgart 1981), pp. 75ff.

3 On the, in any case methodologically difficult, concept of historical continuity
see A. Gerschenkron, 'On the Concept of Continuity in History', in A.
Gerschenkron, *Continuity in History and Other Essays* (Cambridge Mass.
1968), pp. 11ff.

4 An initial attempt was undertaken by W. G. Hoffmann, F. Grumbach and H.
Hesse, *Das Wachstum der deutschen Wirtschaft seit der Mitte des 19.
Jahrhunderts* (Berlin 1965), in the first part, pp. 12–170, placed in front of the
presentation of the evidence. International studies on the quantitative growth-
process, which also include Germany / the Federal Republic, from D. C. Paige,
F. T. Blackaby and S. Freund, 'Economic Growth: The Last Hundred Years',
National Institute Economic Review (July 1961), pp. 24ff.; A. Maddison,
Economic Growth in the West (New York 1964); A. Maizels, *Growth and Trade*
(Cambridge 1970); S. Kuznets, *Modern Economic Growth* (New Haven 1966);
S. Kuznets, *Economic Growth of Nations. Total Output and Production
Structure* (Cambridge Mass. 1971); W. W. Rostow, *The World Economy.
History and Prospect* (London 1978).

5 The figure rests, for the period from 1850 to 1950, on the information in
Hoffmann, *et al.*, *Das Wachstum*.

6 Here too it should explicitly be noted that the construction of this figure can appear dubious for many reasons, because problems of the sources and the methodology of the index statistics can only be determined arbitrarily. For the relatively crude evidence on the growth rates to be discussed here, the doubtful aspects may, however, be regarded as less critical. The occasionally preferred time-series of industrial production also stand on uncertain ground due to the problems of estimating the original material and to the index question which, in such a long-term investigation, is fundamentally insoluble without arbitrariness. They certainly do have the advantage of showing somewhat smaller gaps in the war and post-war years than the statistics for the national product.

7 Borchardt, 'Trend', above, chapter 6.

8 See among others the – hitherto not out-of-date – work by H. Wallich, *The Mainsprings of the German Revival* (New Haven 1955). In the same spirit, also H. Winkel, *Die Wirtschaft im geteilten Deutschland 1945–1970* (Wiesbaden 1974); W. Glastetter, *Die wirtschaftliche Entwicklung der Bundesrepublik Deutschland im Zeitraum 1950 bis 1975. Befunde und Aspekte* (Berlin 1977).

9 J. Schumpeter, *Business Cycles: A Theoretical, Historical and Statistical Analysis of the Capitalist Process* (New York and London 1939), esp. pp. 169ff.

10 For instance, the long waves of the Kondratieff-type were interpreted completely differently by W. W. Rostow than by H. H. Glismann, H. Rodemer and F. Wolter, *Zur Natur der Wachstumsschwäche in der Bundesrepublik Deutschland. Eine empirische Analyse langer Zyklen wirtschaftlicher Entwicklung. Kieler Diskussionsbeiträge*, 55 (Kiel 1978).

11 See also the recent work by R. Spree, Was kommt nach den "langen Wellen" der Konjunktur?' in Schröder and Spree (eds.), *Historische Konjunkturforschung*.

12 F. Jánossy, *Das Ende der Wirtschaftswunder. Erscheinung und Wesen der wirtschaftlichen Entwicklung* (Frankfurt 1969).

13 Among others, see W. Abelshauser, *Wirtschaft in Westdeutschland 1945–1948. Rekonstruktion und Wachstumsbedingungen in der amerikanischen und britischen Zone* (Stuttgart 1975); W. Abelshauser and D. Petzina, *Krise*.

14 Such curves of imagined potentials of growth are used by various authors; see also R. A. Gordon, *Economic Instability and Growth. The American Record* (New York 1974), p. 10 on the long-term curve of the potential national product of the USA; W. A. Lewis, *Growth and Fluctuations 1870–1913* (London 1978), p. 36 – where the log-linear form is also generalised.

15 G. Gehrig, *Ein makroökonomisches Modell für die Bundesrepublik Deutschland (Schriftenreihe des Ifo-Instituts für Wirtschaftsforschung, No 56)* (Berlin 1963) and also contributions in *Ifo-Studien*, 7 (1961), Nos. 1/2.

16 G. Gehrig and K. C. Kuhlo, 'Überprüfung der ökonometrischen Projektion von 1962', *Ifo-Studien*, 18 (1972), pp. 275ff.

16a W. Krug, 'Quantitative Beziehungen zwischen materiellem und immateriellem Kapital', *JNSt*, 180 (1967), pp. 36ff.

16b *Ibid.*, p. 59.

17 The values for 1850 to 1950 are taken from Hoffmann, *Das Wachstum*, pp. 253f. and 172ff. For the following period, they were linked to information in H. Lützel, 'Das reproduzierbare Sachvermögen zu Anschaffungs- und zu Wiederbeschaffungspreisen', *WiSta* (1972/11), pp. 61ff., and C. Stahmer, 'Reproduzierbares Anlagevermögen nach Wirtschaftsbereichen', *WiSta* (1979/6), pp. 411ff.

18 According to Deutsche Bundesbank (see footnote 1), pp. 2 and 4; Hoffmann, *Das Wachstum*, pp. 9825f. and also StatBA, *Lange Reihen zur Wirtschaftsentwicklung* (1978).

19 According to StatBA, *Bevölkerung*, p. 142.

20 *Ibid.*

21 *Ibid.*

22 For further material, see F. W. Henning, 'Der Beginn der modernen Welt im agrarischen Bereich', in R. Koselleck (ed.), *Studien zum Beginn der modernen Welt* (Stuttgart 1977), pp. 97ff. For instance, the numbers of draught animals changed only negligibly between 1910 and 1950. Henning arrives at the conclusion 'that – viewed from the present – one has to place the beginning of the modern world in the fifties of this century for the area of agriculture'.

23 On the significance of the still existing potential of labour forces in agriculture for the development of the economy as a whole after the Second World War, see C. P. Kindleberger, *Europe's Postwar Growth. The Role of Labour Supply* (Cambridge Mass. 1967); N. Kaldor, *Strategic Factors in Economic Development* (London 1967).

24 According to Hoffman, *Das Wachstum*, pp. 250f. and 825f. and also StatBA, *Lange Reihen zur Wirtschaftsentwicklung* (1978), pp. 172–3. See also H. Hesse, 'Strukturwandlungen im Außenhandel der Bundesrepublik Deutschland', in H. König (ed.), *Wandlungen der Wirtschaftsstruktur in der Bundesrepublik Deutschland, SchVfSp N.F.*, 26 (Berlin 1962), pp. 250ff.

25 StatBA, *Lange Reihen zur Wirtschaftsentwicklung* (1978), pp. 116ff.

26 SVR, *Jahresgutachten 1980/1*, pp. 319ff.

27 E. v. Knorring, 'Strukturwandlungen des privaten Konsums im Wachstumsprozeß der deutschen Wirtschaft seit der Mitte des 19. Jahrhunderts', in W. G. Hoffmann (ed.), *Untersuchungen zum Wachstum der deutschen Wirtschaft* (Tübingen 1971) pp. 167ff.; H. Schmucker, 'Die langfristigen Strukturwandlungen des Verbrauchs der privaten Haushalte in ihrer Interdependenz mit den übrigen Bereichen einer wachsenden Wirtschaft,' in F. Neumark (ed.), *Strukturwandel einer wachsenden Wirtschaft, SchVfSp N.F.*, 30/1 (Berlin 1964), pp. 106ff.

28 StJbb, summarised in SVR, *Jahresgutachten* – in each case in the tabular section (for the period before 1960, one can go back to older annual volumes).

29 W. W. Rostow, *Stages of Economic Growth* (Cambridge 1960, 2nd edn 1971), pp. 73ff. Although Rostow has since pushed back the beginning of the age of mass consumption from the original date of 1950 to 1925, see W. W. Rostow, *World Economy*, p. 408.

30 That is, in view of the multiplicity of subjects, already clear to the reader who scans text-books on the economic system or the constitution of the economy of the Federal Republic; see G. Gutmann, W. Klein, S. Paraskensopolous and H. Winter, *Die Wirtschaftsverfassung der Bundesrepublik Deutschland* (Stuttgart 1976); H. Lampert, *Die Wirtschafts- und Sozialordnung der Bundesrepublik Deutschland* (Munich 1981[7]).

31 Usually one refers to patterns only implicitly, for example by describing situations as 'abnormal' without stating precisely when normality had reigned. But in contemporary literature there are also many explicit references to patterns of normality. See for instance a quotation from the Weimar period: 'From year to year, the number of those whose standards of comparison are other than ours grows therewith, while we progressively orientate ourselves toward the 'norm' of the pre-war years, and have our reasons for doing so.' W. Röpke, 'Die Quellen der deutschen Kapitalbildung 1908–1913 und 1924–1929', in B. Harms (ed.), *Kapital und Kapitalismus*, Vol. 1 (Berlin 1931), p. 289.

8 Germany's experience of inflation

1 We will dispense with detailed evidence for the statements here, but to give the reader the possibility of gaining a deeper insight, some recent publications on both the inflations dealt with are given below: K. Borchardt, 'Wachstum und Wechsellagen 1914–1970' in *HdWSG*, 2 (Stuttgart 1976), pp. 698ff., 714ff. and 720ff. – in each case with references to the older literature; Deutsche Bundesbank (ed.), *Währung und Wirtschaft in Deutschland 1876–1975* (Frankfurt 1976), pp. 115ff., 157ff., 367ff., 433ff. – in each case with references to the literature; O. Büsch and G. Feldman (eds.), *Historische Prozesse der deutschen Inflation 1914 bis 1924, Ein Tagungsbericht* (Berlin 1978); C.-L. Holtfrerich, *Die deutsche Inflation 1914–1923, Ursachen und Folgen in internationaler Perspektive* (Berlin 1980) – with an extensive bibliography.

2 H. Brüning, *Memoiren 1918–1933* (Stuttgart 1970), p. 280.

3 See P. Jostock and A. Ander, 'Konzentration von Einkommen und Vermögen', in H. Arndt (ed.), 'Die Konzentration in der Wirtschaft', in SchVfSp N.F. 20/1 (Berlin 1960), pp. 208ff. — Important for the reader: the editor issued a second edition of this volume (1971) in which the contribution cited is missing!

4 See K. Borchardt, *Strukturwirkung des Inflationsprozesses (Munich 1972).*

9 Constraints and room for manoeuvre in the great depression of the early thirties: towards a revision of the received historical picture

1 Overviews of the international crisis: C. P. Kindleberger, *The World in Depression* (London 1973); J. S. Davis, *The World Between the Wars, 1919–39. An Economist's View* (Baltimore 1975); G. Haberler, *The World Economy, Money, and the Great Depression 1919–1939* (Washington 1976); 'Die Weltwirtschaftskrise und das internationale Währungssystem in der Zeit zwischen den beiden Weltkriegen', in Deutsche Bundesbank (ed.), *Währung und Wirtschaft in Deutschland 1876–1975* (Frankfurt 1976), p. 205ff. On the development in Germany, W. Conze and H. Raupach (eds.), *Die Staats- und Wirtschaftskrise des deutschen Reiches 1929/33* (Stuttgart 1967); K. Borchardt, 'Wachstum und Wechsellagen 1914–1970', *HdWSG*, 2 (Stuttgart 1976), pp. 685ff. and 703ff. (with a bibliography); D. Petzina, *Die deutsche Wirtschaft in der Zwischenkriegszeit* (Wiesbaden 1977). The extensive source-edition, *Politik und Wirtschaft in der Krise 1930–1932. Quellen zur Ära Brüning. Eingeleitet von G. Schulz (Quellen zur Geschichte des Parlamentarismus und der Politischen Parteien: Reihe 3, Die Weimarer Republik; Vol. IV)* (Düsseldorf 1980) which has since become available, could not be used in the drafting of this essay.

2 Of course, after its formation the Weimar Republic found itself in a continual crisis, which merely changed in character in the various phases. Those political forces which identified relatively unconditionally with the Weimar system were already a minority before 1930, and plans for altering the constitution were repeatedly considered even at the highest level. (See *inter alia* Graf Westarp's note, 'Montag, 18. März (1929) 5.30 bis 6.15 von Hindenburg eingeladene Besprechung', cited in E. Jonas, *Die Volkskonservativen 1928–1944* (Düsseldorf 1965), pp. 186ff. Summaries: M. Stürmer, 'Der unvollendete Parteienstaat – zur Vorgeschichte des Präsidialregimes am Ende der Weimarer Republik', *VfZ*, 21 (1973), pp. 119ff., reprinted in M. Stürmer (ed.), *Die Weimarer Republik. Belagerte Civitas* (Königstein 1980), pp. 310ff. See also the recent collection of

essays, K. D. Erdmann and H. Schulze (eds.), *Weimar – Selbstpreisgabe einer Demokratie. Bilanz heute* (Düsseldorf 1980).

It is true that, without the crisis, the end of Weimar could have looked different, and might have led for instance to one of those kinds of authoritarian leaderships also realised in other European countries in the twenties and thirties. Several authors (see *inter alia* V. Hentschel, *Weimars letzte Monate. Hitler und der Untergang der Republik* (Düsseldorf 1978)) think that, even in the crisis, no structural compulsion in Hitler's favour is deducible. Over all, one will not be able to explain Hitler's takeover of power in terms of the crisis without taking further very weighty circumstances into account, whereby there is no possibility of apportioning responsibilities precisely. But see B. S. Frey and H. Weck, 'Hat Arbeitslosigkeit den Aufstieg des Nationalsozialismus bewirkt?', *JNSt*, 196 (1981), pp. 1ff.

3 References to German authors above all in W. Grotkopp, *Die große Krise. Lehren aus der Überwindung der Wirtschaftskrise 1929/32* (Düsseldorf 1954); G. Garvy, 'Keynes and the Economic Activists of Pre-Hitler Germany', *JPE*, 83 (1975), pp. 391ff. Further, A. Korsch, 'Der Stand der beschäftigungs-politischen Diskussion zur Zeit der Weltwirtschaftskrise in Deutschland', G. Bombach, H.-H. J. Ramser, M. Timmermann and W. Wittman (eds.), *Der Keynesianismus, Vol. 1: Theorie und Praxis keynesianischer Wirtschaftspolitik. Entwicklung und Stand der Diskussion* (Berlin 1976), pp. 9ff. Unfortunately this contribution contains several errors and does not take account of the dates of the appearances of the purportedly rescuing programmes, which were in part only published after 1932, but are treated here as possible bases for Brüning's decision-making too.

4 Not a few authors have changed their opinions in the course of time. Later statements cannot necessarily count as evidence of earlier views. Understanding the context often depends on the precise dates of publication. L. A. Hahn, often viewed as a critic of the government (see also his book, *Fünfzig Jahre zwischen Inflation und Deflation* (Tübingen 1963)), still wrote on 14 May 1931: 'I do not hold the possibility of kindling a special recovery in Germany to be given.' In *SP*, 40 (14 May 1931).

5 In preference to many pieces of individual evidence, see the following summarising judgements: 'Furthermore, Brüning's economic course is predominantly judged to have been wrong in recent literature . . .', K. D. Erdmann, 'Die Zeit der Weltkriege', in *Gebhardts Handbuch der Deutschen Geschichte*, 4/1 (Stuttgart 1973[9]), p. 314. 'There is agreement as to Brüning's failure . . .', G. Bombach, 'Einleitung', to G. Bombach, H. J. Ramser, M. Timmermann and W. Wittmann, *Keynesianismus, Vol. II: Die beschäftigungs-politische Diskussion vor Keynes in Deutschland*, p. 6. Finally, sharply critical in conclusion, W. Jochmann, 'Brünings Deflationspolitik und der Untergang der Weimarer Republik', in D. Stegmann, B.-W. Wendt and P.-C. Witt (eds.), *Industrielle Gesellschaft und Politisches System. Beiträge zur politischen Sozialgeschichte* (Bonn 1978), pp. 97ff.

In the German-speaking world, the sharpest critic of subjectivist positions to date is T. Kuczynski, 'Das Ende der Weltwirtschaftskrise in Deutschland 1932/33', unpublished thesis (Hochschule für Ökonomie in Berlin 1972). Contrastingly, the comparatively great understanding which H. Sanmann, 'Daten und Alternativen der deutschen Wirtschafts- und Finanzpolitik in der Ära Brüning', *Hamburger Jb. f. Wirtschafts- und Gesellschaftspolitik*, 10 (1965), pp. 109ff. musters for Brüning emerges not from a lesser estimation of the scope for policy in the crisis, but from the readiness to accept the political goal of getting rid of reparations which was held to be paramount.

6 How controversial the opinions as to the appropriate methods of fighting a

crisis are even today is shown in an overview by H. J. Ramser, 'Krisenbekämpfung aus der Sicht verschiedener zeitgenössischer Lehrmeinungen', in W. Petwaidic (ed.), *Wirtschafts- und Gesellschaftspolitik in kritischen Zeiten. Festschrift für Dr. Heinrich Dräger* (Frankfurt 1978), p. 69.

7 The fact that there is still no agreement in respect of the causes of the long and deep crisis contrasts markedly with the unanimity of critical judgement on the purportedly erroneous policy in the crisis and the contribution of this policy to the deepening of the downturn. On the numerous differing explanations of the great depression, see the literature mentioned in footnote 1 and also L. Barber, 'On the Origins of the Great Depression', *SEJ*, 44 (1978), pp. 432ff.; P. Fearon, *The Origins and Nature of the Great Slump 1929–1932* (London 1979).

8 If only the period up to Brüning's fall is taken into consideration, it is not because the actual turn in the crisis policy in the second half of 1932 is uninteresting. But what is at issue here is the image of the Brüning period. In the second half of 1932, the conditions of domestic and foreign policy were different from what they had been before. Furthermore, the trough of the crisis had (in Germany as in other countries) been reached. That altered the prospects for the efficacy of expansionary measures which, as is well known, were taken up not only as late as the Hitler government. See among others D. Petzina, 'Elemente der Wirtschaftspolitik in der Spätphase der Weimarer Republik', *VfZ*, 21 (1973), pp. 127ff.; H. Marcon, *Arbeitsbeschaffungspolitik der Regierungen von Papen und Schleicher. Grundsteinlegung für die Beschäftigungspolitik im Dritten Reich* (Frankfurt 1974); T. Kuczynski, 'Die unterschiedlichen wirtschaftspolitischen Konzeptionen des deutschen Imperialismus zur Überwindung der Wirtschaftskrise in Deutschland 1932/33 und deren Effekt', in L. Zumpe (ed.), *Wirtschaft und Staat im Imperialismus* (Berlin 1976), pp. 215ff. Of course, what H. James writes, for the present just in a review article ('State, Industry and Depression in Weimar Germany', *HJ*, 24 (1981), p. 234), deserves great attention: 'If responsibility for recovery has to be attributed to state activity, it might be better to go back to the Brüning period.'

9 The emphasis is on the word 'expansionist', for the Brüning Government certainly did pursue business cycle politics in 1931/2, if of a sort which one characterises as 'deflationary'. (The Reichsbank certainly did try unconventional things from July 1931 on.) Jochmann (see footnote p. 111) is therefore wrong when he writes that Brüning had rejected all discussion on 'new paths of economic policy'. He certainly did tread new paths, in many areas, just not that of deficit policy financed by the bank of issue. On the attempts of active employment policy in 1930, see note 29.

10 I owe considerable stimulation for the following analysis to a lecture by the ancient historian Christian Meier, *Die Ohnmacht des allmächtigen Diktators Caesar* (Munich 1978, new edition Frankfurt 1980). There, p. 9, he says: 'Were only problems which could have been "solved" with more insight and competence really at issue here? Might it not rather be the case that social conditions, i.e. above all the way in which interests and opinions were arranged at the time, rendered the re-integration of the community completely or next to impossible? And that for everyone, even for the most talented, the most insightful, the most selfless, and not only for a man of Caesar's peculiar character and past?'

11 '. . . to regain the openness of a future of which we already know the way in which it is closed, constitutes a methodological demand on the historian, especially for the examination of the state- and economic crisis of the Weimar Republic', K. D. Erdmann, 'Die Zukunft als Kategorie der Geschichte', *HZ*, 198 (1964), p. 54. In this sense, S. Pollard, 'The Trade Unions and the

Depression of 1929–33', in H. Mommsen, D. Petzina and B. Weisbrod (eds.), *Industrielles System und politische Entwicklung in der Weimarer Republik* (Düsseldorf 1974), p. 237 also canvassed for understanding for the actors. To speak of 'failure' implies a foreknowledge of the disaster to descend on Germany which was quite out of keeping with the reasonable expectations of people who might, in their worst nightmares, visualise a return to Wilhelmine conditions but not to the barbarism which actually ensued (Pollard, *Ibid.*, p. 237).

12 Several authors prefer to retain the concept *Weltwirtschaftskrise* exclusively for the crisis after 1929, because this had not only been a world-wide crisis but, in a special way, a crisis of the world economy and its institutions (thus for instance A. Predöhl, 'Weltwirtschaftskrise', *HdSW*, 11 (1961), p. 618). The others would then have been 'crises on a world-wide scale'. But see also H. Rosenberg, *Die Weltwirtschaftskrise 1857–1859* (Stuttgart 1934, reprinted Göttigen 1974).

13 On this crisis, see D. H. Aldcroft, *From Versailles to Wall Street, 1919–1929* (London 1977), pp. 67ff.

14 On this, see F. Blaich, *Die Wirtschaftskrise 1925/6 und die Reichsregierung. Von der Erwerbslosenfürsorge zur Konjunkturpolitik* (Kallmünz 1977).

15 The theoretical basis for this assertion of the continuing and self-reinforcing downward spiral is of course still weak today.

16 When the great depression began is still debated today. The widespread customary contention that the great depression had commenced on a 'Black Friday' in October 1929 in the USA contains three mistakes in a single sentence. First, there was no 'Black Friday' in the USA, because the two big panic-like collapses of market prices took place on 24 (Thursday) and 29 (Tuesday) October. (There was a 'Black Friday' on 13 May 1927 in Germany.) Second, judging by business cycle indicators in common usage today, the crisis had already set in in the USA before that. Third, in Germany and a number of other countries the turning of the tide should be dated before that in the USA. On this, see e.g. P. Temin, 'The Beginning of the Depression in Germany', *EHR*, 2nd series, 24 (1971), pp. 240ff., and the discussion which followed, including T. Balderston, 'The German Business Cycle in the 1920's. A Comment', *EHR*, 30 (1977), pp. 159ff.

17 There is as yet no precise description and systematic analysis of the movement of the German business cycle indicators. But the time-series available show that one cannot speak of a continuous process of shrinkage. See especially data in the various periodicals of the *Institut für Konjunkturforschung* and the two editions of *Konjunkturstatistisches Handbuch* (1933 and 1935) of the Institute, then the monthly journal 'Wirtschaft und Statistik' (WiSta) published by the *Statistisches Reichsamt* and also the six-monthly reports of the *Reichs-Kredit-Gesellschaft* 'Deutschlands wirtschaftliche Lage . . .' or 'Deutschlands wirtschaftliche Entwicklung . . .'.

18 To the same effect, see J. Schumpeter, *Business Cycles* (New York and London 1939) with the chapter headings 'Incidents, Accidents, and Policy in Germany', pp. 930ff. and 'Incidents, Accidents, and Policy in the United States', pp. 936ff.

19 That political instability fundamentally impaired the aim of economic prognoses as well was the general opinion at the latest since September 1930. On this, see *inter alia* P. Mombert, 'Wandlungen in der Konjunkturgestaltung Deutschlands in der Vor- und Nachkriegszeit', *BkAr*, 30 (15 June 1931), p. 448.

20 The electoral success of the NSDAP on 14 September 1930 (6.4 million votes!) is, on the whole, not to be ascribed predominantly to the economic crisis. That emerges from an analysis of the election campaign themes and methods. See, e.g. Hitler's manifesto to the German *Volk* of 10 September 1930 in the

Völkischer Beobachter No. 215, 10 September 1930, reprinted *inter alia* in J. Hohlfeld (ed.), *Dokumente der Deutschen Politik und Geschichte von 1848 bis zur Gegenwart. Bd. III: Die Weimarer Republik 1919–1933* (Berlin undated), pp. 340ff. That is why we have thought it right to interpret this political result as an external influence on the economic course of the crisis, not as an endogenous development. However, see also Frey and Weck, 'Hat Arbeitslosigkeit . . . bewirkt?' In the winter of 1929–30, Hitler himself prophesied that he would hold power in the Reich 'in two and a half years at most', and he did not at all link this prediction – reckless at the time – to the condition of the sharpening of the economic crisis – see G. Schulz, *Aufstieg des Nationalsozialismus. Krise und Revolution in Deutschland* (Berlin 1975), p. 482.

21 This is true above all of daily and monthly lending rates, of private discount and commercial bill rates. From October 1929 until September 1930, the Reichsbank-rate was reduced from 7.5 per cent to 4 per cent and daily lending rates fell at least from 8.17 per cent (monthly average) to 4.07 per cent. Thus, until September 1930, the crisis ran a 'normal' course which was interrupted by the elections (and, as a second external event, by the bank crisis in the USA and France).

22 The notable interruption in the spring of 1931 which has been noticed in almost every country has not as yet undergone any scientific analysis. Herbert Hoover writes in his *Memoirs, Vol. III: The Great Depression 1929–1941* (New York 1951 and following years), p. 61: 'In the spring of 1931, just as we had begun to entertain well founded hopes that we were on the way out of the depression, our latent fears of Europe were realized in a gigantic explosion which shook the whole foundations of the world's economic, political, and social structure.' See also P. Temin, *Did Monetary Forces Cause the Great Depression?* (New York 1976), p. 172: 'The decline appeared to stop in early 1931, but there is no way of knowing if this was the beginning of potential recovery or simply a random deviation from a downward trend.'

23 Index of production – consumer goods subject to elastic demand. Source: *Konjunkturstatistisches Handbuch*, 1935 and *Wochenberichte IfK* and also own calculations (of the smooth components). Other indicators also showed an upward development which is not only seasonally explicable, such as raw material prices, share prices, sales. It is true that this is not the case with the production of investment goods, which are so important for the course of the business cycle.

24 On 15 May 1931, Secretary of State Hans Schäffer noted in his diary, '. . . economically, the low-point seems to have been reached, if psychological depression does not talk it down further.' See E. Wandel, *Hans Schäffer* (Stuttgart 1974), p. 159. On 13 May 1931, the *Institut für Konjunkturforschung* (Wochenbericht) believed that the 'recession in the business cycle has, on the whole, evidently come to a standstill'. And W. Röpke, a co-author of the Brauns-Report, also wrote on 21 May 1931: '. . . the next phase in the business cycle, which (at however great a distance) is lying before us, is the renewed ascent from the depression. To hasten the reaching of this next phase is the goal which the Brauns-Report has in mind', W. Röpke, 'Das Brauns-Gutachten und seine Kritiker', *SP*, 40 (21 May 1931), pp. 666f. – The proclamation of the government, with which it accompanied the Second Notverordnung zur Sicherung von Wirtschaft und Finanzen (Emergency Decree to Secure the Economy and Finances) on 5 June 1931, also still referred to the springtime hope which had since been disappointed: 'The expectation that the world economic crisis would ebb with the spring of 1931 and that the need and

unemployment of all the industrial countries, and still more of the raw material and agrarian countries, would retreat, has shown itself to have been deceptive', *Schulthess' Europäischer Geschichtskalender, N.F.* 47, 1931 (Munich 1932), p. 120.

25 On this, see also among others R. E. Lüke, *Von der Stabilisierung zur Krise* (Zurich 1958); E. W. Bennett, *Germany and the Diplomacy of the Financial Crisis, 1931* (Cambridge Mass. 1962); K. E. Born, *Die deutsche Bankenkrise 1931. Finanzen und Politik* (Munich 1967); R. Stucken, 'Die deutsche Bankenkrise von 1931', *KuK*, 1 (1968), pp. 390ff.; K. Gossweiler, *Großbanken, Industriemonopole, Staat* (Berlin 1971), pp. 369ff.; G. Hardach, 'Währungskrise 1931: Das Ende des Goldstandards in Deutschland', H. Winkel (ed.), 'Finanz- und wirtschaftspolitische Fragen der Zwischenkriegszeit', *SchVfSp N.F.*, 73 (Berlin 1973), pp. 121ff.; H. Irmler, 'Bankenkrise und Vollbeschäftigungspolitik (1931–1936) in Deutsche Bundesbank, *Währung und Wirtschaft in Deutschland 1876–1975* (Frankfurt 1976), pp. 283ff.

26 For a summary of the international course with references to further literature see Kindleberger (see footnote 1), pp. 153ff.

27 This was already pointed out in the first monographs on the great crisis, see G. Clausing, *Die wirtschaftlichen Wechsellagen von 1919–1932* (Jena 1932). In observing the crisis, J. Schumpeter, 'The Decade of the Twenties', *AER*, 36 (1946), Pap. a. Proc. pp. 1ff. distinguishes between 'depression' and 'disaster'. A. Predöhl is of the opinion that it is only the collapse of the gold standard that justifies the term 'world economic crisis', since it was only then that the possibilities of a rapid automatic passage through a trough were lost. See A. Predöhl, *Weltwirtschaftskrise*, and A. Predöhl, *Das Ende der Weltwirtschaftskrise. Eine Einführung in die Probleme der Weltwirtschaft* (Reinbek 1962).

28 On this, see the literature listed in note 23. It is true that the discussion had precursors in England, because there *structural* unemployment had already given rise to more profound reflections on the state's possibilities of taking action. From this, the suggestions which J. M. Keynes came out with developed too, without, it is true, persuading the experts or the politicians. On this, see among others S. Howson and D. Winch, *The Economic Advisory Council 1930–1939. A Study in Economic Advice During Depression and Recovery* (Cambridge 1977). Yet Keynes' proposals at the time referred substantially to three possible remedies: a lowering of nominal wages (which he rejected on predominantly political grounds), a devaluation of the Pound (which he regarded as being less helpful), the introduction or raising of tariffs (this measure for decreasing real wages was preferred by Keynes at the time).

The work of R. Friedländer (later Friedländer-Prechtl), *Chronische Arbeitskrise, ihre Ursachen, ihre Bekämpfung* (Berlin 1926), often cited as proof of the existence of a 'Keynesianism before Keynes' also proceeds – as is already stated in the title – from the assumption of an *enduring crisis* which required state action in an altogether different way. Even if several of the measures proposed do bear a resemblance to later instruments of business cycle policy, this work may not be counted as an early contribution to the theory of fiscal policy.

29 That the Brüning Government was not fundamentally opposed to directly effective measures of employment policy (as one often reads), also emerges from the extensive plans of the summer of 1930 which did, after all, envisage additional expenditure of between eight and nine hundred million RM in the course of a half-year. On this, see among others C. Landauer, 'Arbeitsbeschaffung', *Der deutsche Volkswirt* (8, August 1930), pp. 1535ff.; W. Frank, 'Das

Arbeitsbeschaffungsprogramm', *WD*, 15 (5 September 1930), pp. 1521ff. The programmes foundered on the impossibility of financing them. The *Deutsche Gesellschaft für öffentliche Arbeiten* (German Association for Public Works) founded by the Reich President's emergency decree of 29 July 1930 could not furnish the necessary financial means (above all, people had foreign credit in mind) either. See K. Wilhelmi, 'Die bisherige Tätigkeit der deutschen Gesellschaft für öffentliche Arbeiten', *SP*, 40 (25 June 1931), p. 854.

That, through increased expenditure, the state could be helpful in periods of crisis, was uncontested. It was the question of finance over which opinion was divided in 1930/2. Herein lay the significant difference to 1925 as well. When, at that time, the Reich government realised what was certainly a programme of fiscal policy, the monetary situation was exceedingly favourable. See the work of F. Blaich mentioned in footnote 14. It is true that the expansive measures of fiscal policy of 1925/6 also contributed to the significantly worsening state which Reich finances were in after 1927, and for that reason alone did not necessarily strike successors as being an example. On this see I. Maurer, *Reichsfinanzen und Große Koalition. Zur Geschichte des Reichskabinetts Müller, 1928–1930* (Bern 1973); R. Morsey, 'Brünings Kritik an der Reichsfinanzpolitik 1919–1929', in E. Hassinger, J. H. Müller and H. Ott (eds.), *Geschichte, Wirtschaft, Gesellschaft. Festschrift für Clemens Bauer* (Berlin 1974), pp. 359ff.

30 Of course, one can only speculate as to the 1931/2 lag in the effectiveness of policy measures, because there is no possibility of testing it empirically. If it has frequently been stated that the Papen programme brought about the rapid change in the business cycle (Korsch, 'Der Stand', p. 95, and H. J. Rüstow, 'Konjunkturtheorie und Konjunkturpolitik vor und nach dem ersten Weltkrieg', in Petwaidic (ed.), *Wirtschafts- und Gesellschaftspolitik*, then this does not, in any event, appear to concur with our knowledge of the lags in the impact of business cyclical policy after 1950. Furthermore, not a few business cyclical indicators already announced the change in the trend *before* the Papen programme. Here, see also T. Kuczynski, 'Das Ende der Weltwirtschaftskrise'. For an analysis of the effects of the Papen and Schleicher programmes it would, it is true, be important to differentiate more precisely between the respective plans and their realisation. In the 'Verwaltungsbericht für das Jahr 1932', p. 5, the Deutsche Reichsbank writes for instance that whereas the tax coupons of the Papen programme had often been used, it was nevertheless the case that 'the credit facilities for purposes of work-creation have so far only been called for to a small extent.' See also note 8 above.

31 On the question of the dating of the trough of the crisis in the various countries, see the literature cited in footnote 1. For Germany especially T. Kuczynski, *'Ende'*, p. 131. Differently, F.-W. Henning, 'Die zeitliche Einordnung der Überwindung der Weltwirtschaftskrise in Germany', in Winkel (ed.), *Finanz- und Wirtschaftspolitische Fragen*, pp. 135ff.

32 The Autonomy Law of 26 May 1922 (*RGBl*, II, p. 135) and the decree of 24 July 1922 regarding the alteration of the Reichsbank Statute (*RGBl*, II, p. 683) had already brought significant changes by comparison with the old Bank Law of 1875. But the Bank Law of 30 August 1924 (*RGBl*, II, p. 235) went considerably further still (Section 1): 'The Reichsbank is a bank independent of the Reich Government, having the character of a juridical person and the task . . .' Respecting the possibility of financing the public purse through the Reichsbank Section 25, para II: 'Notwithstanding the stipulation of para. 4, the Bank may allow the Reich operational credits, but these must in each case be at most for three months and only up to an upper limit of a sum of 100 million Reichsmark. At the end of the financial year, no Reich indebtedness to the Bank

may exist.' For the *Reichspost* and the *Reichsbahn*, Section 25, para. 4 drew up limits of 200 million RM. altogether. That these and several other cases of financial relations between the Reichsbank and the public purse mentioned in Section 25, were supposed to be exceptional emerges clearly once again from Section 25, para 5: 'Beyond this, the Bank may not grant credits either indirectly or directly to the *Länder* or local authorities (local authorities' organisations) or to foreign governments.' The ban on the indirect provision of credit, strictly implemented, excluded circumventions via relief organisations for financing work-creation as well. On the prehistory of the Law and its individual stipulations, see H. Schacht, *Die Reichsgesetzgebung über Münz- und Notenbankwesen* (Berlin 1926[7]).

33 The documents on the Young Plan are printed in E. Heilfron and P. Nassen, *Der Neue Plan. Young-Plan und Haager Vereinbarungen nebst den deutschen Ausführungsvorschriften* (Berlin 1931). In Chapter 8, Section 5 of the experts' plan which, in accordance with the protocol, was a part of the agreement, it is stated that 'The German Government undertakes for the purposes of these stipulations as for the general purposes of the plan that the Reichsmark is and shall remain exchangeable into gold or foreign currency in accordance with Section 31 of the present Reichsbank Act and that for these purposes the Reichsmark shall have and retain a mint par of exchange of 1/2790 kilograms of fine gold, as is provided for in the German Coinage Act of 30.8.1924', Heilfron and Nassen, *ibid.*, p. 66; similarly, at another point in the agreements, see *Ibid.*, pp. 130f. and 227. Theoretically these formulations do not appear to have contradicted a conceivable splitting of the exchange rate, since the protection of the reparations creditors after all appears to have been meant by the 'purposes of these stipulations' – and this protection would have been guaranteed if the agreed rate had been adhered to at least for the reparations payments. The remaining business of international payments could perhaps have been settled at other rates. Yet there is no reference to such considerations to be found in the contemporary sources. They would surely scarcely have been supportable in domestic politics either.

The switch to exchange controls in July 1931 needed no international legal recognition, since Section 31 of the Bank Act remained unchanged. But when, in the late summer of 1932, it was proposed that the stipulation of a minimum discount rate if reserves fell below the legal limit (Bank Act, 29), be suspended for two years, the Papen Government had to request the agreement of the Board of the Bank for International Settlements. This was granted on 19 September 1932. Even the Hitler-Papen Government still observed this law, when in September 1933 it sought agreement from the BIS to three changes in the Bank Act. The BIS Board once more gave its agreement, making it clear in the process that its task was not to judge the 'value or otherwise of the proposed changes' but the question as to 'whether, for instance, the changes are incompatible with the New Plan'. See BIS, 3rd annual report (1932/3), pp. 29f. and 4th annual report (1933/4), p. 38.

In the literature the assertion is repeatedly made that the said international commitments were no longer so restrictive, for did not even important foreign personalities advise Brüning to 'devalue'? On this, see K. Borchardt, 'On the question of Germany's currency policy options during the world economic crisis', in this volume, pp. 184ff.

33a I have since been strengthened in this opinion through further study of the documents. In particular, during the negotiations on the alteration of the Bank Act in order to adapt it to the Young Plan, the international duty to maintain currency parity was never contested on the part of the Germans despite their interest in restoring banking sovereignty. Indeed, from the outset, the German delegation characterised this point as beyond any possible revision. See ZStA, Potsdam Reichswirtschaftsministerium, No. 15578–82.

34 It is not tenable to maintain that a majority of the so-called 'reformers' inclined towards the extreme Right. Yet it appears very doubtful whether one will be able to join Kindleberger (see footnote 1) in saying that the 'reformers' stood in opposition to Hitler. In that case it would be obscure why, for instance, Heinrich Dräger's interesting plan, *Arbeitsbeschaffung durch produktive Kreditschöpfung*, first appeared in March 1932 in the Nationalsozialistische Bibliothek (No. 41), published by G. Feder. Jochman, however (*Brünings Deflationspolitik*), seeks to give the impression that Brüning's inactivity finally drove the reformers into the National Socialists' camp. But, if the precise dates of the development and publication of the plans are followed, then this construction appears to me to lay the burden too heavily on Brüning. A. Barkai, *Das Wirtschaftssystem des Nationalsozialismus. Der historische und ideologische Hintergrund 1933–1936* (Cologne 1977), p. 44 explains the fact that the reformist proposals for deficit-financed work creation were well received almost exclusively among politicians and political formations which, like the NSDAP, occupied a right-wing position in the political arena in the following manner: because most of the proposals contravened the letter and the spirit of binding international agreements, 'politicians and parties which supported first the "fulfilment policy" of Stresemann and then the international endeavours of Brüning which finally led to the agreement of Lausanne [could] scarcely support such proposals. The NSDAP and its fellow-travellers in the "Nationalist Opposition" were completely free of such inhibitions.' (*Ibid.*, p. 56).

An exception in the political spectrum was the WTB-plan accepted by the 'Krisenkongreß' of the ADGB in April 1932 (but not before), which fundamentally also provided for deficit-financing, albeit in so small a measure and with so many curtailments that not much more than a change of mood could have emanated from this plan either. See M. Schneider, *Das Arbeitsbeschaffungsprogramm des ADGB. Zur gewerkschaftlichen Politik in der Endphase der Weimarer Republik* (Bonn 1975).

The KPD's 'work creation plan' of May 1931 was highly traditional in respect of the question of finance which is decisive here. It provided practically only for a politically unrealistic reshuffle of state expenditure and tax burdens, which would surely also have had an economically counterproductive effect. The plan is reprinted in S. Vietzke and H. Wohlgemuth, *Deutschland und die deutsche Arbeiterbewegung in der Zeit der Weimarer Republik 1919–1933* (Berlin 1966), pp. 509ff. How T. Kuczynski, *Ende* could have come to the conclusion that this plan could have helped is incomprehensible. According to a Marxist perspective, all plans which wanted to intervene in the course of the crisis must really be doomed to fail, for after all it was, in principle, the task of the crisis to remove the 'contradictions'. Organised measures of anti-cyclical policy would accordingly have been able only temporarily to diminish the depth of the crisis, but on the other hand would have had to increase its duration. It is in this spirit that the theoretician of the Communist International, E. Varga, judges the Hoover 'Capital-Labor-Pact' in autumn, 1929, see *Internationale Presse-Korrespondenz*, 10/1 (3 February 1930), p. 271: 'Organisierte Krisenbekämpfung – ein aussichtsloser Versuch.' It is noteworthy that, in the question of fighting the crisis, strict Liberals and strict Marxists came to very similar conclusions. It is therefore regrettably one-sided when C. D. Krohn subjects the 'bourgeois theory of business cycles' to a sharp criticism but explicitly excludes an examination of socialist theories of the crisis. See C. D. Krohn, 'Autoritärer Kapitalismus. Wirtschaftskonzeptionen im Übergang von der Weimarer Republik zum Nationalsozialismus' in Stegmann, *et al.* (eds.), *Industrielle Gesellschaft*, p. 114. On the contemporary Marxist interpretation of the crisis, see also the recent work, which could not have been taken into account here, by R. H. Day, *The 'Crisis' and the 'Crash'. Soviet Studies of the West (1917–1939)* (London 1981).

35 *Gutachten zur Arbeitslosenfrage, Teil 1–3. Sonderveröffentlichung des Reichsarbeitsblatts 1931.* The parts were published one after another: Part 1 on 4 April 1931, Part 2 on 29 April/5 May 1931 and Part 3 on 28 May/5 June 1931. Part 2 is relevant here.

36 This is also emphasised by the co-authors of the plan in their publications commenting on the experts' report: 'What we lack is a loans prospect sufficiently appealing to the foreign credit-giver, and the whole Brauns-Report is to be regarded as such a prospect' (Röpke, 'Das Brauns-Gutachten'. See also W. Lautenbach, 'Das neue Gutachten der Brauns-Kommission', *WD*, 16 (8 May 1931), pp. 790ff. and W. Lautenbach, 'Bekämpfung der Arbeitslosigkeit durch Arbeitsbeschaffung', *SP*, 40 (14 May 1931), pp. 617ff. In this respect G. Kroll misrepresents reality when he writes: 'While Lautenbach gradually and carefully broke loose from the idea that foreign credits were absolutely necessary for "cranking up" the business cycle, the report of the Brauns-Commission remained rooted in this notion.' (G. Kroll, *Von der Weltwirtschaftskrise zur Staatskonjunktur* (Berlin 1958), p. 381.) A turn towards domestic sources of financing for increased state expenditure can, in Lautenbach's case, be demonstrated only some time after the publication of the article cited above. See also W. Lautenbach, *Zins, Kredit und Produktion*, edited by W. Stützel (Tübingen 1952). Moreover, see also A. Feiler, 'Auslandskredite – Arbeitsbeschaffung', *SP*, 40 (28 May 1931), pp. 681f.

37 Rather than many references, see H. Graml, *Europa zwischen den Kriegen* (Munich 1969) and in Institut für Zeitgeschichte (ed.), *Deutsche Geschichte seit dem Ersten Weltkrieg*, Vol. 1 (Stuttgart 1971), pp. 383ff.

38 On reparations policy, see W. J. Helbich, *Die Reparationen in der Ära Brüning* (Berlin 1962); now – correcting Helbich too – W. Glashagen, 'Die Reparationspolitik Heinrich Brünings 1930–1931. Studien zum wirtschafts- und außenpolitischen Entscheidungsprozeß in der Auflösungsphase der Weimarer Republik' (Thesis, Bonn 1980); W. Gosmann, 'Die Stellung der Reparationsfrage in der Außenpolitik der Kabinette Brüning', in J. Becker and K. Hildebrand (eds.), *Internationale Beziehungen in der Weltwirtschaftskrise 1929–1933* (Munich 1980), pp. 237ff.; G. Schulz, 'Reparationen und Krisenprobleme nach dem Wahlsieg der NSDAP 1930. Betrachtungen zur Regierung Brüning', *VSWG*, 67 (1980), p. 200 (with two – contradictory – footnotes on my statements in this essay).

39 See Bennett, *Germany and the Diplomacy of the Financial Crisis*; J. L. Kooker, 'French Financial Diplomacy: The Interwar Years', in B. M. Rowland (ed.), *Balance of Power or Hegemony? The Interwar Monetary System* (New York 1976), pp. 83ff.

40 'For the central problem of Germany's economic situation and especially of the German labour market lies in the foreign policy of Europe.' O. v. Zwiedeneck-Südenhorst, 'Die dreifache Wurzel der Notbekämpfung', *SP*, 40 (9 July 1931 and 16 July 1931), here p. 901. Other authorities expressed themselves in similar fashion, e.g. 'There is surely no doubt that the destruction of all positive first signs on the stock market is purely political in origin, and that the key to the situation therefore rests in the Foreign Office.' E. Heimann, 'Zum

deutschen Kapital- und Anleiheprogramm', *WD*, 16 (29 May 1931), p. 931. On
the foreign policy determinants of the scope of German economic policy, see
also F. Tarnow at the Leipzig party conference of the SPD: 'It is impossible to
create sufficient capital in a short time from the national economy, for that
already founders on the whole structure of the capitalist economy itself . . . For
a long time yet we shall be obliged to make use of the world capital market and
our policy must be geared toward extending and facilitating these possibilities.'
*Sozialdemokratischer Parteitag in Leipzig vom 31. Mai bis 5. Juni im
Volkshaus, Protokoll* (Leipzig 1931), p. 48 (new imprint Glashütten 1974). And,
under 10 June 1931, Luther noted in his diary: 'Afternoon visit Geheimrat
Bachem of the Arbeiterbank. Tries to win me over to a policy of capitulation,
to all intents and purposes, to France. Things could not be managed in the way
that had been done with the emergency decree. We should have to fulfil
France's political wishes in order that she would give us money. Discussion
broke off prematurely as I was called to the Bank meeting. I had told Bachem:
even were one to hold such a path to be right, there would be no government in
Germany capable of following it. He disputes that: the German only wanted
bread.' BA NL Luther No. 501 (incomplete), copy thereof in No. 425.

41 The conjecture that France would link granting German requests to political
conditions already surfaced in the first discussion of French credits. Clues also
emerge from the speeches of the politicians responsible, see *Schulthess'
Europäischer Geschichtskalender* N.F., pp. 371ff., yet the seriousness of these
conditions was disputed for some time. It is true that the French conception did
come through clearly to the outside world in the communiqué of the Paris
negotiations of 19 July 1931: 'The representatives of the Fr. Govt. recognised
the seriousness of the crisis and have declared that, with the proviso of certain
financial guarantees and politically calming measures (mesures d'apaisement
politique), they are prepared later to discuss the modalities of financial cooperation in an international framework', *ibid.* p. 376. On this, see also the
literature cited in footnotes 25, 38 and 39.

42 Telegram of the leaders of the 'Nationalist Opposition' to Reich Chancellor Dr
Brüning, 21 July 1931, Para. 4: 'The entire nationalist opposition therefore
formally draws attention to the fact that, in accordance with its fundamental
principles, it will not regard new conditions which are being entered into in
respect of France as being legally binding.' H. Michaelis and E. Schraepler
(eds.), *Ursachen und Folgen. Vom deutschen Zusammenbruch 1918 und 1945
bis zur staatlichen Neuordnung Deutschlands in der Gegenwart, Bd. 8: Die
Weimarer Republik* (Berlin 1963), pp. 1994f.

43 'The Reich President had given notice that he would resign in the event of
acceptance . . . You will find the sources on this in the Koblenz Federal
Archive under the Cabinet minutes and the Pünder Papers and in my diaries at
the "Institut für Zeitgeschichte".' Secretary of State H. Schäffer to Dr Kurt
Wolf, Gräfeling b. München, 7 May 1966 – published in excerpt in a reader's
letter in the *Süddeutsche Zeitung* 16/17 May 1970 and, to my gratitude, sent to
me.

44 Of course Brüning needed no pressure from outside in order to resist the
temptation of a credit which shackled him politically. See Brüning, *Memoiren,
1918–1938* (Stuttgart 1970), p. 330. As early as the bank crisis – according to
the memoirs, p. 317 – he declared 'that we would never capitulate' after the
partner of the Berliner Handelsgesellschaft, O. Jeidels, had named the aid of
French credits as the sole way out of the crisis, which would require the
precondition 'that the Reich government capitulate immediately in its foreign
policy to France . . .'

45 This is above all emphasised by Helbich, *Die Reparationen*. In this, Sanmann, 'Daten und Alternativen', follows him. Contrastingly, H. Köhler, 'Arbeitsbeschaffung und Reparationen in der Schlußphase der Regierung Brüning', *VfZ*, 17 (1969), pp. 276ff., especially, it is argued, as after the cancellation of the reparations, it emerged that the ostensible drawers filled with alternative programmes had never existed. On the weight of Helbich's arguments on reparations policy now, see also Glashagen, 'Die Reparationspolitik', and Gosmann, 'Die Stellung'. Independently thereof, the fact that the removal of reparations was a vital goal of German policy remains undisputed. If, as many people did at the time, one sees in reparations a significant cause of the heavy crisis (which, seen in purely economic terms, is assuredly incorrect), then a policy directed towards the removal of the reparations could even be interpreted as a policy for overcoming the crisis. In this spirit, see for example Ministerialrat Neumann, 'Reparationen und Entstehung der Wirtschaftskrise', *BkAr*, 30 (1 July 1931); Ministerialrat Neumann, 'Reparation und Wirtschaftskrise. Reparation und Überwindung der Krise', *BkAr*, 30 (15 July 1931). But see H. Fleisig, 'War-Related Debts and the Great Depression', *AER*, 66/2 (1976), pp. 52ff.; Haberler, *The World Economy*, pp. 232ff.

46 W. Galenson and A. Zellner, 'International Comparisons of Unemployment Rates' in *The Measurement and Behavior of Unemployment. A Conference of the Universities National Bureau for Economic Research* (New York 1975), pp. 455f.; A. Agthe, 'Übersicht der Arbeitslosigkeit in der Welt', in M. Saitzew (ed.), *Die Arbeitslosigkeit in der Gegenwart*, *SchVfSp, Bd., 185/I* (Munich 1932).

47 O. Büsch and G. Feldman (eds.), *Historische Prozesse der deutschen Inflation 1914 bis 1924. Ein Tagungsbericht* (Berlin 1978); C. H. Holtfrerich, *Die deutsche Inflation 1914–1923* (Berlin 1980). See also K. Borchardt, 'Germany's Experience of Inflation' in this volume, p. 132ff.

48 Instead of much further evidence, W. Albers, 'Finanzpolitik in der Depression und in der Vollbeschäftigung' in Deutsche Bundesbank, *Währung*, p. 340: 'From today's perspective, Brüning's deflationary policy must be perceived as having miscarried. A gap in demand in the private sector must be compensated by additional demand from the public sector, which may be financed without endangering the stability of the currency (!) by the creation of money.' But at the time J. M. Keynes saw the salvation for England precisely in raising the level of prices which was intended to have the purpose of lowering real wages at constant nominal wage rates. See J. M. Keynes, 'Gedanken über Freihandel', *WD*, 16 (1 May 1931), p. 750.

49 For the most part, the more recent economic discussion overlooks the instability of the political framework in 1931/2, which scarcely permitted of trust in measured doses of money creation. Even G. Colm, who is numbered among the reformers today, had a low estimation of the positive possibilities of limited money-creation at the time: 'Today, every inflation would, in a sense, leapfrog over fruitful stages of the sort we came to know in the years 1921 and 1922, and lead very rapidly to the catastrophic situation of 1923. What we understand by inflation here are all those measures which, whether intentionally or by virtue of their perhaps unintended consequences, lead to the fact that in Germany revenues are continually drawn not from the circulation of profits, taxes etc., but from the printing of bank notes.' G. Colm, 'Wege aus der Weltwirtschaftskrise', in *Die Arbeit* (November 1931), pp. 815ff. That Germany was in far greater danger of soon experiencing a collapse of her currency is also emphasised by E. Varga, 'Wirtschaft und Wirtschaftspolitik im

4. Vierteljahr 1931', in *Internationale Presse-Korrespondenz* 12/13 (15 February 1932), p. 354.

50 On this see the wide-ranging work by M. Wolffsohn, *Industrie und Handwerk im Konflikt mit staatlicher Wirtschaftspolitik? Studien zur Politik der Arbeitsbeschaffung in Deutschland 1930–1934* (Berlin 1977); M. Wolffsohn, 'Banken, Bankiers und Arbeitsbeschaffung im Übergang von der Weimarer Republik zum Dritten Reich', in *Bankhistorisches Archiv* 1977/1, pp. 54ff.; M. Schneider, *Unternehmer und Demokratie. Die freien Gewerkschaften in der unternehmerischen Ideologie der Jahre 1918 bis 1933* (Bonn 1975), pp. 118ff.

51 U. Hüllbüsch, 'Die deutschen Gewerkschaften in der Weltwirtschaftskrise', in Conze/Raupach (eds.), *Die Staats- und Wirtschaftskrise*, pp. 126ff.; Pollard, *Trade Unions*; Schneider, *Arbeitsbeschaffungsprogramm*; H. Mommsen, 'Staatliche Sozialpolitik und gewerkschaftliche Strategie in der Weimarer Republik', in O. Borsdorf (ed.), *Gewerkschaftspolitik heute: Reform aus Solidarität. Festschrift für Vetter* (Cologne 1977), pp. 75ff.; M. Schneider, 'Die Stellung des Allgemeinen Deutschen Gewerkschaftsbundes zu den Regierungen Brüning bis Hitler' in W. Luthardt (ed.), *Sozialdemokratische Arbeiterbewegung und Weimarer Republik. Materialien zur gesellschaftlichen Entwicklung 1927–1933*, Vol. 1 (Frankfurt 1978), pp. 150ff.; M. Schneider, 'Arbeitsbeschaffung. Die Vorstellungen von Freien Gewerkschaften und SPD zur Bekämpfung der Wirtschaftskrise', in *Ibid.*, pp. 220ff.

The change of sides of the ADGB at the crisis Congress with the resolution of 13 April 1932, i.e. a few weeks before Brüning's fall, is in substance not quite so very radical as is often claimed. Most of the measures demanded in the resolution had long been uncontroversial – *if* it had been possible to implement them. And for financing them, the resolution foresees in the first instance taxes, loans, and also once again savings in unemployment insurance. Yet the path towards the creation of credit is finally mentioned as well: 'In as much as the loans are not yet fully accommodated in the capital market, they should serve the banks as a basis for intermediate financing of work-creation. In order to increase the security of the payment of interest on, and repayment of, the credits, special administrative unions of the debtors' bodies must necessarily be formed.' Schneider, *Arbeitsbeschaffungsprogramm*, p. 235. The WTB plan which underpinned this resolution was on the whole of very modest dimensions. Then, in the course of the discussion, Naphtali emphasised that a much larger amount of finance – and that means inflation – would immediately become necessary in order to achieve success by this road.

52 That is an important point of difference compared with 1914–23, when the significant political forces (albeit in part for different reasons) supported the inflation policy for the time being.

53 Instead of many references see R. Skidelsky, *Politicians and the Slump. The Labour Government of 1929–1931* (London 1967). A critique of this is R. McKibbin, 'The economic policy of the second Labour Government 1929–1931' in *Past and Present*, 68 (1975), pp. 95ff.

54 For the SPD, currency stability was a substantial point of political dispute with the right. See for example the following excerpt from an article in the late edition of *Vorwärts* of 12 October 1931, in which the author takes up the 'Schacht Case', Schacht's speech in Bad Harzburg: 'His programme means: new inflation in Germany (spaced out in the text) . . . this is where the inflationary front between big landowners, industrialists in heavy industry and fascists was closed, and Herr Schacht is leading it! Fascism means inflation! Its goal is to pay the workers inflationary wages for which they can scarcely buy bread, in order that the bankrupt heavy industrialists and big landowners may

be brought to health at the cost of the workers. Fascism is the means to the end of the political subjugation of the workers, inflation is its economic weapon against the workers.' See also R. A. Gates, 'Von der Sozialpolitik zur Wirtschaftspolitik. Das Dilemma der deutschen Sozialdemokratie in der Krise 1929–1933', in Mommsen *et al.* (eds.), *System*, pp. 206ff.; R. Leuschen-Seppel, 'Budget- und Agrarpolitik der SPD', in Luthardt (ed.), *Sozialdemokratische Arbeiterbewegung*, pp. 83ff.; Schneider, 'Arbeitsbeschaffung', in *Ibid.*, pp. 220ff.

55 In those countries to which a successful anti-cyclical policy was *later* ascribed, the turn came only in 1932/3. In *Sweden*, attempts at a policy of fighting the crisis were first discussed in the autumn of 1932. See B. Thomas, *Monetary Policy and Crisis: A Study in Swedish Experience* (London 1936); C. G. Uhr, 'Economists and Policymaking 1930–1936: Sweden's Experience', *HPE*, 9 (1977), pp. 89ff. For the USA see L. V. Chandler, *America's Greatest Depression, 1929–1941* (New York 1970). Roosevelt still conducted his election campaign against Hoover with bitter accusation respecting his alleged deficit economics and, for his part, promised the resurrection of financial order! In the USA, the two great parties put through the biggest increase in taxation in American history in the trough of the crisis in 1932! On *Great Britain*, see *inter alia* S. Hawson, *Domestic Monetary Management in Britain 1919–38* (Cambridge 1975); S. Pollard, *The Development of the British Economy 1914–1967* (1969²). General critical overviews in H. W. Arndt, *The Economic Lessons of the Nineteen-Thirties* (Oxford 1944) and E. Lundberg, *Instability and Economic Growth* (New Haven 1968).

56 It cannot be emphasised enough that what has often been personalised as 'Brüningite policy' was in great measure, at least until the spring of 1932, the policy shaped by many forces, if only in the sense that there was no other way in which consensus could be formed. What boundaries even modest forms of authoritarian finance policies of a new order came up against is also evidenced by the conflict of the Reich government with the administration of the Reich debts which, among other things, in the aftermath of the emergency decree of 20 February 1932, doubted whether Article 48, Para. 2 of the Reich Constitution permitted additional indebtedness by means of emergency decree (in lieu of a law passed by the Reichstag) at all. This was also what was ultimately at issue during the memorable session of the Reichstag on 9/10 May 1932 (first reading of the law on the liquidation of debts). The National Socialists characterised the take-up of credit by emergency decree as being impermissible, but Gregor Strasser then, on 10 May 1932, announced the economic programme of the NSDAP. On the course of the session, see *Schulthess' Europäischer Geschichtskalender*, New Series, Vol. 48 (1932), pp. 73ff. The ministers of the interior and of finance had requested two legal opinions, which eventually gave a very broad construction to Article 48 II in the interests of the 'healing of the economy' in the context of the 'failure of the parliamentary system'; see G. Anschütz and W. Jellinek, *Reichskredite und Diktatur. Zwei Rechtsgutachten* (Tübingen 1932).

57 That is why it is necessary to relativise the assertion that Brüning had functionalised the crisis with regard to internal, but above all to external, political goals. This view is presented yet again by H. Mommsen, 'Heinrich Brünings Politik als Reichskanzler: Das Scheitern eines politischen Alleinganges', in K. Holl (ed.), *Wirtschaftskrise und liberale Demokratie. Das Ende der Weimarer Republik und die gegenwärtige Situation* (Göttingen 1978), pp. 16ff. We would concur with Petzina, *Elemente*, p. 133: 'The Keynesian critique of Brüning's economic policy taken up in the first instance by

economists, and later also by historians, as a rule neglected to denote the political preconditions of an alternative crisis strategy just as it reduced economic policy unilaterally to the aspect of deflation and restrictive budgetary policy, without simultaneously referring to the active – if, for the purposes of fighting the crisis, ultimately inadequate – policy of state subvention.' Petzina also indicates the result in another context: 'Without being able to examine the question here as to whether there was, under the political conditions of the late phase of Weimar, a realistic chance of a change in course – and scepticism is called for – the repercussions [of the crisis, K.B.] for the public consciousness of the following generations are not in dispute and virtually traumatic in their intensity.' D. Petzina, *Krise gestern und heute – die Rezession von 1974/75 und die Erfahrungen der Weltwirtschaftskrise (Vortragsreihe der Gesellschaft für Westfälische Wirtschaftsgeschichte e. V., H. 21k)* (Dortmund 1977), p. 26.

58 It is not possible to go into the economic and political problems of a devaluation or devaluation in greater detail here. Since October 1931, there had been some suggestions to this effect in Germany. See Borchardt, 'Germany's exchange rate options' in this volume, pp. 184ff.

59 In a strict sense, it will never be possible to prove the theses, since too many circumstances, about which one could only make crude assumptions, would have to be taken into account in an alternative model. This was already recognised by G. Colm in the course of an attempt made in November 1931 to provide quantitative data for the order of magnitude of a crisis programme: 'Here too, the difficulty lies in the fact that statements of size cannot be made because there are too many unknowns in the equation', Colm, *Wege aus der Weltwirtschaftskrise*, p. 830. The assumption made by Friedländer-Prechtl, '16 Thesen zur Wirtschaftskrise', in *Wirtschafts-Wende* (30 September 1931), according to which, with 2 thousand million RM, some 4 million workers could additionally be set in motion through secondary and tertiary effects, was completely illusory. It was this that Heinrich Draeger's plan, *Arbeitsbeschaffung durch produktive Kreditschöpfung, Juni/August 1932* (new edn 1956) soothingly proceeded, for he estimates that, in 1932/3, a programme of 2 thousand million RM would surely initially bring about a diminution of the level of unemployment to the tune of half a million. He then continues: 'Only given a work creation programme of between 3 and 5 thousand million per annum in extent may one anticipate an effect in the sense of a diminution of the high total figures of unemployment worthy of mentioning and really conclusive.' In his later 'Hindenburg-Programm für Arbeitsbeschaffung', printed in Bombach, *et al.* (eds.), *Keynesianismus*, Draeger outlined a programme, to be spread out over a period of years, on a scale of 30 thousand million RM, though admittedly without going into the question of financing it in any detail at this point. A study which estimated the application of alternative tools of financial policy in the USA on the basis of an econometric model, came to the conclusion that a successful counter-cyclical policy would have had in all measure to have exceeded the estimates mooted in even the most balanced notions entertained in the thirties. M. R. Norman, 'The Great Depression and What Might Have Been: An Econometric Model Simulation' (Ph.D. Thesis, University of Pennsylvania 1969). There are as yet no comparable studies on Germany.

60 The gross domestic product for 1929 was calculated at 88.4 thousand million RM, see Statistisches Bundesamt, *Bevölkerung und Wirtschaft 1872–1972* (Wiesbaden 1972), p. 260. Even this GDP lagged behind the possibilities as a result of the high unemployment rate!

61 See Sachverständigenrat zur Begutachtung der gesamtwirtschaftlichen
Entwicklung, *Jahresgutachten 1978/9, Wachstum und Währung* (Stuttgart
1978), pp. 262 and 245. It is true that one cannot regard the total contribution
of the deficits in 1975 as 'stimulating economic activity'. The so-called 'impulse
toward economic activity' of actual state spending is calculated at 36.9 thousand
million DM by the committee of experts – *ibid.*, p. 108. That would
correspond to 3.6 per cent of the gross domestic product. With comparisons
between increased expenditure for work creation discussed in 1931/2 and
increased indebtedness today, it is true that it is also necessary to take into
account the fact that the authors of that time frequently believed that they
would only have to finance a portion of the increased expenditure for these
purposes with loans, so that the amount of the additional means effectively in
circulation would have been even smaller.

62 This is not to take over the thesis that only economic grounds caused Hitler's
seizure of power (see footnote 2). Rather, it is only said that, even if one does
adhere to this thesis, the documents of the period do not permit the conclusion
that effective antidotes existed at the time. A different view is presented by H.-
J. Rüstow, who even gives the impression that Brüning had available to him a
possibility of 'removing unemployment. He would then certainly not have been
overthrown, and the nameless misery which came over us would then have been
spared not us alone but the whole world.' H.-J. Rüstow, 'Entstehung und
Überwindung der Wirtschaftskrise am Ende der Weimarer Republik und die
gegenwärtige Rezession. Überlegungen eines Beteiligten', in Holl (ed.),
Wirtschaftskrise, p. 143. The notion that Brüning could have put an end to
unemployment is certainly utopian, especially as there was, after all, already
considerable unemployment before the crisis and as, even under extremely
favourable conditions, massive state activity later still took years to remove
unemployment, something which was not achieved in any democratic country
before the Second World War. For those who adhere to the thesis that Hitler
would have been avoidable with the aid of economically active programmes, it
would thus necessarily be important to determine by which degrees of higher
employment and profits Hitler could still have been stopped – and whether this
might have been achieved rapidly.

63 It is not permissible to extrapolate the chances of such measures in 1931/2 from
the observation of later successes of expansionary economic policy. Moreover,
there is a great deal of discussion as to whether and to what extent the recovery
of the years after 1932 were really due to the respective policies of the
governments and central banks. From critical examinations of the fiscal policies
of the thirties it emerged in respect of the USA that the expansionary effect of
public spending was at its highest in 1931 of all years, whereas from 1933 to
1939, with the exception of 1936, in the full employment budget, always
surpluses were produced; see E. C. Brown, 'Fiscal Policy in the Thirties: A
Reappraisal', *AER*, 46 (1956), pp. 857ff. Regarding Sweden, E. Lundberg's
appraisal is noteworthy: 'There is no doubt that this new approach (increase in
public spending – financed through the take-up of credit, K.B.) had a great and
lasting significance in the development of ideas, but the actual measures taken
after 1932 were of secondary importance in the revival of 1932–34. The
expansionist plans were impeded by such events as the labour dispute on the
building industry in 1933–1934, and they could not be realized on any large
scale until 1934–1935, by which time the trade revival was already past its first
stage.' E. Lundberg, *Business Cycles and Economic Policy* (London 1957), p.
55.

64 On economic analysis of the development to 1929, see Borchardt, 'Wachstum',

pp. 685ff. and 703ff.; W. Fischer, 'Die Weimarer Republik unter den
weltwirtschaftlichen Bedingungen der Zwischenkriegszeit', in Mommsen *et al.*
(eds.), *System*, pp. 26ff.; D. Petzina and W. Abelshauser, 'Zum Problem der
relativen Stagnation der deutschen Wirtschaft in den zwanziger Jahren', in
Mommsen, *et al.* (eds.), pp. 57ff.; R. Stucken, 'Schaffung der Reichsmark,
Reparationsregelungen und Auslandsanleihen, Konjunkturen (1924–1930)', in
Deutsche Bundesbank, *Währung*, pp. 249ff.; G. Hardach,
*Weltmarktorientierung und relative Stagnation. Währungspolitik in
Deutschland 1924–1939* (Berlin 1976); see also R. Stucken, 'Zur politischen
Ökonomie der Weimarer Republik', in R. Kühnl and G. Hardach (eds.), *Die
Zerstörung der Weimarer Republik* (Cologne 1979[2]), pp. 14ff. For an
international comparison, see Aldcroft (see footnote 13).

65 Net domestic product at 1913 prices per capita and logarithmic-linear trend
1850–1913. Source: W. G. Hoffmann, F. Grumbach and H. Hesse, *Das
Wachstum der deutschen Wirtschaft seit der Mitte des 19. Jahrhunderts* (Berlin
1965), for 1850–1950/9, linked from 1950 on with information from official
statistics, Statistisches Bundesamt, *Lange Reihen zur Wirtschaftsentwicklung
1974*, and current data. For the purposes pursued here, methodological
objections to the construction of such long time-series do not appear to be
significant, because only relatively rough comparisons of growth rates are at
issue.

66 Yet the expression, possibly appropriate to its cultural life, of the 'golden
twenties', is often extended to the economy. But even industrial production only
slightly exceeded the pre-war level until 1928, see R. Wagenführ, 'Die deutsche
Industriewirtschaft', in *VfKf Sonderheft, 31* (Berlin 1933).

67 In 1910/13, the average net rate of investment amounted to 16 per cent, in
1925/9 to 10.5 per cent. See K. Borchardt, 'Changes', in this volume pp. 59ff.

　　In detail, the net investments per capita at constant prices, calculated
according to the evidence in Hoffmann (see footnote 65), p. 828 together with
p. 174 ran to the following sums (in M and RM respectively):

1905	111.25	1910	102.37	1925	85.17
1906	115.12	1911	119.80	1926	51.86
1907	124.81	1912	129.86	1927	126.05
1908	95.76	1913	121.98	1928	106.84
1909	105.15			1929	54.83

　　That these data are subject to several uncertainties does not render them
useless for the purposes of longer-term comparison.

68 According to Hoffmann, *Wachstum*, pp. 828 and 174. A different interpretation
in Schulz, *Aufstieg*, p. 448: 'Neither purchasing power, nor the supply of
consumer goods, nor yet welfare provisions could grow. What happened was
precisely the opposite of what the reformers of capitalism in Germany held to
be required. Even in the relatively good years – good for industry – of 1925 to
1928, any improvement of general conditions among the growing army of the
workforce was lacking.' There is scarcely any evidence for these assertions. See
also the literature referred to in note 70.

69 Labour productivity in the economy as a whole (net national product at 1913
market prices per gainfully employed person). Source: Hoffmann, *Wachstum*
and several calculations on the basis of the official statistics 1950 and following
years. The reader is reminded of the comment in note 65.

70 On the development of wages see above all G. Bry, *Wages in Germany 1871–*

1945 (Princeton 1960); R. Skiba, 'Die langfristige Entwicklung der Reallöhne', *WWI Mitteilungen 1969*, pp. 192ff.; E. H. Phelps Brown and M. H. Browne, *A Century of Pay. The Course of Pay and Production in France, Germany, Sweden, the United Kingdom, and the United States of America, 1860–1960* (London 1968); R. Skiba and H. Adam, *Das westdeutsche Lohnniveau zwischen den beiden Weltkriegen und nach der Währungsreform* (Cologne 1974); M. v. Lölhöffel, 'Zeitreihen für den Arbeitsmarkt. Lohnsatz, Beschäftigungsfälle, Arbeitskosten und Arbeitsstunden (1925 bis 1938 und 1950 bis 1967)', *Ifo Studien*, 20 (1974), pp. 33ff. In consequence of the shorter working hours by comparison with the pre-war period, average real *weekly* wages continued to lag behind the pre-war level until 1927. Of course, developments varied to a considerable extent as between the individual categories of employee. (See Bry, *Wages in Germany*.) As a rule, those at lower wage levels were able to improve their position faster than those on the higher wage levels.

71 According to Phelps Brown and Browne, *A Century of Pay*, p. 210, the increases in the real incomes of wage earners in 1930/1 compared with 1905 or (USA) 1909 amounted to: Sweden 64 per cent, Germany 39 per cent, USA 30 per cent, Great Britain 28 per cent and France 23 per cent. Increases in free time (shortening of the working week) amounted to 31 per cent in Sweden, 33 per cent in Germany, 31 per cent in France, 17 per cent in Great Britain and 8 per cent in the USA. See the source for a more detailed interpretation of the data and the methods on which this information rests.

72 The 'cumulated position of real wages' in Germany (German Reich and Federal Republic of Germany) 1925–77 is taken from H. H. Glisman, H. Rodemer and F. Wolter, *Zur Natur der Wachstumsschwäche in der Bundesrepublik Deutschland. Eine empirische Analyse langer Zyklen wirtschaftlicher Entwicklung (Kieler Diskussionsbeiträge Nr. 55)* (Kiel 1978), p. 29. The data for the calculation are analysed in Glisman *et al.*, *Zur empirischen Analyse langer Zyklen wirtschaftlicher Entwicklung in Deutschland – Datenbasis und Berechnungsmethoden (Kieler Arbeitspapiere Nr. 72)* (Kiel 1978), pp. 13f. On the method employed in the calculation and on the evidential content, see Sachverständigenrat zur Begutachtung der gesamtwirtschaftlichen Entwicklung, *Jahresgutachten 1977/78*, p. 214. 'From the changes in the position as regards real wages, it is possible to see whether changes in the real average wage in the economy as a whole had a neutral effect with respect to the level of costs. We call a rise in the average real wage neutral in terms of the level of costs if this is not greater than the percentage by which the per capita productivity of those in employment changes in the economy as a whole.' (SVR, 64, Ziffer 24). As a result of the limited availability of data, a somewhat simplified calculation has to be made for the years 1925–38, which probably does not, however, substantively influence the levels. The cumulation of changes in the position of real wages (proceding from the basis 1960=0) gives a time-series which indicates the percentage by which the real gross wages and incomes sum diverges from that which would have been neutral in terms of the level of costs. As figure 9.4 shows, the material result is not significantly altered by the selection of any year between 1938 and 1970 as a base-period, and there is much to be said for seeking the 'normal situation' in this rather than any other period.

It is more usual to examine the so-called wage share, that is the proportion of the national income accounted for by non-independent labour, than it is to give the position of real wages. Because this quota, in connection with the trend of decline of the proportion of independents and of family labour (increase in the proportion of the non-independent), rises within the total number of those working for a living without this signalling an 'improvement' in distribution in favour of the workforce, the 'adjusted' wage share, which eliminates the aforementioned effect of the alteration of the social composition of those earning a living is preferred. If one takes the structure of employment for the year 1950 as a base, then the adjusted wage share for 1925–9 of an average of 66.75 per cent stands at some 10 per cent above that of 1950–70. See Skiba and Adam, *Lohnniveau* (see footnote 70), p. 106 and illustration 7. See a similar account of the long-term alterations in distribution relations above, figure 6.8, p. 102.

73 Added to higher wage costs (including social contributions) were the costs of financing, considerably higher than anything known before 1914. On the development of interest rate levels, see Statistisches Bundesamt, *Bevölkerung*, pp. 214f.; Deutsche Bundesbank, *Deutsches Geld- und Bankwesen in Zahlen 1876–1975* (Frankfurt 1976), pp. 3ff. and 274ff.

74 Remembering that these statements refer to the aggregate in the national economy, and thus to averages, which does not preclude there having been enterprises and branches for which the general statement does not hold. On the development of the profitability of capital in the long term see Hoffmann, *Wachstum*, pp. 98ff. In 1925–9, the yield (capital income divided by capital stock) stood far below the levels of 1880–1913 and 1950–9.

75 Unemployment rates 1887–1938 from B. R. Mitchell, *European Historical Statistics 1750–1970* (London 1975), pp. 167ff.; 1950–1971: Statistisches Bundesamt, *Bevölkerung*, p. 148. 1972–4: *Statistische Beihefte zu den Monatsberichten der Deutschen Bundesbank*, 4th Series. The curve up to 1929 refers to the unemployment rate among trade unionists; the curve from 1929 on, to averages of monthly figures of the unemployed registered at labour exchanges. For the period before 1914, figures for the unemployed are often to be gained only through estimates. J. Kuczynski, *Die Geschichte der Lage der Arbeiter unter dem Kapitalismus*, Vol. 3 (1871–1900), p. 266, Vol. 4 (1900–1917/18), p. 315, Vol. 5 (1917/18–1932/3), p. 197 comes to somewhat different (slightly higher) figures. But this series of figures too, confirms the statement that after 1923 unemployment rates stood at a level far above those in the preceding period. The same emerges from a comparison of the figures of those seeking employment per 100 positions vacant before 1914 and from 1924, see Reichs-Kredit-Gesellschaft AG, 'Deutschlands wirtschaftliche Lage . . .' and 'Deutschlands wirtschaftliche Entwicklung . . .'.

76 To provide a complete diagnosis of the 'sickness' of economic development before 1929, which would of course require drawing on far more facts of the case, cannot be the issue here. It would also be quite imaginable that in a correspondingly constructed model, the extremely high share of income from employment and the extremely low profitability of capital are interpreted as being symptoms of other focuses of disease. But this would change nothing as regards the consequences with respect to the question posed as to the goals of a policy of fighting the crisis after 1931. See also the contribution which follows, pp. 161ff.

77 In order to avoid any misunderstanding, I should explicitly emphasise that the remarks about the 'disease' of the development up to 1929 are not intended to represent anything like a comprehensive explanation for the slump. They refer only to structural problems which allowed a recession – which would set in sooner or later, and which was furthermore affected by the simultaneous contraction in all the important world trading countries – to become especially difficult.

78 H. Kaun, *Die Geschichte der Zentralarbeitsgemeinschaft der industriellen und*

gewerblichen Arbeiter und Arbeitnehmer Deutschlands (Jena 1938); G. D.
Feldman, 'German Business Between War and Revolution. The Origins of the
Stinnes-Legien Agreement', in G. A. Ritter (ed.), *Entstehung und Entwicklung
der modernen Gesellschaft. Festschrift Hans Rosenberg* (Berlin 1970), pp.
311ff.; G. D. Feldman, 'The Origins of the Stinnes-Legien Agreement: A
Documentation', *IWK*, 19/20 (1973), pp. 45ff.

79 Alongside this, the revolutionary power intervened directly, see the
proclamation of the *Rat der Volksbeauftragten an das deutsche Volk*, 12
November 1918 (RGB1. 1918, 1303): 'The eight hour working day will come
into effect on 1. 1. 1919 at the latest. The Government will do everything
possible in order to provide for sufficient opportunities for work . . .' The
ordinance on working hours went through as early as 23 November 1918.

80 See *inter alia* G. D. Feldman and I. Steinisch, 'Die Weimarer Republik
zwischen Sozial- und Wirtschaftsstaat. Die Entscheidung gegen den
Achtstundentag', *ASG*, 18 (1978), pp. 353ff. On the following industrial
conflicts and their general political consequences, see *inter alia* G. D. Feldman,
'Aspekte deutscher Industriepolitik am Ende der Weimarer Republik 1930–
1932', in Holl (ed.), *Wirtschaftskrise*, pp. 103ff.; Schneider, *Unternehmer*.

81 On this, see L. Preller, *Sozialpolitik in der Weimarer Republik* (Stuttgart 1949,
new edn, Kronberg 1978); H.-H. Hartwich, *Die öffentliche Bindung
unternehmerischer Funktionen in der Weimarer Republik* (Berlin 1967); U.
Hüllbüsch, 'Koalitionsfreiheit und Zwangstarif. Die Stellungnahme des
Allgemeinen Deutschen Gewerkschaftsbundes zu Tarifvertrag und
Schlichtungswesen in der Weimarer Republik', in U. Engelhardt, V. Sellin and
H. Stuke (eds.), *Soziale Bewegung und politische Verfassung. Festschrift W.
Conze* (Stuttgart 1976), pp. 599ff. On the development of wages see the
literature referred to in footnote 70 and J. H. Müller, *Nivellierung und
Differenzierung der Arbeitseinkommen in Deutschland seit 1925* (Berlin 1954).

82 A dramatic summary of the troubles and arguments of the entrepreneurs may
be found in Denkschrift des Präsidiums des Reichsverbandes der Deutschen
Industrie, '*Aufstieg oder Niedergang? Deutsche Wirtschafts- und Finanzreform
1929*' (Veröffentlichung des Reichsverbandes der Deutschen Industrie Nr. 49
(Berlin December 1929). H. Soell, 'Das Versagen Weimars und die Chancen
Bonns' in *Das Parlament*, 44 (4 November 1978), p. 11 speaks of a 'failure of
the economic and social power elites' in the Weimar period: 'Industry in
particular proved itself incapable of entering into the offer of cooperation,
which the trade unions had made in 1918, with a dynamic strategy for growth,
which would above all have presupposed an increase in domestic purchasing
power through an expansion of real wages.' Unfortunately, Soell fails to give
clearer evidence for this assertion and to show ways in which this would have
been possible given the ruling constellations. By contrast, in his analyses E.
Varga, the then respected theoretician of the Communist International and
Director of the Institute for World Economy and World Politics of the Moscow
Academy of Sciences, regularly emphasised all those circumstances forcing the
German entrepreneurs to exert pressure on costs and especially on wages. See
his interpretations in *Internationale Presse-korrespondenz*, 70/9 (8 August
1929), p. 1609, 107/9 (18 November 1909) and 12/10 (3 February 1930),
pp. 279ff., etc.

83 'That the governments were unsuccessful in correcting this overburdening of
the economic system was surely one of the decisive structural problems of the
Weimar Republic.' Petzina, *Krisen*, p. 21.

84 In 1930, there were attempts at reinvigorating the Central Working
Community. Due to opposition within both participating organisations,

however, these failed to arrive at any result. See U. Wengst, 'Unternehmerverbände und Gewerkschaften in Deutschland im Jahre 1930', *VfZ*, 25 (1977), pp. 99ff. After the departure of the pound from the gold standard, too, voices were raised in the government to the effect that a new central working community would have to be created. On 24 September 1931, during the first cabinet session after the flotation of the pound, Trendelenburg and Treviranus addressed this possibility, but Brüning 'replied that it was not now possible to bring a central working community into being'. BA R 43/11452.

85 When, in England, J. M. Keynes considered the question of how real wages could be lowered (a measure he held to be necessary), he dismissed the possibility of lowering nominal wages, since this would involve 'a sort of civil war or guerilla warfare carried on, industry by industry, all over the country' – in short a political adventure. Of course, his preferred option (a massive increase in import duties by a simple act of legislation given the assumed monetary illusion of the trade unions) was not available in Germany. On J. M. Keynes' views, see Howson and Winch, *The Economic Advisory Council*, p. 58.

86 The theory of the 'purging crisis' has a tradition reaching back far into the nineteenth century and long had a considerable explanatory force for the understanding of general economic movements. It was advanced by both Liberal and Marxist theoreticians. Later, the fact that the crisis was also understood as an opportunity for cleansing after 1929 was termed a 'liberal blindness', but this would only be convincing were one able to demonstrate that there had (already) been other cleansing mechanisms available at that time. In fact, it was only the experience of this crisis that created the intellectual and above all the political preconditions for new kinds of control of the economy as a whole, which do not, of course, work with unambiguously foreseeable success. Moreover, the theoretician of the Communist International, E. Varga, still did not consider a 'capitalist solution to the crisis' to be out of the question even in January 1932. See *Internationale Presse-korrespondenz* 13/12 (15 February 1932), pp. 345f.

87 This concept originates with A. Gehlen, *Urmensch und Spätkultur. Philosophische Ergebnissee und Aussagen* (Bonn 1956), p. 76: 'Whoever has transformed himself into a great task, i.e. a task whose dominance derives from the objective realities, becomes irresistible, because the franchise of things operates through him.'

88 Hitler came to power when, after the deep depression, the economic upturn had again, if haltingly, got going in almost every country. That meant that numerous circumstances of importance to the dynamic of the business cycle had developed to the point where a thrust could emanate from them (see in particular the substantially lowered money wages). After that, the uniquely low level of production and the enormous unutilised capacity rendered it possible for both the civil and the rapidly growing military demand to be satisfied out of the growing GDP. Thus, the vast rearmament did not have to procede at the expense of the standard of living – rather, the opposite appeared to be the case. In foreign policy, Hitler found himself faced with an altered international post-war order, that is a Versailles system which had already collapsed. The norms and institutions of the free world economy had already been swept away before 30 January 1933. All countries turned inward and put national goals far ahead of international ones, feeling themselves bound by no other considerations. Even if one does not put the worldwide depression forward as the explanation for the fact of Hitler's seizure of power, it must be taken into consideration in order to understand why he was able to exercise his power internally and externally in the way he actually did. At least in this sense, the worldwide depression is one of the foundation stones of the Third Reich.

10 Economic causes of the collapse of the Weimar Republic

1 In June 1979, at the invitation of the Fritz Thyssen Stiftung, historians, political scientists, jurists, sociologists and economists met under the direction of K. D. Erdmann to discuss the factors which may have contributed to the collapse of the Weimar Republic. An exposé by Hagen Schulze (which is repeatedly cited here) on the previous results of research and the state of the argument had been submitted to the participants. The exposé and the results of the meeting are published in K. D. Erdmann and H. Schulze (eds.), *Weimar. Selbstpreisgabe einer Demokratie. Eine Bilanz heute* (Düsseldorf 1980). Beyond this, K. D. Erdmann has published an evaluation of the conference in 'Vom Scheitern einer Demokratie. Forschungsprobleme zum Untergang der Weimarer Republik', *GWU*, 32 (1981), pp. 65ff.

The conference paper printed here arose in a temporally direct association with the lecture 'Constraints and Room for Manoeuvre' printed above, which explains the agreement in the basic statement and also in several formulations. But the studies are differently designed in the respective cases and can also be read as reciprocal commentaries.

2 A. Hillgruber, 'Unter dem Schatten von Versailles – die außenpolitische Belastung der Weimarer Republik: Realität und Perzeption bei den Deutschen', in Erdmann and Schulze (eds.) (see footnote 1), p. 63. On this, see also M. R. Lepsius, 'From Fragmented Party Democracy to Government by Emergency Decree and National Socialist Takeover: Germany', in J. J. Linz and A. Stepan (eds.), *The Breakdown of Democratic Regimes: Europe* (Baltimore 1978), p. 44: as early as 1929, Gustav Stolper is said to have remarked that there were now only opposition parties. Lepsius continues with the statement: 'This is the clear perception of the crisis of the parliamentary regime under conditions of the existing party system in 1929, at a time where neither the economic crisis nor the impact of the Nazi movement were dominating the political scene.'

3 See also W. Conze, 'Die politischen Entscheidungen in Deutschland 1929– 1933', in W. Conze and H. Raupach (eds.), *Die Staats- und Wirtschaftskrise des Deutschen Reiches 1929/33* (Stuttgart 1967), p. 177.

4 With reference to cells and molecules, the physicist H. Maier-Leibnitz formulated the problem as follows: 'It appears to me that there are many more building errors than one has hitherto known of, and on the other hand there is a quite unexpected ability (of nature, K.B.) to cope with these building errors, so long as there are not too many of them.' See H. Maier-Leibnitz, 'Atomenergie vor 23 Jahren und heute betrachtet, Vortrag auf der Jahressitzung der Bayerischen Akademie der Wissenschaften am 24. 11. 1979', *Bayerische Akademie der Wissenschaften. Jahrbuch 1980*, p. 94.

5 E. Friesenhahn, 'Zur Legitimation und zum Scheitern der Weimarer Reichsverfassung', in Erdmann and Schulze (eds.), *Weimar*, p. 91.

6 J. J. Linz's work, *The Breakdown of Democratic Regimes: Crisis, Breakdown and Reequilibrium* (Baltimore 1978), is typical. Here, even in the index, there are no key-words like economy, finances, tax burden, budget, business outlook. In J. Habermas, *Legitimationsprobleme im Spätkapitalismus* (Frankfurt 1973), there are a broadly drawn framework and classifications of crises in systems.

7 On this, see K. Borchardt, 'Perspektiven der Wachstumsgesellschaft', in K. v. Beyme, *et al.*, *Wirtschafliches Wachstum als gesellschaftliches Problem* (Königstein 1978), pp. 157ff. If one only gets a fifth of a substantially larger cake as opposed to getting a fourth of a smaller cake previously, then it may be that the amount of cake at one's disposal has grown over all. Of course, the imputation that those interested are interested only in pure quantity is not

necessarily reasonable; but it seems over all to be more sensible than the assumption that they are in reality interested *only* in distributional shares.

8 On the difference between economic and political controls, see A. O. Hirschman, *Exit, Voice, and Loyalty: Responses to Decline in Firms, Organizations, and States* (Cambridge, Mass. 1970).

9 On inflation and specifically its political implications, see K. Borchardt, 'Germany's experience of inflations' in this volume, pp. 132ff, and the recent literature on inflations in Germany referred to there. Further, F. Hirsch and J. Goldthorpe (eds.), *The Political Economy of Inflation* (London 1978).

10 But our attention should explicitly be drawn to two circumstances: (1) A considerable part of the so-called losses in the inflationary process is largely to be ascribed to the war. That it had to undertake the liquidation of the monetary assets which had increased enormously during the war should be numbered among the burdens of the political order of the Weimar Republic. (2) What has often been described as a loss of financial property in the course of inflation would to a large extent have had to be withdrawn even without inflation in a process of explicit redistribution.

11 See G. Stolper, K. Häuser and K. Borchardt, *The German Economy. 1870 to the Present* (New York 1967). Stolper describes a 'trend toward statism that had pervaded all Germany's history after she was resurrected under Prussian leadership' (p. 12).

12 As is well known, this question has constantly been controversially discussed. It is remarkable that even those two high-ranking civil servants of the Reich who, in the banking crisis of 1931, finally participated in the solution of the consequences of the financial collapse had previously stood in the camp of those who played down the problem. Memorandum for the Reich Chancellor, 24 September 1927: 'In so far as the necessary capital cannot be formed in the interior, foreign capital is required. The strong pressure of the President of the Reichsbank for a curbing of foreign loans is, as Secretary of State Trendelenburg has established with Ministerialdirektor Scheffer [*sic*] in week-long studies, not expedient. Even if short term credits are called in in great measure, a danger to the currency is not to be feared. Only a rise in the Reichsbank discount would be needed in order to receive long term foreign moneys in adequate measure', BA R 43 1/2337.

13 K. D. Bracher, *Die Auflösung der Weimarer Republik* (1957), p. 214.

14 In summary, K. Borchardt, 'Wachstum und Wechsellagen 1914–1970', *HdWSG*, 2 (Stuttgart 1976), pp. 685ff. and 703ff.; D. Petzina and W. Abelshauser, 'Zum Problem der relativen Stagnation der deutschen Wirtschaft in den zwanziger Jahren', in H. Mommsen, D. Petzina and B. Weisbrod (eds.), *Industrielles System und politische Entwicklung in der Weimarer Republik* (Düsseldorf 1974), pp. 26ff.; R. Stucken, 'Schaffung der Reichsmark, Reparationsregelungen und Auslandsanleihen, Konjunkturen (1924–1930)' in Deutsche Bundesbank (ed.), *Währung und Wirtschaft in Deutschland 1876–1975* (Frankfurt 1976), pp. 249ff.; G. Hardach, *Weltmarktorientierung und relative Stagnation. Währungspolitik in Deutschland 1924–1931* (Berlin 1976); information on the international comparison of growth rates in S. Kuznets, *Modern Economic Growth. Rate, Structure and Spread* (New Haven 1966); S. Kuznets, *Economic Growth of Nations. Total Output and Production Structure* (Cambridge Mass 1971); A. Maddison, *Phases of Capitalist Development, Banca Nazionale del Lavoro Quarterly Review* (121, June 1977); A. Maddison, 'Per Capita Output in the Long-Run', in *Kyklos*, 32 (1979), pp. 412ff.

15 W. Fischer, 'Die Weimarer Republik unter den weltwirtschaftlichen Bedingungen der Zwischenkriegszeit', in Mommsen, *et al.* (eds.), *System*, pp. 26ff.

16 On this, see also K. Borchardt, 'Trends, Cycle, Structural Breaks . . .', in this volume pp. 85ff. Similarly on various patterns of interpretation, see the recent article by W. Fischer, 'Die Weltwirtschaft im 20. Jahrhundert. Beharrung und Wandel', *HZ*, 229 (1979), pp. 54ff.

17 The (speculative) calculation of potential is based on considerations which I published in Borchardt, 'Trends'. There, Model 1. The quantitative information is taken from W. G. Hoffmann, F. Grumbach and H. Hesse, *Das Wachstum der deutschen Wirtschaft seit der Mitte des 19. Jahrhunderts* (Berlin 1965).

18 The index of industrial production calculated by Wagenführ, in D. Petzina, W. Abelshauser and A. Faust, *Sozialstatistisches Arbeitsbuch III. Materialien zur Statistik des Deutschen Reiches 1914–1945* (Munich 1978), p. 61. I hold the attempts at estimating a national product for the world war and the inflation to be methodologically impermissible. In summary, now C.-L. Holtfrerich, *Die deutsche Inflation 1914–1923* (Berlin 1980), pp. 193ff. and 220ff.

19 Institut für Konjunkturforschung (ed.), *Konjunkturstatistisches Handbuch* (1933), p. 41.

20 Calculated from Statistisches Bundesamt (ed.), *Bevölkerung und Wirtschaft 1872–1972* (Wiesbaden 1972), p. 261.

21 On the very peculiar pattern of the business cycle in the inter-war period, see K. Borchardt, 'Changes in the Phenomenon of the Business Cycle over the Last Hundred Years', in this volume, pp. 59ff.

22 A. Agthe, 'Statistische Übersicht der Arbeitslosigkeit in der Welt', in M. Saitzew (ed.), *Die Arbeitslosigkeit in der Gegenwart*, *SchVfSp*, 185/1 (Munich 1932).

23 Unemployment among members of trade unions comprised 2.1 per cent on average in 1904–13 and 11.4 per cent on average in 1924–9. *Statistische Jahrbücher* (1914 and 1928ff.) Of course it must be born in mind that the level of unionization after the First World War was far higher and also that now relatively more employees in endangered employment situations belonged to trade unions. On the long-term comparison and also the international comparison of unemployment rates, see also W. Galenson and A. Zellner, 'International Comparison of Unemployment Rates', in National Bureau of Economic Research (ed.), *Measurement and Behavior of Unemployment* (New York 1957); B. R. Mitchell, *European Historical Statistics 1750–1970* (London 1975), p. 167 according to *Yearbook of Labour Statistics*; B. R. Mitchell, 'Statistical Appendix', in C. Cipolla (ed.), *The Fontana Economic History of Europe, Vol. VI: Contemporary Economies* (Glasgow 1976), pp. 667ff.

24 K. Littmann, 'Ausgaben, öffentliche II', *HdWW*, 1 (Stuttgart 1977), p. 353.

25 We will not go into the considerable problems of estimating investment activity here. Even if one considers a larger scope for errors, the basic statement remains correct. The figures provided here rest on Hoffmann's estimates (see note 17), p. 828.

26 Here too the problems of getting reliable figures are very great. The information relates to the corresponding sums in D. Keese, 'Die volkswirtschaftlichen Gesamtgrößen für das Deutsche Reich in den Jahren 1925–1936', Conze and Raupach (eds.), *Die Staats- und Wirtschaftskrise*, p. 51.

27 That the proportions discussed above did not possess the quality of economic fates should at least be indicated. In 1925/6, 62 per cent of the means of financing house building stemmed from public sources! In 1929/31 it was still 42 per cent. But this was in large part not to be ascribed to a 'natural' weakness of the capital market, but substantially also to the intention of the state to control the rents for housing. See K. Borchardt, 'Realkredit und Pfandbriefmarkt im Wandel von 100 Jahren', in *Hundert Jahre Rheinische Hypothekenbank* (Frankfurt 1971), pp. 134f.

28 Differently in Hardach, *Weltmarktorientierung*, pp. 34f. and S. Hardach, *Deutschland in der Weltwirtschaft 1870–1970*. Eine Einführung in die Sozial- und Wirtschaftsgeschichte (Frankfurt 1977), p. 45.

29 E. H. Phelps-Brown and M. H. Browne, *A Century of Pay* (London 1968), appendix III and table 19.

30 Keynes further refers to the fact that, after 1924, Germany had transformed its unique competitive advantage into a disadvantage through a rapid increase in real wages. See the reprint of the original publication from *Evening World* (New York 25 March 1929) in *The Collected Writings of John Maynard Keynes, Vol. XVIII: Activities 1922–1932* (London 1978), p. 316. Similar formulations in J. M. Keynes, 'The German Transfer Problem' in *EJ* 39 (1929), pp. 3ff. With that, Keynes addresses one of the 'insoluble' problems, which were seen ahead in 1929.

31 H. Soell, 'Das Versagen Weimars und die Chancen von Bonn', *Das Parlament*, 44 (1978), 4 November 1978.

32 According to Statistisches Bundesamt (ed.), *Bevölkerung und Wirtschaft*, pp. 254 and 250. For closer inquiries, see G. Bry, *Wages in Germany 1891–1945* (New York 1960).

33 Also correct in his tendency: G. Castellan, 'Zur sozialen Bilanz der Prosperität 1924–1929' in Mommsen *et al.* (eds.), *System*, p. 105. It is true that the essay would need re-working in some other respects.

34 Hoffmann, *Das Wachstum*, pp. 828 and 174.

35 The respectively different pairs of figures result from the fact that, in the first case, for the corrected wage share, the quota of employees in the labour force (including self employed and employed family members) of the pre-war period, and in the second case, that of the year 1928 is held constant. The figures are doubtlessly not precise. Furthermore, it was necessary to go back to 1907 for the calculation of the quota of employees and, for the corrected wage share, and to assume that no substantial change in the social structure of employment had emerged up to 1913. The calculation is based on data in Petzina, *Arbeitsbuch*, pp. 102 and 55. If the average wage share of the twenties is compared with that in the Federal Republic 1950–70 (after correcting the changes in employment structure), it emerges that the wage share of the twenties, at 67 per cent, stood at around 10 percentage points above that of the years 1950–70 (underlying the quota of employees of 1950). See R. Skiba and H. Adam, *Das westdeutsche Lohnniveau zwischen den beiden Weltkriegen und nach der Währungsreform* (Cologne 1974), p. 106 and Figure 7.

36 Hoffmann, *Das Wachstum*, pp. 86ff.

37 This emerges from examination of the distribution of income in industry and crafts alone. An international comparison of industrial profit shares shows the extreme compression of profits in Germany. See E. H. Phelps-Brown, *Pay and Profits* (Manchester 1968), pp. 18f.

38 It is true that the rise of the wage share and the share of income derived from all sorts of labour continued after 1929 in the slump. This, however, is a normal phenomenon for downswings, while it is normal for the upturns that these shares decline – which did not occur before in Germany.

39 See also K. Borchardt, 'Constraints and room for manoeuvre' in this volume, pp. 143ff.

40 *Aufstieg oder Niedergang? Deutsche Wirtschafts- und Finanzreform 1929*. Eine Denkschrift des Präsidiums des Reichsverbandes der Deutschen Industrie (Veröffentlichungen des Reichsverbandes der Deutschen Industrie No. 49) (Berlin 1929).

41 D. Petzina, *Krisen gestern und heute – die Rezession von 1974/75 und die*

Erfahrungen der Weltwirtschaftskrise (Gesellschaft für Westfälische Wirtschaftsgeschichte 21) (Dortmund 1977), p. 21.

42 K. H. Minuth (ed.), *Akten der Reichskanzlei: Die Kabinette Luther I und II*, Vol. 2 (Boppard 1977), Document 216, p. 836.

43 *Deutsche Sozialpolitik 1918–1928. Erinnerungsschrift des Reichsarbeitsministeriums* (Berlin 1928), pp. 108f.: 'It [the state's wages policy, K.B.] has upheld the idea of the collective wage agreement with absolute logical consistency in the last ten years and has always let itself be governed by the goal of making the portion of the employees out of the total yield of the economy as large as possible.'

44 H. v. Beckerath, *Reparationsagent und deutsche Wirtschaftspolitik. Eine programmatische Kritik der deutschen Wirtschaft der Gegenwart* (Bonn 1928), p. 22.

45 See H. Wunderlich, 'Aufwertung', *HdSt Ergänzungsband* (Jena 1929[4]), pp. 24ff.; O. Pfleiderer, 'Die Reichsbank in der Zeit der Großen Inflation, die Stabilisierung der Mark und die Aufwertung von Kapitalforderungen', in Deutsche Bundesbank (ed.), *Währung und Wirtschaft*, pp. 194ff. Note that in several other inflationary countries no upward revaluation took place, *inter alia* not in France.

46 Formulation in G. Kessler, 'Die Lage der deutschen Arbeiterschaft seit 1914', in B. Harms (ed.), *Strukturwandlungen der deutschen Volkswirtschaft*, Vol. 1 (Berlin 1928), p. 442.

47 On this, see L. Preller, *Sozialpolitik in der Weimarer Republik* (1949, New Edition, Düsseldorf 1978), pp. 296ff. which is not outdated.

48 On this, see M. Schneider, *Unternehmer und Demokratie. Die freien Gewerkschaften in der unternehmerischen Ideologie der Jahre 1918 bis 1933* (Bonn 1975), pp. 50ff.

49 For mining this is also shown by H. Mommsen, 'Sozialpolitik im Ruhrbergbau', in Mommsen *et al.* (eds.), *System*, pp. 303ff.

50 See *Internationale Presse-korrespondenz* 9/70 (of 8 August 1929), p. 1609 and 9/107 (8 November 1929), p. 2544.

51 On this, above all H.-H. Hartwich, *Arbeitsmarkt, Verbände und Staat 1913–1933. Die öffentliche Bindung unternehmerischer Funktionen in der Weimarer Republik* (Berlin 1967); U. Hüllbüsch, 'Koalitionsfreiheit und Zwangstarif. Die Stellungnahme des Allgemeinen Deutschen Gewerkschaftsbundes zu Tarifvertrag und Schlichtungswesen in der Weimarer Republik', in U. Engelhardt *et al.* (eds.), *Soziale Bewegung und politische Verfassung. Beiträge zur Geschichte der modernen Welt* (Stuttgart 1976), pp. 559ff.; B. Weisbrod, *Schwerindustrie in der Weimarer Republik. Interessenpolitik zwischen Stabilisierung und Krise* (Wuppertal 1978), pp. 395ff.

11 Germany's exchange rate options during the great depression

1 Of the publications which have appeared most recently, see H. Irmler, 'Bankenkrise und Vollbeschäftigungspolitik', in Deutsche Bundesbank (ed.), *Währung und Wirtschaft in Deutschland 1876–1975* (Frankfurt 1976), pp. 249f. W. Jochmann, 'Brünings Deflationspolitik und der Untergang der Weimarer Republik', in Stegmann *et al.* (eds.), *Industrielle Gesellschaft und Politisches System. Beiträge zur politischen Sozialgeschichte* (Bonn 1978), pp. 78ff. On the relativisation of the judgments of the 'mistake' of Brüning's policy see W. J. Helbich, *Die Reparationen in der Ära Brüning. Zur Bedeutung des Young-Plans für die deutsche Politik 1930–1932* (Berlin 1962); H. Sanmann, 'Daten

und Alternativen der deutschen Wirtschafts- und Finanzpolitik in der Ära Brüning', *Hamburger Jahrbuch für Wirtschafts- und Gesellschaftspolitik*, Vol. 10 (1965), pp. 109ff. K. Borchardt, 'Constraints and Room for Manoeuvre', in this volume, pp. 143ff.

1a But not with J. Schiemann, *Die deutsche Währung in der Weltwirtschaftskrise, 1929–1933. Währungspolitik und Abwertungskontroverse unter den Bedingungen der Reparationen* (Bern 1980). The book appeared at the same time as this essay. Schiemann seeks to demonstrate that a devaluation of the Reichsmark would first have been difficult politically and second (given the rate, of 20 per cent, assumed) of relatively little effect with regard to the goal of overcoming the crisis. It is true that he regards the grounds given by those responsible as being highly deficient. But, on p. 176, Schiemann only touches on the question which is the subject of this essay, which is thus not materially superseded by his work. The opportunity to clarify a number of points in regard to Schiemann's arguments was taken in the footnotes marked with the additional letter a.

2 On this, see above all the minutes of the Reich Cabinet meetings, beginning 24 September 1931 up to the passage of the 4th Emergency Decree on 7 December 1931, BA Koblenz R43 I/1452 and 1453. Whence R. E. Lüke, *Von der Stabilisierung zur Krise* (Zürich 1958), p. 334, has derived his information – to the effect that the decisive question of exchange rate policy was indeed discussed in the press, but not in the cabinet – is beyond our understanding. How seriously currency policy was taken is also shown by Secretary of State Trendelenburg's verdict in the morning meeting of 2 October, characterising the 'sinking of the English pound' as 'the greatest economic event since the conclusion of the Peace'.

3 This is reaffirmed by W. Grotkopp, *Die große Krise. Lehren aus der Überwindung der Wirtschaftskrise 1929/32* (Düsseldorf 1954), pp. 209f.

4 Text of the press release in R. S. Sayers, *The Bank of England 1891–1944*, Vol. 3, Appendices (Cambridge 1976), pp. 264f.

5 O. Emminger, *Währungsentwertung und Krisenüberwindung in England, WA*, Vol. 40 (1934/2), pp. 437ff.; S. K. Howson, *Domestic Monetary Management in Britain 1919–38* (Cambridge 1975).

6 This is not an accusation directed exclusively against the critics of the exchange rate policy pursued at the end of the Weimar Republic. Rather, the practice of criticising historical decisions without explicitly naming the alternatives and carefully evaluating them with respect to their (assumed) results is widespread.

7 On the concepts of the exchange rate theory and policy of the thirties, see E. Wagemann, 'Das Devalvationsproblem', in *Wochenbericht des Instituts für Konjunkturforschung* 4/36, 2 December 1931; W. Förster, *Theorie der Währungsentwertung* (Jena 1936), pp. 1ff.

7a Schiemann (*Die deutsche Währung*) also uses the concept, *Abwertung* (devaluation) for quite different policy options, but then bases his investigation of possible effects of an *Abwertung* on the modern concept (new fixing of an exchange rate with higher price of gold in RM). His decision to take as a basis a devaluation rate of 20 per cent is only justified in a single sentence on p. 264: out of political consideration for Britain, the rate of devaluation would have had to lie below the British one (of 30 per cent). The conceptual confusion we have already had occasion to reproach is before us again: the British did not devalue, but freed the pound against gold, thus floating it. If only for that reason, the British rate could not be regarded as an unalterable fact, on which a German '*Abwertung*' of 20 per cent could have been based. As it emerges from British and German sources, one still reckoned with a lesser devaluation of the pound for a relatively long period after 20 September – and later with an upward revaluation (see below, III/6 and note 28).

8 C. Krämer, 'Der Weg des Pfundes' in *Wirtschaftsdienst*, 16 (1931), 25 September 1931; C. Krämer, 'Der Weg der Reichsmark', in *ibid.*, 16 October 1931.

9 This is how H. Luther, *Vor dem Abgrund. Reichsbankpräsident in Krisenzeiten 1930–1933* (Munich 1964), p. 156, among others, argues in retrospect.

10 On the amendments of the bank law in the general context of the Young Plan, see also 'Begründung zum Entwurf eines Gesetzes zur Änderung des Bankgesetzes vom 30. 8. 1924, zugeleitet von der Reichsregierung am 7. 2. 1930', Reichstag IV 1928, Drucksache 1623, p. 3.

11 That in their public statements as to why currency parity had to be adhered to, the German government and the Reichsbank never attempted to strengthen the persuasiveness of their case by referring to the Young Plan does not, by the way, prove how little the matter weighed in the actual decisions. It might have resulted from the fact that such a reference would have been highly unwise in domestic politics since it would have emphasised the dependence of German policy on this controversial treaty and thus only given their opponents more ammunition. Where it was correctly understood, the German spokesmen (in international conversations) certainly did justify their decision not to float the mark also in terms of the obligations imposed by the Young Plan.

11a Schiemann (*Die deutsche Währung*) takes a middle path: first of all, he describes the legal position nationally and internationally with its various contractual effects (pp. 167ff.) and deduces from them the risks of economic and military sanctions in the event of an autonomous German currency policy being pursued. Then, however, he too bases his speculations as to the effect of a 20 per cent devaluation on the most advantageous scenario – without examining foreign reactions in trade policy, political or military measures (pp. 254f.).

12 'Stenographic Notes of the London Conference, 20.–23. 7. 1931.', *Documents on British Foreign Policy 1919–1939*, 2nd Series, Vol. 2, 1931 (London 1947), pp. 435ff., esp. pp. 444ff. and 482f. Brüning fought for the cancellation of regulations on the minimum discount rate and the tax on bank notes in the event of a fall below the minimum cover of the notes; and he asked for formal recognition of the raising of the obligations to hold RM convertible in gold, but not for the right to change the rate of exchange. However, the French participants foresaw this, as may be seen from Finance Minister Flandin's declaration: 'This is why, at any rate so far as France is concerned, we make the most explicit reserves on this point, all the more because the exchange of views between Dr. Brüning and Mr. Stimson has made it appear that, so to speak, there is some question of organising the legal devalorisation of the German currency' (*ibid.*, p. 449). When the question of the alteration of sections 29 and 31 came up again in the 4th session of the heads of delegations, the French President again turned strictly against any alteration of the Haag agreements, and in the process expressed the interesting thought: 'but the Governmental Conference must avoid, even in the indirect way (the British Prime Minister MacDonald had proposed a softer formulation of a resolution, K.B.), recommending inflation to the German Government'. Brüning replied to this in a remarkable fashion: 'I think the proposal put forward by the Chairman of this conference does not recommend any inflation at all. What we have done is the opposite of inflation. We have put forward a policy of deflation for the last few months, and I am prepared to put on the record the declaration of the German Government that the German Government is prepared to do all that is possible to keep the stabilised mark, as was proposed yesterday by Mr.

Francqui' (*ibid.*, p. 482). That the French Government then itself reacted 'very agitatedly' to the decision in favour of foreign exchange controls recommended indirectly and directly in Paris and London is shown by Ambassador Hoesch's telegram of 6 August 1931, PA Büro RM 7 – Frankreich 24 sheet 191ff. On 7 August 1931, the British Foreign Office explained to a member of the staff of the French embassy in London that it held foreign exchange controls to be the lesser evil in view of the other conclusions which Germany would otherwise have to draw. Public Record Office London, FO 371/15210.

13 Grotkopp, *Die große Krise*, p. 202. Schiemann (*Die deutsche Währung*), too, rests his case respecting what Keynes is supposed to have said and meant exclusively on Grotkopp and Brüning (see note 14).

14 Brüning, *Memoiren 1918–1938* (Stuttgart 1970), p. 506.

15 'Memorandum to the Prime Minister's Advisory Committee on Financial Questions' of 20 November 1931 in *Collected Writings of John Maynard Keynes, Vol. XVIII, Activities 1922–1932, Reparations* (London 1978), p. 358.

16 *Hamburger Fremdenblatt*, 9 January 1932. One might be tempted to regard this quotation as evidence that Keynes, at least at this point in time, did not yet wish to characterise the German policy as necessarily erroneous. According to this, he would have been fairly close to the governmental conception, had it not been just one among many remarks of varying kinds.

16a Schiemann, *Die deutsche Währung*, p. 249, appears, by contrast, to view devaluation and exchange controls only as alternatives. On this, see more under 12.

17 The French currency was in fact never endangered at this time and never under suspicion of having to alter the gold parity or of wishing to alter it. From time to time, the position was different in the case of the US dollar. From October 1931 on, the dollar was repeatedly thought to be in danger even if opinions as to whether the USA would have to depart from parity were divided. For a summary of this, see C. P. Kindleberger, *The World in Depression, 1929–1939* (Berkeley and London 1973). The continuing concerns of European central banks about the dollar is also reflected in a travel report by Jay E. Crane, who was responsible for foreign operations at the Federal Reserve Bank of New York, in autumn, 1932: 'Report of European Trip, October 1 to November 10, 1932, J. E. Crane, accompanied by Lewis Galantiere, Federal Reserve Bank of New York' archival copy from the George Leslie Harrison Papers in Columbia University, New York, Binder 34. Also contains notes on discussions with German partners.

18 Reich Cabinet minutes, BA Koblenz, R 43 I/1452.

19 IfZG, 'Tagebücher Hans Schäffer', 26 September 1931, p. 848. See also Luther's own account of the preceding telephone conversation with Hülse (Basle) in the Day Reports of Reichsbank President Luther, 26 September 1931, BA Koblenz Luther Papers No. 366 – sheet 110ff.

20 Proceedings in BA Koblenz, R 43 I/2437. See also BA Koblenz, Luther Papers No. 366 – 26 September 1931.

21 W. Woytinsky, *Internationale Hebung der Preise als Ausweg aus der Krise* (Leipzig 1931).

22 Note by R. Dalberg with an enclosed memorandum for the Reich Chancellor of 3 October 1931: BA Koblenz, R 43 I/2437.

23 *Ibid.* Dalberg did, it is true, harbour considerable illusions regarding the interests and intentions of the English, of whom he not only expected that they would give information on request as to what rate below the old parity they wanted effectively to stabilise the pound, but also that they had a strong interest in the first instance in de facto and later in formal stabilisation, albeit naturally at a lower level.

24 Brüning, *Memoiren*, p. 367.
25 Anon. (R. Dalberg and W. Grävell), 'Ein Programm der Devalvation', *Der Deutsche Oekonomist* (49/49), 11 December 1931.
26 Wagemann, 'Das Devaluationsproblem'. K. E. Born, *Die deutsche Bankenkrise* (Munich 1967), p. 45 mentions there having been devaluation proposals of Wagemann's in 1931. No evidence of this can be found, however. The Wagemann plan which became known in January 1932, which met with enormous resonance at home and abroad, had something else in view, which Wagemann's above-mentioned critical essay already indicated.
27 Sayers, *The Bank of England*, Appendix, p. 265.
28 Emminger, *Währungsentwertung*, p. 437. For the British ambassadors' discussions, see *Documents on British Foreign Policy*, pp. 265ff. On the assumption that England would immediately return to the gold standard, see *inter alia* Ministerialdirigent Norden of the Reich Ministry of Finance in a draft for Secretary of State H. Schäffer of 23 September 1931: 'Erste Gedanken darüber, ob Deutschland dem Beispiel Englands hinsichtlich seiner Währung folgen soll.' BA, Luther Papers No. 366, sheet 94ff. On this memorandum, ordered by Schäffer on 22 September 1931, see IfZG, 'Tagebücher Hans Schäffer', 22 September 1931.
29 Lüke, *Von der Stabilisierung*, p. 334. The evidential basis for this does appear to me to be somewhat questionable, see below.
29a In this connection, Schiemann, *Die deutsche Währung*, p. 188, mentions the German Government having had a devaluation rate of 20 per cent in mind and cites the ministerial discussion of the morning of 2 October 1931 as evidence. But it is very doubtful whether anyone really had 20 per cent in mind. In the minutes, among the Reich Chancellor's arguments for currency stability, it says, amongst other things, only that: 'It is also impossible to hope that one could maintain the position of the currency at a level lowered by 20 per cent', BA Koblenz R 43 I/1453. Brüning appears rather to have taken this figure at random. It is true that one can only speculate as to what exchange regime he had in view at all when he spoke out against alternatives.
30 The source for this is the entry in Hans Schäffer's diary under 21 September after a conversation with Dreyse. The continuation of the note is interesting: 'Dreyse responded to that by saying that he would not gladly do it and would seek to avoid it in any event.' IfZG, 'Tagebücher Hans Schäffer', p. 806.

    Siepmann was, furthermore, one of those leading men in the Bank of England who had already supported abandoning gold for some considerable time before 19 September. Thus J. E. Crane of the Federal Reserve Bank of New York also reports from his European journey of August/September 1931 (text completed 16 September 1931): 'Even at the Bank of England one hears men like Siepmann and Rodd admit quite freely that the only way out is for England and most of the other European countries to go off the gold standard temporarily, leave France and the United States high and dry, and then return to gold at a lower level.' Federal Reserve Bank of New York, archive copy as above, note 17.
31 IfZG, 'Tagebücher Hans Schäffer', 23 September 1931, p. 825.
32 NA Washington RG 59, Diplomatic Branch Decimal File, 862.51/3206. The telegram ends with the interesting hint that Germany would consider giving up the gold standard in the event of the USA doing the same thing.
33 PRO FO 371–15211.
33a BA Koblenz, Luther Papers, No. 340.
34 Luther, *Abgrund*, p. 155. It is evidently on this that the information contained in standard historical works like Gebhardt, *Handbuch der Deutschen Geschichte* Vol. 4/1 (Stuttgart 1973[9]), p. 312 are based.

35 See Grotkopp, *Die große Krise*, p. 206, footnote 206 re personal information received from K. Blessing.

36 IfZG, 'Tagebücher Hans Schäffer', p. 821.

37 *Ibid.*, 21 July 1931; Day Report of Reichsbank president Luther of 21 July 1931, BA, Luther Papers, No. 365. Also *Politik und Wirtschaft in der Krise. Quellen zur Ära Brüning (Quellen zur Geschichte des Parlamentarismus und der politischen Parteien, III Series, Vol. 4/I)* (Düsseldorf 1980), p. 783. In the unpublished memorandum *Marcus Wallenberg und die deutsche Bankenkrise (1934)*, above and beyond what is noted in the diary, Schäffer does admittedly state as Norman's opinion: 'In case of extreme need, however, there would still be the option of the foreign moratorium, whose after-effects on German credit would not last for ever, either. To keep the domestic economy moving, compulsory convertibility to gold and the obligation to maintain a fixed gold cover would have to be suspended for some time.' Cited after E. Wandel, *Hans Schäffer. Steuermann in wirtschaftlichen und politischen Krisen* (Stuttgart 1974), p. 216. Was it then Sprague or Norman who brought up the suspension of the obligation to hold RM convertible in gold or Dollar in the conversation of that day? And what exactly was this supposed to mean?

38 Sayers, *The Bank of England*, Vol. 2, p. 415.

39 BA Koblenz, Luther Papers, No. 337: Hilger van Scherpenberg's notes on discussion with Montagu Norman on 19 October 1931.

40 BA Koblenz, Luther Papers, No. 338: Vocke's notes re visit to the Bank of England on 3 December 1931.

40a PRO FO 371/15936. The Ambassador's report is attached to a memorandum of Commercial Counsellor F. Thelwall's of 14 January 1932. In it, he reports that now (after the emergency measures), the Germans preferred Brüning, who was said to have shown himself to be strong, to Hitler since 'Brüning has stolen Hitler's thunder'. Thelwall's sentence gives an idea of the political impossibility of a departure from the gold standard in Germany: 'I cannot imagine that a programme consisting chiefly of departure from the gold standard and ejection of all Jews really appeals to a large section of the German nation.'

41 G. Haberler, 'Die Weltwirtschaft und das internationale Währungssystem in der Zeit zwischen den beiden Weltkriegen', in Deutsche Bundesbank, *Währung und Wirtschaft*, p. 225.

42 See *inter alia* H. Luther, *Wirtschaftsfragen der Gegenwart* (Jena 1932), p. 74.

43 On 28 September 1931, H. Brüning and H. Luther spoke at the 50th Anniversary of the Deutscher Sparkassenverband. Text of the Brüning speech in *Schulthess' Europäischer Geschichtskalender*, New Series 47, 1931 (Munich 1932), pp. 210ff. It has since become common to estimate the inflationary danger conjured up by Brüning and others to have been negligible; but one has to do justice to those responsible in as much as the few supporters of a policy of devaluation explicitly characterised price increases as the real purpose of the measure at the time. This was, for example, the statement made in R. Dalberg's memorandum, cited above, of 3 October 1931 and of the Quesnay Plan, and it was to this effect that Keynes had expressed himself, too.

44 How widespread 'substitute devaluations' or 'additional devaluations' via trade policy measures were in 1931/2 is demonstrated in a comprehensive overview by W. Greiff, *Der Methodenwandel der europäischen Handelspolitik während des Krisenjahres 1931* (Berlin 1932).

45 BA Koblenz, minutes of ministerial discussion, 15 January 1932 R 43 I/1454.

46 BA Koblenz, Silverberg Papers No. 249: minutes of the meeting of the Präsidial- und Vorstandsbeirat für allgemeine Wirtschaftspolitik, 20 April 1932.

47 B. Josephy, *Währungsschutz, Währungsbeherrschung* (Jena 1933), p. 105 – the

manuscript was, according to the foreword, completed in the autumn of 1932. The author had not wished to recommend this path, but merely to show how sundry 'side-questions' might have been dealt with.

48 The peculiar combination in the British decisions of desiring something and being forced to do it is nicely expressed in the quotation: 'They (the British currency authorities, K.B.) were prepared to have the devaluation of the pound thrust upon them by events.' O. Emminger, 'Die englischen Währungsexperimente der Nachkriegszeit', *WA*, 40/2 (1934), p. 325.

49 As late as 1976, this point prompted J. L. Kooker to a polemical observation: 'At the London Conference of July 1931, the US attempt to rescue Germany from the severe French demands dismayed and disheartened the French. By proposing the freezing of short-term foreign credits in Germany and rigid exchange control, the Americans, in effect, were instigating the stringent financial controls and autarkic policies later perfected by the Nazis.' J. L. Kooker, 'French Financial Diplomacy: The Interwar Years', in B. M. Rowland (ed.), *Balance of Power or Hegemony: The Interwar Monetary System* (New York 1976), p. 113.

50 Of course, this was nothing peculiar to Germany. In 1931/2 there were only very few countries in Europe which did not regulate the acquisition of foreign currency in one way or another. From 22 September 1931 until 3 March 1932, even Great Britain took refuge in controls of capital movement in order to brake the collapse of the exchange rate.

50a Schiemann, *Die deutsche Währung*, appears to overlook this on p. 281 and at other points in his analyses.

51 Krämer, 'Der Weg des Pfundes', pp. 1625f.

52 Of the extensive literature on monetary policy after the floatations in the various countries, reference should be made especially to the substantial comparative account in Vol. 43 of the *WA* (1936/I) and also to O. Pfleiderer, *Pfund, Yen und Dollar in der Weltwirtschaftskrise. Monetäre Konjunkturpolitik in Großbritannien, Japan und den Vereinigten Staaten, ihre volks- und weltwirtschaftliche Bedeutung* (Berlin 1937), and Kindleberger (see footnote 17).

53 IfZG, 'Tagebücher Hans Schäffer', 23 September 1931, p. 822.

54 Report of the meeting of the board of the Reichsverband der Deutschen Industrie on 28 September 1931, and the statement by the Reichsverband der Deutschen Industrie of 29 September 1931 in *Schulthess' Europäischer Geschichtskalender*, Vol. 72, 1931 (Munich 1932), pp. 213f.

55 On this – political – problem, see also Borchardt, 'Constraints and Room for Manoeuvre', above pp. 150f.

56 National Industrial Conference Board, *The Situation in Germany at the Beginning of 1933* (New York 1933), p. 49.

Index